EUROPEAN CONTRACT LAW IN THE DIGITAL AGE

EUCOLATH
EUROPEAN CONTRACT LAW AND THEORY SERIES

EUROPEAN CONTRACT LAW AND THEORY SERIES, Volume 3

EUROPEAN CONTRACT LAW IN THE DIGITAL AGE

Edited by
Stefan Grundmann

intersentia
Cambridge – Antwerp – Portland

Intersentia Ltd
Sheraton House | Castle Park
Cambridge | CB3 0AX | United Kingdom
Tel.: +44 1223 370 170 | Fax: +44 1223 370 169
Email: mail@intersentia.co.uk
www.intersentia.com | www.intersentia.co.uk

Distribution for the UK and Ireland:
NBN International
Airport Business Centre, 10 Thornbury Road
Plymouth, PL6 7PP
United Kingdom
Tel.: +44 1752 202 301 | Fax: +44 1752 202 331
Email: orders@nbninternational.com

Distribution for Europe and all other countries:
Intersentia Publishing nv
Groenstraat 31
2640 Mortsel
Belgium
Tel.: +32 3 680 15 50 | Fax: +32 3 658 71 21
Email: mail@intersentia.be

Distribution for the USA and Canada:
International Specialized Book Services
920 NE 58th Ave. Suite 300
Portland, OR 97213
USA
Tel.: +1 800 944 6190 (toll free) | Fax: +1 503 280 8832
Email: info@isbs.com

European Contract Law in the Digital Age

ISBN 978-1-78068-477-2
D/2018/7849/3
NUR 822

British Library Cataloguing in Publication Data. A catalogue record for this book is available from the British Library.

CONTENTS

PART V. DIGITAL OBJECTS OF CONTRACT – CESL II AND MORE

TABLE OF CASES

COURT OF JUSTICE OF THE EUROPEAN UNION

AUSTRALIA

CANADA

HONG KONG

UNITED KINGDOM

UNITED STATES

OPINIONS

LIST OF AUTHORS

Roger Brownsword
Professor at King's College London and at Bournemouth University

Carmen Estevan de Quesada
Professor at the University of Valencia

Stefan Grundmann
Professor at the European University Institute, Florence and at Humboldt-University, Berlin

Philipp Hacker
Max Weber Fellow at the European University Institute, Florence and Postdoctoral Researcher at Humboldt-University, Berlin

Florian Idelberger
Researcher at the European University Institute, Florence

Vanessa Mak
Professor of Private Law at Tilburg University

Przemysław Jacek Pałka
Researcher at the European University Institute, Florence

Christina Ramberg
Professor at Stockholm University

Giovanni Sartor
Professor at the European University Institute, Florence

Kristoffer Schollin
Researcher at the University of Gothenburg

Gerald Spindler
Professor at the Georg-August University of Göttingen

Dan Jerker B. Svantesson
Professor and Co-Director at the Centre for Commercial Law, Bond University and Researcher at the Swedish Law and Informaties Research Institute, Stockholm University.

PART I

THE OVERALL ARCHITECTURE

THE DIGITAL DIMENSION AS A CHALLENGE TO EUROPEAN CONTRACT LAW – THE ARCHITECTURE*

Stefan GRUNDMANN and Philipp HACKER

ABSTRACT

In this introductory chapter, we offer an overview of the interactions between digital technologies and contract law. We identify three pillars in this architecture: the

* This chapter draws on and develops further the article on 'Digital Technology as a Challenge to European Contract Law' published in *European Review of Contract Law*. We thank de Gruyter for their permission.

regulatory framework; digital interventions over the life-cycle of the contract; and digital objects of contracting. The regulatory framework, which itself may draw on digital technology to effectively pursue its ends, shapes, and is shaped by, the other two pillars. More specifically, on the one hand, we show how four key technologies – digital platforms, Big Data analytics, artificial intelligence, and blockchain – are being used at different stages of the contractual process (from the screening for contractual partners to formation, enforcement and interpretation) and engender novel market dynamics that, in many instances, necessitate regulatory responses. On the other hand, digitally facilitated contracting increasingly relates to digital content as the object of the contract. However, while this area has notably been shaped by the proposed Directive on Contracts for the Supply of Digital Content, we argue that a number of important blind spots remain that fail to be addressed by the directive. All in all, the digital dimension of contracting will likely reinforce an adaptive, relational view and practice of contracting. This increased fluidity engenders a vast potential for preference-conforming, time-sensitive contracts; however, to the extent that it also mirrors novel asymmetries of information and power, the ordering mechanisms of the law may simultaneously be more needed than ever.

1. CHALLENGES AND CORE FEATURES OF AN 'ARCHITECTURE'

The digital dimension and its challenges and repercussions for contract law in Europe – or 'European Contract Law' – are not a narrow issue.

It may therefore be wise to specify three things in a bird's-eye view first: (i) what kind of contract law and contract law perspective we are mainly interested in; (ii) what vision of 'European Contract Law' we base our discussion on; and finally (iii) what the main thrust of the chapter (and book) is and, linked to this question, which ingredients are included as being important for this purpose.

1.1. WHAT PLACE FOR CONTRACT LAW IN THE DIGITAL ARENA?

The broader the issue, the more *a certain understanding of law and contract law* may have a bearing on how to treat the issue (one could also say a certain 'preconception' of how to so). As German scholars who are internationally oriented, we see (public interest) *regulation* as an (important) integrative part of contract law. We certainly concede that they are quite different in aim, with regulation primarily furthering the public interest, and genuine private and contract law dealing primarily with the adequate balance of individual, private party interests. Despite this, however, we see them as strongly functionally linked. We would even want to suggest that (a large part of) the regulatory body nowadays is more intimately embedded in genuine private law issues or regimes than it was in the concept of the ordo-liberal school when the relation between contract and (public interest) regulation was first conceptualised – but where both regimes were quite neatly kept apart.[1] Finally, not including regulation – and even not featuring it very prominently – would also mean not including that part of the regime where EU Law in the technical sense is strongest. In fact, if one distinguishes between regulatory parts of the regime and private law parts of it, the latter is more often still national – or mainly national – while the former is mostly enacted at the EU level.[2] As German scholars with international orientation, we also want to highlight that a good part of the most innovative ideas in the last half century have been developed – at least for German law – in areas which really constitute *cross-sections* of several areas. The 'creation' of a banking law is a relevant example; that of a capital market law another one.[3] Finally, when it comes to *input from the social sciences*

---

1 F. Böhm, 'Privatrechtsgesellschaft und Marktwirtschaft', *ORDO* 17 (1966), 75–151; translation (and discussion) in S. Grundmann / H. Micklitz / M. Renner, *Private Law Theory – Global, European, Social Sciences Based* (Antwerp/Cambridge: Intersentia, 2017), chapter 6 (forthcoming); discussion and in part further development of the theory: E.-J. Mestmäcker, 'Macht – Recht – Wirtschaftsverfassung', *Zeitschrift für das gesamte Handels- und Wirtschaftsrecht (ZHR)* 137 (1973) 97–111; E.-J. Mestmäcker, 'Auf dem Weg zu einer Ordnungspolitik für Europa', *Festschrift für Hans von der Groeben* (Baden-Baden: Nomos, 1987), pp. 9–49; translation (and discussion) of this last text in S. Grundmann et al. (above) chapter 24; see also S. Grundmann, 'The Concept of the Private Law Society after 50 Years of European and European Business Law', 4 *European Review of Private Law (ERPL)*, 553–581 (2008); G. Schnyder / M. Siems, 'Ordoliberal Variety of Neoliberalism' in S. Konzelmann / M. Fovargue-Davies (eds.), *Banking Systems in the Crisis: the Faces of Liberal Capitalism* (London / New York: Routledge Taylor & Francis Group, 2013), pp. 250–268.

2 On this disposition of bodies of the law, see path-breaking, Ch. Kirchner, 'Europäisches Vertragsrecht' in L. Weyers (ed.), *Europäisches Vertragsrecht* (Baden-Baden: Nomos, 1997), 103–137 at 106 (he therefore characterises European contract law as 'harmonisation coming from the edges'); more broadly S. Grundmann, 'The Structure of European Contract Law', 9 *European Review of Private Law*, 505–528 (2001); S. Grundmann (end of n. 3 below); and also C. Quigley, *European Community Contract Law* (London: Kluwer, 1997); J. Basedow, 'A Common Contract Law for the Common Market' 33 *Common Market Law Review* 1169–1195 (1996).

3 The scholars who most prominently represent these areas are certainly among the key figures nationally and internationally, see below nn. 5–6. One could mention here competition law as well, as it is really about how to supplement contract and company law with a regime which helps to guarantee best possible material freedom (regulation and private law). See references in n. 2 above. For a comprehensive view on the interplay between competition law (more generally, business regulation in its interplay with traditional private law): see W. Fikentscher, *Wirtschaftsrecht* (Munich: Beck, 1983) (2 volumes on German and European Business Regulation Law); E.J. Mestmäcker / H. Schweitzer, *Europäisches Wettbewerbsrecht* (3rd edn., Munich: Beck, 2014); see also W. Fikentscher / Ph. Hacker / R. Podzun, *FairEconomy. Crises, Culture, Competition and the Role of Law* (Heidelberg: Springer, 2013). More recently and more focused on the relationship (as such) between regulation and private law: A. Hellgarth, *Regulierung und Privatrecht – Staatliche Verhaltenssteuerung mittels Privatrecht und ihre Bedeutung für Rechtswissenschaft, Gesetzgebung und Rechtsanwendung* (Tübingen: Mohr Siebeck, 2016); S. Grundmann, 'Privatrecht und Regulierung', *Festschrift für C.-W. Canaris* (2017), pp. 907–948 (forthcoming also in English in the *European Review of Private Law*).

into law, we are inclined to think that at least economic theory (information economics, game theory), new economic sociology with its network analysis,[4] behavioural insights (including behavioural economics)[5] and more generally theories of choice, including also collective choice, are paramount – with all these theoretical approaches related to the social sciences now being supplemented, and complicated, by the technical side, including computing (algorithms) and robotics. In the following considerations and namely in quite a few of the papers that constitute this book, these cross-disciplinary dimensions play a significant, in some even a dominant role.

For the digital arena, these ideas – namely the intimate link between private law contractual drafting, regulation, and the cross-sectional character of the area – can shortly be described as follows. While banking law was of the highest practical importance, and as well a powerful source of emerging ideas and research mainly in the 1970s and 1980s[6] – and similarly capital

---

4 On network theory and its relationship to the digital dimension (Internet, platforms, network effects for the digital economy like Google etc.), see (with particular attention to private law and regulation) M. Stucke / A. Grunes, *Big Data and Competition Policy* (Oxford: Oxford University Press, 2016), particularly Part IV and chapter 18; D. Rubinfeld / M. Gal, 'Access Barriers to Big Data', 59 *Arizona Law Review* 339 (2017), ssrn.com/abstract=2830586; early contribution in M. Lemley / D. McGowan, 'Legal Implications of Network Economic Effects', 86 *California Law Review* 479–611 (1998); groundbreaking, of course, for the overall concept: M. Castells, *The Information Age: Economy, Society and Culture, vol. 1: The Rise of the Network Society* (2nd edn., Chichester: Wiley Blackwell, 2010; 1st edn. 1996).

5 On behavioural approaches to problems of the digital dimension – as dealt with in the context of contract law and regulation – see in particular: R. Calo, 'Digital Market Manipulation', 82 *George Washington Law Review* 995, 1002–1012; 1015–1018 (2014); E. Mik, 'The Erosion of Autonomy in Online Consumer Transactions', 8 *Law, Innovation and Technology* 1 (2016); N. Helberger, 'Profiling and Targeting Consumers in the Internet of Things', in R. Schulze / D. Staudenmayer, *Digital Revolution: Challenges for Contract Law in Practice* (Baden-Baden: Nomos, 2016), pp. 135-161; Y. Hermstrüwer, *Informationelle Selbstgefährdung* (Tübingen: Mohr Siebeck, 2016); Ph. Hacker, *Verhaltensökonomik und Normativität* (Tübingen: Mohr Siebeck, 2017), §13; Ph. Hacker, 'The Ambivalence of Algorithms. Gauging the Legitimacy of Personalized Law' in M. Bakhoum et al. (eds.) *Personal Data in Competition, Consumer Protection and IP Law – Towards a Holistic Approach?* (Berlin: Springer, forthcoming); Ph. Hacker., 'Personalizing EU Private Law. From Disclosures to Nudges and Mandates', 25 *European Review of Private Law* 651 (2017), http://ssrn.com/abstract=2914393.

6 Among the main issues and insights we 'owe' mainly to banking law are these: Contracts are adequately assessed only once one sees their regime from the pre-contractual phase via the contractual to the post-contractual phase down into insolvency (C.-W. Canaris, *Bankvertragsrecht = Großkommentar HGB, Bankvertragsrecht*, (3rd and 4th edn., Berlin / New York: de Gruyter, 1975 / 1988)); the reality of contracts is often one of multi-party regimes, i.e. of various relations linked with each other (C.-W. Canaris, ibid. (1988) paras. 425–430; C.-W. Canaris, 'Bereicherungsausgleich im bargeldlosen Zahlungsverkehr', *Wertpapier-Mitteilungen (WM)* 1980, 354–371; W. Möschel, 'Dogmatische Strukturen des bargeldlosen Zahlungsverkehrs', *Archiv für civilistische Praxis (AcP)* 186 (1986), 187–236; G. Teubner, *Networks as Connected Contracts* (Oxford / Portland OR: Hart Publishing, 2011)); in no area one set of rules created by the business sector has been object of and has contributed as much as banking practice has to standard contract terms law and control.

market law[7] and both areas of law are certainly of supreme importance again today[8] – one can equally well say that today the digital economy and more generally the digital dimension are of similar importance practically speaking – dealing as they do with another key factor: information – and in their potential as a source of emerging ideas. The digital dimension, of course, raises questions of regulation in many areas: in IP law, in the law of unfair competition, with respect to antitrust law. Certainly, however, the relationship between contract law and regulation is one of the most prominent relationships in the digital arena too. The law of the digital age – now concerning the key factor of data and broadly available information – would seem to play a role analogous to the one which the law of banking and capital markets plays for the key factor of capital. Also with respect to the digital dimension, the relationship to (public interest) regulation is omnipresent, and again this is a cross-sectoral area. The relationship to regulation will be taken up below (section 2), specifying that regulation mainly affects platforms for contracting on the one hand and single contracts on the other. Similarly important is the cross-sectoral character of the area. Whilst in banking and capital market law, principally contract law, company law and some of property law come together and banking law cuts across these areas – adding then regulation in the form of prudential supervision of the institutions and in the form of a market publicity, integrity and stability regime – the law of the digital arena would seem to be even more multifaceted and dispersed. With respect to contract law, formation, implementation and performance are specifically regulated, but also (digital) contents are clearly 'specific' whenever the digital dimension comes in (see below). For company law, instruments such as the digital company register or digital voting have revolutionised publicity and the structure of governance[9] – but capital market law has been affected even

---

7 Capital market law has brought – very practically speaking – the most striking example of how 'voice' and 'exit' as strategies on markets are alternatives and complement each other at the same time (K. Hopt, *Kapitalanlegerschutz im Recht der Banken* (Munich: Beck, 1975); before and ground-breaking H. Manne, 'Mergers and the Market for Corporate Control', 73 *Journal of Political Economy* 110–120 (1965)); it also has brought about a whole international and interdisciplinary approach to research, the (corporate) governance approach (among so many: K. Hopt / H. Kanda / M. Roe / E. Wymeersch / S. Prigge (eds.), *Comparative Corporate Governance – the State of the Art and Emerging Research* (Oxford, University Press, 1998); summary in S. Grundmann, *European Company Law: Organization, Finance and Capital Markets*, (2nd edn., Antwerp / Oxford: Intersentia, 2012), §14).

8 The financial crisis has certainly brought about again a new awareness of the links between robust supervisory regimes and solid private law protection – for instance in contract law. As this, however, is a core topic namely for the digital arena as well, this aspect will rather be taken up and more deeply discussed for the digital arena than for banking law (on banking, see only S. Grundmann, 'The Banking Union Translated into (Private Law) Duties – Infrastructure and Rulebook', *EBOR* 16 (2015), 357–382).

9 On these issues, see summary in S. Grundmann, *European Company Law* (above n. 7), §9 paras. 2–19, 36 et seq. and §13 paras. 23–29).

more deeply. Securities have long been digitalised; the securities transactions even more radically, namely when algorithms have taken over the actual decision-making process as in high-frequency trading. The transfer of 'property' (title) was fundamentally modified when digital registrations replaced transfers of documents;[10] the transfer of securities ownership stands to be taken one step further with the advent of blockchain-facilitated ledgers recording securities transactions.[11] The law of money has not only seen the digital 'storing' of legal tender in accounts, but also a (partial) replacement of legal tender by digital alternatives such as Bitcoins (see below Part III Schollin).

1.2. EUROPEAN CONTRACT LAW IN PARTICULAR

We look at the digital dimension – with regulation and in its multi-faceted appearance – more specifically in *European Contract Law*. By European contract law, three dimensions are addressed in particular.

1.2.1. The EU Substantive Law Basis – Three Lines of Specific Legislation

The first dimension – and in the future perhaps the most important one – is that of EU Law in the technical sense. There are three main legal measures with respect to contract law. All three have considerable importance, develop a certain model – albeit fragmented, namely in the first case – and thus can serve as an 'anchor' for the overall consideration of 'contract law in Europe in the digital age'.

The first legal measure is the EC Directive on electronic commerce of June 2000 in which a certain model of formation of contract is enshrined – more specifically, those mechanisms which were seen as being necessary to adapt the general model of formation of contract (in the various national contract laws) to the particular environment of electronic contracting, namely adaptations

10 On questions of transfer of digital rights (representing securities) see, for instance: H. Potter / D. McLean, 'Introduction to Book Entry Transfer of Securities', 28 *Business Law* 209–214 (1972); E. Guttman, 'Toward the Uncertificated Security: A Congressional Lead for States to Follow', 37 *Washington & Lee Law Review* 717–738 (1980); J. Dalhuisen, *Dalhuisen on Transnational Comparative, Commercial, Financial and Trade Law*, Vol. 1 (6th edn., Oxford: Hart Publishing, 2016), pp. 513 et seq.

11 H. Kakavand et al., 'The Blockchain Revolution: An Analysis of Regulation and Technology Related to Distributed Ledger Technologies', Working Paper (2017), https://ssrn.com/abstract=2849251, pp. 14–16; M. Iansiti / K. Lakhani, 'The Truth About Blockchain', *Harvard Business Review* 118–127 (January–February 2017), https://hbr.org/2017/01/the-truth-about-blockchain, under 'localization'; cf. also J. Brito / H. Shadab / A. Castillo, 'Bitcoin Financial, Regulation: Securities, Derivatives, Prediction Markets, and Gambling', 16 *Columbia Science & Technology Law Review* 144–221 (2014).

required due to the 'fluidity' of the clicks and expressions of will made in this context, the diminished clarity and the increased ambiguity and possibility of errors.[12]

The *second legal measure* – more precisely, group of legal measures – deals with the distance character of most digital contracting. This dimension was first regulated in the so-called EC Distance Selling Directive, then reformed and integrated in the EU Consumers Rights Directive.[13] In 2015, this line of legislation became the object of a broader strategy on the digital economy – extending, however, also well beyond it.[14] In fact, two proposals were based on this strategy paper, both adopted by the EU Commission on 9 December 2015, the *first proposal* referring to *online sale of goods*[15] and thus continuing

---

12 Directive 2000/31/EC of the European Parliament and of the Council of 8 June 2000 on certain legal aspects of information society services, in particular electronic commerce, in the Internal Market ('Directive on electronic commerce'), *EC OJ* 2000 L 178/1; on this measure, see, for instance C. Ramberg, 'The e-commerce directive and formation of contract in a comparative perspective', 26 *European Law Review* 429–450 (2001); M. Kightlinger, 'A Solution to the Yahoo! Problem? The EC E-Commerce Directive as a Model for International Cooperation on Internet Choice of Law', 24 *Michigan Journal of International Law* 719–766 (2003); M. Hellner, 'The Country of Origin Principle in the E-commerce Directive – A Conflict with Conflict of Laws', 12 *European Review of Private Law* 193–213 (2004); see in more detail below in section 3.3 and in the chapter by R. Brownsword in Part III of this book; see also Directive 1999/93/EC of the European Parliament and of the Council of 13 December 1999 on a Community framework for electronic signatures, *EC OJ* 2000 L 13/12; and on this measure, for instance H. Rossnagel, 'Mobile Qualified Electronic Signatures and Certification on Demand' in S. Katsikas / S. Gritzalis / J. López (eds.), *Public Key Infrastructure* (Berlin / Heidelberg: Springer, 2004), pp. 274–286; C. Thiel / A. Fiedler, 'Der grenzenlose digitale Binnenmarkt', 37 *Datenschutz und Datensicherheit (DuD)* 2013, 14–19; A. Mitrakas, 'Information security and law in Europe: Risks checked?', 15 *Information & Communications Technology Law* 33–53 (2006).

13 Directive 2011/83/EU of the European Parliament and of the Council of 25 October 2011 on Consumer Rights, amending Council Directive 93/13/EEC and Directive 1999/44/EC of the European Parliament and of the Council and repealing Council Directive 85/577/EEC and Directive 97/7/EC of the European Parliament and of the Council [Consumer Rights Directive], *EU OJ* 2011 L 304/64; much further reaching (encompassing sales law and unfair contract terms law) was the Proposal by the EU Commission for a Directive of the European Parliament and of the Council on consumer rights of 8 October 2008, COM(2008) 614 final; see in more detail on this measure (and also on the EC Distance Selling Directive which it replaced): E. Hall / G. Howells / J. Watson, 'The Consumer Rights Directive – An Assessment of its Contribution to the Development of European Consumer Contract Law', 8 *European Review of Contract Law* 139–166 (2012); S. Grundmann, 'The EU Consumer Rights Directive – Optimizing, Creating Alternatives or a Dead-End', 18 *Uniform Law Review*, 98–127 (2013); V. Mak, 'Standards of Protection: In Search of the Average Consumer of EU Law in the Proposal for a Consumer Rights Directive', 19 *European Review of Private Law* 25–42 (2011).

14 Digital Single Market Strategy for Europe, COM(2015) 192 final; on this strategy paper, see S. Arnerstål, 'Licensing digital content in a sale of goods context', 10 *Journal of Intellectual Property Law & Practice* 750–758 (2015).

15 Proposal for a Directive of the European Parliament and of the Council on certain aspects concerning contracts for the online and other distance sales of goods of 9 December 2015, COM(2015) 635 final; on this proposal (online sales), see, for instance J. Smits, 'New

(and extending) the regime established in the EC Distance Selling and the EU Consumer Rights Directives. As the E-Commerce Directive, this line of measures mainly focuses on the formation of contracts (see below section 3).

Conversely, the other proposal – the *third legal measure* (yet to come) – goes well beyond known territory. It is based on rules on aspects of the digital arena already proposed in the project on a Common European Sales Law[16] and deals with the supply of *digital content* in particular – and hence no longer mainly the formation, but the content of the contract and duties based on it too.[17] In fact, digital content is about the problem of an object of the contract which poses considerably, or even completely, new problems in large quantity: namely non-rivalrous and/or non-excludable use of the goods and questions of compensation; alternative modes of compensation (namely giving personal data instead of payment); services which have strong IP implications, but also network effects, etc. Digital content poses these new problems to such a degree that a truly new dimension of object of contract and questions of performance would seem to be opened.

Besides these three specific measures, EU law for the digital economy consists, however, also of the application of 'general' EU law (not specifically focusing on the digital arena) – namely measures of market regulation – to digital transactions. Thus, for instance, high-frequency trading can be scrutinised under the rules on insider trading in the EU Market Abuse Regulation or rules on market manipulation in the same legal measure[18] and be subject to a particular ban

---

European Union Proposals for Distance Sales and Digital Contents Contracts: Fit for Purpose?' *Zeitschrift für europäisches Privatrecht* 2016, 319–324; F. Zoll, 'The Remedies in the Proposals of the Online Sales Directive and the Directive on the Supply of Digital Content', *EuCML* 2016, 250–254; D. Staudenmeyer, 'Digitale Verträge – Die Richtlinienvorschläge der Europäischen Kommission', *Zeitschrift für europäisches Privatrecht* 2016, 801–831, at 806–825.

16 On these rules in CESL (and as its model: the [Academic] Common Frame of Reference), see, for instance, H. Eidenmüller et al., 'The proposal for a regulation on a common European sales law: Deficits of the most recent textual layer of European contract law' (2012) 16 *Edinburgh Law Review* 301–357, at 310–311 and 333; N. Helberger et al., 'Digital Content Contracts for Consumers', 36 *Journal of Consumer Policy* 37–57, 47–48 and 53 (2013).

17 Proposal for a Directive of the European Parliament and of the Council on certain aspects concerning contracts for the supply of digital content of 9 December 2015, COM(2015) 634 final; on this proposal (supply of digital content), see, for instance Smits, above n. 15; G. Spindler, 'Verträge über digitale Inhalte', *MultiMedia und Recht* (*MMR*) 2016, 147–153 and 219–224; Zoll, above n. 15; Staudenmeyer, above n. 15, pp. 825–830; see in more detail below section 4 and chapters by G. Spindler and C. Ramberg in Parts IV and V of this book.

18 On the application of these two regimes to high-frequency trading, see, for instance, K. Alexander, 'Market structures and market abuse' in G. Caprio, *The Handbook of Safeguarding Global Financial Stability* (London / Waltham / San Diego: Elsevier, 2013), pp. 375–385; G. Forst, 'Ist der Hochfrequenzhandel in der Europäischen Gemeinschaft gestattet?', *Bank- und Kapitalmarktrecht (BKR)* 2009, 454–462; E. Jaskulka, 'Das deutsche Hochfrequenzhandelsgesetz – eine Herausforderung für Handelsteilnehmer, Börsen und Multilaterale Handelssysteme (MTF)', *Bank- und Kapitalmarktrecht (BKR)* 2013, 221–233, at 231; P. Kasiske, 'Marktmissbräuchliche Strategien im Hochfrequenzhandel', *Wertpapier-Mitteilungen (WM)* 2014, 1933–1940.

under the stability rules in the new banking supervision architecture.[19] Another example, crowdfunding, irrespective of whether digital tools are prominent in its creation or use, is mainly about adapting requirements of (EU or national) capital market law to a changed environment. This environment is characterised by smaller amounts of investment and often more direct, substantive interest in the purpose of the investment (other than just an interest in returns). Even though crowdfunding is not conditional on digital forms of marketing, these are particularly suited for the particular characteristics of this type of investment scheme (small amounts, and a large number of dispersed potential investors who should, however, be directly approached during the time-scale of the investment). This example shows as well how such an adaptation was first put in place at the national level and now is proposed at the EU level.[20]

1.2.2. A Broader Concept of 'European Contract Law'

The example given just now, however, is also telling insofar as it represents a broader concept of 'European Contract Law'. Besides EU law measures this broader vision encompasses at least two more types of instruments, models or perspectives.

The first is a comparative law perspective in the EU – for instance on national measures already taken with respect to crowdfunding. This can be seen as part of a 'European Contract Law' especially if there is an interplay with existing EU law (e.g. capital market requirements set at the EU law level; in other cases EU antitrust law requirements) or if EU law is emerging in that area (as in the case of crowdfunding). Similarly, there is a strong 'European' dimension already whenever there is a model which may be based on one national law, but circulates in an unchanged form across all the European Union market or large parts of it. The most famous example stems probably from company law, the Company Limited by Shares (Ltd.) under English law – an example again

---

19 On this possibility, see arts. 17, 4(1)(40), 2(1)(d)iii of Directive 2014/65/EU (MiFID II); and, for instance, N. Moloney, *EU Securities and Financial Markets Regulation* (4th edn., Oxford: Oxford University Press, 2014), pp. 525–530.

20 On crowdfunding and its regulation (both at national and at EU level), see, for instance, E. Sixt, *Schwarmökonomie und Crowdfunding* (Wiesbaden: Springer, 2014), pp. 161–189 (chapter: 'legal regime of crowdfunding platforms'), overview on the crowdfunding national regulation in several EU Member States: T. Aschenbeck-Florange et al., 'Regulation of crowdfunding in Germany, the UK, Spain and Italy and the impact of the European single market', European Crowdfunding Network. June 2013, available at http://eurocrowd.org/wp-content/blogs.dir/sites/85/2013/06/20130610_Regulation_of_Crowdfunding_ECN_OC.pdf; G. Dorfleitner / L. Hornuf / M. Schmitt / M. Weber, 'The Fintech Market in Germany' (2016), available at: https://papers.ssrn.com/sol3/papers.cfm?abstract_id=2885931; and in more detail below, chapter by C. Estevan in Part II of this book.

where digital registration is paramount for success.[21] For contract law, Hugh Collins has suggested for such models 'in circulation across the EU' a 'freedom to circulate documents [i.e. models]'.[22]

A 'European Contract Law' in the broad sense may even be emerging or existing where a distinctly European way of looking at certain problems can be found or a distinctly European way of drafting particular contracts in the field can be discerned. One example may be duties arising at the pre-contractual stage: while duties of fair dealing are virtually non-existent under US contract law at this stage, European contract law extends core principles of contract law into the pre-contractual negotiation phase (below, section 3.1).

How this integrates into a digital market which in many cases may even be global, is a delicate issue – encompassing conflict of laws issues with respect to standard terms, private law and public interest regulation.[23] This clash between (partly) national legal frameworks and transnational markets is omnipresent in the digital arena.

1.3. THE MAIN PIECES OF THE ARCHITECTURE

In the following, this ocean of (new) phenomena and – increasingly – also of rules and legal regimes is structured in a way which is aimed at furthering the perception of an 'architecture' by referring to known structures – namely, given that the focus is on European Contract Law, known contract law structures. A first, sharp distinction should be drawn between two different *pillars* of the architecture: (i) on the one hand, digital content as the *object* of contract and, (ii) on the other hand, the use of digital technologies in a variety of procedures during the *contractual life-cycle*. Digital content, i.e. digital goods and services, data, and instruments of storage for digital information in the broader sense, may constitute the performance or the counter-performance of the contract. Irrespective of this contractual content, different digital technologies (such as digital platforms; Big Data analytics; artificial intelligence (AI); or blockchain)

---

21 On this phenomenon, see summary of the law applicable and the background in the freedom of establishment: S. Grundmann, *European Company Law* (above n. 7), §3 paras. 13–16, §4 para. 14, §7 paras 12–27 and §25 paras. 15–38, 42–48; on English Law in this respect, see S. Mayson / D. French / C. Ryan, *Mayson, French and Ryan on Company Law* (22nd edn., Oxford: Oxford University Press, 2005), p. 45.

22 H. Collins, 'The Freedom to Circulate Documents: Regulating Contracts in Europe', 10 *European Law Journal* 787–803 (2004); see as well S. Wittacker, 'On the Development of European Standard Contract Terms', 2 *European Review of Contract Law* 51–76 (2006).

23 On the problems of law applicable to digital platforms and transactions, see, for instance, D. Svantesson, *Private International Law and the Internet* (3rd edn., Alphen aan den Rijn: Wolters Kluwer, 2016); D. Svantesson, 'A new jurisprudential framework for jurisdiction: Beyond the Harvard Draft', 109 *American Journal of International Law* 69–74 (2015); and below the chapter by D. Svantesson in Part II.

also intervene at different stages of the contractual life-cycle: in the screening of prospective contractual parties; in drafting the contract (AI selection of contractual clauses); during contract formation (match-making by platforms); in the definition of concrete contractual obligations, their continuous development over time, and their automated enforcement (smart contracts); in the linkage of contracts (networks of (smart) contracts or decentralised (autonomous) organisations); and, finally, in contractual interpretation (AI interpretation). Over these different stages, the contractual basis is subjected, more than in traditional contexts, to the possibility of perpetual adaptation, revision, and renegotiation via the updating of the information, codes and methods used by contractual digital technology.

The first two pillars of the digital architecture of contracts may, but do not have to, come together in a single contract: contracts over the licensing of e-books may be negotiated and concluded in an offline scenario; contracts governing the sale of old-fashioned, hardcopy books may be initiated, formed and enforced entirely in the digital world, using technologies that span from Big Data analytics via digital platforms to AI and blockchain. Besides these two, a *third pillar* is found (iii) in the *regulatory* framework within which private law and the law made by private parties has to take place. Its instruments, in turn, may shape the other two architectural elements with conventional methods of regulation, but they may also actively harness digital technology to more effectively pursue regulatory aims.

We deal with the three pillars in the following order: starting out from the overall framework, i.e. the regulatory framework (see below section 2), followed by the two – more traditionally contract-law-related – pillars mentioned first: the contractual basis (from formation to adaptation, see below section 3); and the object of the contract (see below section 4). We thereby take a market approach to the conceptualisation of (European) contract law in the digital age.

These parts are strongly interconnected with each other, most prominently in the following two respects. As already mentioned, the regulatory regime – focusing primarily on public interests such as market structure – is nowadays often intimately embedded in private law regimes – aimed primarily at striking an adequate balance between individual private parties' interests. Moreover, in contracts whose basis has been formed in the digital arena often the formation and the subsequent ongoing development of the contractual basis are more intimately interconnected with one another than in traditional contracting (and in fact often cannot be severed at all). Particularly in the case of blockchains, the 'information' for the ongoing further development of the contract is already inbuilt in the preceding phase, i.e. in the formation of the instrument.[24]

---

[24] See below, n. 32 and accompanying text.

An example on point is the Bitcoin protocol: it not only creates Bitcoins, but also governs exhaustively the possibility of their transfer.

Hence, the choice of where to place a phenomenon, and a chapter discussing it, is sometimes difficult – to some extent even arbitrary. For instance, both crowdfunding and high-frequency trading are novel financial transactions, heavily influenced by an interplay between freedom of choice and regulatory framework. The former is characterised by some leniency with respect to capital market law requirements imposed on issuers looking for capital (in order to further this type of investment and the goals which investors in this setting typically pursue). Conversely, the latter is characterised by a large amount of freedom – as high-frequency trading consists of transactions on the part of (professional) investors – which, however, has to be limited in case of excesses. While high-frequency trading is investor action, because of its speed and volume it nevertheless also creates particular risks for other investors. Nevertheless, with respect to the main focus of 'novelty' which these two financial techniques deploy, it would seem that both differ considerably. Crowdfunding issues would seem to mainly revolve around questions of platforms and a relaxing of regulatory requirements (see therefore Part II Estevan). Conversely, high-frequency trading would seem to create most problems because of the automated creation and performance of transactions in high numbers. It would thus seem to particularly characterise the 'automatic' transformation of digital contracts when they are executed (Part III of the book and section 3 of this chapter).

In any case, to give architecture to the subject, allocating phenomena to core phases and modes of regulation of contracts would seem to be useful nevertheless and – with the proviso made – also possible. The discussion of such allocation of the problems and system-building in the contract law of the digital age has, however, just started. The allocation in the following therefore constitutes a mere 'first sketch'.

In this structure, the EU law measures named above – two already existing (of which one is to be amended soon), and a third one just emerging – serve as 'anchors'. They have been given particular attention, namely the latter two with two chapters, mapping them, analysing them, in one case very critically (see below Part V Spindler and Ramberg). In fact, over the last 18 months – and certainly once the two proposals of December 2015 are adopted – all the above-mentioned phases and perspectives would seem to be covered substantially also with respect to private law phenomena. The regulatory side, on the other hand, is strong at the EU level anyhow – also with respect to digital phenomena. Specifically capital market law, data protection law, antitrust and unfair competition law are already broad and thorough with respect to digital phenomena and, in addition, quite a few of the digital phenomena (such as crowdfunding and high-frequency trading) are also dealt with more specifically in their regulatory side. This does not imply that regulation for the digital arena in these areas of the law cannot be shaped in a more convincing and appropriate way – more appropriate for the digital dimension in particular[25] – but a solid basis from which to start in this endeavour certainly already exists. These anchors – establishing a certain framework-system already at the EU level, hence for all of Europe – allow to group the diverse phenomena of digital contracting around them. This includes national views on other legal issues (comparative law) and supranational practices ('*selbstgeschaffenes Recht der Wirtschaft*' / 'private ordering originating in business practices and terms').[26] The latter focuses either on the individual transactions (contracts) or on the establishment and functioning of platforms on which such contracts can be entered into.

While this introductory chapter is, of course, also about 'mapping' the area and the new challenges (and the chapters included in this book), we want to stress mainly the 'architecture' in all this. And just like real architecture (namely good architecture) is often telling a story (a story of power, of spirit, of light, of emotion and dynamics, sometimes of sweeping ascension to heaven (e.g. Sant'Andrea al Quirinale) or of death, darkness, powerful belief in resurrection and relief (e.g. Notre Dame du Haut, Ronchamps)), also 'architecture' in this more virtual sense is about a 'narrative' of what the digital dimension does or will do to contract law in the larger sense. The digital perspective is certainly a cross-sectional perspective. This perspective will further enhance the view that there is not just one rather one-dimensional image of contracts – namely as contracts

---

25 See, for instance, Hacker, above n. 5; Ph. Hacker / B. Petkova, 'Reining in the Big Promise of Big Data. Transparency, Inequality, and New Regulatory Frontiers', 15 *Northwestern Journal of Technology and Intellectual Property* 1 (2017), http://ssrn.com/abstract=2773527.

26 See very early: H. Grossmann-Doerth, 'Selbstgeschaffenes Recht der Wirtschaft und staatliches Recht' (Freiburg/Breisgau: Wagner'sche Universitätsbuchhandlung, 1933); and from the abundant flow of literature on 'private ordering': G. Bachmann, *Private Ordnung. Grundlagen ziviler Regelsetzung* (Tübingen: Mohr Siebeck, 2006); L. Bernstein, 'Private Commercial Law in the Cotton Industry: Creating Cooperation through Rules, Norms, and Institutions', 99 *Michigan Law Review* 1724–1790 (2001) (still more pertinent in this respect than her more famous piece on the diamond industry of 1992); R.C. Ellickson, *Order Without Law: How Neighbors Settle Disputes* (Cambridge, MA: Harvard University Press, 1991); J. Köndgen, 'Privatisierung des Rechts. Private Governance zwischen Deregulierung und Rekonstitutionalisierung', *Archiv für die civilistische Praxis* 206 (2006) 477–525; G. Teubner, 'Societal Constitutionalism' in Ch. Joerges / I.J. Sand / G. Teubner (eds.), *Constitutionalism and Transnational Governance* (Oxford: Hart Publishing, 2004), pp. 3–28. For transnational law as an area for which this discussion is particularly rich, see L.C. Backer, 'Economic Globalization and the Rise of Efficient Systems of Global Private Law Making: Wal-Mart as Global Legislator', 39 *Connecticut Law Review* 1739–1784 (2007); F. Cafaggi, 'The Many Features of Transnational Private Rule-Making: Unexplored Relationships between Custom, Jura Mercatorum and Global Private Regulation', 36 *University of Pennsylvania Journal of International Law* 875–938 (2015); G.-P. Calliess / J. Freiling / M. Renner, 'Transnational Governance and Evolutionary Theory' in G.-P. Calliess / P. Zumbansen (eds.), *Law, Economics and Evolutionary Theory* (Cheltenham: Edward Elgar 2010), pp. 353–368; G. Teubner, 'Global Bukowina: Legal Pluralism in the World Society' in G. Teubner (ed.), *Global Law Without a State* (Aldershot: Dartmouth, 1997), pp. 3–28; also G. Teubner, 'Societal Constitutionalism' (above).

for exchange – but more than one,[27] perhaps even many. The digital dimension will also further a less mechanical view of contracts – first formed or not formed, then properly performed or breached – in favour of a more relational view of contracting. In this relational view, the issues of constant reshaping of contracts (as an ongoing process) will play a larger role, and, of course networks[28] and platforms[29] will play a larger role – the view of contract as the basis of a (long-term) organisation.[30]

A particular challenge, for drafting as well as regulation, may lie in squaring this realistically relational approach with smart contracts in which, as a general

---

27 G. Dorfleitner / L. Hornuf / M. Schmitt / M. Weber, 'The Fintech Market in Germany' (2016), available at: https://papers.ssrn.com/sol3/papers.cfm?abstract_id=2885931; Dorfleitner / Hornuf / Schmitt / Weber, *FinTech in Germany* (Berlin: Springer International Publishing, forthcoming 2017).

28 G. Teubner, *Networks as Connected Contracts* (Oxford: Hart Publishing, 2011); Teubner, *Netzwerk als Vertragsverbund – Virtuelle Unternehmen, Franchising, Just-in-time aus sozialwissenschaftlicher und juristischer Sicht* (Baden-Baden: Nomos, 2004); Teubner, 'Coincidentia oppositorum: Hybrid Networks beyond Contract and Organization' in M. Amstutz and G. Teubner (eds.), *Networks: Legal Issues of Multilateral Cooperation* (Oxford: Hart Publishing, 2009), pp. 3–30; S. Grundmann, 'Contractual networks in German private law' in F. Cafaggi (ed.), *Contractual Networks, Inter-Firm Cooperation and Economic Growth* (Cheltenham: Edward Elgar Publishing, 2011), pp. 111–162; based mainly on the groundbreaking work by: W.W. Powell, 'Neither Market nor Hierarchy – network forms of organization', 12 *Research in Organizational Behaviour* 295–336 (1990) V.P. Goldberg, 'Relational Exchange – Economics and Complex Contracts', 23 *American Behavioral Scientist* 337–352 (1980); more in particular with respect to *networks* with a digital contractual basis: A. Wright / P. de Filippi, 'Decentralized Blockchain Technology and the Rise of Lex Cryptographia', https://ssrn.com/abstract=2580664, pp. 15–17; 30–33 and 54–56; V. Buterin, 'DAOs, DACs, DAs and More: An Incomplete Terminology Guide', *Ethereum Blog* (6 May 2014), https://blog.ethereum.org/2014/05/06/daos-dacs-das-and-more-an-incomplete-terminology-guide/; and F. Idelberger's chapter in Part III of this book.

29 On digital platforms, see, for instance: Research group on the Law of Digital Services, 'Discussion Draft of a Directive on Online Intermediary Platforms', *EuCML* 2016, 164–169; German Federal Ministry of Economics and Energy, *Grünbuch Digitale Plattformen* (May 2016): http://www.bmwi.de/DIGITAL/Navigation/DE/Gruenbuch/gruenbuch.html; C. Busch et al., 'The Rise of the Platform Economy: A New Challenge for EU Consumer Law?', *EuCML* 2016, 3–10; C. Cauffman, 'The Commission's European Agenda for the Collaborative Economy – (Too) Platform and Service Provider Friendly?', *EuCML* 2016, 235–243; Ch. Wendehorst, 'Platform Intermediary Services and Duties under the E-Commerce Directive and the Consumer Rights Directive', *EuCML* 2016, 30–33; for a US perspective, see, e.g., V. Katz, 'Regulating the Sharing Economy', 30 *Berkeley Technology Law Journal* 1067–1126 (2015); R. Calo / A. Rosenblat, 'The Taking Economy: Uber, Information, and Power', Columbia Law Review (forthcoming), https://ssrn.com/abstract=2929643.

30 For the sweeping importance of this other image of contract see S. Grundmann / F. Cafaggi / G. Vettori (eds.), *The Organisational Contract* (Farnham: Ashgate, 2013), especially the introduction; more in particular with respect to contractual organisation on a *digital* basis, see: A. Norta, 'Creation of Smart-Contracting Collaborations for Decentralized Autonomous Organizations' in R. Matulevičius / M. Dumas (eds.), *Perspectives in Business Informatics Research* (Cham: Springer, 2015), pp. 3–17; Wright / de Filippi, above n. 28; Buterin, above n. 28.

rule, the terms and conditions of execution are fixed at the onset in code, allowing for automatic enforcement *irrespective* of novel factual developments outside the conditions specified in the original contract.[31] However, while automatic enforcement of clauses specified at the moment of the formation of the contract is the paradigmatic case in smart contracts, different strategies exist to update and partially rewrite smart contracts as well.[32] For example, the contract may be consensually terminated if the parties so wish, and the monetary value already exchanged will be restored to the original owner. Furthermore, the original smart contract may include coding provisions that enable an updating later during the contractual relationship. Even if such updating mechanisms were not embedded initially into the smart contract, parts of it may be cancelled and rewritten after formation. Hence, the contractual base, and even the code base, of smart contracts may evolve over time as well.

Finally, digital content sheds a completely new light on the question of how to shape and characterise the object of performance – what both parties owe, namely also the user. Here again, the overall thrust may be summarised with the statement that this object is also more fluid and its definition truly challenging, from a contract theory perspective, but also very practically when it comes to personal data[33] – again with the exception of those smart contracts in which performance is exactly pre-specified in code.

2. INSTITUTIONAL FRAMEWORK – REGULATORY ISSUES, PLATFORMS, AND GLOBAL SURROUNDINGS

2.1. THE CORE COMPONENTS AND DIMENSIONS – SURVEY

The substantive discussion of an 'architecture' is probably best approached by starting out from the institutional and regulatory framework. The regulatory environment for contracts in the digital world separates into two distinct subfields. On the one hand, digital technology may be actively harnessed by legislators and regulators in order to shape a proactive, adaptive environment for contracts, both non-digital and, particularly, digitally mediated ones.

31 See the chapter by F. Idelberger in this book, in Part III below.

32 We would like to thank Florian Idelberger for comments on these updating mechanisms; cf. also V. Buterin, 'A next-generation smart contract and decentralized application platform', Ethereum White Paper (2014), pp. 20–21.

33 See, for instance, Hacker / Petkova, above n. 25, particularly pp. 17–24; H. Schweitzer et al., 'Digitale Plattformen: Bausteine für einen künftigen Ordnungsrahmen', ZEW Discussion Paper No. 16-042 (2016), ftp.zew.de/pub/zew-docs/dp/dp16042.pdf, pp. 21–23; H. Schweitzer, 'Daten als neue Währung', *Frankfurter Allgemeine Zeitung* (24 February 2017) p. 18.

Such regulation *with* algorithms may draw on the seminal work by Lessig that parses out how societal and legal values may be infused directly into code.[34] Recently, regulation by technology has again been recognised as a promising road forward for the establishment of a facilitative and effective framework for governing the digital economy.[35] For example, scholars have discussed the need for, and the drawbacks of, regulators creating or improving digital intermediaries that help consumers find the products best matching their preferences;[36] others have suggested that regulators ought to use Big Data and blockchain technology to tailor contractual (and other) rules to individual addressees in 'personalised law';[37] and finally, it is suggested that central banks should build centrally-banked cryptocurrencies as tools for monetary policy, potentially enabling novel types of financial contracts and means of legal tender in the future.[38]

On the other hand, the digital component may reside not in the instrument, but in the object of regulation: regulation *of*, not *with* digital technologies. This is certainly the dimension of the institutional and regulatory framework on which most ink has already been spilled, and which therefore forms the centre of our overview and of the chapters in the book. Concerning digital contracts, three aspects seem paramount: the first is (i) the divide between individual contracts and platforms on which masses of (typically highly standardised) contracts are prepared or formed – prepared by indication of occasions for contract and exchange (match making), formed when such a mechanism is part of a platform regime. Digital contracting thus is characterised by an extraordinarily intimate link between the law of contracts and the law of markets.[39] Equally important as a framework parameter of digital contracting is (ii) the regulatory regime and framework for both individual contracts and platforms as such. Finally, the framework is immensely conditioned by (iii) the positioning of digital contracts

---

34 L. Lessig, *Code version 2.0* (New York: Basic Books, 2006).

35 G. Spindler, *Regulierung durch Technik*, Short Report (Berlin: Sachverständigenrat für Verbraucherfragen, 2016); Ph. Hacker, 'The Ambivalence of Algorithms. Gauging the Legitimacy of Personalized Law' in M. Bakhoum et al. (eds.) *Personal Data in Competition, Consumer Protection and IP Law – Towards a Holistic Approach?* (Berlin: Springer, forthcoming).

36 Cf. R. van Loo, 'Rise of the Digital Regulator', 66 *Duke Law Journal* 1267–1329 (2017), https://ssrn.com/abstract=2902238.

37 A. Porat / L. Strahilevitz, 'Personalizing Default Rules and Disclosure with Big Data', 112 *Michigan Law Review* 1417–1478 (2014); O. Ben-Shahar / A. Porat, 'Personalizing Negligence Law', 91 *NYU Law Review* 627 (2016); Ph. Hacker, 'Personalizing EU Private Law. From Disclosures to Nudges and Mandates', 25 *European Review of Private Law* 651 (2017), https://ssrn.com/abstract=2914393.

38 D. Danezis / S. Meiklejohn, 'Centrally banked cryptocurrencies', Working Paper (2015), arXiv preprint, arXiv:1505.06895.

39 The link would seem much more intimate than in the traditional analogue world, see references above nn. 1–3.

or of platforms for digital contracting – and their regulation – in a global environment.[40] In fact, the latter might even be the starting point (see below, section 2.2).

These three divides or types of regime are institutional and have a framework character indeed. Institutions are characterised by their features creating stability for the arena analysed and by their broad relevance for shaping such arena. Thus, (i) markets – and digital platforms as a particular form of organised market – are different from individual contracts precisely in that their regime may also contain important contractual rules, but that they reach far beyond that. They form a constant organisation not only between the parties of the contract, but for many other actors as well. Thereby, the platform may also favour some clients to the detriment of others – a phenomenon strongly regulated, for instance, in financial markets, also in less formally organised ones such as systematic internalisers.[41] Third-party effects are omnipresent particularly when there is scarcity of demand or supply – similarly, then, the need of stability and foreseeability is increased (owed in good part to the fact that participants cannot shape individual solutions). Hence, it is understandable that at least in institutional economics, markets/platforms are indeed seen as 'institutions',[42] while individual contracts are not. Moreover, the above-mentioned characteristics call as well (ii) for a further increased need of regulation – based not only on concerns of structural inequalities between the parties to the contract (information, 'bargaining power'), but also on greatly increased concerns for externalities (third-party effects). Regulation as such, again, is more 'institutional' and has more of a framework character than traditional contract law in that it is primarily aimed at furthering the public interest – for all participants of that digital arena – and

---

40 On digital platforms, see, references above n. 29; and for different types and examples, but also cross-section issues such as the binding character of certain standards, the chapters in Part II below (V. Mak, Airbnb), (C. Estevan, Crowdfunding) and (P. Pałka, Platform standards and their role as contractual terms). See all three chapters very substantially also on the regulation of platforms and/or contracts. On digital contracting in a global environment, see, for instance, L.A. Bygrave, *Internet Governance by Contract* (Oxford: Oxford University Press, 2015); and below the chapter by D. Svantesson in Part II. This contribution is in addition the one which approaches digital contracting most decidedly also from an overall 'institutional' perspective and therefore serves as starting point.

41 For a duty to offer all participants in such regimes 'best execution' – not giving preferential treatment to some – see art. 27 MiFID II; and L. Enriques / M. Gargantini, 'The Overarching Duty to Act in the Best Interest of the Client in MiFID II' in D. Busch / G. Ferrarini (eds.), *Regulation of the EU Financial Markets – MiFID II and MiFIR* (Oxford: Oxford University Press, 2017), chapter 4; S. Grundmann / Ph. Hacker, 'Conflicts of Interest' in D. Busch / G. Ferrarini (eds.), *Regulation of the EU Financial Markets – MiFID II and MiFIR* (Oxford: Oxford University Press, 2017), pp. 165–204, at 194–197.

42 See, for instance, A. Morrison / W. Wilhelm Jr ., *Investment Banking – Institutions, Politics, and Law* (Oxford: Oxford University Press, 2007), p. 37 ff.; H. Hirte / A. Heinrich (eds.) *Kölner Kommentar zum WpHG* (2nd edn., Cologne: Heymanns, 2014), Introduction (*Einl.*) para. 14 et seq.

not primarily at striking an adequate balance between individual interests 'only'. Public interest regulation often also not only channels transactions more powerfully because of its (typically) mandatory character, but is also enforced by supervisory institutions in the narrow sense.[43] Finally, the overall legal regime and its arrangement, namely (iii) questions of its application in the international and even global arena, are also both an institution and a framework.[44] As questions of their application are fundamental for the effect of such regimes, this perspective would seem to be a natural starting point for a legal analysis of contract law in the digital age. With these three institutions or institutional divides, most of the architecture of contracting in the digital age would seem to be captured: the relevant markets, encompassing also mass transactions; the relevant legal/regulatory regimes; and their application in a setting which is globalised to an extent largely unparalleled in other areas of contracting.

We shall now take up these points in turn. The regulatory component is inherent both in the discussion of the levels of regulation and in the difference between platforms and contracts; these two dimensions of the institutional framework for the digital world of contracts are thus scrutinised in greater detail in the following two sections, always with an eye on the interrelations between private law and regulation.

2.2. NATIONAL AND GLOBAL – THE LEVELS OF REGULATION

When it comes to the level of regulation, the starting point would seem to be that many phenomena of digital platforms and contracting are more decidedly cross-border than the regulation of these phenomena.[45] A common perception (and criticism) is therefore that phenomenon and regulation do not match,

---

43 Their character as institutions is even more universally accepted than that of markets/platforms. See, for instance, A. Morrison / W. Wilhelm Jr. (n. 42 above), pp. 88–92 (technical and organisational equipment – in addition to the features named – characterising those institutions which are seen by all as the 'inner circle' of institutions).

44 For the – largely undoubted – characterisation also of legal rules and whole regulatory regimes as 'institutions' see, for instance, E. Furubotn / R. Richter, *Institutions and Economic Theory* (2nd edn., Ann Arbor: University of Michigan Press, 2005), pp. 6–7; G. Geyer / A. Venn, *Ökonomische Prozesse – Globalisierung und Transformation: Eine institutionenökonomische Analyse aus der Perspektive des institutionellen Wandels und der Transaktionskostenökonomik* (Münster: Lit, 2001), p. 89.

45 See, for instance, Digital Single Market Strategy for Europe, COM(2015) 192 final, pp. 3–6; D. Svantesson, 'Time for the Law to Take Internet Geolocation Technologies Seriously', 8 *Journal of Private International Law* 473–487 (2012); and in this volume, the chapter below by D. Svantesson – observing as well that the digital arena produces more contracting or at least more contracting with choice of law and choice of forum clauses than analogue environments and (after a passage of fundamental critique) then indeed analysing mainly the validity of such clauses and one core choice of laws connecting factor (whether a particular market has been 'targeted').

namely that regulation is territorial and the phenomenon is global – with one core consequence being that many laws may apply cumulatively.[46] From this perspective, it may even be doubtful whether the most important regulatory forces still take sufficient effect in the digital arena – for instance law, code, market and norms (as prominently identified by L. Lessig).[47]

While such concerns are justified to some extent and while certainly more than just an adaptation of traditional regimes for the analogue world is needed for a coherent regulatory regime for the digital arena,[48] two structural features should nevertheless not be overlooked when the image of an allegedly chaotic state of fragmentation is conjured up.

The first is about the level where regulation typically takes place. At least in the EU – but in areas such as capital market law, competition law and banking regulation also in the United States – regulation tends to concentrate on the federal, i.e. the EU level, while national law (or State law) is dominant for the private law regime – in contract law typically default rules. Thus, public interest regulation as that part of the regime which is not open to private law contracting – and boilerplate law which can indeed largely circulate across territories and thus create a legal platform transcending state territories – is typically designed for such large entities as the entire European internal market. Seen from this perspective, it may be less unforeseeable and burdensome to adapt to such regimes (in the EU just one regime for 28 states!), and the impact principle which reigns supreme in business regulation[49] may justify the application of EU Law to platforms and to contracts with EU clients (consumers). When indeed a contract is formed, the 'genuine link' with the market where it is formed would seem to be strong enough, and also with the profit derived. Thus, while in tort law or with respect to injunctions, the territoriality principle may lead to hyper-regulation by fragmentation, in contract law the risk seems less considerable. The argument would be that while there may be a strong territoriality principle, it does not excessively fragment a world-wide digital arena, at least not with respect to contract law and standards of conduct relating to contracting.

---

46 See, for instance, J. Goldsmith / T. Wu, *Who Controls the Internet? Illusions of a Borderless World* (Oxford: Oxford University Press, 2006), chapter 9; and in this volume, section 2.3 of the chapter in Part II below by D. Svantesson, 'hyper-regulation'.

47 L.A. Bygrave, *Internet Governance* (above n. 40), p. 4 et seq. – taken up by D. Svantesson, in Part II below, section 2.4 and fns. 8–9.

48 See, for instance, Hacker, above n. 5; J. Kroll et al., 'Accountable Algorithms', 165 *University of Pennsylvania Law Review* (2017), ssrn.com/abstract=2765268.

49 The so-called effects doctrine ('impact' principle) – as opposed to the principle of territoriality (seat of the actors or place of actions taken) –, was most prominently introduced in antitrust law: see ECJ judgment of 27 September 1988 – Joined Cases 89, 104, 114, 116, 117 and 125–129/85 *Ahlstrom and Others v. EC Commission (Re Woodpulp Cartel)*, [1988] ECR 5193. It is paramount, however, also in other areas such as capital market law or unfair competition law.

The second feature which calls for some caution with respect to an allegedly excessive fragmentation is the constitutionalisation of private law and private ordering. Indeed, most of the platforms are based on a legal regime combining private law rules with some regulatory content. If such legal regimes set up by private ordering constitute a significant part of a cross-border legal regime in the digital arena of contracting, one other development may become increasingly important, and discussion should focus on directing the endeavours in an appropriate direction. Constitutional principles more generally speaking have indeed increasingly been used, namely with respect to rule-setting by private bodies ('private ordering'), ultimately based on party autonomy. Here, they have been used to call for subjecting private ordering to rules such as proper representation of all parties affected, transparency, accountability etc. This trend is prominent for example in the conceptualisation of large parts of transnational law.[50] All these trends can ultimately be traced back to the – already mentioned – concept of market regulation and private law as mutually influencing and supporting each other, as so-called 'mutually enforcing backdrop orders' ('*wechselseitige Auffangordnungen*') – the two orders now being the constitutional system on the one hand and private law or private ordering on the other.[51]

2.3. PLATFORM MARKETS AND INDIVIDUAL CONTRACTS

The second component of the institutional framework that merits special consideration is platforms and the markets that they constitute. Regulation features in almost all aspects of the intersections between digitalisation and contract law, be it contracts for digital content or digital interventions in the contractual life-cycle. However, regulation seems particularly important with respect to platforms for three reasons. First, historically, platforms were the first clear instantiations of the novel, data-driven economy that were subjected to regulatory scrutiny.[52] This perspective, however, was not one derived from

---

50 For all these issues, both private ordering and in particular the transnational arena, see references above n. 26.

51 See already references above n. 4. On the concept of 'schemes mutually supporting each other' ('*wechselseitige Auffangordnungen*' in the sense of W. Hoffmann-Riehm and E. Schmidt-Assmann) see recently S. Grundmann / M. Renner, 'Vertrag und Dritter – System der Wechselwirkungen zwischen Marktregulierung und Vertragsrechtsdogmatik', *Juristenzeitung (JZ)* 2013, 379–388.

52 From the academic literature, see, e.g., K. Devine, 'Preserving Competition in Multi-Sided Innovative Markets: How Do You Solve a Problem Like Google?', 10 *North Carolina Journal of Law & Technology* 59–117 (2008); D. Evans, 'Competition and regulatory policy for multi-sided platforms with applications to the web economy', 2 *Concurrences* 57–62 (2008); for the investigations by the EU Commission into Google, see Case COMP/C-3/39.740, *Foundem v. Google* (30 November 2010); Case COMP/C-3/39.775, *Ciao v. Google Inc.* (30 November 2010); COMP/C-3/39.768, *1plus v. Google Inc.* (30 November 2010).

traditional contract law, but rather from antitrust law. Here, the economics literature on multi-sided platforms, and the specific market dynamics they engender,[53] was applied to digital platforms in an attempt to analyse how far dominant platforms could potentially hinder competition, abuse competitors and customers, and forestall innovation in the long run.[54] An important literature has now developed on barriers to entry into the digital economy,[55] and platforms, precisely because they constitute the hubs of, or gateways to many services in the digital economy, figure prominently in this literature.

Second, platforms not only play a special role with respect to the maintenance of an effective or workable competition, but they also are a crucial ingredient for the environment in which digitally facilitated contracts all too often take place. They provide the framework, as it were, that frames the way in which supply and demand are matched, in which products are perceived, and hence in which a vast number of individual contracts are formed. The importance of framing effects, underlined by behavioural economics,[56] points to the specific importance of this type of decision architecture that brings formerly diffuse agents together in specific channels that must be thoroughly analysed in order to uphold basic principles of consumer or investor protection, fair and efficient exchange, as well as innovation.

Third, platforms also more concretely shape the contractual relationships and economic incentives for their users. Scholars have argued that liability of platforms may follow from the reliance of users on the predominant influence of the platform over the supplier.[57] Going beyond the reliance criterion, we complement this proposal by suggesting that regulation may be necessary if contractual 'predetermination' by the platform leads to an unacceptable imbalance in the allocation of risks between the platform users. When platforms supply default contractual terms or provide for specific support for certain users, they act as de facto 'law-makers' for the platform environment. This is so because in most cases, users will accept the given arrangements, and the allocation of risks that

53 J.-C. Rochet / J. Tirole, 'Platform Competition in Two-Sided Markets', 1 *Journal of the European Economic Association* 990–1029 (2003); M. Armstrong, 'Competition in Two-Sided Markets', 37 *Rand Journal of Economics* 668–691 (2006).

54 I. Lianos / E. Motchenkova, 'Market Dominance and Search Quality in the Search Engine Market', 9 *Journal of Competition Law & Economics* 419–455 (2013).

55 Rubinfeld / Gal, above n. 4.

56 A. Tversky / D. Kahneman, 'The Framing of Decisions and the Psychology of Choice', 211 *Science* 453–458 (1981); A. Kühberger, 'The Influence of Framing on Risky Decisions: A Meta-Analysis', 75 *Organizational Behavior and Human Decision Processes* 23–55 (1998); overview in Ph. Hacker, *Verhaltensökonomik und Normativität* (Tübingen: Mohr Siebeck, 2017), §4 B.I.2.

57 Busch et al., above n. 29, pp. 8–9; Research group on the Law of Digital Services, above n. 29, pp. 167–168, Art. 16(2)(b) and Art. 18.

accompany them, rather than adapting them to their real needs and preferences. Contractual terms are a case in point: if a platform supplied a default contractual framework that users may adopt to govern the relationships between them, it would be rational for most users to just accept this framework and not invest time and cognitive effort to understand the terms and negotiate a better agreement with the counterparty, i.e., another user;[58] and boundedly rational users would ignore the terms and conditions most likely, anyway.[59] This does not necessarily invite regulatory intervention; however, if rational (and boundedly rational) apathy leads to the adoption of a contractual framework supplied by a platform that engenders serious imbalances in the allocation of risks *and* runs counter to the legitimate expectations of users, regulatory solutions would seem to be needed to account for the lack of market-based bargaining solutions that would address these shortcomings. For example, Airbnb at the moment only supplies a 'host guarantee' that, to a certain extent, covers damage to the host's property caused by Airbnb guests.[60] There is no corresponding 'guest guarantee' covering damage to guests caused by the host (not even for cancellation at extremely short notice without cause).[61] This does create an imbalance in the allocation of risks between hosts and guests; clearly, Airbnb wants to incentivise hosts to offer their housing on the platform, and believes that hosts are more sensitive about damage to their property than guests are about being damaged themselves. However, this does not leave guests entirely without recourse in case of damage; rather, guests may rely on the rental contract with the hosts to seek damages from them. What is missing for guests is the *additional* benefit of the guarantee by the platform. This, in turn, does not seem to contradict legitimate expectations of users since such guarantees are not part of other rental contracts, either; a real estate broker, for example, that brings a tenant and a landlord together would never, under reasonable circumstances, offer such a guarantee to the tenant.

However, imagine that Airbnb supplied a default rental agreement that users might adopt which included a provision excluding host liability for damages to the extent legally possible, for example excluding negligent damage to guests' property. This would not only create an imbalance in the allocation of risks, but might also run counter to the legitimate expectations of guests. Here, a specific kind of control of unfair contractual terms may be needed that takes account of the multipolar relationship between users and platforms. As a result, platforms

58 Cf. I. Ayres / A. Schwartz, 'The No-Reading Problem in Consumer Contract Law', 66 *Stanford Law Review* 545–609, 546–548 (2014).

59 Cf. O. Ben-Shahar / C. Schneider, *More Than You Wanted to Know* (Princeton NJ: Princeton University Press, 2014), chapter 4; Ph. Hacker, *Verhaltensökonomik und Normativität* (Tübingen: Mohr Siebeck, 2017), §9 D.

60 https://www.airbnb.com/guarantee.

61 See the contribution of Vanessa Mak (below in Part II) for a detailed analysis of the issues of guarantees by Airbnb.

might be required by future regulation to cover the risks, vis-à-vis their users, that they inappropriately and unexpectedly shifted onto those users. A crucial point, and difficulty, of such a regulatory framework would be to determine what the legitimate expectations of users are. On the one hand, a normative concept could be employed that would have to take account of both boundedly and more fully rational expectations of users.[62] On the other hand, an empirical concept could be used, governed by empirical surveys.[63]

Future regulation, therefore, will have to take into account the fact that platforms to a large extent dictate the decision environment of users. Quite obviously, such regulation must be introduced in a prudent way so as to not stifle innovation or render impossible services that most users continue to enjoy. However, as always in the regulation of novel technologies, the safeguarding of innovation must not be understood as a prohibition of regulation;[64] rather, the specific risks posed by certain new technologies, and the effectiveness of regulation to reduce them, must be analysed and weighed against their innovative potential.

Finally, regulation could also be harnessed to specifically foster innovation, for example by providing safe legal harbours for introducing novel, experimental features that, from an *ex ante* perspective, do not pose grave risks for users, but that nevertheless introduce an element of legal uncertainty, for example concerning liability.[65] For instance, platforms may fear that if they offer not only mechanisms of search and matchmaking, but also advice, they may be held liable if the advice turns out to be inappropriate. Airbnb might introduce an automated piece of advice that recommends specific apartments to potential guests based on the user's previous booking and rating history. On average, users may benefit from such advice, particularly if novel techniques of automated advice (using, for example, AI agents) are employed. At least in an introductory phase (e.g., beta versions), it is conceivable that regulation provides a safe harbour, shielding the platform from liability in case some pieces of advice point in the 'wrong' direction.

---

62 Cf., for the related issue of consumer expectations, Ph. Hacker, 'The Behavioral Divide. A Critique of the Differential Implementation of Behavioral Law and Economics in the US and the EU', 11 *European Review of Contract Law* 299–345, 317–318 (2015).

63 Cf. the recent proposal for interpreting contracts using empirical surveys by O. Ben-Shahar / L. Strahilevitz, 'Interpreting Contracts via Surveys and Experiments', University of Chicago Coase-Sandor Institute for Law & Economics Research Paper No. 791 (2017), https://ssrn.com/abstract=2905873.

64 R. Brownsword, 'The shaping of our on-line worlds: getting the regulatory environment right', 20 *International Journal of Law and Information Technology* 249–272, 267 et seq. (2012).

65 See, e.g., the 'regulatory sandbox' introduced by the UK Financial Conduct Authority, <https://www.fca.org.uk/firms/regulatory-sandbox> (last accessed on 26 June 2017).

At the moment, the factual regulatory depth varies from platform to platform. As Estevan de Quesada argues in her contribution to this book in Part II, crowdfunding is already subject to a deep thicket of securities regulation in the EU; the current regulatory structure, she suggests, should be simplified and amended so that crowdfunding platforms can unfold their full potential, and so that informed decisions by investors are facilitated. National legislatures have taken the first steps, and the EU legislature is about to follow. Vanessa Mak, in turn, finds in her contribution that housing platforms like Airbnb are currently operating in a regulatory blind-spot that leaves most of the decisions, and allocations of risk, to the platforms and users themselves. While some regulatory interventions from public law, particularly addressing concerns about competition to hotels and the crowding out of rental space for local inhabitants, have started to target Airbnb, a coherent regulatory framework for the contractual interactions seems to be patently lacking at the moment.

Platforms are a particularly noteworthy component of the digital economy, especially with respect to regulation. As the next section of this Introduction will show, however, platforms are far from the only digital phenomena interacting with contractual relationships at different stages of their genesis and development, and they are not the only technological innovations that merit novel responses from contract law and regulation, either.

3. THE USE OF DIGITAL TECHNOLOGY OVER THE LIFE-CYCLE OF A CONTRACT – FROM SCREENING FOR PARTIES TO ENFORCEMENT AND INTERPRETATION

The regulatory framework analysed in the previous section shapes the incentives and possibilities for the use of digital technology at various stages of the life-cycle of a contract. As we walk through these different stages, it will become apparent that the intersections between digitalisation and contracting draw on different technologies which, in turn, generate different contractual possibilities and regulatory challenges. This shows again to what extent private law, understood as the facilitation of legal arrangements by individual parties, and regulation are intertwined in the field of novel technologies.

3.1. FINDING CONTRACTUAL PARTNERS

Digital technologies are increasingly used by individuals and companies to find, screen and select potential contractual counterparties. These activities take place at the pre-contractual stage. Nevertheless, since they are undertaken with a view to forming contracts, and since contractual obligations extend into this phase under EU law, they form an important first stage in the life-cycle of a contract.

As we have seen, platforms play a major role in this phase by providing services of match-making. For example, eBay provides an effective tool of channelling buyers toward potential sellers; Uber connects drivers and travellers; Airbnb links hosts and guests; and crowdfunding platforms bring issuers and investors together. As noted above (sections 2.1 and 2.2), the greater part of Part II of this book is dedicated to an extensive analysis of the possibilities and regulatory issues surrounding platforms in European contract law.

However, we would like to note that the use of digital technologies in the pre-contractual phase is not limited to platforms and the specific market dynamics they engender. On the one hand, companies of all kinds (not only platforms) are increasingly relying on data mining and scoring techniques, enhanced by machine learning, to identify targets for marketing and contracting.[66] As is well-known, personal data about potential addressees of marketing material or contractual offers is collected to this end by a variety of companies and advertising networks.[67] The data is then stored and subjected to data mining techniques that increasingly use machine learning algorithms to extract valuable patterns of behaviour from seemingly unrelated data points.[68] This leads to the establishment of, for example, scores that determine what exact advertisement is served to which users in order to promote a sales or services contract.[69] In this way, personal data is converted into a valuable commercial product, which pays for many of the 'free' services most consumers nowadays take for granted in the digital world.[70] The disclosure

---

66 See I. Witten et al., *Data Mining: Practical Machine Learning Tools and Techniques* (4th edn., Amsterdam: Morgan Kaufman, 2016), pp. 26–27; F. Pasquale, *The Black Box Society* (Cambridge MA: Harvard University Press, 2016), chapter 2; V. Mayer-Schönberger / K. Cukier, *Big Data* (Boston MA: Houghton Mifflin Harcourt, 2013), chapter 6; A. Gandomi / M. Haider, 'Beyond the hype: Big data concepts, methods, and analytics', 35 *International Journal of Information Management* 137–144 (2015); for a particularly critical perspective, see, e.g., C. O'Neil, *Weapons of Math Destruction* (New York: Crown, 2016).

67 See, e.g., F. Borgesius, *Improving privacy protection in the area of behavioural targeting* (PhD thesis, 2014), http://dare.uva.nl/search?identifier=c74bdba6-616c-4cd9-925e-33a5858935e5, chapter 2; see also, for novel tracking techniques employing cross-browser device fingerprinting with a unique user identification rate of over 99%, Y. Cao et al., '(Cross-) Browser Fingerprinting via OS and Hardware Level Features', *24th Annual Network and Distributed System Security Symposium NDSS* (2017), www.yinzhicao.org/TrackingFree/crossbrowsertracking_NDSS17.pdf.

68 Cf. D. Kamarinou et al., 'Machine Learning with Personal Data', *Queen Mary University Legal Studies Research Paper* 247/2016 (2016), papers.ssrn.com/sol3/papers.cfm?abstract_id=2865811.

69 D. Citron / F. Pasquale, 'The Scored Society: Due Process for Automated Predictions', 89 *Washington Law Review* 1–33, 13–16 (2014).

70 C. Hoofnagle / J. Whittington, 'Free: Accounting for the Costs of the Internet's Most Popular Price', 61 *UCLA Law Review* 606–670 (2014); Hacker / Petkova, above n. 25, pp. 17–24.

of data between data-collecting companies, such as digital platforms, data brokers or advertising networks, not only raises data protection concerns;[71] it also creates novel informational asymmetries between those companies having access to the relevant data and algorithms, and the data subjects who, in most cases, do not.[72] As Przemysław Pałka shows in his contribution to Part II of this book, the algorithms, and hence the code, are most often unilaterally controlled by tech-savvy companies. Harnessing predictive analytics, the algorithmically advanced party often knows more about the future preferences and likely behaviour of a data subject than the data subject herself. As a growing literature in theoretical and empirical economics shows, this leads to the possibility of so-called exploitative contracting.[73] In this, contractual offers are tailored, by data-savvy companies, to the behavioural vulnerabilities of current or future clients.[74] For example, consumers with significant present bias may be served offers for teaser rates that, for these consumers, have negative expected value. This raises the question of the enforcement of the principle of fairness at the pre-contractual stage, where on the one hand innovative contracting, minimising search costs, should be facilitated, but exploitative schemes mitigated. As Giovanni Sartor shows in his contribution in Part IV, companies may increasingly rely on AI agents for the very marketing purposes that make up the pre-contractual stage. Therefore, an important avenue of future research will be to inquire how notions of fairness can be squared with automated screening procedures enhanced by artificial intelligence.[75] This is particularly relevant to European contract law where, in contrast to US contract law, notions of fair bargaining during the pre-contractual process are recognised.[76] As Roger Brownsword suggests in Part III of this book, an updated reading of the

---

71 Borgesius, above n. 67, pp. 82 et seq.; O. Lynskey, *The Foundations of EU Data Protection Law* (Oxford: Oxford University Press, 2016), pp. 196 et seq.

72 Calo, above n. 5, pp. 1002–1012; 1015–1018; Mik, above n. 5, pp. 12 et seq.

73 B. Kőszegi, 'Behavioral Contract Theory', 52 *Journal of Economic Literature* 1075–1118, 1104–1110 (2014); M. Grubb, 'Overconfident Consumers in the Marketplace', 29 *Journal of Economic Perspectives* 9–35 (2015); see, more generally, O. Bar-Gill, *Seduction by Contract* (Oxford: Oxford University Press: 2012), pp. 14–18; G. Akerlof / R. Shiller, *Phishing for Phools* (Princeton NJ: Princeton University Press, 2015).

74 See again R. Calo, above n. 5.

75 See, e.g., C. Dwork et al., 'Fairness Through Awareness', *Proceedings of the 3rd Innovations in Theoretical Computer Science Conference* 214–226 (2012); R. Zemel et al., 'Learning Fair Representations', *Proceedings of the 30th International Conf. on Machine Learning*, 28 *Proceedings of Machine Learning Research* 325–333 (2013).

76 See, for the European perspective, Study Group on a European Civil Code / Research Group on EC Private Law (Acquis Group), *Principles, Definitions and Model Rules of European Private Law*, Outline Edition (Munich: Sellier, 2009), Principles 7, 8 and 10, pp. 65–68; for the US perspective, Restatement (Second) of Contracts §205 cmt. c (Philadelphia: American Law Institute, 1981); §1-304 UCC (both restricting the obligations of good faith to the performance and enforcement of a contract).

Directive on Unfair Commercial Practices, or even an entirely novel regime, may be necessary to tackle these issues.

On the other hand, besides the issues of data protection and potential exploitation, discrimination is a further concern when automated algorithmic decisions are employed to screen potential contractual parties.[77] For example, data mining and machine learning techniques are increasingly used to select job applicants.[78] As a number of articles have shown, however, bias may enter these algorithmic processes at various instances of the design and application of the algorithm.[79] For example, in the case of machine learning, if the data set used to train the algorithm exhibits sample bias, the algorithm itself will 'learn' this bias and replicate it in the selection process even if the company had no intention of discriminating. This is a real concern when, for instance, the data of historically successful candidates constitute the training data; if, for societal or historical reasons, these candidates were mostly white males, the algorithm will likely find white and male applicants more attractive.[80] It remains doubtful how far antidiscrimination law can tackle this problem.[81] Algorithmic discrimination is thus another problem for a digitalised contract law that merits further scrutiny. Procedures of algorithmic fairness may offer a way forward here, a topic increasingly explored in the computer science literature[82] that is only just beginning to make an impact on legal analysis.[83]

However, companies are not the only players using digital technology in the pre-contractual phase; increasingly, individual clients and consumers also use technical support to find contractual offers that fit their preferences, or to ensure that they belong to a particular, advantageous group of consumers. Gal and Elkin-Koren call these digital assistants 'algorithmic consumers'.[84] Scholars have

---

77 S. Barocas / A. Selbst, 'Big Data's Disparate Impact', 104 *California Law Review* 672–732 (2016); Hacker / Petkova, above n. 25.

78 P. Kim, 'Data-Driven Discrimination at Work', 58 *William & Mary Law Review* 857–936 (2017), https://ssrn.com/abstract=2801251.

79 B. Custers, 'Data Dilemmas in the Information Society: Introduction and Overview' in B. Custers et al. (eds.), *Discrimination and Privacy in the Information Society* (Berlin: Springer, 2013), pp. 3–26, at 9, 12–18; T. Calders / I. Žliobaitė, 'Why Unbiased Computational Processes Can Lead to Discriminative Decision Procedures' in B. Custers et al. (eds.), *Discrimination and Privacy in the Information Society* (Berlin: Springer, 2013), pp. 43–57; A. Datta et al., 'Automated experiments on ad privacy settings', *Proceedings on Privacy Enhancing Technologies* 92–112 (2015); A. Lambrecht / C. Tucker, 'Algorithmic Bias? An Empirical Study into Apparent Gender-Based Discrimination in the Display of STEM Career Ads', Working Paper (2016), ssrn.com/abstract=2852260.

80 Cf. S. Lowry / G. MacPherson, 'A Blot on the Profession', 296 *British Medical Journal* 657–658 (1988).

81 See the references above, nn. 77 et seq.

82 See references above, n. 75.

83 Kroll et al., above n. 48.

84 M. Gal / N. Elkin-Koren, 'Algorithmic Consumers', *Harvard Journal of Law and Technology* (forthcoming), https://ssrn.com/abstract=2876201.

argued that a key challenge for regulation in the digital economy is for regulators to bring about, or at least facilitate, the effective, efficient and fair functioning of such digital intermediaries.[85]

All in all, methods of search, signalling, and screening – practices thoroughly analysed in the past century in information economics[86] – are being radically changed, for better or worse, by the advent of algorithms in the pre-contractual phase, on platforms and beyond.

3.2. DRAFTING

Once a potential contractual partner has been identified, or in many cases even before, the concrete terms of the contract need to be drafted. Here, both AI and blockchain technology may be used, and increasingly in fact are being used in practice. The art of drafting a contract on the one hand consists in finding the right contractual clauses that fit the situational pattern. Increasingly, the identification of such clauses, and of relevant factual documents to support and complement a contract, can be delegated to AI agents.[87] For example, given certain parameters as to the factual environment of the contract (goods sold; quantities; time and place of performance; concrete counterparty), such agents could then find clauses that are least likely to be litigated over, or that are least likely to trigger a longer negotiation process. Traditionally, lawyers would have consulted handbooks written by practitioners which condense the experience of many authors into practical, step-by-step drafting instructions. With the right set of training data, this experience can be 'learned' by an AI agent, and applied with greater speed to a given contractual situation than any human lawyer could deliver. In his contribution to this book, Giovanni Sartor in Part IV discusses some limitations of the use of AI agents for such purposes; and indeed, it seems premature to declare the full substitutability of lawyers drafting contracts by machines.[88] However, it seems plausible that an AI agent could at least provide

---

85 van Loo, above n. 36; Bar-Gill, above n. 73, at 5.

86 M. Spence, 'Job Market Signaling', 87 *Quarterly Journal of Economics* 355–374 (1973); J. Stiglitz, 'The Theory of "Screening", Education, and the Distribution of Income', 65 *American Economic Review* 283–300 (1975); M. Spence, 'The Contributions of the Economics of Information to Twentieth Century Economics', 115 *Quarterly Journal of Economics* 1441–1478 (2000).

87 J. McGinnis / R. Pearce, 'The Great Disruption: How Machine Intelligence Will Transform the Role of Lawyers in the Delivery of Legal Services', 82 *Fordham Law Review* 3041–3066, 3050–3052 (2014); H. Surden, 'Machine Learning and Law', 89 *Washington Law Review* 87–115, 110–114 (2014).

88 Cf. also Surden, above n. 87, pp. 105–107; D. Katz, 'Quantitative Legal Prediction – or – How I Learned to Stop Worrying and Start Preparing for the Data Driven Future of the Legal Services Industry', 62 *Emory Law Journal* 909–966, 958 et seq. (2013).

a decent first draft of a given contract, similar to the one now produced by the legal associate and submitted to a partner for review. As technology proceeds, we shall see to what extent drafting can be incrementally automated. At any rate, the advent of technology in the drafting sphere would seem to foretell a greater potential for personalising contracts and adapting them to the specific circumstances of the environment; technology may thus fill some, but certainly not all, gaps in incomplete contracts by decreasing the costs of fitting contractual terms to specific parameters, and by providing estimates of the likely evolution of the contractual relationship.[89] Such application of AI-facilitated contractual drafting is different from the AI applications discussed in the previous section that gave rise to the problems of exploitation or discrimination: in drafting, while it cannot be excluded that issues of exploitation or discrimination may arise there as well, the focus in these cases is on the adaptation of contractual clauses to given environments. Hence, if negative externalities are a smaller problem in this context, the need for regulation would also be diminished, and the resulting legal relationships would seem to be governed to a greater extent by classical private law.

However, it is not only the selection of clauses that can draw on digital technology; as Florian Idelberger describes in his contribution to Part III of this book, with smart contracts even the very obligations of the parties themselves can be expressed in code.[90] They can be written into a blockchain (specifically, the Ethereum blockchain) in order to make obligations clear, verifiable, and (partially) automatically executable. Smart contracts build on an early contribution by Nick Szabo[91] and are a variety of what Harry Surden later called 'computable contracts', i.e. contracts in which obligations or conditions are specified as computer data and which were pioneered particularly in the financial sector.[92] Their implementation in code triggers a whole set of questions concerning, for example, the effect of the illegality of certain obligations on

89 On contractual gaps, see I. Ayres / R. Gertner, 'Filling Gaps in Incomplete Contracts: An Economic Theory of Default Rules', 99 *Yale Law Journal* 87–130 (1989).

90 On smart contracts, see also R. Weber, 'Contractual Duties and Allocation of Liability in Automated Digital Contracts', in R. Schulze / D. Staudenmayer, *Digital Revolution: Challenges for Contract Law in Practice* (Baden-Baden: Nomos, 2016), pp. 163-187; G. Peters / E. Panayi, 'Understanding Modern Banking Ledgers through Blockchain Technologies: Future of Transaction Processing and Smart Contracts on the Internet of Money' in P. Tasca et al. (eds.), *Banking Beyond Banks and Money* (Switzerland: Springer International Publishing, 2016), pp. 239–278; Wright / de Filippi, above n. 28, pp. 10–12 and 24–26; Ch. Lim et al., 'Smart Contracts: Bridging the Gap Between Expectation and Reality', *Oxford Business Law Blog* (11 July 2016), https://www.law.ox.ac.uk/business-law-blog/blog/2016/07/smart-contracts-bridging-gap-between-expectation-and-reality; Buterin, above n. 32.

91 N. Szabo, 'Formalizing and securing relationships on public networks', 2(9) *First Monday* (1997): http://ojphi.org/ojs/index.php/fm/article/view/548/469.

92 H. Surden, 'Computable Contracts', 46 *UC Davis Law Review* 629–700, 634 et seq. (2012).

the nature of their automated execution, or the limited congruence between 'contracts' in a blockchain and 'contracts' in a legal sense. As was noted above, smart contracts may be rewritten to a certain extent if the parties so agree.[93] Therefore, if the parties, after initially drafting the contract, note that a certain contractual provision runs contrary to a certain regulatory provision or proves sub-optimal, they may adapt the contract consensually accordingly. However, neither of the parties may unilaterally invalidate any of the contractual provisions even if those provisions clearly violate the law. This poses a problem insofar as the self-executing character of the provisions means that the provision will be enforced nevertheless.[94] Hence, we suppose that the drafting stage in smart contracts assumes an importance that is possibly even greater than under 'dumb' contracts: parties must be aware of the fact that they cannot unilaterally withhold performance once it has been written into a smart contract. Whether nullity or substantive control of standard terms are instruments which will still be developed in this context is an open question. We shall come back to some of these issues in the subsection addressing performance (below, section 3.4). What remains clear, at this point already, is that the blockchain environment links the different stages of a contractual life-cycle together in a closer way than is the case with traditional contracts.

3.3. FORMATION

Now that the parties of the contract have been identified and the terms of the contract have been established, the contract still needs to be legally formed. Here, three types of digital mediation may be distinguished that run from more mainstream and established digital technology all the way to cutting-edge innovations of artificial intelligence. The first type comprises contracts formed using declarations of will that are exchanged electronically, for example by email. Already since the year 2000, these practices have been governed on the European level by the E-Commerce Directive (ECD, above section 1.2.1) that, importantly, contained specific information duties meant to ensure that both parties are fully informed about the identity of the counterparty, the main parameters of the object of the contract, particularly the price (Articles 5 et seq. ECD), and the most important steps of contract formation and content (Article 10 ECD). The ECD complemented the Directive governing Distance Contracts,[95] which had been adopted three years earlier, and which has now been entirely refashioned in the Directive on Consumer Rights and will likely be

93 Above, n. 32 and accompanying text.

94 Wright / de Filippi, above n. 28, pp. 25–26.

95 Directive 97/7/EC of the European Parliament and of the Council of 20 May 1997 on the protection of consumers in respect of distance contracts, *EC OJ* 1997 L 144/19.

modified again by the envisioned Directive on Online and other Distance Sales of Goods (see both, above section 1.2.1). Furthermore, the ECD ensured that national contract law allowed for the formation of valid contracts by electronic means (Article 9(1) ECD), thus treating online and offline contracts essentially similarly with respect to most legal requirements and consequences (other than the ones just discussed). As Roger Brownsword writes in his contribution to Part III, the key aim of this provision, and a key aim of the ECD in general, was to provide certainty about the legal validity of online transactions in an early age of online contracting. However, with the advent of the new world of profiling, scoring and personalisation (above, sections 2.1 and 3.1), he argues, another regime for contractual formation might be needed, that clearly differentiates between the diverging challenges of offline and online contracts. To some extent, if we accept this point, it is unclear whether such a regime would best be developed on a national or a European level, or (probably) on both; nevertheless, the novel asymmetries of information and power that digital technologies give rise to have already provoked a host of regulatory ideas to re-establish a balance of interests, and the possibilities of informed decisions, at the stage of the formation of contract.[96] Whether this will eventually lead to an entirely separate environment for formation, and general legal governance of, digital contracts awaits further scrutiny.[97]

The second type of digitally mediated contractual formation is reached where not only declarations of will are exchanged electronically, but where their exchange, and the market, is additionally structured by a digital platform that facilitates the matching of contractual parties. Beyond match-making, the platform may also serve as a device for the formation and storage of the terms of the contract (above, section 2.3). In her contribution to Part II, Vanessa Mak explores how far platforms may be considered intermediaries in the legal sense, and may incur civil liability even for matters pertaining primarily to the relationship between the users of the platform. While facilitating the formation of contracts, platforms also gather a quantity of personal data from their users,

---

96 See, e.g., Sachverständigenrat für Verbraucherfragen, *Verbraucherrecht 2.0 – Verbraucher in der digitalen Welt*, Report (Berlin, 2016), pp. 19–24 and 46–48; Hacker / Petkova, above n. 25, discussing, inter alia, mandatory data-free services, to be chosen in an active choice regime at the moment of contract formation, the control of contractual terms concerning privacy via the unconscionability / unfair contractual terms doctrine, and democratisation of data collection; Calo, above n. 72, p. 1047, suggesting a paid-option regime; Hoofnagle / Wittington, above n. 70, pp. 657 et seq., promoting, inter alia, mandatory price-setting for 'free' offers.

97 The Commission seems to be taking preliminary steps towards such a separate regime in the proposed Directive on Contracts for the Supply of Digital Content, which cuts across contractual typologies and differentiates, instead, between contracts with, and without, digital content (see below, section 4); however, the proposal does not include novel provisions governing the formation of contracts; similarly, rules on contractual formation are absent from the proposed Directive on Online and other Distance Sales of Goods.

contributing to the scoring process described above for the pre-contractual stage (above, section 3.1). As Przemysław Pałka argues, also in Part II it remains doubtful, however, whether the terms of service that online platforms disclose to their users constitute fully-fledged contracts when 'accepted' by users.[98] Rather, his contribution reorients the relationship between users and platforms away from contract and in the direction of property law.

The third type of digitally mediated contract formation is reached with the advent of artificial intelligence.[99] As Giovanni Sartor explains in his contribution to Part IV of this book, the acceptance of an offer, or even the formulation of a counteroffer, may be delegated to AI agents who, acting with different degrees of autonomy, conclude the contract on behalf of their principal. While platforms, therefore, facilitate the formation of the contract, AI agents may take the very steps of contract formation themselves. Obviously, both technologies (platforms and AI agents) may come together, particularly as machine-to-machine communication becomes more important with the spread of the Internet of Things.[100] If intelligent, personal digital assistants take over many of the more – and increasingly perhaps even the less – mundane tasks of ordering goods and services for consumption, the real challenge for contract law at the formation stage will likely not involve the 'automated consumption' (Brownsword's chapter (Part III), section 4.2), and contracts, between these agents, but the original, 'contractual' acts of delegation between humans and their digital assistants. Here, we believe that concepts developed in the tradition of commercial and company law may prove fruitful that deal with the adequate empowerment and monitoring of agents in small companies, as consumers increasingly approximate to principals that delegate authority and discretion to their digital agents/assistants – with the necessary adaptation of these rules from the business to the consumer world. For example, we can imagine differentiating between types of authority of different reach (from the fully authorised signatory (*Prokurist*) to the simple shop(ping) assistant)[101] that are standardised as consumers choose from a menu of digital assistants they would like to 'hire'. To facilitate this choice, the different types of authority that different digital assistants imply could be marked, in a 'traffic light system', with different colours, spanning from green (for limited authority)

---

98 See, however, also 'Sachverständigenrat für Verbraucherfragen', above n. 96, at 48; A. Metzger, 'Dienste gegen Daten: Ein synallagmatischer Vertrag', 216 *Archiv für die civilistische Praxis* 817–865 (2016).

99 For a primer on AI, see, e.g. S. Russell / P. Norvig, *Artificial Intelligence: A Modern Approach* (3rd edn., Upper Saddle River: Prentice Hall, 2010), chapter 1; for applications, see Witten et al., above n. 66, chapter 1; McKinsey Global Institute, *The Age of Analytics*, Report (London, 2016), pp. 81–93.

100 Cf. Surden, above n. 92, pp. 694 et seq.; M. Weyrich et al., 'Machine-to-Machine Communication', 31(4) *IEEE Software* 19–23 (2014).

101 Cf. §§48–58 German Commercial Code (*Handelsgesetzbuch – HGB*).

to red (extensive authority). Similar risk assessment and information tools are currently discussed to help retail investors in the choice of securities[102] – another potential analogy between the law of finance and the law of digital assistants. The automated transactions between digital assistants themselves might become less relevant for contract law as the focus will be on their factual implementation and execution; nevertheless, some contractual regime at least will need to govern the property dimension of these exchanges, under which, e.g. depleted olive oil may be reordered, the latest software installed, and licences for potentially inspiring e-books bought.[103] Meanwhile, more explicitly regulatory approaches will then be needed to, where necessary, shape the design of and the interactions between the digital assistants themselves to ensure that the very asymmetries of information and power that shape relationships between humans, and that are then subject to legal review and regulation, are not re-created between digital assistants of various stages of development and capacities. A related challenge is presented by predatory and exclusionary conduct, or contracts, undertaken by digital assistants, to be answered by future antitrust law.[104]

In all of these novel methods of drafting and formation, the use of adaptive, intelligent systems to us seems to harbour the possibility of making contracts more amenable to the continuous adaptation of their terms to novel developments. If both parties so wish, they could agree on an adaptation of, for example, the coded provisions of a smart contract to reflect a change in the present state of the world, or in the estimation of the likelihood of future events. It does not even seem far-fetched to imagine that both parties to a contract could use AI agents, as legal agents, and delegate to them the task of agreeing on mutually beneficial contractual updates as new information becomes available (for example, on a shift of supply or demand in the market concerning goods that are the object of a sales contract). This would certainly strengthen, as noted before, the relational character of the contract. Florian Idelberger further investigates this phenomenon under the heading of 'agreement technologies' in this book (section 4.1 of his contribution to Part III).

3.4. PERFORMANCE

Importantly, even the performance of a contract may, partially or entirely, be delegated to digital technology. In computable or smart contracts, this goes

102 See Ph. Hacker, *Verhaltensökonomik und Normativität* (Tübingen: Mohr Siebeck, 2017), §12 B.III.2.c.i.(1).

103 On the property dimension of smart contracts, see also B. Arruñada, 'Blockchain's Struggle to Deliver Impersonal Exchange', Pompeu Fabra University Economics and Business Working Paper Series 1549 (2017), https://ssrn.com/abstract=2903857, pp. 17 et seq.

104 Gal / Elkin-Koren, above n. 84, pp. 38–47.

beyond mere payment with electronic payment systems, for example. Rather, the fulfilment of any number of conditions upon which the performance is contingent may be electronically verified; upon verification, automated performance mechanisms may be initiated. Again, blockchain technology is particularly suitable for these tasks as it provides a consensus mechanism for the verification of certain conditions, for example the payment of specified amounts of cryptocurrency, such as Bitcoins, to the designated recipient. The controversial monetary status of Bitcoin is explored in depth, both analytically and historically, by Kristoffer Schollin in his contribution to Part III of this book. Similarly, the transfer of other assets may be recorded on electronic ledgers using blockchain technology. A central problem of this approach remains the verification of events that happen 'off-chain'; Ethereum, for example, has introduced so-called 'oracles' that could monitor and verify external events that trigger contractual consequences, similar to a panel of arbiters.[105]

As is well-known, probably the most important technological contribution of blockchain is the solution of the problem of the 'trusted third-party'.[106] Blockchains operate in a trustless way because of the distributed consensus mechanism that ties the verification of each additional block to a majority vote of the nodes running the chain. Hence, there is no central party that needs to be trusted to verify and guarantee the authenticity of the information contained in the blockchain. Similarly, smart contracts offer a way of mitigating the problem of trust concerning the willingness of the party to perform the contract. Since performance is enforced automatically once the conditions specified in the contract are met, there is no way for the bound party to unilaterally withhold performance.[107] The need for verification of off-chain events does reintroduce a certain amount of necessary trust (in oracles, for example); but to the extent that verification by multiple independent nodes (oracles) – rather than by the (conflicted) counterparty of a contract – is perceived as more objective, the required level of trust is still lower than in a traditional contract.[108] Additionally, as the transfer of more and more movable and immovable objects (such as securities; real estate; cars) is executed on blockchains, both performance and counter-performance can be verified on the chain, making trusted oracles

---

105 V. Buterin, 'Ethereum and Oracles', Ethereum Blog (22 July 2014), https://blog.ethereum.org/2014/07/22/ethereum-and-oracles/; see also Weber, above n 90, pp 166–167.

106 S. Nakamoto, *Bitcoin: A Peer-to-Peer Electronic Cash System*, Bitcoin White Paper (Without Place of Publication, 2008), p. 2; J. Witte, 'The Blockchain: A Gentle Introduction', Working Paper (2016), https://ssrn.com/abstract=2887567, p. 4; see also the contributions by Idelberger and Schollin in Part III of this book.

107 Lim et al., above n. 90.

108 Cf. J. Weldon, 'Building an "Oracle" for an Ethereum Contract', *Medium* (11 October 2016), https://medium.com/@mustwin/building-an-oracle-for-an-ethereum-contract-6096d3e39551#.f335uyw5a; Arruñada, above n. 103, at 31.

obsolete for these purposes.[109] To be sure, automated enforcement potentially creates other problems in contract law, for example when the party would have a right to withhold performance even though the conditions specified in the original contract are met. Nevertheless, automated performance and enforcement generally lower the level of trust needed between the parties,[110] and hence make cooperation, and mutually beneficial contracts, more likely to occur.

3.5. LINKING CONTRACTS

As Florian Idelberger explores in his contribution to Part III of this book, different contracts may be linked into contractual networks using a system of smart contracts. One particular, and particularly noteworthy, instantiation of such smart contractual networks is that of decentralised autonomous organisations (DAOs), i.e., systems written in code that function with a large degree of independence from human intervention and that are endowed with some internal capital they allocate to certain functions.[111] They may be used, for example, as investment vehicles that automatically collect contributions by investors, invest the collected funds, and distribute the returns according to a pre-specified algorithm. Again, using blockchain technology, such vehicles may leverage the verification processes inherent in cryptocurrency systems. Moreover, the investment decisions can be subjected, to different degrees, to the votes of investors; this promises to minimise monitoring costs for (the non-existent) human managers while, at the same time, allowing for shareholder voting to remain meaningful.

However, as the spectacular hack of the best-known DAO in June 2016 showed,[112] such contractual networks give rise to questions not only of the application of securities regulation, investor protection or company law, but also, and prominently, of the (cyber)security of invested funds. The complexity of such linked contracts therefore not only permits novel forms of investment

---

109 See Iansiti / Lakhani, above n. 11, for the growing potential for transferring ownership via blockchains.

110 Cf. A. Kosba et al., 'Hawk: The Blockchain Model of Cryptography and Privacy-Preserving Smart Contracts', *Proceedings of the 2016 IEEE Symposium on Security and Privacy (SP)* (San José CA: IEEE, 2016), pp. 839–858; for a cautious account and the re-introduction of centralising facilities and intermediaries, however, see Arruñada, above n. 103.

111 Buterin, above n. 28.

112 J. Wong / I. Klar, 'Everything you need to know about the Ethereum "hard fork"', *Quartz* (18 July 2016), http://qz.com/730004/everything-you-need-to-know-about-the-ethereum-hard-fork/; D. Siegel, 'Understanding The DAO Attack', *Coindesk* (25 June 2016), http://www.coindesk.com/understanding-dao-hack-journalists/; Ph. Hacker, 'Corporate Governance for Complex Cryptocurrencies? A Framework for Stability and Decision Making in Blockchain-Based Monetary Systems', Working Paper (2017, on file with authors).

packages, and contractual networks or network contracts to be offered, but also highlights the risks of cyber security that increase with the number of attack points that a complex system offers.[113] Given that many see in its informality and in the role an open system of reciprocity plays, the core advantages of the organisational contract (long-term and typically arranged in networks),[114] a word of caution would seem to be required before one derives lessons from arrangements in digital networks (typically highly formalised) for those in the analogue world.

3.6. INTERPRETATION

A final issue that will likely arise as digitally mediated contracts become more popular in mainstream commerce is the question of interpretation. To start with, it is an open question whether specific rules of interpretation should apply to smart contracts written in code rather than natural language. There seems to be a patent lack of literature on this issue, and we shall restrict our observations in this overview to pointing out specific problems and avenues for future research. Interpretation is important if a smart contract is challenged in court, for example when one party aims to reverse the self-executed performance because the counter-performance was allegedly defective. The interpretation of smart contractual terms will certainly depend on whether the provisions in a smart contract are standard terms or not. If they are, the specific interpretative methods for standard terms should, at least generally, apply.[115] Therefore, the terms will be subject to an interpretation that is more objective than general contractual interpretation, geared toward seeing the clause in the context of the general legal problem which it typically aims to resolve. Furthermore, if the smart contract is concluded between a professional party and a consumer, doubts about the meaning of the term would generally have to be resolved to the benefit of the consumer (Article 5 Sentence 2 of the Directive 93/13/EEC of 5 April 1993 on unfair terms in consumer contracts (UTD)); more generally, they are resolved to the detriment of the party supplying the terms. However, this provision immediately raises further questions, beyond the principled

---

113 Cf. B. Schneier, 'Click Here to Kill Everyone', *New York Magazine* (27 January 2017), nymag.com/selectall/2017/01/the-internet-of-things-dangerous-future-bruce-schneier.html.

114 See references above n. 28 and O. Williamson, 'Transaction-Cost Economics: The Governance of Contractual Relations', 22 *Journal of Law & Economics* 233–261 (1979); O. Williamson, *The Economic Institutions of Capitalism – Firms, Markets, Relational Contracting* (New York / London: Macmillan 1985), esp. chapter 2.

115 See, e.g., J. Basedow in *Münchener Kommentar*, BGB (7th edn., Munich: Beck, 2016), §305c BGB, paras. 18 et seq.

concerns which Roger Brownsword, in his contribution to Part III of this book, voices over the possibility of applying the UTD, written for an offline world, to online transactions.

First, with smart contracts, it seems more difficult than in traditional contracts to decide whether the terms employed are indeed standard terms. On the one hand, even if a contractual term is used only once, it might be drawn from a generic coding database that has been set up for use on many occasions; on the other hand, even if terms are used on multiple occasions by one contractual party, they might vary in their concrete coded expression given their interaction with the other terms or the general environment of the blockchain that the smart contract is implemented on. Therefore, future scholarship will need to parse out what variations in code, and even in programming languages, still preserve the character of standard terms vis-à-vis individually negotiated ones. Furthermore, even if a contractual term is considered to be a standard term under the UTD, it is unclear what the obligation to draft terms in plain, intelligible language would entail for provisions written in programming language, cf. Article 5 Sentence 1 UTD; certainly, the yardstick of intelligibility would have to be adapted to the fact that smart contracts, at least at the moment, are almost exclusively concluded between technologically savvy contractual parties who are able, at least generally, to read and judge the underlying code. However, if smart contracts become more common, they might be concluded even between parties unable to read the code, in which case the condition of intelligibility seems to be difficult to fulfil; 'translations' of the coding provisions in plain, natural language may then become obligatory. Finally, it remains to be seen how courts will grapple with the difficulty of 'interpreting' a programming language that, in many respects, differs from a natural language – independently of whether the clauses are classified as standard terms or not.

On a different note, AI technology may be used to estimate the outcome of legal disputes, be they over smart or traditional contracts.[116] For example, an algorithm could be designed to predict the likely interpretation of contractual clauses by the courts, taking note of specific parameters such as court districts or the situation and identity of the contractual parties. Here again, the future will show to what extent AI agents will prove superior in this prediction task to their human counterparts.[117] What is clear is that, with increasing granularity of

116 Empirical studies can be found in: D. Katz et al., 'A General Approach for Predicting the Behavior of the Supreme Court of the United States', Working Paper (2017), https://ssrn.com/abstract=2463244; T. Ruger et al., 'The Supreme Court Forecasting Project: Legal and Political Science Approaches to Predicting Supreme Court Decision-Making', 104 *Columbia Law Review* 1150–1210 (2004); overviews in: Katz, above n. 88, pp. 936 et seq.; Surden, above n. 87, pp. 102–105 and 108–110; McGinnis / Pearce, above n. 87, pp. 3052 et seq.

117 For limitations of predictive machine learning techniques, as applied to legal outcomes, see references above, n. 86.

the prediction of court interpretation of clauses, the results of this prospective interpretation can be fed back into the drafting stage of the contract. Hence, it becomes clear that, with the digitalisation of contracting, the life-cycle of a contract quite literally, in many aspects, becomes a real cycle in which beginning, end and other stages tend to overlap and mutually influence one another.

4. DIGITAL OBJECTS OF CONTRACT – CESL II AND MORE

In this last substantive section of the introduction, we shall turn to the third pillar of the architecture we are describing: digital objects of contract. From a bird's-eye perspective, the following contracts with digital content may be distinguished: first, the digital component may reside in the performance or in the counter-performance of a contract. The performance may, on the one hand, be related to personal or, on the other hand, to non-personal data. In the former instance, European data protection law, parts of which may be viewed as a specific regulatory framework for contracts concerning the processing of personal data, governs the legal relationships.[118] For example, when personal data is sold or rented to third parties by data brokers, the main questions of data protection law are now dealt with in the General Data Protection Regulation (GDPR). However, the object of performance may also be related to non-personal data. For example, contracts govern the download of e-books or the provision of certain digital services on the manifold platforms that constitute the backbone of the digital economy. As Przemysław Pałka argues in his contribution to Part II, however, the provision of digital services need not necessarily be understood as governed by contracts; rather, the use of platforms by users may take place within a property regime offered by the platforms. The contrary view, probably dominant in the mainstream literature, would hold that, at least implicitly, contracts are formed between users and platforms concerning the digital services that these platforms offer.[119]

It has become a common understanding, however, that digital content need not only be the object of the contractual performance, but may also constitute the counter-performance. Non-monetary forms of 'payment' have become particularly important whenever digital services are provided free of monetary charge.[120] The data transferred is almost always personal data of the users, or,

118 See Article 2 of Regulation (EU) 2016/679 of the European Parliament and of the Council of 27 April 2016 on the protection of natural persons with regard to the processing of personal data and on the free movement of such data (General Data Protection Regulation), *EU OJ* 2016 L 119/1; for an overview of European data protection law, see LYNSKEY, above n. 71.

119 See, e.g., 'Sachverständigenrat für Verbraucherfragen', above n. 96, at 48.

120 See references above, n. 70.

in the language of the GDPR, of the 'data subjects'. On the one hand, this data enables the provision of targeted, personalised advertising to these very users (above, section 3.1), for which providers of multi-sided platforms are able to charge higher prices to advertisers than for non-targeted advertisements.[121] On the other hand, the analysis of personal data provided helps the platforms, and other companies, to continuously improve their analytic and predictive models, which may then be applied to *other* users, thus contributing to the very essence of the algorithmic prowess that makes these companies so economically valuable today.[122]

Hence, we want to note that whenever personal data constitutes the counter-performance, it becomes questionable what the characteristic performance of the contract is.[123] Traditionally, in the provision of goods or services in exchange for money, the monetary component is regarded as uncharacteristic.[124] However, since personal data is the very fuel that keeps the engine of the data-driven business models running, and is put to multiple kinds of analytic and predictive uses that money is not, one might be tempted to conclude that, in many cases, it becomes as, or even more, characteristic as the service for which it is exchanged. This holds particularly true when the service is quite trivial in nature, such as a simple flashlight app for a smart phone. This may have repercussions (i) within private international law as the characteristic performance determines, if no contractual type can be easily identified, how a contract is classified and the law of what country is applicable to it;[125] and (ii) for the default legal regime applying to a contract that, often, will also follow the characteristic performance, particularly in so far as this regime is not fully contained in the proposed Directive on certain aspects concerning Contracts for the Supply of Digital Content (CSDC, above section 1.2.1), to which we now turn.

Intended as a continuation of the Common European Sales Law (CESL) with other means, and with a different scope,[126] the two proposed directives

---

121 Hacker / Petkova, above n. 25, pp. 17–24.

122 Cf. E. Siegel, *Predictive analytics: The power to predict who will click, buy, lie, or die* (Hoboken: Wiley, 2013); Gandomi / Haider, above n. 66, at 143; Mayer-Schönberger / Cukier, above n. 66, chapters 2 and 6; Witten et al., above n. 66, pp. 28–30; H. Chen et al., 'Business intelligence and analytics: From big data to big impact', 36 *Management & Information Systems Quarterly* 1165–1188 (2012).

123 Cf. Recital 19 of Regulation (EC) No 593/2008 of the European Parliament and of the Council of 17 June 2008 on the law applicable to contractual obligations (Rome I), *EC OJ* 2008 L 177/6.

124 D. Martiny in *Münchener Kommentar*, Rom I-VO, (6th edn., Munich: Beck, 2015), Art. 4, para. 172.

125 Art. 4(2) of the Rome I Regulation.

126 This is not the place to retell the story of CESL and its predecessors; for references, see above, n. 16; for the connection of CESL to the digital era, see, e.g., R. Schulze, 'The New Shape of European Contract Law', *EuCML* 2015, 139–144; for the different scope of CESL and the proposed directives, see, e.g., Smits, above n. 15, under Section 3; Staudenmeyer, above n. 15, p. 803; and Spindler's chapter in Part V, sections 2 and 3.

on contracts for the supply of digital content and for online sales assimilate the framework of obligations and remedies from the Directive on the Sale of Consumer Goods[127] to digital contracts.[128] However, in sticking to (a narrowed version of) the CESL frame of specifying general rules of contractual conformity and remedies, the directives fail to address some of the biggest challenges that digital contracting poses and that were described in the previous section (the second pillar of the 'architecture' discussed here). For example, the phenomenon of data as a novel currency is clearly recognised and covered by Article 3(1) CSDC. Nevertheless, none of the crucial questions following from this observation are addressed, such as: (i) What is the value of data?[129] And may this lead to serious imbalances in the contractual obligations? (ii) How far is the data processing enabled by the exchange of data for services and goods excessive, and how can the law mitigate exploitative schemes (above, section 3.1)? (iii) How can issues of discrimination that arise in the pre-contractual phase be addressed (above, section 3.1)? It seems that the Commission, with its focus on spurring economic growth through the digital economy,[130] and by restricting its regulatory ambitions to a set of obligations and remedies mostly taken from the CESL, is missing some of the important, novel dynamics that digital contracting has engendered.

Another key difficulty in the legal framework governing contracts with digital content will be the reconciliation of the CSDC with the novel EU data protection law that applies whenever personal data are processed. Gerald Spindler in Part V touches on a number of palpable contradictions between the GDPR and the CSDC; the most notable probably is the right to withdraw consent to the processing of personal data according to Article 7(3) GDPR, which seems to conflict with the enforceable duty to provide accurate personal information once personal data is perceived as the counter-performance in a contract exchanging economically valuable goods – which is precisely the perspective of the CSDC. One potential regulatory option would be to make such contracts only enforceable by the data subject, not by the data-collecting entity (just as contracts for sexual services are enforceable only for the monetary obligation under German Law).[131] The alternative might be to

---

127 Directive 1999/44/EC of the European Parliament and of the Council of 25 May 1999 on certain aspects of the sale of consumer goods and associated guarantees, *EC OJ* L 1999/12.

128 For differences, see, e.g., Smits, above n. 15; Staudenmeyer, above n. 15, pp. 829–830.

129 See, e.g., Hacker / Petkova, above n. 25, pp. 17–24; A. Acquisti et al., 'What Is Privacy Worth?', 42 *Journal of Legal Studies* 249–274 (2013); A. Acquisti et al., 'The Economics of Privacy', 54 *Journal of Economic Literature* 442–492 (2016).

130 Digital Single Market Strategy for Europe, COM(2015) 192 final, p. 3; Staudenmeyer, above n. 15, pp. 803 and 830.

131 §1 of the German Law on Prostitution (*Prostitutionsgesetz*).

distinguish between contracts with monetary compensation (fully enforceable) and those – much more informal ones – where an online 'service' is rendered accessible to those who give their personal data 'in consideration' and deal with these situations without having recourse to the concept of a 'binding' contract at all (no intention of being bound). As regards the law as proposed in the two regulations, it remains an open question whether Article 7(3) GDPR would mandate a right of rescission for contracts where personal data constitutes the counter-performance, and what the consequences of the use of this right would be for the contractual relationship. Article 13(2)(b) CSDC holds that, upon termination, 'the supplier shall … refrain from the use of the counter-performance other than money which the consumer has provided in exchange for the digital content and any other data collected'; this seems consonant with Article 7(3) GDPR, which provides that '[t]he withdrawal of consent shall not affect the lawfulness of processing based on consent before its withdrawal'. This should, however, not contradict any improvement already made that can still be used after termination without any impact on the personal data. The most important example might be the incrementally improved performance of the predictive model which will continue to accrue to the provider even after the contract is terminated or consent withdrawn.[132]

Another troubling divergence between GDPR and CSDC lies in the extent to which users may use personal data as a means of counter-performance.[133] Article 3(1) CSDC treats monetary and non-monetary forms of counter-performance identically; hence, one may suppose, payment with data is not subjected to any substantial limits, similar to the payment with money (except provisions in general contract law governing the adequate balance of performance and counter-performance – which again are difficult to apply when personal data with uncertain value is at stake). The novel Article 7(4) GDPR, however, stipulates that for the assessment of freedom, and hence validity, of consent to process personal data,

> utmost account shall be taken of whether, *inter alia*, the performance of a contract, including the provision of a service, is conditional on consent to the processing of personal data that is not necessary for the performance of that contract.

The provision is meant to push back against the ever-increasing demand for more personal data on a take-it-or-leave-it basis by providers of digital content, and to limit the amount and type of personal data that can be 'used' as a medium of exchange (cf. Recitals (42)–(43) GDPR). To be sure, it remains highly doubtful what data exactly are necessary for the performance of a contract – as

---

132 Cf. Staudenmeyer, above n. 15, pp. 819–820; Metzger, above n 98, p. 825–826.

133 Cf. Metzger, above n 98, p. 824; Schweitzer, above n. 33.

we have seen, it is increasingly difficult to attach a single, characteristic purpose to a contract in which data is exchanged against goods or services. Rather, economically speaking, the purpose of the contract precisely lies in this very exchange. The interpretation of Article 7(4) GDPR by the CJEU therefore is difficult to forecast. Meanwhile, Article 3(7) CSDC specifies that other Union enactments take precedence over the CSDC, and Article 3(8) CSDC reiterates this for EU data protection law. However, to the extent that Article 3(1) CSDC wants to subject the very contracts that the GDPR governs to the CSDC regime of obligations and remedies, it would be premature to brush the differences between the two legislative acts aside by reference to the subsidiary character of the CSDC – otherwise, some of its most novel provisions would be hollowed out before even taking effect without discussing normative issues at all.

Those are only some of the problems that plague the CSDC. Whether it will fulfil its promise to facilitate cross-border trade and contracting, remains to be seen. Christina Ramberg, in her sweeping critique of the CSDC in Part V of this book, draws a bleak picture of a directive provoking confusion rather than providing useful direction for the future of digital contracting. Gerald Spindler is more optimistic; while acknowledging its shortcomings, he describes it as a 'bold step in the right direction'. The future of digital contracting, and the future of the academic discussion, will tell which prediction will be closer to the economic and legal reality, and will gather more support among commentators. The purpose of the present book, certainly, is to provide a broad platform of thought-provoking discussions that ought to shape these discussions as the digital economy continues to unfold, in European contract law and beyond.

5. CONCLUSIONS

The purpose of this introductory chapter was to provide an overview of the interactions between digital technologies and European contract law. The general architecture of these interactions, as it were, rests on three distinct yet interrelated pillars: (1) the regulatory framework, which may even harness digital technology for regulatory purposes; (2) digital technology employed at different stages of the contractual life-cycle, from pre-contractual searches, screening and signalling to drafting, formation and performance, and even all the way to the linking and interpretation of contracts; and finally (3) digital content as the object of (traditional or, more often, digitally mediated) contracts.

We have tried to show that, like every good piece of architecture, the contractual digital architecture also subscribes to a certain narrative; it knows exceptions, but it nevertheless captures a tendency that will likely become ever more impactful as digitalisation proceeds. We see four main storylines in this narrative that all have to do with a growing interpenetration of different contractual parameters. First, national and global markets, contracting partners, and thus contractual regimes become increasingly interlinked as services are exchanged, and data is transferred, across borders, and as the regulatory environment is shaped by global dynamics. Second, the contractual basis is subject to ever greater modification and continuous updating over time; intelligent agents may even adapt contractual provisions in real time as new information becomes available. Third, the different stages of contracting, from the search for contractual partners to formation and enforcement, and even interpretation, are increasingly linked by digital processes in which feedback on, and predictions for, one or more of these stages are directly implemented into the other stages, bringing the contractual life-cycle closer than ever to full circle. Fourth, in the supply of digital content, it is becoming increasingly unclear which contractual obligation may be deemed characteristic of the contract, and which a mere 'counter-performance'; this holds particularly true when this counter-performance is effectuated by the provision of personal data instead of money which, amazingly enough, also brings back 'exchange in kind' in high volumes to a society which seemed to have left behind such transactions as mass transactions for a long time. The normative discussion on these transactions, namely on the bases of evaluation, has only just started.

Regulatory challenges arise at many different stages and levels of these interlinking pieces of the architecture. We suppose that, as the processes underlying digital contracting become more fluid and interwoven, users will benefit insofar as new information can be integrated in evolving contractual arrangements; however, where this adaptive environment leads to severe imbalances of information, power, and agency, the ordering forces of the law may be needed more than ever to provide for the safeguarding of core legal values in the digital economy. After all, many important pieces of architecture include some version of *Iustitia* in their narrative.

PART II

INSTITUTIONAL FRAMEWORK – PLATFORMS, REGULATION ISSUES, GLOBAL SURROUNDINGS

DIGITAL CONTRACTS IN GLOBAL SURROUNDINGS*

Dan Jerker B. Svantesson

ABSTRACT

Currently, questions around Internet jurisdiction – in a general sense – are gaining an unprecedented level of attention. Yet, progress is both slow and limited. This chapter argues that the most significant obstacle for progress is found in the fact that our current thinking on jurisdiction is largely dominated by, and rooted in, notions

* This chapter draws and expands on research findings previously presented in: D. Svantesson, *Private International Law and the Internet*, 3rd edn., Kluwer Law International, The Hague 2016. Professor Svantesson is the recipient of an Australian Research Council Future Fellowship (project number FT120100583). The views expressed herein are those of the author and are not necessarily those of the Australian Research Council.

of territoriality. The problem is that it is not always easy – or indeed possible – to determine *where* (in real-space geographical terms) events take place online. Thus, this chapter advances an alternative. More broadly, this chapter aims to bring attention to several themes of central importance for digital contracts in global surroundings. Apart from the already mentioned reliance on territoriality, those themes are: (i) that the Internet cannot be allowed to be a lawless space; (ii) that cross-border online interaction fulfils a valuable function; (iii) that we presently are experiencing a state of 'hyper-regulation' and (iv) that the role of contracts has increased with our use of the Internet. This chapter is also aimed at bringing attention to important considerations of the extent to which we uphold party autonomy in the context of choice of forum and choice of law clauses online. In addition, the prevalent 'targeting' focus is discussed and analysed in detail.

1. INTRODUCTION

The world is changing dramatically and rapidly due to advances in information technology, in particular the Internet. But despite these changes, the central role of contracts remains. In fact, it seems the role contracts play in our lives is increasing. And arguably, this trend is particularly clear in the context of cross-border interactions raising questions of which court(s) may claim jurisdiction, and which (country's) substantive law will govern the interaction.

This chapter commences by examining this theme and four other clear themes discernible in digital contracts in global surroundings, namely:

- that the Internet cannot be allowed to be a lawless space;
- that cross-border online interaction fills a valuable function;
- that we presently are experiencing a state of 'hyper-regulation'; and
- that there is a strong focus on territoriality.

Some of these trends are so self-evident that we often take them for granted, but they are all worth taking note of: the first three because of the fact that they were much less obvious not so long ago, and the fourth because it, in fact, now represents a roadblock for serious – and much needed – reform of our approach to jurisdiction.

Following that introductory part, the next section focuses on two selected problem areas in which the intersection of private international law rules, contracts and Internet interaction produces undesirable outcomes or, at best, uncertainty. The first is the central question of the validity of choice of court and choice of law terms in digital contracts. In this context, special account is taken of the most recent development visible in *Verein für Konsumenteninformation v. Amazon EU Sarl* (C-191/15), delivered by the Court of Justice of the European Union (CJEU) on 28 July 2016. The second problem area examined is that associated with the so-called 'targeting' test – a test that despite its questionable merits is steadily gaining momentum.

Finally, the chapter concludes by making a set of summarising observations and speculations.

2. SOME CENTRAL THEMES

To set the scene for the discussion below, it is important to keep in mind certain central themes[1] that colour our thinking on digital contracts in global surroundings. As already noted, these themes will not surprise the reader. However, even where self-evident, they are nevertheless of great importance and must always be kept in mind.

Further, the last of the five themes is important in that it is deserving of close scrutiny, hopefully leading to serious reform of our approach to jurisdiction.

2.1. THE INTERNET CANNOT BE ALLOWED TO BE A LAWLESS SPACE

If someone today made the claim that the Internet should be exempt from the law, few would take them seriously. Today, it is well established that the Internet cannot be allowed to be a lawless space. A lawless Internet is, quite simply, useless from a commercial perspective, and our Internet of today is very much commercialised. Almost everything we do online has a commercial dimension, not least due to the fact that our data – whether personal or not – is of commercial value. Even the most mundane data we share online may be used to create a picture of our lives and our preferences: information of commercial value.

Nevertheless, we would do well to recall that until 1992 commercial activity online was banned,[2] and less than 20 years ago, there was a serious debate regarding whether laws should apply online. Most famously, John Perry Barlow proclaimed in his 'Declaration of the Independence of Cyberspace': 'Governments of the Industrial World, you weary giants of flesh and steel, I come from Cyberspace, the new home of Mind. On behalf of the future, I ask

---

1 See further: D. Svantesson, *Private International Law and the Internet*, 3rd edn., Kluwer Law International, The Hague 2016, pp. 1–14.

2 OGC-00-33R Department of Commerce: *Relationship with the Internet Corporation for Assigned Names and Numbers* (PDF). Government Accountability Office. 7 July 2000. p. 6.

you of the past to leave us alone. You are not welcome among us. You have no sovereignty where we gather …'[3]

It is worth pointing out that even if one were inclined to pursue this agenda – of a lawless Cyberspace – today, the difficulty of distinguishing what belongs to Cyberspace and what is part of the 'real world' would be unsurmountable. After all, our lives – characterised by a constant social media presence, big data and the Internet of things – transcend the border between Cyberspace and the 'real world' to such a degree that a distinction is not possible.

Where the above is conceded, an obvious question arises; that is, from where can we then expect the necessary law to originate? Many commentators (myself included) have at some stage reached the conclusion that the best path forward is to work towards an international agreement addressing the complications that plague the online environment. While resorting to such a conclusion perhaps ought to be added to the list of *peccata mortalia*, such a conclusion is not necessarily reached out of naivety; most commentators stress the considerable obstacles that stand in the path of this Holy Grail. However, the reality is unfortunately that if this is the best proposal we manage to come up with, we are failing. Indeed, such suggestions, due to their slim prospects of success, are simply not good enough.

A more viable path forward is found in what has been termed 'legal interoperability'. Discussing legal interoperability as a normative tool, Weber draws upon the work of Palfrey and Gasser and makes the point that:

> The supranational realization of the process of legal interoperability (as the process of making legal rules work together across jurisdictions) can fluctuate between two poles: full harmonization and a complete fragmentation on a bilateral, plurilateral or multilateral level.[4]

At any rate, the discussion as to the vital role of law should not be seen as an endorsement of law to the exclusion of other forms of regulatory forces. I acknowledge the role of 'soft law'. I also, obviously, acknowledge the vital role that contracts play in Internet regulation.[5] In other words, it is 'law vs lawlessness' I am dealing with here, not 'law vs other forms of regulation'.

---

3 J.P. Barlow, 'A Declaration of the Independence of Cyberspace', 8 February 1996 <https://projects.eff.org/~barlow/Declaration-Final.html> accessed 13.08.2016. For academic writings adopting a similar view, see e.g., D. Johnson and D. Post, 'Law and Borders – The Rise of Law in Cyberspace' (1996) 48 *Stan. L.R. (Stanford Law Review)* 1379.

4 R.H. Weber, 'Legal Interoperability as a Tool for Combatting Fragmentation', Global Commission on Internet Governance, Paper Series No. 4 (December 2014) at 6.

5 See further: L.A. Bygrave, *Internet Governance by Contract*, Oxford University Press, Oxford 2015.

2.2. CROSS-BORDER ONLINE INTERACTION FULFILS A VALUABLE FUNCTION

In my view, one of the most profound statements that legal philosophy giant Fuller made is his observation regarding the importance of communication:

> Communication is something more than a means of staying alive. It is a way of being alive ... if I were asked, then, to discern one central indisputable principle of what may be called substantive natural law – Natural Law with capital letters – I would find it in the injunction: Open up, maintain, and preserve the integrity of the channels of communication by which men convey to one another what they perceive, feel, and desire.[6]

This brings attention to an important theme – it is widely recognised that cross-border interaction fulfils a valuable function. Thus, the need to be pro cross-border interaction must colour our design, and guide our application, of private (and public) international law rules.

2.3. WE ARE PRESENTLY EXPERIENCING A STATE OF 'HYPER-REGULATION'

Given the nature of the Internet, virtually everything we do online may place us at risk of being exposed to foreign laws and the jurisdiction of foreign courts. Consider, for example, a mundane example of social media use, such as a posting on Facebook or LinkedIn. Where we post content to social media, we need to – as every contract lawyer would be aware – take account of the agreement between users and social media providers. As most major social media platforms are based in the United States and nominate US (typically Californian) law as their governing law, and purport to give exclusive jurisdiction to US courts, we need to consider US law. But that is by no means the 'end of the story'.

Typically, we need also to be mindful of the law of the country we are in at the time of making the posting. Further, we may also need to consider the law of the country in which we are habitually residing (and/or domicile) and the law of our country of citizenship (if different). In addition, if our posting relates to another person, we may need to take into account the laws of that person's location, residence, domicile and citizenship. And, in addition, we could be required to have regard for the laws of any country in which that person has a reputation to protect.

---

6 L.L. Fuller, *The Morality of Law*, 2nd edn., Yale University Press, New Haven CT 1969, p. 186.

But then, under the law of many, not to say most, countries, the focus may be placed on where content is downloaded or read. This means that we would also need to make allowance for the laws of all the countries in which our Facebook 'friends' or LinkedIn 'connections' are found and, less predictably, the laws of all the countries in which they may be located when reading our posting. It goes without saying that the number of additional legal systems to be considered grows with the number, and geographical diversity, of our friends or connections. Furthermore, in light of the mobility of people, these jurisdictions may never be fully ascertained at the time of posting.

Then things get even more complicated. Given that our postings may be re-posted, we may also need to take into account the laws of all the countries in which re-posted versions of our posting may be downloaded or read. Here the original poster obviously loses all possibility of predicting the scope of laws to which she or he may be exposed.

As if this were not complicated enough, we must also bear in mind that content placed on social media platforms often is stored in 'the cloud', and while we as users may not necessarily be able to find out where our content is stored, we may be legally obligated to consider the laws of the country in which the content is stored. Finally, content posted may, depending on both our settings and on how our social media platform treats those settings, be available to third-parties, and we may then need to also let the laws of the locations of those third-parties guide our conduct.

This legal situation, of extraordinary complexity, is what billions of social media users expose themselves to on a daily basis. Admittedly, for the absolute majority, social media postings will not lead to any legal drama – the risks are more theoretical than real. However, this does not prevent us from drawing several conclusions based on the discussion above.

First of all, it is obviously a concern that our legal system is structured in such a way that people are expected to abide by laws that (1) they may be unaware of, (2) they may be unable to access, (3) they may be unable to understand and (4) may be directly contradicting other laws by which they also are required to abide.[7] In fact, this can be seen to shake the very core of legitimacy of law.

Second, the complex patchwork of partially overlapping, potentially contradictory, laws that Internet users are exposed to can arguably be seen to undermine the idea that the standard terms users are required to 'click' that they agree to are forming some type of new '*lex mercatoria*'. This matter will, however, not be explored further here.

7 See further, C. Reed, *Making Laws for Cyberspace*, Oxford University Press, Oxford 2012, p. 71, noting: 'Ignorance of foreign law is not just common in cyberspace; it is inevitable.'

2.4. INTERNET TECHNOLOGY HAS INCREASED THE IMPORTANCE OF CONTRACTS

As noted in the introduction, the role of contracts has only increased with our constantly deepening dependence on Cyberspace. We now enter into more contracts than we did before. And more importantly, we enter into considerably more contracts with choice of forum and choice of law clauses nominating foreign courts and foreign laws than we did before.

Prior to the Internet revolution, people in general entered into few contracts with choice of forum and choice of law clauses nominating foreign courts and foreign laws, since most consumer contracts were entered into locally. This changed with the Internet and the number of click-wrap and browse-wrap agreements we all have to enter into when visiting websites and downloading content. The situation has become even more extreme due to the 'app revolution'. With apps being the principle features of smart phones and tablets, we now enter into even more contracts with choice of forum and choice of law clauses pointing to foreign courts and foreign laws. To get a picture of the scale of this phenomena, we can observe the download figures for the two dominant Operating Systems; in 2015, the total number of iOS app downloads was 25 billion and the total number of Android app downloads in 2015 was 50 billion. The conclusion is obvious; the need for consumer understanding of private international law issues has never been greater.

But it is of course not merely a quantitative matter – a numbers game – in the sense that contracts are more important for us due to the volume of contracts into which we enter. There is also a qualitative aspect. As we live an increasingly large part of our lives in, or via, Cyberspace, the contractual terms we are bound to online play an increased role for how we live our lives. Put differently, as almost everything we do online is governed by contracts, not least via terms of use, and as the percentage of our lives lived online increases, we are subjected to an increased percentage of our lives being governed by contracts.

In light of the important role that contracts play online, it is surprising that not more academic writing has been directed at examining that role in detail. Nevertheless, in 2015, Bygrave published an excellent book doing just that.[8] The aim of his book was to examine the role of contract in Internet governance. In more detail, the book sets out to examine the reasons contracts hold such a special and prominent role in Internet governance, as well as the utility and legitimacy of this contractual governance mechanism. The role of contracts is placed in contrast and comparison with the role played by statutes, and two case studies are provided: one dealing with the contractual matrix associated with

---

[8] L.A. Bygrave, *Internet Governance by Contract*, Oxford University Press, Oxford 2015.

Internet Corporation for Assigned Names and Numbers (ICANN) and the other dealing with the contracts surrounding Facebook.

Just how important such research is becomes clear when one places it in the context of conventional thinking on Internet governance. Consider, for example, how Bygrave convincingly illustrates that Lessig's classic description of the four regulatory forces (law, code, market and norms) – a description that has guided and indeed dominated much thinking on Internet governance – clearly fails to account for the distinctive role of contracts.[9] This is particularly significant since contracts often have a more direct impact on our lives than does legislation.

In this context, it should be noted that domestic statutes restricting freedom of contract are, at least in the short-term, the most obvious competitor to governance via contracts. And given the well-known fact that genuine consent is a fairy-tale creature absent in virtually every single online contract entered into by individuals online, a move towards a 'nanny state', where domestic statutes impose certain contract terms and prohibit others on a much greater scale than today, is a serious contender deserving of attention. I will have reason to return to this matter below.

The claim above – that Internet technology has increased the importance of contracts – depends on the assumption that the agreements we enter into online are indeed contracts. While commonly accepted – indeed taken for granted – this assumption is not universally shared, as we have learnt in this volume. In his thought-provoking contribution in Part II, Pałka asserts that 'on the descriptive level, terms of online services are not contracts for service in the traditional sense, since they often do not contain any obligations or promises on the side of the providers.'[10] Further he argues that 'the question of whether these documents are contracts at all remains open.'[11]

These are interesting claims indeed, deserving of careful scrutiny. And Pałka presents what I see as convincing arguments proving that platform terms of service agreements, while commonly approached as contracts for service, do not fit well with traditional notions of such contracts.[12] I have no quarrel with this.

In contrast, personally I have no hesitation in viewing platform terms of service agreements as contracts. I suspect our differences of view may be traced to the following reasoning, central to Pałka's thinking on the matter:

> Imagine a person enters a bookstore, with a clear 'no ice cream' sign at the entrance. Yet, he holds an ice cream in his hand. The shop owner approaches him and asks the person to leave, which that person agrees to and complies with the request. Should

---

9 See further, ibid. pp. 4–5.

10 Przemysław Jacek Pałka in Part II of this volume, Abstract.

11 Przemysław Jacek Pałka in Part II of this volume, Abstract.

12 Przemysław Jacek Pałka in Part II of this volume.

> one accept that the shop owner had a right to ask the person to leave her store … the question is: what was the legal basis of this right? Was it a contractual right or a property right?
>
> To claim the former would be to claim that whenever one enters a private space under some condition, or even without it, or actually whenever one uses someone else's property with the owner's consent, there is a contractual relationship between the user and the owner. This would mean that every time someone lends a pen to a friend, or invites a guest to their house for a beer, there is a contract. However, there is no legal, statutory, judicial or doctrinal reason to believe that this is a case.[13]

When I taught contract law, I used to encourage – force, they may say – my students to memorise the following summary of what is a contract:

> A legally enforceable contract is formed if the party making an offer, with the intention that it be an offer, receives the acceptance of that offer from a party intending to make an acceptance and being in a position to make an acceptance, and the following requirements are met: (a) the contract is for consideration by both parties; (b) both parties have capacity to enter into a legally enforceable contract of the kind entered into; and (c) the terms of the contract are certain.

I think platform terms of service agreements, just like the 'no ice-cream' sign by the bookstore entrance tick all boxes alluded to in my summary of what is a contract. In contrast, I think the situation involving a guest invited to drink some beers, and the lending of a pen to a friend, both lack the element of intention, and may thus be distinguished. In other words, it seems to me that Pałka's conclusion may be based on an underappreciation of how we may use the intention requirement as a filtering mechanism.

Furthermore, my claim that platform terms of service agreements amount to contracts is unaffected by the observation that such agreements neither require the platform provider to provide the 'service', nor indeed do they require the 'customer' to actually use the platform. I do not think this means that they 'do not contain any obligations or promises on the side of the providers' as Pałka suggests. The terms of service provide obligations and promises applicable for the situation where the platform provider provides the platform and the customer uses that platform.

To the somewhat theoretical discussion above, we may add some rather serious practical considerations. As discussed by Pałka, where his claim is accepted 'a significant part of consumer law, including the Unfair Contract Terms Directive 93/13 and the currently worked on Digital Content Directive, will not apply to them [the platform providers]'.[14] This clearly speaks heavily

---

13 Przemysław Jacek Pałka in Part II of this volume, Section 3.1.

14 Przemysław Jacek Pałka in Part II of this volume, Section 2.2 (footnotes omitted).

against the reclassification of these agreements, even if it would have been a theoretical possibility.

Nevertheless, I think Pałka has done a commendable service by analysing this issue in detail and in raising it for discussion (see section 1 of his chapter). Complacency and academic sleep-walking – in the form of an unthinking acceptance of what is commonly taken for granted – are the greatest threats to progress.

2.5. THERE IS A STRONG FOCUS ON TERRITORIALITY

The focus on territory runs like a *fil rouge* throughout contemporary private, and public, international law, and its history is long:

From ancient times a person was subject to the law of his tribe. This law followed the person wherever he moved. However, over time, both the influence of and the connection to the tribe faded. The principle of personality weakened and the principle of territory grew stronger.[15]

In other words, territoriality had arguably come to prominence already at the fall of the tribal society.

In some areas of law, territoriality is, if possible, even more pronounced than generally is the case. Looking at private international law, the intellectual property setting provides an example of this. Nevertheless, it is worth recalling that already at the time of the birth of private international law, it was recognised that, for trade to run as smoothly as possible, neither the principle of personality nor the principle of territoriality 'could be applicable alone or in their purest content'.[16] And indeed, the focus on territoriality has been called into question also in relation to intellectual property rights.[17]

Further, there is a clearly increasing recognition that strict territoriality is ill-equipped for today's modern society.[18] This is particularly so given that the

---

15 B.R. Konow, 'Observations on Some Points of Contact between Private and Public International Law in Sweden' in P. Lindskoug et al. (eds.), *Essays in Honour of Michael Bogdan*, Jurisförlaget I Lund, Lund 2013, p. 207.

16 Ibid., p. 208.

17 B. Ubertazzi, *Exclusive Jurisdiction in Intellectual Property*, Mohr Siebeck, Tübingen 2012, p. 139.

18 See e.g., C. Ryngaert, Jurisdiction in International Law, 2nd edn., Oxford University Press, Oxford 2015; A. Mills, 'Rethinking Jurisdiction in International Law' (2014) 84 *The British Yearbook of International Law* 87–239; A. Slaughter, 'The Future of International Law Is Domestic (or, The European Way of Law)' (2006) 47 *Harvard International Journal of Law* 327; P.S. Berman, *Global Legal Pluralism: A Jurisprudence of Law beyond Borders*, Cambridge University Press, Cambridge 2012; J. Oster, 'Rethinking *Shevill*. Conceptualising the EU Private International Law of Internet Torts against Personality Rights' (2012) 26 *International Review of Law, Computers & Technology* 113–128; T. Schultz, 'Carving up the Internet: Jurisdiction, Legal Orders, and the Private/Public International Law Interface' (2008)

society of today is characterised by constant, fluid and substantial cross-border interaction, not least via the Internet. In fact, in the Internet context, a strict application of the territoriality principle is quite simply both unworkable and destructive, and it is one of the key reasons we are suffering under the hyper-regulation described above.

Examples of the destructive impact of strict territoriality abound. Consider, for example, how cross-border data communications often transit servers in states located between the sender and the receiver. It is an undisputable fact that during such a journey, data is temporarily located in the territory of the states other than the state of the sender and the state of the receiver. Under a strict application of the territoriality principle, the states of the transit servers could claim jurisdiction. Thus, for example, where a person in state A sells an e-book to a person in state C, she may be exposed to the jurisdiction of state B if the e-book's journey happens to pass through state B (a fact that the seller may, of course, not be able to know in advance). If the content of the e-book is illegal in state B, the seller may, with no warning or real possibility to predict it, violate state B's law. Further, the owner of the server in state B may also be violating that state's laws. Such a situation is clearly undesirable, and several examples can be found of legal solutions put in place to avoid this destructive impact of a strict application of the territoriality principle.[19] In light of this, the step toward accepting that data being (temporarily and randomly) stored on a server within a state, for example due to a multi-state cloud computing arrangement, should not always give that state jurisdiction over the data, may not be so dramatic.

In light of this, it is unsurprising that we are already seeing the supreme position of the territoriality principle eroding. In his interesting article 'Rethinking Jurisdiction in International Law', Mills highlights:

> The fact that these connecting factors are used and widely accepted in private international law itself suggests that the treatment of territory and nationality as discrete

19 *The European Journal of International Law* 799–839; C. Magnusson Sjöberg, 'Rättens internationalisering i det digitala informationssamhället – Folkrätt och rättsinformatik' in R. Stern and I. Österdahl (eds.), *Folkrätten i svensk rätt*, Liber AB, Stockholm 2012 and, somewhat more carefully, H.L. Buxbaum, 'Territory, Territoriality, and the Resolution of Jurisdictional Conflict' (2009) 57 *American Journal of Comparative Law* 631, 674, noting how: 'the use of territoriality as a mechanical standard used to link particular conduct with a particular country's law – rightly rejected – must be distinguished from the use of territoriality as an expression of a specific understanding about fairness and legitimacy in cross-border regulation.'

19 Consider e.g., Art. 4(1)(c) of Directive 95/46/EC of the European Parliament and of the Council of 24 October 1995 on the protection of individuals with regard to the processing of personal data and on the free movement of such data [1995] *OJ* L281: '[T]he controller is not established on Community territory and, for purposes of processing personal data makes use of equipment, automated or otherwise, situated on the territory of the said Member State, *unless such equipment is used only for purposes of transit through the territory of the Community*.' (emphasis added).

> grounds for jurisdiction in traditional formulations of international law jurisdiction is too restrictive. The practice of states instead supports the idea that jurisdiction may be based on a flexible combination of both territorial and personal connecting factors – connections between a person and a place which do not depend on nationality, such as domicile or habitual residence.[20]

Given the contractual focus of this volume, we may here usefully pause to recall the fact that the *Rome I Regulation* does indeed rely, in important respects, on the concept of 'habitual residence'.[21]

At least one leading commentator prefers to view the domicile principle as 'a variation on the active personality principle [another term for the nationality principle]'.[22] This may be so, but this does not necessarily undermine Mills' assertion that the focus on 'domicile' and 'habitual residence' highlights that state practice has moved beyond the territoriality principle and the nationality principle as originally conceived. And it may indeed be argued that if the domicile principle is to be viewed as a variation on the nationality principle, then the nationality principle has been stretched beyond recognition.

Another example of private international law thinking going beyond territoriality is found in the 'centre of interests' or 'centre of gravity' test. While this test most famously, in recent times, was employed by the Court in the *eDate* case,[23] Oster emphasises that this test is not a recent discovery and points to its use in the United States, Canada and by the House of Lords.[24] Furthermore, he correctly links the test to Savigny's 'seat of the legal relationship'.[25]

Importantly, Oster also draws attention the fact that the adoption of the 'centre of interests' test in the *eDate* case was made necessary by the failure of current – territoriality-focused – connections tests, such as the 'place where the information has been published', which in Oster's accurate assessment 'is rendered almost valueless with a view to the global accessibility of online publications':[26]

> Instead of a determination based on objective facts such as physical publication of a newspaper as under Shevill, the 'centre of gravity of the conflict' doctrine introduces an evaluating interest analysis considering different criteria in order to establish the

---

20 A. Mills, above n. 18, p. 207.

21 Regulation (EC) No 593/2008 of the European Parliament and of the Council of 17 June 2008 on the law applicable to contractual obligations (see below), Article 4.

22 C. Ryngaert, above n. 18, p. 108.

23 Case C-509/09, *eDate Advertising GmbH v. X*, ECLI:EU:C:2011:685 and Case C-161/10, *Olivier Martinez and Robert Martinez v. MGN Lmited*, ECLI:EU:C:2010:656.

24 J. Oster, above n. 18, p. 120.

25 Ibid.

26 Ibid.

appropriate forum most suitable for the interests of all the parties, that is, essentially the most convenient or 'natural' forum.[27]

In the context of contracts, issues such as those discussed arise much more seldom. However, that is not to say that the problematic territoriality thinking is absent in cross-border contractual situations. Below, I will examine some particularly important contractual private international law situations in which the weakness of the territoriality thinking is obvious.

2.5.1. The Location of Contract Formation

The location of contract formation is widely used as a ground for jurisdiction.[28] Furthermore, the location of contract formation is used in determining choice of law (however, in a less determinative manner). This is clearly a factor grounded in territoriality thinking, and states typically deem a contract to be formed upon the acceptance by a party having legal capacity to enter into a contract of an offer from a party having legal capacity to enter into a contract.[29] This principle applies online as well as offline. Yet it has been subject to severe, and well-founded, criticism:

> The rule that contracts have to be judged by the law of the place of making is very old. It was developed at a time when the conclusion of contracts through the mail was unknown. When parties made a contract they were both present on one spot. Very often a judge or notary was called in to give the contract the proper form. In this situation the application of the law of the place of making is reasonable. This is the law the application of which the parties expect, and it is convenient and often even unavoidable to observe the formalities prescribed by the law of the place of making.
>
> As soon as a contract is concluded through the mail or over the telephone between persons residing in different jurisdictions all these considerations lose their force. Only in a figurative sense one of the places where the parties acted or resided can be called the place of the making.

---

27 Ibid.

28 See further: D. Svantesson, *Private International Law and the Internet*, 3rd edn., Kluwer Law International, The Hague 2016, pp. 436–437.

29 See, e.g., Chapter V of *The Contract law of the People's Republic of China*, at <http://www.ncp.gpv/englishnpc/Law/2007-12/11/content 1383564.htm> accessed 13.8.2016; The Swedish contracts law ('*Lag (1915:218) om avtal och andra rättshandlingar på förmögenhetsrättens område*'); and M. Davies, A.S. Bell and P.L.G. Brereton, *Nygh's Conflict of Laws in Australia*, 9th edn., Sydney, Lexis Nexis Butterworths, 2014, pp. 460–477. It is, in addition, not uncommon for the law to provide the parties with the opportunity to agree upon where the contract is said to have been formed. Such party discretion does, however, not normally preclude a court from determining the actual place of contract formation. See B. Fitzgerald et al., *Jurisdiction and the Internet*, Law-book Co., Sydney 2004, p. 13, referring to *Sheldon Pallet Manufacturing Co. Pty. Ltd. v. New Zealand Forest Products Ltd.* [1975] 1 NSWLR 141, 147. Note, however, the so-called 'Postal acceptance rule'.

> Under the prevailing American doctrine [and the doctrine of many other states] one finds the place of contracting by asking where the last act necessary to make the contract binding occurred. This is an objectionable method because it transposes a rule, which was developed for quite different purposes to a field where it is possibly wholly inappropriate. The rule has been developed in order to answer the question when the power of the offeror to revoke the offer ends and when the offeree is bound. Even to these questions different answers would be possible. No policy argument has as yet been made for the proposition that the same act should fix the applicable law. The task of the jurist in this situation is not to find through some construction, even if it were as simple as Beale strongly asserts, the place of making, but to find policy considerations, which indicate which of the different legal systems to which the factual situation is related should be given preference.[30]

These quoted words were written back in 1942 – almost 75 years ago. The critique expressed against the location of contract formation being used to determine the question of jurisdiction and choice of law is even more justified and potent today, not least due to the widespread use of the Internet. Any determination of the location of contract formation is necessarily artificial when the parties are not in the same place at the time of the contract formation.

While it typically is reasonable to say that a contract is formed where the last act necessary to make the contract binding occurs (i.e., where the offeror receives the acceptance), since only then is the contract actually concluded, one must still question why this should decide the jurisdictional and choice of law questions. What makes that place the proper focal point? One can picture a situation where two parties exchange offers and counter-offers only to come to an agreement after several rounds of counter-offers. In such a situation, the place of formation and thereby the jurisdictional and choice of law questions are determined rather by coincidence under a rule focused on where the last act necessary to make the contract binding occurs.

Against this background, it could be submitted that placing focus on the artificially constructed place of contract formation makes little sense in cross-border contracts, and is an inappropriate foundation for jurisdictional claims. However, it may not be necessary to disregard the location of contract formation completely.

The solution adopted in Swedish law illustrates that a suitable balance can be found. Swedish law attaches significance to the location of contract formation only when both parties are present at the location of contract formation. This approach seems reasonable. However, a slight clarification is necessary in the online context. The location of contract formation should be of relevance only

30 R. Neuner, 'Policy Considerations in the Conflict of Laws' (1942) XX *The Canadian Bar Review* 498–499 (footnotes omitted).

where both parties *knowingly* are at the same location when the contract is concluded. This avoids significance being attached to the location of contract formation where parties are unaware that they are located in the same place during the formation of the contract.[31]

On a more general note, it could be said that grounding jurisdictional rules, or choice of law rules, on concepts stemming from substantive law areas such as the concept of contract formation is associated with the risks of: (1) inheriting any or all of the substantive law rule's weaknesses; and (2) the substantive law concept developing and thereby taking on a new direction which the private international law rule has to follow.

2.5.2. The Location of Contract Performance/Breach of Contract

Another example of strong territoriality thinking in private international law as it relates to cross-border contracts is found in the relatively pervasive focus on the location of contract performance and/or the location of contract breach.[32]

Most notably, a focus on the location of performance can be found in the *Brussels I bis Regulation*. There the place of performance is determined to be the place of delivery of goods or performance of a service, unless otherwise agreed.[33] However, the role of this thinking in private international law is clearly broader as it has been adopted into the proposed resurrected 'Judgments Project'.

The Hague Conference on Private International Law has made significant progress with its new 'Judgments Project'. In October 2015, a draft text was produced for version 2.0 of this ambitious initiative aimed at putting in place a workable yet robust structure for the recognition and enforcement of foreign judgments. One of the provisions – Article 5(1)(e) – makes clear that:

> a judgment is eligible for recognition and enforcement if … the judgment ruled on a contractual obligation and it was given in the State in which performance of that obligation took place or should take place under the parties' agreement or under the law applicable to the contract, unless the defendant's activities in relation to the transaction clearly did not constitute a purposeful and substantial connection to that State.[34]

However, ascertaining where the performance of certain e-commerce obligations takes place or should take place is notoriously difficult and can only be done by

31 This type of situation may not be as rare as it first may appear. It would, for example, not be unusual for a contract to be formed online between a seller and a buyer, both located in New York, without either of the parties being aware of the other party's location.

32 See further: D. Svantesson, *Private International Law and the Internet*, 3rd edn., Kluwer Law International, The Hague 2016, pp. 438–439.

33 Regulation (EU) No. 1215/2012, Article 7 (*Brussels I bis Regulation*).

34 The Hague Conference on Private International Law, 'Report of the Fifth Meeting of the Working Group on the Judgments Project', p. iii.

reference to legal fictions. For example, where does the performance take place when a person who lives in state A for part of the year, but who spends part of the year in state B and works in and spends a lot of time in state C, subscribes to an online streaming service? In light of this type of difficulty, the wisdom of placing reliance on such a concept is questionable unless more guidance is provided, and more generally I agree with the view expressed in a press release from the Geneva Round Table on Electronic Commerce and Private International Law:

> For on-line contracts in general, in the matter of jurisdiction and applicable law, if the performance of the relevant obligation takes place off-line, the existing rules of private international law referring to the place of performance remain relevant. If the performance takes place on-line, the place of performance is not appropriate as a connecting factor.[35]

Courts may also be authorised to claim jurisdiction over a contractual dispute where the contract was breached within the forum state. While it is ordinarily easy to identify the place of breach when one party has actively done something wrong, it is harder to identify the place where the contract was breached when the breach stems from inactivity (e.g., failure to deliver a product). In the latter situation, the breach is often considered to have taken place where the contractual obligation in question is due to be performed.[36] However, it is of course possible to imagine situations where the nature of the Internet contributes to making it hard to establish the location where a contract was breached.

While the location of contractual breach could be said to have a more direct connection to a contractual dispute than the place of contract formation, this jurisdictional ground may nevertheless interfere with the parties' legitimate expectations, and its legitimacy is limited to those situations where the state where the breach occurred is the more convenient forum due, for example, to the location of witnesses and evidence (i.e., simplicity and efficiency concerns). Furthermore, this jurisdictional ground could be rather easily abused in the online context due to the inherent mobility, not least when it comes to cloud computing.

2.5.3. A Better Alternative

The above has hinted at the fact that, whatever the status of the territoriality principle *de lege lata*, it is unsustainable as the jurisprudential core of our

---

35 Hague Conference on Private International Law, 'Press Release from the Geneva Round Table on Electronic Commerce and Private International Law' (25 April 2006) <http://www.hcch.net/upload/wop/press01e.html> accessed 13.08.2016.

36 See, e.g., Australian law as discussed in M. Davies, A.S. Bell and P.L.G. Brereton, above n. 29, pp. 58–59.

thinking on jurisdiction *de lege ferenda*. In light of this, I have advanced the following jurisprudential framework for jurisdiction – consisting of three core principles:

> [I]n the absence of an obligation under international law to exercise jurisdiction, a State may only exercise jurisdiction where:
>
> (1) there is a substantial connection between the matter and the State seeking to exercise jurisdiction;
> (2) the State seeking to exercise jurisdiction has a legitimate interest in the matter; and
> (3) the exercise of jurisdiction is reasonable given the balance between the State's legitimate interests and other interests.[37]

It is this jurisprudential framework which I envisage as the starting point for a new paradigm for jurisdiction. Importantly, as I see it, these core principles represent the foundation of both private international law and public international law. While I will not pursue that matter here, it should be noted that, where that is accepted, we have in these principles found something that actually unites public and private international law as far as jurisdiction is concerned.

3. THE VALIDITY OF CHOICE OF COURT AND CHOICE OF LAW TERMS IN DIGITAL CONTRACTS

Respect for the parties' choice of forum and choice of law is shared by a large number of states around the world.[38] To understand why this is so, and to see how this should work online, it is useful to consider the role of *legitimate expectations* in some detail. The importance of people's legitimate expectations as to the law is neatly described by Krygier:

> We do better, too, in large societies, where we are constantly interacting with non-intimates, if we can know important things about people we may not know well in other respects. Such things include their and our rights, responsibilities, risks and constraints. In small and pre-modern societies, as in families, we can know many of these things

[37] D. Svantesson, 'A New Jurisprudential Framework for Jurisdiction: Beyond the Harvard Draft' (2015) 109 *American Journal of International Law* 69 <https://www.asil.org/blogs/new-jurisprudential-framework-jurisdiction-beyond-harvard-draft> accessed 13.08.2016.

[38] See P. Nygh, 'The Reasonable Expectation of the Parties as a Guide to the Choice of Law in Contract and in Tort' (1995) 251 *Recueil des cours*. See also: D. Svantesson, *Private International Law and the Internet*, 3rd edn., Kluwer Law International, The Hague 2016, pp. 430–431 and 500–501.

> from personal everyday experience. In larger, more various, agglomerations such knowledge and the shared normative understandings that make it possible, are often not available. Where the rule of law matters in a society, however, we can know many of these things even about strangers. That makes their and our activities more predictable to each other and might make us less fearful of and more cooperative with them, and, of course, them of and with us. This can lead to a productive spiral of virtuous circles, where each gains by reasonable trust in others.[39]

Following the reasoning above, it would seem that the rule of law has a particularly large role to play in relation to online interactions, as such interactions frequently involve parties who lack knowledge of each other.

Arguably, the most obvious situations in which parties' legitimate expectations may be met are contracts.[40] If the parties actively and in an informed manner reach an agreement as to, for example, which law shall be applied in, or which court shall determine, a potential dispute, we can speak of *genuine party expectations* being created from the point when such agreement is reached. By allowing for party autonomy (i.e. allowing the parties to make such choices and ensuring that the parties' choice is respected), private international law rules can be predictable.[41] This *predictability*,[42] in turn, ensures that legitimate party expectations are met. The term predictability is, thus, given a very specific meaning here: a predictable rule is a rule that aims at the fulfilment of genuine party expectations.

The desirability of upholding party autonomy is widely recognised, and Keyes has provided a summary of why this is so:

> The justifications for enforcing mutual agreements as to jurisdiction and arbitration are widely agreed to be compelling. The fundamental justification is that the parties' freedom to contract should be respected by enforcing their agreements. This gives effect to certainty and predictability, which are essential to supporting international trade and commerce. Upholding the parties' agreements as to venue and type of dispute resolution should simplify and discourage litigation about venue, and this should save both public and private costs.[43]

---

39 M. Krygier, 'False Dichotomies, True Perplexities, and the Rule of Law' in A. Sajo (ed.) *Human Rights with Modesty. The Problem of Universalism*, Martinus Nijhoff, Leiden/Boston 2004, pp. 251–277 (footnote omitted).

40 P. Nygh, above n. 38, p. 297.

41 Authors have gone as far as to suggest a 'human rights basis for party autonomy' (ibid., p. 303).

42 Or 'certainty'. Predictability and certainty are, of course, if not the same, variations of the same theme and will consequently be treated as one quality for the purpose of this discussion.

43 M. Keyes, 'Jurisdiction under the Hague Choice of Courts Convention: Its Likely Impact on Australian Practice' (2009) 5 *J. Priv. Int'l. L. (Journal of Private International Law)* 181.

Furthermore, Pertegás has pointed to the following beneficial characteristics of party autonomy:

> First, the principle of party autonomy defers to the expectations of the parties and protects legal certainty. Second, insofar as the parties' choice of law is seen as being part of the contractual regime concerning dispute settlement, the exercise of part autonomy helps to achieve efficiency by reducing the legal costs of dispute resolution. Third, the principle of party autonomy promotes cross-border economic activity by enabling the parties to choose the applicable law, which facilitates their intended transaction. Lastly, increased international mobility and communication accentuate the relevance of party autonomy as the most practical solution for international commercial contracts.[44]

These are strong arguments, and holding the parties to their agreement would clearly address the risk of vexatious litigation in a court other than the chosen one, aimed at delaying the process or even sabotaging the proper resolution of the dispute. At the same time, it must be remembered that a valid choice of court provision, nominating a forum that is inaccessible to the other party, is likely to represent an effective barrier preventing legal action being taken against the party nominating the forum. Indeed, where the selected forum is out of reach for the other party (e.g., due to the costs associated with taking action there), it does not matter which law that forum would have applied or whether that other party would have been likely to succeed in an action taken there – that other party is, in effect, blocked from access to justice. Consequently, no other type of contractual clause (including choice of law and limitation of liability clauses) can be as detrimental to the power balance between the contractual parties as a choice of forum clause, and no other type of contract clause can be as severely misused as a choice of forum clause.

In light of this, while it is unsurprising that the concept of 'party autonomy' is held up as a corner stone of private international law,[45] we must not lose sight of the fact that party autonomy is merely a subsidiary of legitimate party expectations – the value of party autonomy depends on, and indeed stems from, the fulfilment of legitimate party expectations.

While predictability often is the safest way of ensuring the fulfilment of legitimate party expectations, the instances where predictability can be relied upon are limited to those fact-scenarios that involve the aforementioned genuine party expectations. In cases not involving genuine party expectations,

44 M. Pertagás, 'Hague Principles on Choice of Law in International Contracts' in P. Lindskoug et al. (eds.), *Essays in Honour of Michael Bogdan*, Jurisförlaget I Lund, Lund 2013, p. 464.

45 A. Jaroszek, 'European Online Marketplace – New Measures for Consumer Protection against "Old Conflict of Laws Rules"' (2015) 9 *Masaryk University Journal of Law and Technology* 22.

we must also rely upon *flexibility* to provide for legitimate party expectations to be met. As used here, a flexible rule is a rule that takes account of the individual circumstances of the case at hand.

There are several situations in which one cannot speak of any genuine party expectations. For example, a consumer entering into a cross-border contract might not at all have considered in which forum a potential dispute would be heard or which laws would be applied if a dispute should arise. Indeed, most consumers would not have sufficient legal knowledge to properly evaluate the relevance of these questions.

Web-based choice of forum and choice of law clauses are associated with particular difficulties.[46] First and foremost, a large percentage of people simply do not read the online contract but still click 'I agree' or the equivalent. This obviously raises the question: why do people in general not read the terms and conditions to which they agree? One explanation is that people do not think the terms and conditions are binding. Thus, consumer protection organisations worldwide may have to intensify their efforts to increase consumers' understanding of the relevant issues – a difficult task that requires substantial governmental spending.

Another reason – indeed probably the main reason – for people's lack of interest in reading web-agreements is perhaps found in the fact that this type of contract is not negotiable. If we cannot change the terms and conditions, our only real choice is whether or not we want to go through with the action regulated by the terms and conditions. Thus, a person will weigh his/her desire to go through with the action regulated by the terms and conditions on the one hand, and the potential risks associated with going through with the action on the other. In performing this balancing, most people rely on their constructive party expectations instead of spending the time and effort of reading the terms and conditions to obtain an understanding amounting to genuine party expectations.

A problem in this context is that those drafting the terms are typically doing little to encourage people to read those terms. Indeed, one can legitimately question whether those who construct the terms really want people to read them. For example, it is still relatively rare for there to be any convenient 'print button' on the web pages containing the contractual terms.

Yet, we may still speak of a party expectation in relation to these types of situations. After all, it could be said that each and every one of us has some basic expectation as to how we will be treated in the eyes of the law, in case something happens. We could here speak of *constructive party expectations*, as opposed to the genuine party expectation of a party who has properly considered the issues

46 See further: D. Svantesson, *Private International Law and the Internet*, 3rd edn., Kluwer Law International, The Hague 2016, pp. 105–111.

to which the expectations relate. Bearing in mind that party expectations may be both constructive and genuine, a rule of private international law aiming to meet the parties' expectations must balance the two different, and competing, sub-qualities mentioned above – predictability and flexibility. However, the respective importance of these two sub-qualities varies depending on the context.

As defined above, predictability and flexibility are each other's opposites. However, they are not opposites in a binary sense; rather, they are the opposites in the sense that light is the opposite of darkness – a particular situation can be more light than dark, just as a rule can be more predictable than it is flexible.

At any rate, as far as contractual situations are concerned, the relationship between predictability and flexibility can be described in the following terms: while sophisticated[47] contracts, such as a multimillion dollar contract between Microsoft and LinkedIn, require a high level of predictability and a much lower level of flexibility, unsophisticated contracts, such as a low-value business-to-consumer (B2C) contract, require a high level of flexibility and a lower level of predictability. The reason for this is primarily that high-value contracts between large corporations are invariably under the supervision of legally trained experts. This means that, in most cases, there is an inherent high level of legal awareness behind any such contract.[48] The parties may have negotiated and agreed upon a certain law to apply and a certain forum to decide any potential dispute. With that degree of planning, certainly amounting to genuine party expectations, the most important sub-quality of private international law rules is predictability – the parties expect their expectations to be met. In contrast, in low-value contracts between less sophisticated parties, such as among smaller businesses, between smaller companies and consumers, or among consumers, the above-mentioned level of legal planning and awareness, and consequently genuine party expectations, are lacking – there are only constructive party expectations. In such circumstances, the importance of predictability is obviously at a minimum while the importance of flexibility is at its peak.

Particular considerations are present in relation to contracts between one sophisticated party and one unsophisticated party. In such contractual relations there are never, or very rarely, any real negotiations, and all the legal planning is done by the sophisticated party. An emphasis on predictability, in such a case, may lead to the fulfilment of only one party's expectations – the stronger party's

47 No absolute line can be drawn between sophisticated and unsophisticated contracts. However, generally, it could be said that the level of sophistication of a contractual relation must be judged based on several different factors including: the parties' level of sophistication, the monetary value of the transaction, and the extent of legal knowledge applied in forming the contract.

48 Since it allows the parties to make conscious decisions, this legal awareness is of greatest importance also in a situation where the parties are not evenly matched, and perhaps one party is seeking to impose certain conditions on the other party.

genuine party expectations would be met, while the weaker party's constructive party expectations would be unlikely to be met.[49] On the other hand, too strong an emphasis on flexibility may create an undesirable degree of uncertainty. Such uncertainty may discourage business and, thus, amount to a barrier to e-commerce.

Determining the respective importance of predictability and flexibility in such a situation necessarily involves a value-judgement as to the respective rights of, for example, businesses and consumers: a topic upon which reasonable people may disagree. It also involves practical considerations such as whether the stronger parties would be willing to contract at all if they were not allowed to dictate the terms, including the choice of the forum and choice of law.

However, whether one takes an idealistic approach wanting to safeguard the rights of the weaker party, or whether one takes a more pragmatic approach simply wishing to encourage e-commerce, one cannot ignore the inherently unequal bargaining powers present in many online contracts. One could argue that as long as the consumer was not coerced into the contract, despite the unequal bargaining powers it could represent both parties' will. However, such an argument would only be valid if two separate requirements were met: first, that the consumer was informed enough to evaluate the potential impact of the relevant contractual terms; and second, that the particular contractual terms in question were not common practice so that the consumer could obtain the same goods or services from another provider that did not try to impose the relevant contractual terms, or equally unfair contractual terms.

For the past 15 years or so, I have suggested that in order to optimise the potential of e-commerce, legal rules must ensure: 'a healthy balance between the consumer's need for protection and the business' need to be able to conduct business in an effective manner'.[50] While this line of reasoning seems appropriate in the context of private international law, it may not be immediately clear how it can be applied in relation to the balance between predictability and flexibility. However, drawing upon some available statistics, we can get an insight into consumer behaviour.

Approximately 46 per cent of Internet users think that only about half of the content on the Internet is reliable and accurate.[51] Furthermore, '47 per cent

---

49 This can of course be avoided where the rules of private international law can be made clear to the businesses, while at the same time be structured so as to protect consumer interests. For example, a rule allowing consumers to always have B2C disputes settled under the law of the consumer's home state are of course *prima facie* predictable while at the same time providing protection for the consumer.

50 D. Svantesson, 'Optimising the potential of e-commerce: a win-win solution' (2001) 3(10) *Internet Law Bulletin* 136.

51 USC Annenberg School Center for the Digital Future, 'The 2014 Digital Future Report: Surveying the Digital Future – Year Twelve' (2014), p. 44 <http://www.digitalcenter.org/wp-content/uploads/2014/12/2014-Digital-Future-Report.pdf> accessed 13.08.2016.

of respondents age 18 and older who have a credit card are very concerned or extremely concerned about credit card security when or if buying online.'[52] It must be noted that the use of credit/debit cards is by far the most common payment form in B2C e-commerce.[53] According to a 2014 Pew Research Center report:

> The percentage of U.S. adults who report they've had personal data, such as their Social Security, credit card or bank account numbers, stolen as a result of their online activities jumped to 18% in January 2014, up from 11% last July [2013].[54]

Statistics suggest that, while the majority of those concerned about their credit card information cited hacking and 'too many unknowns' as the reason for the concern, no less than 7.4 per cent said the concern was based on personal experience, 8.7 per cent said they know someone who has experienced credit card fraud and the same percentage said the concern was based on reading about credit card fraud in the media.[55] This distrust is not entirely unjustified.

With this in mind, it is difficult to imagine trust being created among consumers in the event that businesses can force choice of law and choice of forum clauses onto them through, for example, the use of non-negotiated click-wrap agreements (i.e. non-negotiated contracts of adhesion that normally are entered into when one party clicks on the 'I agree' or 'Accept' button on a website). As noted by Ong, such trust is indeed a necessity if e-commerce is to bloom: '[t]he success of electronic commerce is dependent on consumer confidence.'[56]

---

52 Ibid., p. 76.

53 Ecommerce News, 'The most common payment methods in Europe' (4 June 2013) <http://ecommercenews.eu/the-most-common-payment-methods-in-europe/> and S. Schuh and J. Stavins, 'The 2013 Survey of Consumer Payment Choice: Summary Results' (2015) (15-4) *Research Data Reports* <https://www.bostonfed.org/publications/research-data-report/2015/the-2013-survey-of-consumer-payment-choice-summary-results.aspx> accessed 13.08.2016.

54 As cited in A. Dusto, 'Reports of personal data theft are on the rise' (14 April 2014) https://www.digitalcommerce360.com/2014/04/14/reports-personal-data-theft-are-rise/ accessed 13.08.2016.

55 As reported in UCLA Center for Communication Policy, 'The UCLA Internet Report – Surveying the Digital Future – Year Three' (2003), p. 52 <http://www.digitalcenter.org/wp-content/uploads/2013/02/203_digital_future_report-year3.pdf> accessed 13.08.2016. For more information regarding consumer trust in e-commerce, see, e.g., Consumers International, 'Credibility on the Web: An international study of the credibility of consumer information on the internet' (2002) <http://www.consumersinternational.org/media/304133/credibility%20on%20the%20web.pdf> accessed 13.08.2016; A. Dusto, above n. 54; and R. Clarke, 'Trust in the Context of e-Business' (Version of 1 October 2001) <http://www.rogerclarke.com/EC/Trust.html> accessed 13.08.2016.

56 R. Ong, 'Consumer Based Electronic Commerce: A Comparative Analysis of the Position in Malaysia and Hong Kong' (2004) 12 *Int'l. J.L. & Info. Tech. (International Journal of Law and Information Technology)* 101–122, 121.

Furthermore, while consumer displeasure is increasingly aimed at issues such as data privacy violations, the risks involved with Internet use in general and e-commerce in particular are still gaining considerable media attention. And if e-commerce continues to get 'bad press' due to horror stories of defrauded consumers, trade over the Internet will never reach its full potential.

Yet, the very idea of providing consumers with special legal protection often comes under attack. Perhaps this is only logical given that it imposes a cost – a cost businesses need to either absorb or pass onto the consumers themselves. And that is where the standard opposition to consumer protection typically draws its strength from. The argument is that, as consumer protection imposes a cost on all consumers, but only benefits those few consumers who actually experience difficulties, the majority of consumers would benefit from the removal of consumer protection.

This reasoning is clear, logical and has an immediate appeal. However, upon a sober minded consideration of the real state of things, its flaws are obvious. The trouble is that the same reasoning can be applied, for example, to child labour and to food hygiene standards.

Had it not been for the applicable safety standards, the employers of child labour could have afforded to pay the children more. From this point of view, all the children miss out on higher salaries to protect the few that would have had accidents in the absence of the safety standards. And had it not been for the applicable food hygiene standards, restaurants could have kept their prices down. That would have saved all guests money, at the expense of a few more people getting food poisoning.

I do not think many people would accept the reasoning applied in the setting of child labour or in food hygiene standards. So why do we still see that same reasoning when it comes to consumer protection? The only explanation I can think of is that those relying on this reasoning in the context of consumer protection simply do not view consumer protection as particularly important. But whether consumer protection is important or not is, of course, a different question – an important question that should not be hidden by a flawed reasoning of what actually benefits consumers.

In addition, there are several factors indicating that businesses are in a better position to adapt their conduct to the risks involved in e-commerce than are consumers; businesses can adopt business models that minimise their risks. This can be done in a multitude of ways but, for example, they can employ technological measures – so-called geo-location technologies[57] – to limit the

[57] See e.g., D. Svantesson, 'Time for the law to take Internet geo-location technologies seriously' (2012) 8 *Journal of Private International Law* 473–487 and D. Svantesson, 'Geo-location technologies and other means of placing borders on the "borderless" Internet' (2004) XXIII *John Marshall Journal of Computer & Information Law* 101–139.

geographical extent of their legal exposure. In addition, as is already the case, businesses can demand payment by credit card before delivery of goods or services is made. Finally, business organisations can help work out appropriate business behaviour.

Against this background, it is submitted that, in any contractual case involving at least one unsophisticated party, flexibility is more important than predictability, both in relation to jurisdiction and the choice of law. Indeed, even the greatest advocates of party autonomy acknowledge the need for flexibility in consumer contracts.[58]

It is desirable that rules (or at least guidelines) be developed on an international level, outlining the manner in which web-based agreements are to be formed. The solution, however, obviously does not lie in banning web-based agreements or holding them generally unenforceable. The better approach is to regulate what types of terms and conditions are deemed unfair, as is done, for example, in the EU and in Australia.[59]

In this context, it should be noted that there often is a big difference between the terms to which we agree online and the rights that EU consumer law grants us. And in few other settings has that been more obvious than when it comes to so-called choice of law and choice of forum clauses. Under the *Rome I Regulation*, for example, consumers have the right to enjoy the protection of their home state's laws, and similarly, the *Brussels I bis Regulation* gives consumers the right to litigate on home-ground. Yet consumers are routinely clicking 'I agree' to terms nominating the business's chosen law as applicable, and terms providing that the consumer must litigate where the business is established. The legality of such terms has now been called into question via a judgment by the CJEU, reflecting the thinking of the Opinion issued on 2 June 2016 by Advocate General Saugmandsgaard Øe in the same matter, Case C-191/15 (*Verein für Konsumenteninformation v. Amazon EU*).

The case in question stems from an Austrian consumer organisation (*Verein für Konsumenteninformation*) seeking an injunction preventing Amazon EU from imposing a term to the effect that Austrian consumers are bound by Luxembourg law (the law of the place where Amazon EU is established) in their dealings with Amazon EU. The dispute involves several important legal questions stemming from a range of Regulations and Directives, showcasing just how complex this area of EU law can be.

58 P. Nygh, above n. 38, e.g., pp. 346 and 356.

59 Council Directive (93/13/EEC), 5 April 1993, on unfair terms in consumer contracts <http://eur-lex.europa.eu/legal-content/EN/TXT/HTML/?uri=CELEX:31993L0013&from=EN> accessed 13.08.2016.

Most significantly for our purposes, Advocate General Saugmandsgaard Øe, and subsequently the Court, had to tackle the question of whether Amazon EU's choice of law clause was unfair under Council Directive 93/13/EEC of 5 April 1993 on unfair terms in consumer contracts. In his admirably clear and well-reasoned Opinion, Advocate General Saugmandsgaard Øe essentially broke this question down into two parts. First, he concluded that the clause cannot override the option of litigating under the consumer's home state law. In other words, since consumers doubtless have the protection provided under the *Rome I Regulation* (despite Amazon EU's choice of law clause), the clause does not unfairly exclude the consumer from litigating under the consumer's relevant home state law.

However, and this is important, the clause Amazon EU uses may mislead consumers into believing that they do not have the right they do in fact have under the *Rome I Regulation*, and this potential to mislead makes the term unfair under Council Directive 93/13/EEC of 5 April 1993 on unfair terms in consumer contracts.

In its decision, the CJEU embraced Advocate General Saugmandsgaard Øe's reasoning concluding that:

> Article 3(1) of Council Directive 93/13/EEC of 5 April 1993 on unfair terms in consumer contracts must be interpreted as meaning that a term in the general terms and conditions of a seller or supplier which has not been individually negotiated, under which the contract concluded with a consumer in the course of electronic commerce is to be governed by the law of the Member State in which the seller or supplier is established, is unfair in so far as it leads the consumer into error by giving him the impression that only the law of that Member State applies to the contract, without informing him that under Article 6(2) of Regulation No 593/2008 he also enjoys the protection of the mandatory provisions of the law that would be applicable in the absence of that term, this being for the national court to ascertain in the light of all the relevant circumstances.[60]

This logic is beyond intelligent dispute, and contract lawyers will presumably now be kept busy for some time updating the many choice of law (and choice of forum) clauses that purport to give the business home-ground advantage. In fact, the potential implications of this approach go well beyond the limited sphere of choice of law and choice of forum clauses. The same reasoning that leads to the conclusion that such clauses are unfair, based on their being misleading, can of course be applied to every single clause in a consumer contract that does not accurately enough align itself with applicable consumer protection law or, for

60 Case C-191/15, *Verein für Konsumenteninformation v. Amazon EU Sarl*, ECJ judgment of 28 July 2016, ECLI:EU:C:2016:612, para. 82.

example, data protection law; that is, any contractual term that can be seen to mislead a consumer as to the rights established through EU consumer protection and data protection law needs to be addressed.

This means that lawyers will need to go through all such contracts with a fine-tooth comb in order to seek out those clauses that potentially mislead consumers as to their actual consumer rights. If such an exercise is carried out, I suspect that will be the first time in a long while that anyone actually reads those terms.

More broadly, perhaps the *Verein für Konsumenteninformation* matter is indicative of a greater scrutiny directed at the choice of law and choice of forum clauses we are faced with online? Support for such a proposition may be found in the June 2017 decision by the Supreme Court of Canada in *Douez v. Facebook, Inc.*, 2017 SCC 33. There the majority of the Court held Facebook's forum selection clause, nominating a California court, unenforceable. Time will tell whether this is a temporary set-back for the far-reaching 'party-autonomy' commonly held as holy in private international law, or whether flexibility has finally prevailed in the consumer context.

4. THE 'TARGETING' TEST

Under the *Brussels I bis Regulation* (recast), a person should be sued in his or her place of domicile. However, consumers enjoy a special 'home-ground' advantage in that they can always sue the other party in the consumer's home court and may themselves only ever be sued in their home court. The special protection only applies where the other party (the business) has directed activities to the consumer.[61] The question is then when a website can be seen to 'direct such activities'[62] in the context of Internet-based contracting, which is not clear from the Article as such.

In its explanatory memorandum to an earlier draft of the Regulation, the EC Commission appeared to limit the scope of Article 17(1)(c) to *interactive* websites; the mere fact that a vendor's website is accessible from a particular state would thus apparently not be sufficient to deem the vendor as having 'directed' activity to that state for the purposes of Article 17(1)(c).[63] The Commission did not elaborate on what it meant by an interactive website. It seems safe to assume that the interactivity referred to entails a facility for exchange of information between the website and those visiting it, including a facility for placement of purchase orders. On the other hand, the Commission has also stated that

61 See further: D. Svantesson, *Private International Law and the Internet*, 3rd edn., Kluwer Law International, The Hague 2016, pp. 470–480.

62 Regulation (EU) No. 1215/2012, Art. 17(1)(c) (*Brussels I bis Regulation*).

63 COM(1999) 348 final, 14 July 1999, p. 16.

the new Regulation 'equates the offer of goods and services via the Internet with an invitation or advertising by businesses which "by any means … direct their activities towards that Member State."'[64] A range of other uncertainties is discussed in an interesting article written by Foss and Bygrave.[65]

The year 2010 saw an important development relating to Article 17(1)(c) and the meaning of the expression 'directs such activities'. The European Court of Justice (ECJ) had to consider two cases directly on point, and dealt with the two cases, *Pammer v. Reederei Karl Schlüter GmbH & KG*[66] and *Hotel Alpenhof GesmbH v. Oliver Heller*[67] together. The key question common to the two cases was whether the ability of a website to be consulted on the Internet in the Member State of the consumer's domicile is sufficient to justify a finding that commercial or professional activities are being directed to that Member State within the meaning of Article 15(1)(c) of Regulation No. 44/2001, (now Article 17(1)(c) of Regulation 1215/2012).

The facts of the two cases are interesting as they illustrate the two different ways in which consumers are protected under the *Brussels I Regulation*. In *Pammer*, the claimant (Mr. Pammer – a consumer) sought to take action against the defendant (Reederei Karl Schlüter GmbH & KG – a business) to recover certain payments made to the defendant. The action was taken in the claimant's home jurisdiction (Austria) and was met by the defendant (based in Germany) arguing that the Court lacked jurisdiction.

In *Hotel Alpenhof*, the defendant (Mr. Heller – a consumer) had stayed at the claimant's hotel but had not paid the full amount contracted for. Hotel Alpenhof (the claimant – a business) based in Austria, sought to take action against the defendant who lived in Germany. Mr. Heller argued that the Austrian Court lacked jurisdiction.

---

64 Opinion of the Economic and Social Committee on the Proposal for a Council Regulation (EC) on jurisdiction and the recognition and enforcement of judgments in civil and commercial matters, CES 233/2000-99/1054 CNS, March 2000. See, M. Berliri, 'Jurisdiction and the Internet, and European Regulation 44 of 2001' in D. Campbell and S. Woodley (eds.), *E-Commerce: Law and Jurisdiction*, Kluwer Law International, The Hague 2003, p. 7.

65 M. Foss and L. Bygrave, 'International Consumer Purchases through the Internet: Jurisdictional Issues pursuant to European Law' (2000) 8 *Int'l. J.L. & Info. Tech.* 99. An interesting discussion of the matter can also be found in: G. Krog, 'The Brussels I Regulation Article 15.1(c)' in G. Krog and A. Bekken (eds.), *Yulex 2004*, Institutt for Rettsinformatikk, Oslo 2004.

66 Case C-585/08, *Pammer v. Reederei Karl Schlüter GmbH & KG* ECLI:EU:C:2010:740, [2010] ECR I-12527.

67 Case C-144/09, *Hotel Alpenhof GesmbH v. Oliver Heller* ECLI:EU:C:2010:740, [2010] ECR I-12527.

To understand the jurisdictional matters arising in the two cases, one must turn to Article 18(1) (previously Article 15(1)). That Article provides the consumer with the right to

> bring proceedings against the other party to a contract either in the courts of the Member State in which that party is domiciled or, regardless of the domicile of the other party, in the courts for the place where the consumer is domiciled.[68]

Thus, provided that Reederei Karl Schlüter GmbH & KG's conduct fell within Article 18(1)(c), Mr. Pammer would be entitled to take action in an Austrian court.

At the same time, Article 18(2) (previously Article 15(2)) also states that '[p]roceedings may be brought against a consumer by the other party to the contract only in the courts of the Member State in which the consumer is domiciled.'[69] Consequently, if it is concluded that Hotel Alpenhof's conduct falls within Article 18(1)(c), Mr. Heller should be successful in his argument that the Austrian Court, in which Hotel Alpenhof had instigated the proceedings, lacked jurisdiction.

As to the ECJ's approach, it suffices to note that the Court reached the following main conclusions:

(1) the mere fact that a website can be accessed in the consumer's jurisdiction does not mean that the business has directed its activities to that state;[70] and
(2) whether a trader has directed its activity to the Member State of the consumer's domicile, should be ascertained by reference to:

> whether, before the conclusion of any contract with the consumer, it is apparent from those websites and the trader's overall activity that the trader was envisaging doing business with consumers domiciled in one or more Member States, including the Member State of that consumer's domicile, in the sense that it was minded to conclude a contract with them.[71]

It is also worth taking note of Gillies' observation that:

> despite the aim for uniformity, it is for the courts of the Member State to determine whether the activities were directed to consumers in that Member State using the criteria provided by the CJEU. One wonders if reference back to the national court will provide

68 Regulation (EU) No. 1215/2012, Article 18(1) (*Brussels I bis Regulation*).
69 Regulation (EU) No. 1215/2012, Article 18(2) (*Brussels I bis Regulation*).
70 Joined Cases C-585/08 and C-144/09, ECLI:EU:C:2010:740, [2010] ECR I-12527, para. 95.
71 Joined Cases C-585/08 and C-144/09, para. 95.

> a consistent approach to the interpretation of 'Europeanised' conflicts rules whilst at the same time observing developments towards the maximisation of consumer protection. If there was ever a connecting factor that merited an autonomous interpretation from the CJEU, the connecting factor 'directing activities' qualified as such.[72]

And this is only the start of the problems that flow from the 'targeting approach'. First of all, as often is the case, the 'devil is in the detail' and the 'targeting' test can be applied in both appropriate and inappropriate ways. In other words, the usefulness of such an approach is, of course, directly dependent on how one defines what type of conduct amounts to a party having directed its activities to the forum state. The guidance then amounts to a useful first step, but it can hardly make the claim of providing for certainty and predictability.

Having noted how 'all clear expressions of the intention to solicit the custom of that State's consumers'[73] must be considered, the Court went on to discuss a non-exhaustive list of factors that may be taken into account when deciding whether a business has directed its activities to the consumer's state. Some of those factors ought to be uncontroversial. For example:

(1) 'mention that it [the trader] is offering its services or its goods in one or more Member States designated by name';[74]
(2) 'the disbursement of expenditure on an internet referencing service to the operator of a search engine in order to facilitate access to the trader's site by consumers domiciled in various Member States';[75]
(3) 'the international nature of the activity at issue, such as certain tourist activities';[76]
(4) 'mention of telephone numbers with the international code';[77]
(5) 'the description of itineraries from one or more other Member States to the place where the service is provided';[78] and
(6) 'mention of an international clientele composed of customers domiciled in various Member States, in particular by presentation of accounts written by such customers.'[79]

---

72 L. Gillies, 'Clarifying the "Philosophy of Article 15" in the Brussels I Regulation: C-585/08 Peter Pammer v Reedere [sic] Karl Schluter GmbH & Co and C-144/09 Hotel Alpenhof GesmbH v Oliver Heller' (2011) 60 *International and Comparative Law Quarterly* 557–564, 563.

73 Joined Cases C-585/08 and C-144/09, para. 80.

74 Ibid, para. 81.

75 Joined Cases C-585/08 and C-144/09.

76 Ibid, para. 83.

77 Ibid.

78 Ibid.

79 Ibid.

Whether the use of a certain language and/or currency could be seen as an indication that the business has directed its activities to a particular Member State was discussed at length by both the Advocate General and the ECJ. In the end, the ECJ concluded that the 'use of a language or a currency other than the language or currency generally used in the Member State in which the trader is established with the possibility of making and confirming the reservation in that other language'[80] is a factor capable of constituting evidence from which it may be concluded that the trader's activity is directed to the Member State of the consumer's domicile. I will address the currency and language issues separately, starting with the currency issue.

It is not uncommon for e-businesses, engaging in some degree of cross-border trade, to adopt wholesale e-commerce solutions that, for reasons of simplicity, allow prices to be displayed in a large number of different currencies. Thus, it may not be accurate to assume that an e-business is directing its activities to all the states whose currency is represented on the business's website. For example, a Finnish e-business dealing with consumers from all the Scandinavian countries may adopt an e-commerce solution that allows prices to be displayed in all the different currencies of the EU Member States without that being an indication of the e-business directing its activities to, for example, Germany, France or Spain.

Turning to the issue of whether the use of a certain language, or languages, may be relied upon to establish that the business's activity is directed to the Member State of the consumer's domicile, the Advocate General makes two interesting observations:

> In my view, language can be a relevant criterion in two respects. First, the fact that a website is written only in a language that is not very widespread and is the official language only in one particular Member State can be an indication that the undertaking is directing its activities to that Member State alone ... Secondly, I consider it to be significant whether a website that is written in a particular language provides a facility whereby another language can be selected.[81]

I agree with both these observations, with only a slight reservation: that is, some countries are multilingual and thus websites from such countries may be multilingual without that feature signalling any international ambitions.

In addition, at least one factor may not be quite as generally an accurate indicator as the ECJ and the Advocate General consider it to be. The ECJ stated that the 'use of a top-level domain name other than that of the Member State in which the trader is established, for example ".de", or use of neutral top-level

80 Ibid, para. 93.

81 Opinion of Advocate General Trstenjak delivered on 18 May 2010, paras. 81–83.

domain names such as ".com" or ".eu"'[82] amounts to evidence that the trader's activity is directed to the Member State of the consumer's domicile. The Advocate General discusses the matter in detail and states, amongst other things:

> First, the mention of the internet domain name of a Member State is a clear indication that the undertaking is directing its activities to the Member State with that domain name. If the undertaking – such as Internationale Frachtschif-freisen Pfeiffer in Pammer, for example – sets up a website with the domain name '.de', this must necessarily mean that it is directing its activities to the German market. Secondly, the use of a Member State's internet domain name does not preclude the directing of activities to other Member States.[83]

While the second point made here is legitimate, the first one is questionable as can be illustrated by the very example the Advocate General used to support her assertion. The Advocate General noted that the main issues relating to domain names arise where a business established in state A uses a domain name of state B: 'If, for example, an undertaking with its place of establishment in the United Kingdom sets up a website with the domain name ".es", it is apparent that it is directing its activities in whole or in part to the Spanish market.'[84]

The flaw in this reasoning can be made clear by the use of an example. Imagine that the mentioned undertaking, with its place of establishment in the United Kingdom, set up a website with the domain name 'parti.es', or 'famili.es'. The choice of top-level domain may then very well have been made to achieve a play on words rather than as an attempt at attracting customers from the Spanish market. Indeed, it is common for businesses to favour top-level domains with inherent meanings like '.tv'. In light of this, care must be taken when assessing the true impact of the choice of top-level domain.

The Court also noted some factors that are not of relevance. For example, the mere fact that a website states the trader's e-mail or geographical address, or a phone number without an international code, does not signal an international targeting.[85] This is of course only natural as the provision of such information is in fact mandated by the E-commerce Directive.[86]

Furthermore, both the Advocate General and the ECJ emphasised that whether a website is 'interactive' or 'passive' is not determinative of whether the business operating the website is directing its activities to the consumer's

---

82 Joined Cases C-585/08 and C-144/09, ECJ judgment, para. 83.

83 Opinion of Advocate General Trstenjak delivered on 18 May 2010, para. 84.

84 Ibid, para. 85.

85 Joined Cases C-585/08 and C-144/09, ECJ judgment, para. 77.

86 Directive 2000/31/EC of the European Parliament and of the Council of 8 June 2000 on certain legal aspects of information society services, in particular electronic commerce, in the Internal Market ('Directive on electronic commerce') ([2000] *OJ* L178, p. 1).

state.[87] This is significant, as in its explanatory memorandum accompanying the original proposal for the regulation, the Commission suggested:

> that the dividing line between websites that fall within the scope of the concept of the directing of activities and websites to which this does not apply is to be drawn according to the interactivity of a website, that is to say, it depends upon whether the website permits a contract to be concluded directly.[88]

All in all, it seems clear that the list of factors provided by the Court provides limited guidance only and leaves a wide discretion for the national courts.[89] However, the most worrying aspect of the ECJ's approach is its focus on the trader's subjective intentions prior to the conclusion of the contract with the consumer. Not only is this approach not supported by Article 15(1)(c) of the *Brussels I Regulation*, there is insufficient justification for it in the judgment. In fact, the misguided focus on the subjective intentions of the trader begins already in the second paragraph of the Opinion of the Advocate General. In discussing the matters being balanced in the cases, she states:

> When interpreting this term it is therefore necessary to achieve a balance between protection of the consumer, who is entitled to call upon the special rules of jurisdiction under Regulation No 44/2001, and the consequences for the undertaking, to which these special rules of jurisdiction can only apply once it has made a conscious decision to direct its activities to the consumer's Member State.[90]

Both the Advocate General and the ECJ seem to take the view that the phrase 'directs such activities' implies a conscious decision executed without mistakes. The Advocate General states that '[i]t is ... essential for there to be active conduct on the part of the undertaking, the *objective* and *outcome* of which is to win customers from other Member States.' (emphasis added).[91]

While I agree that there must be some active conduct on the part of the undertaking, the problem with this approach is found in the words in italic. We can have a situation in which the *objective* of an activity is to win customers from other Member States, but no such *outcome* is realised. And we can have a situation in which the *outcome* of an activity is to win customers from other Member States, without it being the trader's *objective*. Imagine the following scenario.

---

87 Joined Cases C 585/08 and C 144/09, ECJ judgment, para. 79.
88 Opinion of Advocate General Trstenjak delivered on 18 May 2010, para. 68.
89 See further, J. Trzaskowski et al., *Introduction to EU Internet Law*, Ex Tuto Publishing A/S, Copenhagen 2015, p. 323.
90 Opinion of Advocate General Trstenjak delivered on 18 May 2010, para. 2.
91 Ibid, para. 63.

A trader in Greece wishes to carry out an extensive marketing campaign in Switzerland, but miscommunicates its wishes so that the marketing company it has hired is under the impression that the country to be targeted is Sweden. The result is that every Swedish household receives marketing materials from the Greek business, and the Greek business accepts a large number of orders from consumers in Sweden. In such a scenario, the Greek business has never made a conscious decision to direct its activities to the consumers in Sweden. Similarly, it would be incorrect to say that the Greek business envisaged doing business with consumers domiciled in Sweden, in the sense that it was minded to conclude a contract with them prior to any contracts were entered into. Put simply, it was never the Greek business's objective to win customers from Sweden.

Applying the standard set by the ECJ, and promoted by the Advocate General, the Swedish consumers would then not be protected by the *Brussels I bis Regulation*. Surely this cannot be in line with the intent of the drafters of the Regulation?

The better approach is to distinguish between *objective* and *outcome* and only focus on the *outcome* when determining whether the business has directed its activities to the consumer's state. Such a move from subjectivity to objectivity promotes certainty and fairness.

Both the Advocate General and the ECJ concluded that the mere fact that a website can be accessed in the consumer's jurisdiction does not mean that the business has directed its activities to that state. This conclusion is supported by Recital (24) in the preamble to Regulation (EC) No. 593/2008 of the European Parliament and of the Council of 17 June 2008 on the law applicable to contractual obligations (Rome I) which states that:

> the mere fact that an Internet site is accessible is not sufficient for Article 15 to be applicable, although a factor will be that this Internet site solicits the conclusion of distance contracts and that a contract has actually been concluded at a distance, by whatever means.[92]

When viewed in isolation from the then applicable Article 15(1)(c) of the *Brussels I Regulation*, this conclusion seems reasonable. Thus one cannot disagree with the ECJ's observations as to the difference between intention in classic forms of advertising and intention in the context of website advertising:

> The classic forms of advertising ... involve the outlay of, sometimes significant, expenditure by the trader in order to make itself known in other Member States and they demonstrate, on that very basis, an intention of the trader to direct its activity towards those States.

92 Recital (24), Preamble to Regulation No. 593/2008.

> That intention is not, on the other hand, always present in the case of advertising by means of the internet. Since this method of communication inherently has a worldwide reach, advertising on a website by a trader is in principle accessible in all States, and, therefore, throughout the European Union, without any need to incur additional expenditure and irrespective of the intention or otherwise of the trader to target consumers outside the territory of the State in which it is established.
>
> It does not follow, however, that the words 'directs such activities to' must be interpreted as relating to a website's merely being accessible in Member States other than that in which the trader concerned is established.[93]

The problem with this line of reasoning is, of course, that Article 15(1)(c) did not regulate advertising as such, it regulated contractual situations only. Thus, while the correctness of this conclusion cannot be called into question, its relevance can, and indeed must, be so called into question. After all, it must be remembered that the only situation in which the matter of whether a business has directed its activities to the consumer's state arises is where that business has entered into an actual contract with the consumer. Consequently, there can quite simply never be a situation where a provision such as the then Article 15(1)(c) comes into play based on the mere fact that a website can be accessed in the consumer's jurisdiction. Indeed, to me, it seems contrary to intuition to conclude that a business that has contracted with a consumer did not, at least *prima facie*, direct its activities to the consumer's state.

The Advocate General suggested that:

> [i]f the legislature had wanted jurisdiction to be determined by the special rules governing consumer contracts simply on the ground that a website can be consulted on the internet, it would have made the mere existence of a website a condition for the application of those provisions rather than the directing of activities.[94]

The ECJ endorsed this view.[95] However, this conclusion is highly questionable given the general tendency to draft in technology-neutral language.

It is my view that placing the focus on whether or not a business has directed its activities to the consumer's state is misguided. Nevertheless, I think that such an approach may work reasonably well where the existence of a contract between the business and the consumer gives rise to a strong, but rebuttable, presumption that the business directed its activities to the consumer's state. That is, in every case where a business has contracted with a consumer in another Member State, it should be presumed that the business has directed its activities

93 Joined Cases C-585/08 and C-144/09, paras. 67–69.

94 Opinion of Advocate General Trstenjak delivered on 18 May 2010, para. 64.

95 Joined Cases C-585/08 and C-144/09, ECJ judgment, para. 71.

to that Member State. After all, the business has made the choice to reap the benefits of contracting with a consumer from that Member State. Bearing this in mind, the special rule for consumers is not that far detached from the general rule on contracts which focuses on the place of performance:

> [A]s regards contracts in general, article 15(1)(b) of the [Brussels I] Regulation allocates jurisdiction to the courts for the place of performance of the supplier's obligation; if the supplier's obligation is to deliver goods to the consumer at the consumer's home address (or to perform services there), the courts for the place where the consumer is domiciled would have jurisdiction in any event – even if the Brussels I Regulation contained no provisions relating specifically to consumer contracts.[96]

In any case, with the aforementioned presumption as the starting point, it would then be for the business to rebut that presumption. This can, for example, be done by showing that it did in fact seek to avoid contracting with consumers from that Member State.

Unfortunately, the ECJ adopted a different, more complex and less certain, interpretation of the then Article 15(1)(c) of the *Brussels I Regulation*, and both businesses and consumers will pay the price.

In light of the above, I am unfortunately inclined to conclude that 'targeting', although it in theory comes across as providing certainty, predictability and simplicity, is hopelessly difficult to apply in too large a number of practical situations – it is quite simply the legislator's dream, but the judge's (and indeed lawyer's) nightmare. And the problems with 'targeting' will be even more noticeable where this approach is applied outside contractual situations, as will be the case via Article 3(2) of the EU's General Data Protection Regulation that will come into effect in May 2018.

5. CONCLUDING REMARKS

Currently, questions around Internet jurisdiction – in a general sense – are gaining an unprecedented level of attention as is evidenced by the number of initiatives e.g. the Internet and Jurisdiction project,[97] events e.g. 'A Western Digital Renaissance: drivers and boundaries', held by the Aspen Institute Italia (Italy) in October 2015, and by academic writing. Yet, progress is both slow and limited.

As discussed above, the most significant obstacle for progress is found in the fact that our current thinking on jurisdiction is largely dominated by, and rooted in, notions of territoriality. It is fair to say that in our current paradigm,

---

96 J. Hill, *Cross-border Consumer Contracts*, Oxford University Press, Oxford 2008, p. 152.

97 <http://www.internetjurisdiction.net/> accessed 14.08.2016.

the territoriality principle represents the jurisprudential core of our thinking on jurisdiction – a state has jurisdiction over all that occurs in its territory for the simple reason that it occurs in its territory. But as is outlined above, it is not always easy – or indeed possible – to determine *where* (in real-space geographical terms) events take place online.

The fact that the territoriality principle is a poor fit for the largely border-disregarding, if not 'borderless', Internet is well established. However, apart from (now largely discredited) calls in the mid-'90s for the law not to apply to the Internet at all,[98] few real alternatives to territoriality as the cornerstone of jurisdiction have been advanced until recently. This chapter has advanced one alternative.

More broadly, this chapter has sought to bring attention to several themes of central importance for digital contracts in global surroundings. Apart from the already mentioned reliance on territoriality, those themes are:

- that the Internet cannot be allowed to be a lawless space;
- that cross-border online interaction fills a valuable function;
- that we presently are experiencing a state of 'hyper-regulation' and
- that the role of contracts has increased with our use of the Internet.

The discussion above has also been aimed at bringing attention to important considerations of the extent to which we uphold party autonomy in the context of choice of forum and choice of law clauses online. In addition, the prevalent 'targeting' focus was discussed and analysed in detail.

While considerable progress has been made already, much work lies ahead. And in pursing that work, we must not shy away from seeking solutions 'outside the box'. There is something unwholesome about statements such as:

> The law must develop and adapt, as it always has done down the years in response to other revolutionary technologies. We must not simply throw up our hands in despair and moan that the internet is uncontrollable. Nor can we simply abandon basic legal principles.[99]

Indeed, this is arguably nothing but a useless truism misrepresenting what our real alternatives are. First of all, not even the Cyber libertarians suggested that a lack of legal regulation should stem from despair or moaning. Their idea of a lawless dimension was very much an intentional, and preferred, choice. Second, and more important, statements such as this mask the real issue – that

98 See e.g., D. Johnson and D. Post, above n. 3.

99 Sir James Munby P in *Re J (A Child)* HCMP590/2014 (unreported, 21 March 2014) as referred to in *Dr Yeung, Sau Shing Albert v. Google Inc.* [2014] HKCFI 1404, para. 54.

technological developments frequently do not come with obvious application of current legal norms and that, therefore, we are always made to make important choices of how we apply existing legal norms to new technologies.

Finally, given that even some basic questions, such as whether e-mails fall within the Common Law postal acceptance rule, remained for a very long time, or still remain, unsettled, it is perhaps overly optimistic to point to history as evidence that the law always will adapt to revolutionary technologies.

REGULATING ONLINE PLATFORMS – THE CASE OF AIRBNB

Vanessa Mak*

ABSTRACT

Platform services, such as Airbnb, Uber, eBay, Amazon, TaskRabbit and many more have rapidly emerged and taken over parts of existing markets for services. Airbnb's peer-to-peer accommodation rental platform competes with hotels in many cities, whereas Uber has entered existing markets for taxi services in many large cities around the world. Innovative services such as these have been welcomed by many users but they also create new challenges: how can users be protected against health and safety risks, are payment systems safe, are effective dispute resolution mechanisms available? Besides typical private law issues concerning the division of responsibilities between the platform and its users, also broader concerns have arisen in relation to market regulation and public order. The aim of

* An earlier version of this contribution was published as 'Private Law Perspectives on Platform Services. Airbnb: Home Rentals between AYOR and NIMBY' (2016) 5 *Journal of European Consumer and Market Law* 19–25.

this contribution is to 'unpack' the legal relationships within one platform service – Airbnb – to provide a basis for discussion of the question whether regulation of platform services is needed and if so, in what form.

1. INTRODUCTION

Like other platform services, Airbnb has become a favourite of digitally savvy consumers who know that some of the greatest benefits of our globalising society can be found online. Offering a platform through which hosts can advertise their apartments to potential guests worldwide, Airbnb provides a real, and in many ways attractive, alternative to visitors who are looking for something else than a hotel room. Tourists who would normally have booked a hotel room on a city trip to New York, Paris or Barcelona, can find a fully furnished apartment with all amenities instead – and often cheaper than a hotel too.

Behind the gleaming façade, the housing platform provided by Airbnb may, however, have some hidden cracks in terms of legal protection that both hosts and guests should be aware of. This chapter discusses the private law relationships that arise between the three parties involved in a home rental through the website: the online platform (Airbnb), the host and the guest. As will be seen, although some improvements have been made, the legal relationships that hosts and guests enter into are strongly characterised by an 'at your own risk' (AYOR) approach. Airbnb as a platform tries to stay out of the rental agreement itself as much as possible, and to have recourse to a host or a guest for damage suffered can – both in legal and in practical terms – prove to be a cumbersome journey.

Besides the private law aspects of Airbnb rentals, it should be realised that the main legal problems that challenge the continuance of the platform are in areas of public law, such as local administrative law and tax regulation. Hotel owners, landlords and disgruntled neighbours of hosts refer to the legal framework to put a stop to rentals in their city or neighbourhood. Whether this 'not in my backyard' (NIMBY) mentality will curtail Airbnb's growth remains to be seen. The final part of this chapter will consider these legal challenges and discuss some recent case law.

The structure of the chapter is as follows. After a brief description of the model through which Airbnb operates (section 2), the private law relationships between the platform and its users will be unpacked (section 3). This part focuses on the platform's general terms and conditions, its privacy policy and its host guarantee. Section 4 shifts the focus to the relationship between host and guest, discussing liability for non-performance and other liabilities that may arise. Section 5 discusses Airbnb's online dispute resolution centre, followed by a discussion of challenges to Airbnb that go beyond the platform and its users – and affect e.g. hotel owners and landlords – in section 6. Section 7 concludes.

2. AIRBNB – HOME AWAY FROM HOME

Airbnb's format is simple. Through the company's website – airbnb.com – hosts can post their spaces online, indicating the price that they wish to charge for rental per night, per week or per month. Most listings are for residential spaces, i.e. apartments or houses, although the platform's terms and conditions allow for the posting of other properties. Airbnb even offers a photography service that enables hosts to have high-resolution, professional photos taken to showcase their space.[1]

Guests – or at this stage, people looking for accommodation – can browse host listings on the website to see availability during their required dates, location, prices, and in most cases also some personal information from the host about the place and the neighbourhood. Airbnb encourages hosts to share their 'favorite places' and to 'teach [guests] something local and unforgettable'.[2] One listing for Amsterdam that I came across while doing some research for this chapter was certainly written in this vein, starting: 'Welcome to our laid-back, "smoke friendly" house, where you will find a vaporiser in almost every room. It is Amsterdam after all and you'll find us in the heart of it.' Amusement aside, most listings do provide quite detailed information about things to see in the neighbourhood and how to find one's way around town.

Hosts as well as guests can only make use of Airbnb's website for bookings once they have registered as users. This is a fairly straightforward procedure. One can either register and create a new account on airbnb.com or sign in to the website using an existing third-party social networking site, such as Facebook or Google.[3]

Guests can contact hosts through their listings to make a reservation. The site makes it possible to send messages to hosts to request further information and, if desired, to negotiate further terms about the rental. Once host and guest agree on a booking, the guest can confirm the booking and pay for it through the Airbnb website. Airbnb holds the payment in escrow until the guest has arrived at the accommodation, and releases it to the host 24 hours after the guest has checked in.[4]

For its services, Airbnb charges hosts a fee of three per cent (often plus VAT) on every booking. Guests pay an additional 6–12 per cent in service fees. Obviously these charges constitute the main income that Airbnb itself makes from the website and that enable the company to make a profit. What users,

---

1 https://www.airbnb.com/help/article/297/how-do-i-apply-for-professional-photography. References in this text are to the US website. Airbnb offers the same services in most places in the rest of the world.

2 https://www.airbnb.com/hospitality.

3 See for a full description, the Terms of Service: https://www.airbnb.com/terms.

4 https://www.airbnb.com/help/article/51/how-does-airbnb-process-payments.

in particular guests, get for their money is, however, harder to see. In addition to the rental price paid to the host and the Airbnb service fee, hosts generally charge separate fees to guests for cleaning and for other amenities (e.g. an extra bed or mattress).

In this three-party relationship between Airbnb, host and guest, several private law relationships can arise. First, host and guest enter into a rental agreement, thereby taking on contractual obligations towards each other. They may also, for matters falling outside the contract, incur other (e.g. tortious) obligations towards each other. Second, Airbnb has a contractual relationship with the host, and a separate one with the guest. Here also liability might arise on other grounds, e.g. tort. Finally, the question arises as to whether Airbnb could perhaps be considered an intermediary. If that were the case, Airbnb could be liable in its own right towards the guest if something goes wrong, for example if there are shortcomings in the rental space or otherwise in the performance of the contract.[5]

Whether a liability claim will be successful in any of the three relationships mentioned here depends on rules of national law. In this chapter I will not seek to answer such specific liability questions, but will rather seek to unpack the main legal issues with a view to giving a basis to future discussions on how liability *should* be divided between the platform, the host and the guest. Such an overview can provide a helpful framework for identifying where current laws perhaps fall short e.g. in protecting consumers who rent spaces through Airbnb as guests, or where Airbnb is taking on responsibilities that go beyond its position of a simple facilitator and might give rise to liability of the platform. It might also be a starting point for discussing the need for a harmonising instrument from the EU legislator. In some cases – e.g. in relation to unfair terms – EU legislation may already provide rules of consumer protection and I will mention those where relevant. I will now first consider the relationships between Airbnb and its users.

3. THE LEGAL RELATIONSHIP BETWEEN AIRBNB AND THE USER

According to its general terms and conditions, Airbnb's 'Site, Application and Services can be used to facilitate the listing and booking of residential and other properties ("Accommodations").'[6] The word to take note of here is

5 Although the precise conditions for liability of intermediaries are often unclear, also at EU level. See for a discussion of this problem in the context of travel law, Anne de Vries, 'Travel Intermediaries and Responsibility for Compliance with EU Travel Law: A Scattered Legal Picture' (2016) 5 *Journal of European Consumer and Market Law* 119.

6 https://www.airbnb.com/terms.

'facilitate'. Airbnb presents itself as a platform that connects hosts and guests, but otherwise seeks to stay outside their rental agreement, at least as much as possible. Use of the platform is, almost literally, 'at your own risk' (AYOR). Airbnb nonetheless has some legal obligations towards its users. I will briefly highlight the terms that seek to establish Airbnb's status as 'only a platform' and that seek to limit its liability towards users, and also say a few words about legal obligations that do arise, e.g. in relation to privacy protection and the so-called Host Guarantee. It is fitting, also, to pay brief attention to the obligation that Airbnb places on hosts to act as 'responsible hosts', even if this obligation is not legally enforceable.

3.1. 'ONLY A PLATFORM', TERMS AND DISCLAIMERS

Confirmation of Airbnb's intention to be a facilitator, rather than a party, to the rental agreement between host and guest is reflected in a number of clauses in the general terms that seek to limit liability of the company. The most prominent one is found towards the beginning of the terms of service. After stating that the site, application and services comprise an online platform through which hosts may create listings and guests may book accommodation directly with the hosts, the terms continue:

> You understand and agree that Airbnb is not a party to any agreements entered into between hosts and guests, nor is Airbnb a real estate broker, agent or insurer. Airbnb has no control over the conduct of hosts, guests and other users of the Site, Application and Services or any accommodations, and disclaims all liability in this regard to the maximum extent permitted by law.

The terms also state that Airbnb 'does not endorse any Member or any Accommodation'. Under the heading 'Disclaimers' another set of limitation clauses follows, starting with: 'If you choose to use the Site, Application, Services or collective content or participate in the referral program, you do so at your sole risk.' The disclaimer also states that

> Airbnb makes no warranty regarding the quality of any listings, accommodations, hosts, guests, your accrual of Airbnb travel credits, the services or collective content or the accuracy, timeliness, truthfulness, completeness or reliability of any collective content obtained through the Site, Application, Services or referral program.

The terms of service further include an entire agreement clause.[7]

[7] As well as choice of law and jurisdiction clauses, on which section 5 below.

Is Airbnb then in no way legally bound to its users, i.e. the hosts and guests making use of the platform? Not entirely. Some obligations undertaken by Airbnb seem to point towards an involvement of the company that goes beyond being a mere platform on which hosts and guests can connect. For example, Airbnb maintains an online dispute resolution centre through which parties can apply for mediation to obtain payment from their host or guest in relation to their rental. Airbnb also offers assistance in cases where the accommodation that was booked is cancelled by the host within 24 hours before the guest's arrival, or where the actual accommodation is materially different from the description in the listing.[8] To what extent these obligations give rise to liability of Airbnb if the company does not fulfil them, however, is not immediately clear. Since they are either phrased as obligations to undertake reasonable efforts, or – in case of dispute resolution – available only on the condition that users accept the decision as final,[9] it will be hard for a dissatisfied user to bring a successful legal action against Airbnb.

3.2. LEGAL OBLIGATIONS – PRIVACY POLICY

Other obligations between Airbnb and its users arise in relation to privacy protection. The platform gathers data from users in several ways, most importantly information about the user, log data and mobile data from devices on which the Airbnb application is run (e.g. a smartphone), which may contain information such as the user's IP address and their location.[10] Data can also come from so-called third-party social plug-ins, such as Facebook's 'like' button.

Although Airbnb is careful in informing users about the purposes for which the gathered data may be used – such as to operate and optimise the platform, or even to monitor behaviour that may constitute fraud – some of the terms of its privacy policy seem contentious or even directly at odds with EU law. The policy for example states (in bold) that '[w]hen you use the Platform, your data may be sent to the United States and possibly other countries.' In the light of the judgment of the Court of Justice of the EU in Case C-362/14 *Maximillian Schrems v. Data Protection Commissioner* one may wonder for how much longer the sharing of data of EU citizens with US-based companies will be allowed.[11] The Court declared Commission Decision 2000/520/EC (the 'Safe Harbour Decision') invalid. That Decision allowed data transfers from the EU to the

8 https://www.airbnb.com/help/article/544/what-is-airbnb-s-guest-refund-policy?topic=250.

9 https://www.airbnb.com/help/article/783/when-can-i-involve-airbnb-in-my-resolution-center-request.

10 https://www.airbnb.com/terms/privacy_policy.

11 See CJEU 6 October 2015, Case C-362/14 *Schrems v. Data Protection Commissioner*, ECLI:EU:C:2015:650.

US on the basis of the European Commission's finding that the US offered an adequate level of protection of the personal data transferred. Since then, Edward Snowden's revelations of NSA data gathering have cast a different light on the protection of personal data in the United States. Against that background, it is not strange that EU citizens such as Mr. Schrems are concerned about the processing in the US of data gathered by social networks – such as in this case Facebook – in Europe. The task is now for the Irish Data Protection Commissioner, as the supervisory authority overseeing Facebook's Irish subsidiary, to decide whether the transfer of data of Facebook's European subscribers to the United States should be suspended. It seems likely that the authority will decide that US privacy protection is not adequate and that therefore data transfers should be suspended. In that case, Airbnb's data sharing policy could also be challenged.

Another term in Airbnb's privacy policy that seems questionable in light of EU law is the one relating to policy changes. Airbnb reserves the right to change how they collect and then use personal information 'at any time and without prior notice, at our sole discretion.'[12] Changes to the privacy policy in general are also said to be allowed at any time, and, it seems, only notified to the user if material changes are made, but not actually prior to making the amendment. This provision seems at odds with rules of EU law that prescribe that terms and conditions must set out in a clear and intelligible manner under what conditions a right to unilateral variation of contract terms may be exercised.[13] Despite Airbnb's designation of Californian or US law as the law applicable to the contract between the platform and the user, European consumers can challenge the unfair nature of these terms. Article 6(2) of the Rome I Regulation provides that the protection that consumers enjoy under mandatory provisions of their national laws (which includes implemented rules of EU law) cannot be derogated from even if a choice of law is made for another law.[14] Of course, whether consumers will in fact challenge unfair terms is another question.

3.3. LEGAL OBLIGATIONS – HOST GUARANTEE

Another obligation that Airbnb assumes and that makes it perhaps closer to being a party to the relationship between host and guest rather than a mere

---

12 See https://www.airbnb.com/terms/privacy_policy, under 'Changes to this Privacy Policy'.

13 Arts. 3 and 5 of Directive 93/13/EEC on unfair terms in consumer contracts [1993] OJ L95/29, and Art. 3(3) of Directive 2003/55/EC concerning common rules for the internal market on natural gas [2003] OJ L176/57, as interpreted by the CJEU 21 March 2013, Case C-92/11 *RWE Vertrieb AG v. Verbraucherzentrale Nordrhein-Westfalen eV*, ECLI:EU:C:2013:180; and Art. 3(1) and (3) of Directive 93/13/EEC as interpreted by the CJEU 26 April 2012, Case C-472/10 *Nemzeti Fogyasztóvédelmi Hatóság v. Invitel Távközlési Zrt*, ECLI:EU:C:2012:242.

14 Regulation (EC) 593/2008 on the law applicable to contractual obligations (Rome I) [2008] OJ L177/6.

platform concerns its 'Host Guarantee'. The Host Guarantee gives coverage for up to $US1,000,000 for certain damage caused by guests to a host's property.[15] Perhaps not surprisingly, considering Airbnb's substantial list of limitation clauses, this guarantee also comes with a number of conditions.

First, the Host Guarantee is not meant to substitute damages payments that can be obtained from elsewhere, in particular from the guest who caused the damage or through (their or the host's) insurance. The terms of the Host Guarantee policy stipulate:

> Any amount of any Covered Losses payable under the Airbnb Host Guarantee will be reduced by the amount already paid to you or for your benefit by a Responsible Guest, Invitee or other source (such as an insurer or other responsible party) for the same Covered Loss.[16]

Second, not all losses are covered. Only those losses covered by Airbnb's insurance policy, and paid out under it, can be compensated for to the host. In other words, Airbnb is not taking on risks that go beyond the insurance policy that it has taken out for its company. Further, the Host Guarantee policy contains a large number of excluded items which cannot be compensated for in damages under the policy. These are, for example, loss of cash and securities, damage to pets, damage to scooters, cars and other vehicles, and – perhaps not the most common – damage to an underground mine or mine shaft.

Despite its limitations, the Host Guarantee gives a reasonable degree of security to hosts that they will be able to obtain financial compensation if guests do damage to their property. As will be seen in the next section, the position of guests is less protected.

3.4. RULES OF CONDUCT – HOST'S RESPONSIBILITY

Finally, Airbnb not only provides rules concerning its own obligations and (limitations of) liability; it also places duties on hosts. These duties relate primarily to hospitality and 'responsible hosting' and are for the most part rules of conduct rather than legally enforceable obligations.

The rules on hospitality are reflected in a list of 'hospitality standards', which refer to designated aspects of the process of listing, taking bookings and actually hosting guests: accuracy, communication, availability, commitment, cleanliness, amenities, welcome, support and reviews.[17] Each of these is explained in more

---

15 https://www.airbnb.com/info/guarantee.

16 ibid.

17 https://www.airbnb.com/help/topic/206/hosting-standards.

detail on Airbnb's website. Most aspects are, however, quite common sense points that one would expect hosts to be aware of: to make sure that the space is clean and tidy, to arrange for an easy way in which the keys can be picked up on arrival and dropped off when the guests are leaving, to be available or to have someone available to support guests with minor mishaps such as leaking taps or finding the toaster (both examples from the website).

Airbnb has also published a 'Responsible Hosting' policy on its website, encouraging hosts to make their accommodation safe for guests, to inform or otherwise consider the interests of neighbours, and to comply with local tax and tenancy regulations.[18] In particular the safety aspects have given rise to discussion. A blog post entitled 'Living and Dying on Airbnb' by journalist Zak Stone recounts the story of his dad's death in an accident at an Airbnb rental.[19] Apart from signalling to everyone who thinks of renting a space through Airbnb that safety standards are not checked by the company or anyone else, the article puts the finger on another sore spot: the lack of insurance or guaranteed damages payments for guests. Whereas hosts can invoke Airbnb's Host Guarantee, no such scheme is available for those who rent a space through the platform. Whereas Stone's family obtained a financial settlement through the hosts' homeowner's insurance policy, which did not exclude coverage for commercial activity, many guests are likely to be left empty-handed. Their hosts are unlikely to have deep enough pockets to pay compensation for personal injury or death, and Airbnb cannot be called upon as an alternative. The company does indeed seem to be too far removed from the tenancy – especially since they do not carry out safety checks – to be held responsible for accidents at the host's accommodation.

One thing that Airbnb has done in response to safety concerns, or likely even in response to actual accidents, is to encourage hosts to make their spaces safe. Airbnb encourages them to have working smoke and carbon monoxide (CO) detectors in their listing and has even offered CO detectors for free through its website.[20] The webpage also gives some other safety tips, e.g. to comply with health and safety regulations, to fix exposed wires, and to remove other hazards around the home.

Although these are not duties that guests can legally enforce against hosts, Airbnb's review mechanism through the website can exercise some pressure on hosts to keep up their standards. Guests can leave reviews in which they give between one and five stars to indicate the quality of their experience, rating things such as accuracy, communication, cleanliness, location, check-in and

18 https://www.airbnb.com/help/responsible-hosting.

19 https://medium.com/matter/living-and-dying-on-airbnb-6bff8d600c04#.lcj7jb9yw.

20 https://www.airbnb.com/help/article/515/i-m-a-host--am-i-required-to-have-a-smoke-and-co-detector-installed?topic=359.

value for money. Hosts can, vice versa, also give star ratings to their guests. Even if not legally enforceable, reputational feedback mechanisms can in this way contribute to decent behaviour from both hosts and guests.[21]

4. THE RELATIONSHIP BETWEEN HOST AND GUEST

Whilst it is probably of the greatest practical importance to users of Airbnb, the relationship between host and guest is not the most intriguing from a private law perspective. It is primarily governed by the agreement between the parties and relevant provisions of contract law – national contract law, that is. Since Airbnb has not stipulated any choice of law or choice of jurisdiction clauses for this relationship – whilst it has done so for claims against the company itself – the rules of private international law will determine which law applies. In the absence of a choice by the parties, and presuming that the contract qualifies as a tenancy agreement, the contract between host and guest will almost always be governed by the law of the country in which the property is located.[22]

Some questions may arise as to whether the contract between host and guest is one between peers, and therefore governed by general contract law, or whether it is a consumer contract. If the definition from EU consumer law is followed, a party can only be considered a trader or supplier if they are a natural or legal person acting 'for purposes relating to his trade, business, craft or profession'.[23] It begs the question whether a host who is renting out an apartment through Airbnb is acting in a professional capacity. Arguably, someone who rents out a flat only for a few days or weeks each year and only during the time that they are on holiday themselves, is not acting for business purposes. Someone, on the other hand, who lists one or more spaces on Airbnb more or less continuously throughout the year might be considered to be running a profitable business, even if that person would not consider himself a professional landlord. Where to draw the line is not that easy to say. Discussions in recent case law show that public and legal opinions are divided about the question of how many days of touristic rental can be considered acceptable under a tenancy

21 A helpful analysis of online review mechanisms in the context of European contract law has been made by Christoph Busch, 'Crowdsourcing Consumer Confidence. How to Regulate Online Rating and Review Systems in the Collaborative Economy' in Alberto De Franceschi (ed.), *European Contract Law and the Digital Single Market. The Implications of the Digital Revolution* (Intersentia 2016) 223.

22 For Europe, Art. 4(1)(c) of the Rome I Regulation confirms that this is the rule applying to tenancies of immovable property.

23 cf the definition in e.g. Art. 2(2) of Directive 2011/83/EU on consumer rights [2011] OJ L304/64. See also Art. 2(c) of Directive 93/13/EEC on unfair terms.

agreement, if renting out to others is allowed to tenants in the first place.[24] Some uncertainty will remain until these points get settled in case law or perhaps by new legislation.

Presumably, many cases will be considered peer-to-peer contracts if the rentals are short-term and only take place during the normal occupant's holidays. These types of rentals will be governed by rules of general contract law of the country in which the property is located. The terms of the contract are primarily determined by the host and the guest, who decide amongst themselves for how many days the rental will be, for what price, and whether other conditions apply (e.g. whether guests are allowed to bring pets). An aspect for which the parties' contractual freedom is limited concerns the terms of cancellation. Airbnb gives hosts the possibility to choose among three standardised cancellation policies. The 'Flexible' policy allows for a full price refund in cases where a cancellation is made at least 24 hours before the listing's local check-in time, with the deduction only of the Airbnb service fee. The 'Moderate' policy gives a refund minus service fees only if the cancellation is made five full days prior to the check-in time. The 'Strict' policy, finally, only gives a 50 per cent refund and requires the cancellation to be made seven full days prior to the check-in time, again with the deduction of service fees. Besides the gradations of cancellation options, the policies also put restrictions on the possibilities for refunds at early check-out.[25]

The main source of concern in the relationship host–guest, however, is not related to the terms of the contract but rather to the potential lack of financial recourse for a guest who suffers damage in the host's rental space. If liability can be established, for example, for a death by CO poisoning caused by a lack of maintenance on the host's property,[26] the host might not be in a financial position to compensate the guest for his loss. Nor may the host's insurance cover such damages. As said above, in section 3.4, the safety standards that Airbnb imposes on hosts to prevent such tragic situations from arising are rules of conduct that are not legally enforceable.

To conclude this section, I mention one final problem that might arise between host and guest: discrimination on the basis of race, or other characteristics. Without having made a full investigation into this problem, I note that cases have started to emerge. An example is an – unsuccessful – complaint by a guest who rented an apartment in Vancouver, Canada for himself and his family, only to be turned away by the host upon arrival.[27] More generally,

---

24 See District Court Amsterdam, 26 May 2015, ECLI:NL:RBAMS:2015:3903, paras. 12–15. See also section 6 below.

25 For details, see https://www.airbnb.com/home/cancellation_policies#flexible.

26 A real-life example described in Zak Stone's blog post: 'Living and Dying on Airbnb', https://medium.com/matter/living-and-dying-on-airbnb-6bff8d600c04#.lcj7jb9yw.

27 British Columbia Human Rights Tribunal, *Rai v. Airbnb and another*, 2015 BCHRT 167.

it has emerged that it is often harder for African-American users of Airbnb in the United States to rent rooms through the site. In response to this finding, Airbnb introduced a non-discrimination policy in 2016.[28]

5. DISPUTE RESOLUTION

Airbnb engages actively with dispute resolution between its users, which is somewhat unusual for a platform service. Others, such as Uber or Amazon do not provide for 'in-house' dispute resolution. The procedure is as follows. If a problem arises, host and guest should first try to work it out between themselves. They may do so through Airbnb's Resolution Center, which enables either party to submit a request for payment to the other party, e.g. for a refund or in relation to other compensation, for example for damage to the apartment. If parties are unable to reach an agreement after 72 hours from when the request was made, they may involve Airbnb. If they do so, the parties agree to hand over the dispute to a team from Airbnb who will make a final decision in the dispute based on Airbnb's policies and the documentation provided by the host and guest.[29]

Although this process seems straightforward, some critical comments may be made in relation to Airbnb's dispute resolution service. First, it should be noted that the 'policies' referred to by Airbnb are not immediately transparent from the website. Of course the terms and conditions and other policies, e.g. concerning privacy, cancellations or refunds, can be found online, yet they are not sufficiently detailed or comprehensive to cover specific disputes. It remains a bit of a gamble, therefore, to submit a dispute to Airbnb's team. Since parties' agree that the decision is final, it will be very hard to contest it in court if one disagrees with the outcome.

Furthermore, if Airbnb infringes consumer rights – e.g. a right to information or to withdrawal that a European consumer may enjoy under current regulation – the consumer is in a weak position to enforce his rights. The only possibility, if Airbnb is unwilling to amend its position, is to litigate. That is of course a cumbersome and often expensive road that not many consumers will be willing to take, in particular if the costs of the procedure outweigh the loss suffered (e.g. payment of the price for one night under a 'Flexible' cancellation policy).

A related problem is that Airbnb in its general terms and conditions includes a choice of law clause that designates the laws of California and the

---

28 *New York Times*, 8 September 2016, 'Airbnb adopts rules to fight discrimination by its hosts'. See also https://www.airbnb.com/help/article/1405/airbnb-s-nondiscrimination-policy--our-commitment-to-inclusion-and-respect?topic=533.

29 https://www.airbnb.com/help/article/435/what-happens-when-i-involve-airbnb-in-my-resolution-center-request.

US as the applicable law to the contract. In addition, Airbnb's general terms and conditions contain an arbitration clause that prescribes that almost all disputes between Airbnb and its users are referred to arbitration. This type of 'forced arbitration' clause is valid under US law.[30] Both clauses would be unfair under EU law,[31] and Airbnb has therefore adopted a different rule for users outside the United States. Users in that case contract with Airbnb's subsidiary in Ireland, and submit to the jurisdiction of the Irish courts. Although the terms indicate that the Irish courts do not have exclusive jurisdiction, and that therefore a dispute may also be litigated before a court in the user's jurisdiction,[32] one may wonder how much this helps users. Many consumers will not be aware of their rights and even if they are, they may spend precious time and money in satellite litigation concerning jurisdiction, rather than dealing with the material dispute. Furthermore, the costs of the dispute might well be too low to warrant litigation in the first place.

6. 'NIMBY' – DISGRUNTLED HOTEL OWNERS, NEIGHBOURS AND LANDLORDS

Besides the private law problems that can arise in relation to Airbnb rentals, the platform has provoked much broader discussions amongst lawyers as well as other members of the public. Like Uber, and perhaps also other innovative platforms that break into traditional markets, Airbnb has encountered resistance from established businesses. In particular hotel owners and those offering similar services (e.g. bed and breakfasts) regard Airbnb as an unfair competitor. Their main objection to the platform is that it enables private parties to offer accommodation services to (primarily) tourists at a cheaper rate than hotels can because these parties, unlike hotels, do not comply with tax regulations – e.g. tourism taxes levied by most cities – and other regulations.[33]

Hotel owners are not the only ones who say 'not in my backyard' (NIMBY) to Airbnb. Residents of various cities have taken to the streets to demonstrate

30 cf *American Express Co. v. Italian Colors Restaurant* 570 US_(2013).

31 Directive 93/13/EEC, Annex sub q.

32 There could be an opening for consumers under Art. 17(1)(c) of Regulation (EU) 1215/2012 on jurisdiction and the recognition and enforcement of judgments in civil and commercial matters (Brussels Ia); formerly Art. 15(1)(c) of Council Regulation (EC) 44/2001 (Brussels I). For that rule to apply, it should be established that Airbnb directs its activities to the user's Member State or to several states including that Member State. The Court of Justice has set out which factors can be taken into account in making that assessment in CJEU 7 December 2010, Joined Cases C-585/08 *Pammer v. Reederei Karl Schlüter GmbH & KG* and C-144/09 *Hotel Alpenhof GmbH v. Oliver Heller* [2010] ECR I-12527.

33 Interestingly, Amsterdam signed an agreement with Airbnb under which 5% tax is charged on every Airbnb rental in the city. Amsterdam is, so far, the only city in the Netherlands to have done so. Some cities in the US have entered into similar agreements with Airbnb.

against the platform, in particular in places where rental practices have become so common that many hosts are continuously renting out their places to tourists. Neighbours suffer from noise – such as the wheels of suitcases on the cobble stones of Amsterdam, but also late-night parties – and are in general unhappy to see a constant stream of tourists in their buildings or in their streets since it takes away the residential nature of their neighbourhood.[34]

Legal action in private law has been taken by another group of affected parties: landlords whose tenants sublet rooms or apartments through Airbnb.[35] For this short chapter I have only made a quick scan of the Netherlands and Germany, in which some cases have reached the courts. In Germany, the Bundesgerichtshof (BGH) ruled that a tenant who had rented out his apartment on a continuous basis for a number of years had been acting in breach of his tenancy contract.[36] Although the tenant had been granted approval from the landlord for renting out the apartment for short periods without pre-approval, the continuous rental to tourists through Airbnb was deemed to go beyond the parties' agreement. This is in line with the subletting policies in many places – renting out is often not allowed to tenants unless they have obtained the approval from their landlords. As Airbnb stated in a response to the BGH decision, the platform already asks hosts to seek permission from their landlord and includes that point on its 'hosting responsibilities' page.[37]

In the Netherlands, lower courts have started to deal with litigation concerning Airbnb use by tenants. It is common for tenancy agreements to include a provision that prohibits subletting without the permission of the landlord. Three cases have come from the Amsterdam District Court in which breach of such provisions could lead to termination of the tenancy agreement and eviction. In two of the three cases, the court held that tenants who had acted in breach of such a provision by renting out their apartments on a continuous basis through Airbnb could be evicted.[38] In the third case, the same outcome could have followed, but the court made an exception based on the specific circumstances of the case.[39] A single mother with two small children had rented out one room in her apartment to tourists through Airbnb, and on one occasion the entire apartment for one weekend. Considering the circumstances of the

---

34 *NRC*, 6 November 2015, W van Noort, 'Hoe Airbnb voor problemen zorgt'. https://www.nrc.nl/nieuws/2015/11/06/hoe-airbnb-voor-problemen-zorgt-1554218-a1233970.

35 In some cases, tenants renting out their spaces through Airbnb have had fines imposed on them under administrative law: see e.g. ECLI:NL:RVS:2015:3086 and for a brief discussion Shanna Derksen and Nathalie Amiel, 'Streng toezicht op hotelmatige verhuur' [2015] *Tijdschrift voor Bouwrecht* 1140.

36 BGH, 8 January 2014, VIII ZR 210/13.

37 http://publicpolicy.airbnb.com/court-decision-germany/.

38 District Court Amsterdam, 7 July 2015, ECLI:NL:RBAMS:2015:4335; District Court Amsterdam, 22 October 2014, ECLI:NL:RBAMS:2014:7231.

39 District Court Amsterdam 26 May 2015, ECLI:NL:RBAMS:2015:3903.

case – the rentals mainly concerned one room and did not seem to take place on a continuous basis; the tenant could use the money to pay part of the rent; and eviction would mean that the woman and her two children were left homeless – the court held the eviction notice unenforceable. Since this was an interim judgment only, it remains to be seen how the case will be judged in substance. Yet, the judgment could be seen as a signal that some judges are willing to weigh broader considerations in their judgment and to acknowledge that (room) rentals for a limited time each year could perhaps be allowed, even within the scope of existing regulations.

An interesting judgment came from the Rotterdam District Court in 2015.[40] The case concerned unapproved subletting by a tenant through Airbnb of one room in her apartment, with the special circumstances that the apartment was situated within a social housing estate, i.e. where tenants paid below-market rental rates. The court held that whilst the tenancy agreement contained a strict prohibition on subletting, breach of which entitled the landlord to terminate the contract, leniency would be granted to the tenant on the basis of the circumstances of the case. First, as the tenant had correctly stated, the practice of subletting through Airbnb was non-existent at the time that the tenancy agreement was drafted and could therefore not have been taken into account by the drafter. Second, the existing case law – i.e. the three cases from Amsterdam – does not yet provide a clear line on how these types of cases should be dealt with, albeit that it indicates that the degree of subletting may be a relevant factor. If a tenant rents out only one room and continues to live in the apartment, they are more likely to be 'forgiven' for breaching the terms of the tenancy agreement than if they rent out their entire apartment and stay elsewhere themselves. Third, the tenant did not seem to be abusing her position as someone enjoying social (and hence cheaper) housing, since she did not rent out the entire apartment and did not intend to make a profit. In these circumstances, the court did not find the breach sufficiently serious to warrant termination of the contract – although the court did indicate that the progression of societal debate might lead to a different conclusion in future cases.

7. CONCLUDING REMARKS

In conclusion, it seems that Airbnb poses a number of challenges for European consumer and market law. Its terms and conditions are in some respects directly at odds with EU regulation and should be brought up-to-date to reflect the (stronger) protection that consumers enjoy under EU law. One of the first terms to be scrapped is the 'forced arbitration' clause that

---

40 District Court Rotterdam, 6 November 2015, ECLI:NL:RBROT:2015:7899.

directs almost all disputes between the platform and its users to arbitration in the United States, and that can be regarded as an unfair term in Europe.

Further, the concept of 'platform services' deserves further consideration in order to determine whether current law adequately responds to the expectations of users. Whilst Airbnb presents itself as a 'facilitator', it is not unimaginable that some responsibility should be directed towards the platform, in particular where it directly involves itself in the rental agreement between host and guest. That is to some extent the case in the standardisation of cancellation policies; in the assistance offered by Airbnb in cases where a guest loses his or her booking due to a 'travel issue'; and in the involvement of Airbnb in dispute resolution. Although private law does not seem to place binding obligations on Airbnb in these cases, one wonders whether regulation should not be introduced that caters specifically to these types of platform services, in which consumers might expect to have a claim not just against the other party – here, their host or their guest – but also against the platform. The possibilities for devising rules of this kind are currently being explored by the Research Group on the Law of Digital Services, which was founded in 2015 in Osnabrück, and is now drafting model rules under the aegis of the European Law Institute (ELI).[41]

Despite the critical comments put forward in this chapter, one thing should not be forgotten. Even if platform services like Airbnb create new challenges and sometimes seem to diminish the rights or safety of consumers, they can also have great benefits to society. Through innovative business models, a boost is given to society to consider ways of cooperation that stimulate sharing – the famous 'sharing economy' – and that create new connections between people from many different corners of the world. The law should perhaps not be a barrier to such developments, but should rather seek to support them.[42]

---

41 The first draft was published in 2016; see Research Group on the Law of Digital Services, 'Discussion Draft of a Directive on Online Intermediary Platforms' (2016) 5 *Journal of European Consumer and Market Law* 164.

42 That view is also held by the European Commission; see Communication from the Commission to the European Parliament, the Council, the European Economic and Social Committee and the Committee of the Regions, 'A European Agenda for the Collaborative Economy' COM(2016) 356 final.

CROWDFUNDING IN EUROPE

Carmen Estevan de Quesada

ABSTRACT

This chapter studies the multifaceted nature of crowdfunding and focuses especially on the investment-based model, particularly the area of so-called 'securities crowdfunding' and its regulation in Europe. It starts by enunciating a general concept of crowdfunding and identifying its defining characteristics. The different business models falling under the general concept are then examined, in order to determine the different legal natures of the key underlying transactions in each of the models. The chapter then focuses on investment-based crowdfunding, describing the different structural options used in the practice to implement these transactions, and directs its attention to securities crowdfunding, the most relevant type in this category. After analysing the complex realms of regulations, both at EU and a national level, that could potentially affect this specific type of crowdfunding, the chapter finally concludes by advocating regulatory intervention by the European Union in this field in order to simplify the current complex situation.

1. INTRODUCTION

Crowdfunding has become a very popular alternative source of funding in the last few years. Its success is partly due to the difficulties faced by small and medium-sized enterprises, start-ups and cultural projects to get finance in the context of the recent global economic crisis. The most common sources of finance such as bank loans, retained earnings, equity or venture capital, are often difficult to obtain for these types of initiatives,[1] and other sources more frequently associated with small and innovative businesses, like 'business angels', money from family, friends and acquaintances, or public subsidies in the case of cultural projects, are often insufficient. This traditional financing problem has been exacerbated at the beginning of the twenty-first century by the global crisis, as a consequence of which all financing channels have been strongly restricted. Banking finance has diminished dramatically and has concentrated on well-established, low-risk firms, while venture capital and business angels have also reduced their activity in this context. Family, friends and acquaintances have been less able to help, since the crisis has impacted on their own budgets, and public subsidies have been sharply reduced.

In this tough economic environment, small businesses have started to use a new way of getting finance that had been developed previously in the charitable and cultural sectors, where financing difficulties have always been an issue. By the mid-1990s some creative minds from the musical world came up with a

1 P. Belleflamme, T. Lambert, A. Schwienbacher: 'Crowdfunding: Tapping the right crowd' (2014) 29 *Journal of Business Venturing* 585, 586.

new way of raising finance, by asking their fans for funds through the Internet.[2] At the start of the twenty-first century, the first contract platforms were founded, initially to help with charity fundraising[3] and then to fund musical projects.[4] In fact, pure charity crowdfunding, as a type distinct from that directed to small business, is still rather substantial according to recent figures,[5] and it is also still one of the most popular crowdfunding types for the general public.

With its proven success in these fields – charity and cultural projects – and progressively as a response to the increasing difficulties of obtaining finance in the context of the global crisis, crowdfunding developed very quickly in the first decade of the twenty-first century, when some of the now most renowned crowdfunding platforms were launched, like Kiva in 2005, Lending Club in 2006, IndieGoGo in 2008 and Kickstarter in 2009. By the beginning of the second decade of this century the idea had extended to other business models and the first investment-based contract platforms were created, such as GrowVC in 2010 and Crowdcube in 2011 among others. They enable the general public to invest in different types of businesses, mostly but not only in start-ups and innovative small businesses, which has led to prestigious economists describing crowdfunding as a financial innovation that democratises finance.[6]

In the European Union, recent data[7] has shown that while this fund-raising mechanism is still relatively small in economic terms when compared

---

2 E. Burkett: 'A crowdfunding exemption? Online investment crowdfunding and U.S. Securities regulation' (2011–2012) 13 *Transactions: The Tennessee Journal of Business Law* 63. The author gives as a first example the case of the rock band Marillion that financed their 1997 US tour and several subsequent albums through online fundraising by their fans (p. 71). This case did not involve any contract platform though, but was instead conducted through the rock band's own website.

3 In 2000 Zarine Kharas and Anne-Marie Huby funded the donations contract platform JustGiving.

4 ArtistShare was launched in 2003 by Brian Camelio, a Boston musician and computer programmer. Its first crowdfunding project was Maria Schneider's jazz album 'Concert in a Garden' the campaign for which raised about $130,000, enabling her to compose the music, pay her musicians, rent a large recording studio, and produce and market the album, which won a 2005 Grammy Award (see D.M. Freedman, M.R. Nutting: 'A Brief History of Crowdfunding. Including Rewards, Donation, Debt, and Equity Platforms in the USA' <http://www.freedman-chicago.com/ec4i/History-of-Crowdfunding.pdf> accessed 11.08.2016, p. 2).

5 In the European Union, donation-based crowdfunding amounted to €25,264,527 in 2015 (*European Commission Staff Working Document: Crowdfunding in the EU Capital Markets Union* (SWD(2016) 154 final), p. 10, citing data from Crowdsurfer Dashboard (www.crowdsurfer.com)).

6 R.J. Shiller: 'Capitalism and Financial Innovation' (2013) 69 *Financial Analysts Journal* 21, 22.

7 *Crowdfunding: Mapping EU markets and events study*, EU 2015. Other studies, like *Moving Mainstream. The European Alternative Finance Benchmarking Report*, University of Cambridge, 2015, refer to and include other types of alternative finance (e.g. p. 10: 'Examples of alternative finance are crowdfunding, peer-to-peer lending, third-party payment systems, SME mini-bonds, private placements and other 'shadow banking' mechanisms, social impact bonds, community shares and alternative (virtual) currencies such as Bitcoin') and therefore the percentages may vary.

to traditional financing, it is already significant. During 2013 and 2014, €2.3 billion was raised for 206,908 successful projects, and by the end of 2014 there were 510 contract platforms operating in the EU.[8] The figures kept on growing the following year, €4.2 billion being successfully raised through crowdfunding platforms across the EU in 2015.[9] Even if the amount is relatively modest in absolute terms, an important aspect shown by the data is the upward trend in the figures. From 2013 to 2014 the data reflect an increase of 119 per cent in the total amount raised, of 112 per cent in the number of projects successfully financed, and of 23 per cent in the number of platforms operating in the EU. And this is a global tendency: in 2014 the crowdfunding volume increased by an average of 167 per cent worldwide, 145 per cent in North America and 320 per cent in Asia where the crowdfunding market is now ahead of Europe.[10] Crowdfunding is not only already significant in economic terms but also, and more important perhaps, it is growing exponentially.[11]

This chapter studies the multifaceted nature of crowdfunding and focuses especially on investment models, particularly the area of so-called 'securities crowdfunding'. To this end the chapter is structured as follows. After this short introduction, section 2 enunciates a concept of crowdfunding and its defining characteristics. Section 3 analyses the different business models falling under the general concept and shows the different legal natures of the key underlying transactions in each of these models. Section 4, in turn, focuses more specifically on the investment-based model of crowdfunding. This section describes first the different structural options used in practice, and then directs its attention to securities crowdfunding – the type of investment crowdfunding that raises the most significant issues from both an economic and legal point of view – analysing the complex realms of regulations that could potentially affect it. Section 5 concludes by advocating regulatory intervention by the European Union in this field in order to simplify the current complex situation.

---

8 *Crowdfunding: Mapping EU markets and events study*, above n. 7, p. 26 (Figure 12).

9 *European Commission Staff Working Document*, above n. 5, p. 9.

10 *European Commission Staff Working Document*, above n. 5, p. 12: Data from 2014 shows that North America is still the first region in terms of crowdfunding volumes (with a total of US$9.46 billion), followed by Asia (US$3.4 billion) and Europe (US$3.26 billion).

11 *European Commission Staff Working Document*, above n. 5, p.12: crowdfunding worldwide volume reached US$16.2 billion in 2014, from US$6.1 billion in 2013. According to a study commissioned by the World Bank, the total market potential of crowdfunding by 2025 is estimated to be up to US$90–96 billion per year, the greatest potential lying in China, followed by the rest of East Asia, Central Europe and Latin America/the Caribbean (see Crowdfunding's Potential for the Developing World. 2013. infoDev, Finance and Private Sector Development Department. Washington, DC: World Bank, p. 43).

2. CONCEPT AND MAIN CHARACTERISTICS OF CROWDFUNDING

2.1. CONCEPT

It is difficult to give an exact definition of the term crowdfunding[12] given that it is an evolving phenomenon. However, in general terms it can be described as a way, tool or channel of raising finance for a specific project or business, typically through contract platforms on the Internet, from a mass of small investors or funders – therefore the use of the term 'crowd' – who usually contribute with small amounts of money.[13] The contract platform puts the calls on its website, where it remains open for a certain period of time and, in most cases, contributions are only formally vested if the project reaches an amount previously stated by the promoter.

---

12 There are some legal definitions of crowdfunding but they usually relate to the business models regulated by the rules in question, typically limited to investment-based crowdfunding and/or loan-based crowdfunding. See for instance: s. 302 of the Jobs Act, referring to 'transactions involving the offer or sale of securities by an issuer ... conducted through a broker or funding portal'; art. L547-1 of the French Code monétaire et financier (created by Ordonnance n° 2014-559 du 30 mai 2014 and modified by the Ordonnance n° 2016-520 of 28 April 2016) defining investment-based crowdfunding as 'activité de conseil en investissement mentionnée au 5 de l'article L. 321-1 portant sur des offres de titres de capital et de titres de créance définis par décret ... menées au moyen d'un site internet remplissant les caractéristiques fixées par le règlement général de l'Autorité des marchés financiers', and L548-1 of the French Code monétaire et financier (created by Ordonnance n° 2014-559 du 30 mai 2014) referring to loan-based crowdfunding as 'mettre en relation, au moyen d'un site internet, les porteurs d'un projet déterminé et les personnes finançant ce projet dans les conditions suivantes'; art. 46 of Spanish Ley 5/2015 describing the crowdfunding activity as 'poner en contacto, de manera profesional y a través de páginas web u otros medios electrónicos, a una pluralidad de personas físicas o jurídicas que ofrecen financiación a cambio de un rendimiento dinerario, denominados inversores, con personas físicas o jurídicas que solicitan financiación en nombre propio para destinarlo a un proyecto de financiación participativa, denominados promotores'.

A more general legal definition can be seen in art. 2 of the Portuguese Lei 102/2015 of 24 August 2015 stating 'O financiamento colaborativo é o tipo de financiamento de entidades, ou das suas atividades e projetos, através do seu registo em plataformas eletrónicas acessíveis através da *Internet*, a partir das quais procedem à angariação de parcelas de investimento provenientes de um ou vários investidores individuais'.

In the UK, the most important crowdfunding market in Europe, the FCA's definition of crowdfunding stated in the FCA's Policy Statement PS14/4 (published together with the *Crowdfunding and the Promotion of Non-Readily Realisable Securities Instrument 2014*) is also relevant: 'Crowdfunding is a way in which people, organisations and businesses, including business start-ups, can raise money through online portals (crowdfunding platforms) to finance or re-finance their activities' (FCA's Policy Statement PS14/4, §1.4 <http://www.fca.org.uk/static/documents/policy-statements/ps14-04.pdf> accessed 11.08.2016).

13 There are many doctrinal definitions of the term crowdfunding. One of the firsts can be found in J.M. Heminway and S.R. Hoffman: 'Proceed at Your Peril: Crowdfunding and the Securities Act of 1933' (2010–2011) 78 *Tennessee Law Review* 879, 881.

2.2. CHARACTERISTICS

From this general concept we can extract the main characteristics of crowdfunding.

2.2.1. The Use of Internet and Social Media

This is the first and probably the most defining characteristic of crowdfunding. As the legal and economic literature frequently point out, the basic idea behind this alternative financing channel is not new. Crowdfunding is rooted in the broader and older concepts of crowdsourcing – getting small contributions from a large number of people in order to achieve a common goal – and microfinance or micro-lending – lending very small amounts of money, typically to poorer borrowers.[14] But its specificity, and what makes it new, comes from the use of the technology related with the social media and the Internet.[15] The Internet makes it possible for the promoters of a project or business to contact a mass of potential funders at little cost – namely just the fees paid to the contract platform, which are usually a small percentage of the total amount obtained, and those charged by payment systems.

In this sense, crowdfunding can be seen as one of the many technological innovations that have had an impact on the financial system and that raise a number of different legal questions.[16] Some of the issues and concerns it raises are not specifically related to crowdfunding itself but are present in all types of products or funding channels,[17] like the problems that may derive from the use of electronic contracts, concerns regarding data protection, or the risk of money laundering, for example. Other concerns – like the different risks for the participants depending on the legal nature of the transaction or, in some cases, the risks for financial stability – are more specific to the chosen business model. In the case of crowdfunding the main area of concern for regulators is investor protection and not so much financial stability, given the relatively modest size of the crowdfunding market when compared to traditional financial services.[18]

---

14 C.S. Bradford: 'Crowdfunding and the federal securities law' (2012) *Columbia Business Law Review* 1, 27.

15 J.M. Heminway: 'Business Lawyering in the Crowdfunding Era' (2014) 3 *American University Business Law Review* 149, 155.

16 J.M. Heminway: 'What is a Security in the Crowdfunding Era?' (2012) 7 *Ohio State Entrepreneurial Business Law Journal* 335, 336.

17 *European Commission Staff Working Document*, above n. 5, p. 12.

18 European Securities and Markets Authority (ESMA): *Opinion: Investment-based crowdfunding*, 18 December 2014, ESMA/2014/1378, p. 11 (in relation to investment-based crowdfunding). Similarly, the *Opinion of the European Banking Authority on lending-based crowdfunding* (EBA/Op/2015/03, 26 February 2015) identifies the potential risks to participants in the market for lending-based crowdfunding (i.e. lenders, borrowers and platform providers) but does not mention any risks for financial stability.

2.2.2. Multifaceted Business Model

A second important characteristic of crowdfunding is the many different forms it can take.[19] The fact that crowdfunding is not regulated from a contractual perspective in any jurisdiction has enabled the economic agents involved to design it in the way that best suits their needs and this has given birth to different forms, types or models of crowdfunding. All of them match the general concept described above but they have specific and very different features, and this has strong legal implications, related basically to the different legal nature of the main transaction (i.e. the one between the funders and the promoters) in each business model.

As further developed below,[20] there are four main crowdfunding business models: the donation-based, the rewards or pre-purchase, the investment-based, and the loan-based model. Each one of them in turn, especially the last two, may present sub-categories or different scenarios according to which the operation is structured.

2.2.3. Tripartite Business

Another characteristic of crowdfunding is that it is a tripartite business involving the promoters of the call, the funders and the contract platform. The promoters, who can be entrepreneurs, artists or non-profit organisations, come up with a project or business for whose development they need funds which they usually cannot get from traditional financing sources and therefore ask for via crowdfunding. The funders are usually individuals who contribute to that project or business with a certain amount of capital, but they can also be legal persons – a trend that is increasing quickly in certain models of crowdfunding like the loan-based one. Finally, the contract platform is a legal entity that operates though a website on which the promoters' calls are published so that the potential funders can see and evaluate them, and which coordinates the whole operation in exchange for a fee.

It could be argued that the tripartite nature of the operation is not a defining characteristic, since the promoters could put this mechanism in place though

---

19 This characteristic was already pointed out in the first studies on crowdfunding (see for instance J.M. Heminway and S.R. Hoffman, above n.13, p. 881) and highlighted also by authorities and regulators (e.g. *Communication from the Commission to the European Parliament, the Council, the European Economic and Social Committee and the Committee of the Regions 'Unleashing the potential of Crowdfunding in the European Union'*, Brussels, 27.03.2014 COM(2014) 172 final, p. 3).

20 See section 3 of this chapter, analysing the main different business models of crowdfunding that can be seen in practice.

their own websites, i.e. without the help of an external contract platform. In fact, the origins of crowdfunding are to be found in this type of call, especially those made by some musical groups that have used their own websites in order to raise money from their fans to finance various types of activities, such as the organisation of a tour or the recording and releasing of a CD. But these cases are less common nowadays due to the birth and growth of specialised contract platforms whose professional activity is the intermediation between the promoters and the funders, together with a whole range of additional services, both for the promoters – like helping them to plan the campaign, to build a community to support it, to launch and manage the campaign, or to use social media to help it succeed – and for the funders – like providing them with information on how to evaluate a campaign, or on acceptable means of payment and its use, the running of algorithms to detect fraud, etc.

Therefore, the currently accepted concept of crowdfunding includes the activity of contract platforms, as a third-party between the promoters and the funders. As a consequence of this tripartite nature, there are two sets of legal relationships in which conflicts can arise: on the one hand, the relationship between the funders and the promoter, which could be termed the 'principal or main transaction'; and on the other, the relationship between the contract platform and its users, be they funders or promoters.

The presence and intervention of the contract platform raises other relevant legal issues from the viewpoint of contract law, especially those connected with contracts through intermediaries, but also those related to standard form contracts, since the contract platform usually designs not only its legal relationship with the other two parties but also the main transaction between them.[21]

2.2.4. Some Relevant Contractual Features

A final characteristic of crowdfunding is the fact that the main transaction is usually affected by some typical features whose presence is relevant because they affect and nuance the legal nature of the underlying contract and the corresponding rights and duties of the parties. Some of these features may even make it slightly more difficult to include or assimilate the specific crowdfunding model to already existing contractual categories.

The first relevant feature is the fact that the main transaction is very often subject to the condition that the fund-raising project has to reach a certain

---

21 See for example Kickstarter Terms of Use, point 4: 'Kickstarter is not a part of this contract – the contract is a direct legal agreement between creators and their backers. Here are the terms that govern that agreement: …', <https://www.kickstarter.com/terms-of-use?ref=footer> accessed 11.08.2016.

amount in order for the promoter to receive the funds. This is the so-called 'all or nothing' system. Alternatively, some contract platforms give the option to conduct the calls through the so-called 'keep it all system', according to which the promoters would receive all the funds obtained at the end of the fixed period even if the amount originally requested in the call is not reached. There are also variations on these two main systems, stating for example that the funds will be transferred to the promoters when the contributions reach a certain percentage of the amount demanded initially. The 'all or nothing' clause operates as a condition precedent expressly stated in the contractual terms. If the stated amount is not reached, the contract will not deploy its normal effects: the promoter will not get the funds and the funders will not be charged or will get their contributions back. In this context, the presence of this condition implies some related duties for the contract platforms and related payment systems regarding the way and the time in which funds are transferred or simply temporary authorised via a credit card or a similar method of payment.

A second relevant clause which is usually present in all types of crowdfunding is that the promoters must use the funds for the specific project as described in the call, and therefore cannot dedicate any sums to other uses. Theoretically, this means that the promoters should return the sums received if they do not use the funds in the manner described in the call. In practice however, since most of the contract platforms expressly state in their own terms of use that they do not guarantee that contributions will be used by promoters as promised, the funders will have to exercise their right to recover the funds directly against the promoters and this may make any claim difficult in practice since some promoters may be insolvent or even impossible to find. In addition to this, it is unclear whether, and under what circumstances, the contract platforms could be held liable for false or fraudulent statements made by the promoters.[22]

Finally, in most types of crowdfunding (except the donation-based and the non-interest loan-based crowdfunding) the promoter has to give some compensation, financial or non-financial, to the funders in exchange for their contributions. But, as in the case of the previous obligation, most contract platforms expressly decline any liability for breach of this obligation and state that the promoter is solely responsible for its fulfilment.

22 See for instance C.S. Bradford: 'Shooting the Messenger: The Liability of Crowdfunding Intermediaries for the Fraud of Others' (2014–2015) 83 *University of Cincinnati Law Review* 371, 379–381, who argues that contract platforms involved in securities crowdfunding should only be liable in three cases: (1) if they know the posted material is fraudulent; (2) if they deliberately ignore 'red flags' that should have alerted them to the fraud; and (3) if they recommend a particular security or issuer without an adequate investigation.

3. BUSINESS MODELS OF CROWDFUNDING AND THE LEGAL NATURE OF THE MAIN TRANSACTION

As briefly mentioned above, a pretty standard and accepted classification of the crowdfunding phenomenon distinguishes four (sometimes five) types of business model: the donation-based, the rewards or pre-purchase, the investment-based, and the loan-based.[23]

This classification is relevant because it is directly linked with a significant legal issue, that of the legal nature of the main transaction between the funders and the promoters. Crowdfunding is not currently being regulated from the contractual perspective in any jurisdiction, and both the interpretation of the contract and the finding of solutions in the case of a dispute between the funders and the promoters are governed by the contractual terms as stated by the parties. Since these terms are usually not very detailed (they are stated by the contract platform in a very brief way without legal qualification), the role of supplementary rules is essential, and these have to be found in the legal category that is most similar to the main legal relationship.

3.1. DONATION-BASED CROWDFUNDING

In so-called 'donation-based crowdfunding' the funders contribute to the project without any compensation or return. This model is typically used for non-profit or charitable causes, but this is not a condition *sine qua non*, i.e. the promoter can use these funds for a profit-making enterprise, as long as the contract platform allows it and the promoter discloses that fact in the call.[24]

This was one of the first types of crowdfunding and its success contributed to the visibility and popularity of this new funding mechanism, but in fact it

---

23 See C.S. Bradford, above n. 14, pp. 14–27. There are of course other classifications: some authors identify other types of crowdfunding (e.g. S.M. O'Connor: 'Crowdfunding's Impact on Start-up IP Strategy' (2013–2014) 21 *George Mason Law Review* 895, 897–899, who distinguishes between 'project crowdfunding' and 'enterprise crowdfunding'; T. Kappel: 'Ex Ante Crowdfunding and the Recording Industry: A Model for the U.S.?' (2008–2009) 29 *Loyola of Los Angeles Entertainment Law Review* 375, differentiates *ex ante* and *ex post* crowdfunding); others do not consider the loan-based model as a type crowdfunding at all (e.g. E. Burkett, above n. 2, p. 67); and others consider 'no-interest lending' and 'interest-based debt' as two different types of crowdfunding (e.g. J.W. Parsont: 'Crowdfunding: The Real and the Illusory Exemption' (2014) 4 *Harvard Business Law Review* 281, 288). For a discussion of the different taxonomies used to describe the types of funding site and financial interests, see J.M. Heminway, above n. 16, pp. 358–359.

24 In practice this possibility obviously depends on the contract platform's policy, since those specialised in charitable or non-profit causes may decide not to publish such calls. In any case, this is not the most common scenario and, as mentioned in the text, the most common use of this model is raising funds for charitable causes.

is not the most significant one in economic terms. In the European context, taking data of the activity of EU platforms on EU projects, the total amount raised with this type of crowdfunding was €5,675,000 in 2013 (approximately 0.8 per cent of the total) and €9,295,000 in 2014 (approximately 0.6 per cent of the total).[25] Later studies show a similar situation in 2015, when donation-based crowdfunding amounted to €25,264,527 in the European Union (approximately 0.6 per cent of the total crowdfunding volume of that year).[26]

As for the legal nature of the contract, this model does not present big problems for its characterisation, since it is clearly a donation, even if it is subject to certain conditions, as explained above.

3.2. REWARD AND PRE-PURCHASE MODELS OF CROWDFUNDING

Reward and pre-purchase models of crowdfunding are usually described together since they present important similarities. Their characteristic common feature is that the funders receive a non-financial compensation for their contribution.

In the 'reward model' this compensation varies greatly and can take the form of a small present, like a t-shirt or a CD/DVD, or recognition of the funders' participation in the project (such as having their names on the credits of a movie), or any other task or service performed by the promoters for them, such as a private concert given by the musical group promoting the call.[27] In the 'pre-purchase model' the non-financial compensation consists of the manufactured product for whose production the crowdfunding was put in place, usually at a discount in relation to the expected retail price.

These two types of crowdfunding have become very popular thanks to platforms such as Kickstarter or IndieGoGo – especially the 'reward model' which is widely used by artists who want to raise funds for a project, and in general for cultural activities – but in reality they, too, do not represent a very big part of the total. In the European Union these models raised €64,266,000 in 2013 (representing approximately 9 per cent of the total) and €99,445,000 in 2014 (around 6.4 per cent of the total).[28] Data from 2015 show that the relative economic significance of these crowdfunding models is diminishing, with €96,899,235 raised, representing only about 2.3 per cent of that year's total volume.[29]

---

25 *Crowdfunding: Mapping EU markets and events study*, above n. 7, p. 20 (Figure 5).

26 *European Commission Staff Working Document*, above n. 5, p. 10 (Table 1).

27 For an example of the great variety of rewards that can be offered in practice, see C.S. Bradford, above n. 14, pp. 18–19, explaining those offered by the music band Nine-Inch Nails in the call for funding an album.

28 *Crowdfunding: Mapping EU markets and events study*, above n. 7, p. 20 (Figure 5).

29 *European Commission Staff Working Document*, above n. 5, p. 10 (Table 1).

From the legal point of view these two models raise more delicate issues than the previous one. The main transaction between the promoter and the funders is similar to a sales contract, especially in the pre-purchase model but also in the reward one. However, the lack of correspondence between the contribution and the value of the reward or the pre-purchased item may cause some problems for the characterisation of this contract in certain jurisdictions. Since the funder's contribution is usually (significantly) higher than the value of the reward or item, it may be difficult for the transaction to be considered a sales contract in some civil law systems where, even if the price does not need to be adequate, one of the essential elements of any such contract is its cause.[30] This is so because especially in the reward model (and sometimes also in the pre-purchase one), the cause of the contract does not really fit the onerous nature typical of a sales contract but is closer to an act of generosity on the part of the funder, which makes it more analogous to a gratuitous contract like a donation.

On the other hand, this issue might be simpler to resolve in legal systems where the cause is not an essential element of the contract and where consideration or payment need not be adequate. In these jurisdictions it may be less problematic to consider both the reward and the pre-purchase models of crowdfunding as sales contracts, even if subject to certain conditions. A more delicate issue arises in the reward model when the reward includes both a product and a task or service to be performed by the promoters. In such cases, the underlying transaction has a more intermediate nature, between a sales and a service contract.

3.3. LOAN-BASED CROWDFUNDING

In the loan-based or lending model of crowdfunding, also called peer-to-peer lending, the funders (the lenders) give a certain amount of money to the promoters (the borrowers) expecting repayment at the end of the fixed period. Depending on whether the lenders receive interest or not in addition to the principal, 'interest loan crowdfunding' or 'non-interest loan crowdfunding' can be distinguished. This is a very popular model, whereby sites like Kiva move huge amounts of money, and in fact it is the most relevant one in economic terms. In the European Union it amounted to €531,095,000 in 2013

---

30 Like Spain or Italy, for example: article 1261 of the Spanish Civil Code and article 1325 of the Italian Civil Code. In France the Ordonnance n° 2016-131 du 10 février 2016 portant réforme du droit des contrats, du régime général et de la preuve des obligations (in force from 1 October 2016) eliminates the rule contained in the previous article 1108 of the French Civil Code so the cause is no longer an essential element of the contract according to French Contract Law (nevertheless the new article 1107 of the French Civil Code still distinguishes between onerous and gratuitous contracts so that the characterisation problem might continue to exist).

(74.6 per cent of the total) and to €1,126,994,000 in 2014 (approximately 72 per cent of the total).[31] The 2015 figures show that its economic relevance is growing, with a volume of €3,209,368,439, which represents 76 per cent of that year's total.[32]

A significant point in this type of crowdfunding is the growing intervention of institutional investors. 'Peer-to-peer lending' started as an alternative lending mechanism where individuals would lend small amounts of money to other individuals, but in recent years it has become dominated by institutional investors, including hedge funds, and also by banks. According to some commentators, these lenders currently fund between two-thirds and 80 per cent of these types of loans.[33]

As for the legal nature of the contract, this business model is easy to characterise in general terms since the underlying contract is clearly a loan. A different issue is the different ways in which the loan can be structured, because there are many variations in practice.[34]

3.4. INVESTMENT-BASED CROWDFUNDING

In this model the promoters offer the funders (called in this case 'investors') an interest in the business they finance, in the form of either a right to participate in the profits, or debt, equity or other form of securities. Two distinct sub-types can therefore be included in this model: the one involving the issuance of securities – be that equity or debt – and so-called 'profit sharing crowdfunding'

---

31 *Crowdfunding: Mapping EU markets and events study*, above n. 7, p. 20 (Figure 5).

32 *European Commission Staff Working Document*, above n. 5, p. 10 (Table 1).

33 K. Judge: 'The future of direct finance: The diverging paths of peer-to-peer lending and Kickstarter' (2015) 50 *Wake Forest Law Review* 603, 613; E. Macchiavello: 'Peer-to-peer lending and the "democratization" of credit markets: Another financial innovation puzzling regulators' (2014–2015) 21 *Columbia Journal of European Law* 521, 537.

See also N. Athwal: 'The disappearance of peer-to-peer lending' <http://www.forbes.com/sites/groupthink/2014/10/14/the-disappearance-of-peer-to-peer-lending/#31cf4c150e6d> accessed 11.08.2016, who claims that institutional investors account 'for up to 80–90% of the capital deployed through Prosper and LendingClub' and that 'institutions have managed to infiltrate this once retail industry from every angle. Board members at the largest P2P platforms include executives at some of the largest banks in the world including Morgan Stanley and Citigroup, and WellsFargo, through its venture capital arm, is the largest investor in LendingClub'.

34 See *Staff Working Paper of the IOSCO Research Department* (by E. Kirby and S. Worner): 'Crowd-funding: An infant industry growing fast', OICV-IOSCO [SWP3/2014], <http://www.iosco.org/research/pdf/swp/Crowd-funding-An-Infant-Industry-Growing-Fast.pdf> accessed 11.08.2016, where the authors describe three peer-to-peer lending business models: the Client segregated account model, the Notary model and the 'Guaranteed' return model (pp. 16–19).

that builds a different type of relationship between the investor and the promoter, as explained in more detail in section 4.2 below. In any case, even if the economic significance of this type of crowdfunding in the European Union was relatively modest until a couple of years ago – €39,212,000 (5 per cent of the total) in 2013 and €104,802,000 (6.7 per cent of the total) in 2014[35] – it increased significantly in 2015 when it reached €422,039,462 (10 per cent of the total).[36]

Regarding the legal nature of the main transaction, this crowdfunding model is more complex than the previous ones.[37] Since the compensation for the contribution of the funder takes the form of participation in the venture of the project or business, the transaction between the investor and the promoter is not a single exchange contract, or a loan, but it has instead a more associative nature that approximates it to the field of corporate law. In practice there are quite different models to instrument that participation, and this in turn affects the legal nature of the main transaction and consequently the rules that will apply to the on-going relationship between the investor and the promoter. Because of the variety and complexity of the different possible scenarios these will be analysed in more detail below.[38]

3.5. A RELEVANT DISTINCTION – FINANCIAL-RETURN AND NON-FINANCIAL RETURN CROWDFUNDING

The crowdfunding models described in the previous sub-sections can be grouped into two categories. On the one hand is the so-called 'financial (or financial-return) crowdfunding' that would include the loan and investment models, and on the other hand is the 'non-financial (or non-financial return) crowdfunding' including the donation, reward and pre-purchase models. This is an important distinction because the financial types of crowdfunding raise serious legal issues, in addition to being much more relevant from the economic point of view.

In economic terms, financial-return crowdfunding raised €4.1 billion of the total of €4.2 billion that was successfully raised through contract platforms in 2015 across the EU.[39] This type of crowdfunding has a significant potential for broadening access to finance for innovative projects, start-ups and small and medium enterprises that have been denied bank finance during the economic

---

35 *Crowdfunding: Mapping EU markets and events study*, above n. 7, p. 20 (Figure 5).

36 *European Commission Staff Working Document*, above n. 5, p. 10 (Table 1).

37 It has been called 'the most meaningful crowdfunding type' (D. Groshoff: 'Kickstarter My Heart: Extraordinary Popular Delusions and the Madness of Crowdfunding Constraints and Bitcoin Bubbles' (2014) 5 *William and Mary Business Law Review* 489, 543).

38 See section 4.2 below.

39 *European Commission Staff Working Document*, above n. 5, p. 9.

crisis and still suffer these restrictions. And the expansion of such companies is key for the creation of jobs and for the increase of Europe's competitiveness.

From a legal perspective, financial-return crowdfunding is more challenging than the non-financial type, since it poses a number of significant potential risks that might need to be tackled by regulation. On the one hand, there are relevant risks related to investor protection, both in the pre-investment phase and over the life of the investment – like for example the risk of losing the investment or not getting the expected returns, the inability to exit the investment, conflicts derived from the misalignment of interests between the parties involved, the insolvency of the platform, etc. On the other hand, more general legal issues arise in this context which are common to all activities in the field of financial technologies – such as those related to data protection, the distance marketing of financial services, or the use of platforms for illicit activities.

In this sense, the financial-return models of crowdfunding have been regulated in some jurisdictions, with rules developing quickly in the recent years. By the last quarter of 2016, eight countries in the European Union had already adopted domestic rules for investment crowdfunding – Italy, the United Kingdom, France, Spain, Germany, Austria, Portugal and Finland – and five of them also for loan crowdfunding – the United Kingdom, France, Spain Portugal and Finland.[40] The need for crowdfunding regulations is being discussed in a number of other European countries[41] and, in addition to that, some self-regulation in the form of codes of conduct has been put in place.[42]

On the other hand, there is not an EU general regulatory framework for crowdfunding, either in the form of a European regulation or a Directive

40 In Italy, the Decreto-legge 18 ottobre 2012, n. 179 (converted to Law by Legge 17 dicembre 2012, n. 221), implemented by CONSOB Delibera n. 18592 of 23.06.2013 (later on, the Decreto-legge 24 gennaio 2015, n. 3, converted to Law by Legge 24 marzo 2015, n. 33, introduced some minor modifications in the Italian regime of crowdfunding). In the UK, the *FCA's Crowdfunding and the Promotion of Non-Readily Realisable Securities Instrument 2014* (FCA 2014/13), of 27.02.2014. In France, the Ordonnance n° 2014-559 du 30 mai 2014 relative au financement participatif. In Germany, the Kleinanlegerschutzgesetz, of 23.04.2015. In Spain, the Ley 15/2015, de 27 de abril de 2015, de fomento de la financiación empresarial. In Portugal, the Lei n.º 102/2015, de 24 de agosto de Regime jurídico do financiamento colaborativo (the rules on investment-based and loan-based crowdfunding were subsequently developed by Regulamento da CMVM nº 1/2016 de Financiamento Colaborativo de capital ou por empréstimo). In Austria, the Alternativfinanzierungsgesetz – AltFG, of 19.05.2015. In Finland, the Crowdfunding Act 734/2016, approved by the Parliament on the 21.06.2016 and in force from the 01.09.2016.

41 Like for instance in Belgium, Croatia or the Netherlands (vid. CrowdfundingHub: *Current State of Crowdfunding in Europe* (2016), available at <http://www.crowdfundinghub.eu/the-current-state-of-crowdfunding-in-europe>, accessed 21.11.2016).

42 See for example the Code of Conduct of the European Crowdfunding Network (ECN), the Code of practice of the UK Crowdfunding Association, the Code of Conduct of the French Crowdfunding Association, or the Code of Conduct of the German Crowdfunding Network.

harmonising this field,[43] so at present the applicable rules are only domestic ones. This may represent a problem for the development of cross-border financial crowdfunding activity, that has been relatively modest until now but which has significant growth potential. As stated by the industry, even if only 38 per cent of the European financial-return platforms currently operate cross-border, almost half of them would like to extend their business to other EU Member States in the future.[44]

4. INVESTMENT-BASED CROWDFUNDING

4.1. INTRODUCTION

Investment-based crowdfunding is the last model that appeared in practice. It is a new, alternative, financing mechanism used mainly by small businesses and start-ups that was developed at the beginning of the second decade of the twenty-first century by some contract platforms mimicking the successful 'reward model' used mainly for cultural projects. Instead of receiving tangible, non-financial compensation, investors in this crowdfunding model receive an interest in the business they help to finance. Even if still relatively small in economic terms when compared to the other financial-return model, loan-based crowdfunding, this financing mechanism has been growing exponentially in Europe over the last few years.[45]

As further analysed below, this crowdfunding model can be structured in different ways but in all cases it builds an on-going relationship between the promoter and the investor that raises a number of problematic issues. In addition

---

43 The European Commission does not seem to preoccupied by this lack of harmonisation (see *European Commission Staff Working Document*, above n. 5, p. 31 stating 'there is no strong case for EU level policy intervention at this juncture'), but the European Parliament has already recommended that the Commission should start to work in that direction (see European Parliament: *Amendments adopted by the European Parliament on 15 September 2016 on the proposal for a regulation of the European Parliament and of the Council on the prospectus to be published when securities are offered to the public or admitted to trading* (COM(2015) 0583 – C8-0375/2015 – 2015/0268(COD))1, Recital 12(a) stating 'in the spirit of the Capital Markets Union and in order to unlock investment, the Commission should propose a regulatory initiative to regulate and harmonise crowdfunding practices across the Union').

44 *Communication 'Unleashing the potential of Crowdfunding in the European Union'*, above n. 19, p. 8.

45 A trend that can be seen clearly in the United Kingdom, the most relevant crowdfunding market in Europe: £28 million in 2013, £84 million in 2014 and £332 million in 2015 (Financial Conduct Authority: 'Call for input to the post-implementation review of the FCA's crowdfunding rules', July 2016 <https://www.fca.org.uk/your-fca/documents/call-input-crowdfunding> accessed 11.08.2016, p. 9).

to the above-mentioned risks connected to the use of financial technologies and investor protection in general, investment-based crowdfunding poses other relevant problems, especially when the transaction involves the issuance of securities – like, for instance, the rights of the investor as a partner in the issuer, or the potential dilution of its stake in case of further financing campaigns, etc.

4.2. STRUCTURE OF THE OPERATION AND THE LEGAL NATURE OF THE MAIN TRANSACTION

The specific investment-based crowdfunding models are varied but three main types can be distinguished.

A first and quite common scenario is that the promoter issues securities that are purchased by the investors.[46] In this case, the latter invest directly in the promoter's company, be this by means of equity or debt. The two possibilities present in turn some differences as regards the future on-going relationship between the investor and the company, depending on the type of security issued. If the return takes the form of equity, the investor becomes a partner in the company and will therefore have all the corresponding rights that would in turn depend on the type of company issuing the stock and the type of stock bought – for example, common or preferred shares, non-voting shares, etc. If the promoter issues debt securities the on-going relationship will differ depending of the characteristics of the bonds – fixed or variable-interest bonds, ordinary or convertible bonds, etc.

A second scenario is that the securities are issued by someone different from the promoter, in which case the investors do not invest directly in the promoter's company, but instead in a different entity that in turn holds stock or another interest in the former. The issuer of the securities is usually a Special Purpose Vehicle (SPV) or a Collective Investment Scheme (CIS) that may be established either by the contract platform itself or by another party.[47]

An important point in those two first scenarios is whether the securities received by the investors are transferable or not, since this connects directly

---

46 See for example the case of Crowdcube, one of the most important contract platforms operating in investment-based crowdfunding in Europe. The specific type of securities that can be purchased varies from one country to another due to the national rules on crowdfunding: for example, in the Crowdcube campaigns the UK investors can invest either in equity or bonds (see <https://www.crowdcube.com/investments> accessed 11.08.2016), while in Spain they can only invest in the stock of limited liability companies (see <https://www.crowdcube.es/pg/terminos-inversor-1122> accessed 11.08.2016).

47 *ESMA Opinion*, above n. 18, p. 6, commenting also that other, more complex, models are developing (fn. 3: 'one platform which also enables direct investment in equities/mini-bonds also hosts a venture capital fund managed by a third party which invests in certain projects in which the crowd has committed at least a third of the target amount. Another says that it will, on occasion, offer funds investing in a group of projects').

with one of the main risks of crowdfunding, which is the difficulty of exiting the investment. This is a relevant issue, since even if the securities are transferable it is unlikely that a secondary market for them exists. And even if it does, because the contract platform itself or a connected third-party creates such a market, it might be quite limited.

A last possibility is that the investors do not receive securities in return for their contributions, but only a right to participate in the profits, like the right to receive the payment of a certain percentage of benefits during a certain time, for example. This 'profit-sharing crowdfunding' is more often used when the promoter is not a legal entity and therefore cannot issue equity or bonds, or even if it is, but does not wish to do so. Even though used in the first developments of investment-based crowdfunding, the relevance of this option in practice seems to be diminishing in recent years.[48]

This is a quite different scenario from the two previous ones, since there are no securities involved but another kind of relationship between the investors and the promoters is created. This may explain why this business model is not always included in the category of investment-based crowdfunding.[49] Nevertheless, it does fit into it conceptually, since it is a form of crowdfunding that aims at investing in a project or business in exchange for financial compensation in the form of an interest in the profits obtained. The difference with the two other scenarios is more technical than conceptual: in this case the participation in the profits is articulated in the form of a right instead of through the purchase of securities.

It follows from this that the legal nature of this last business model most resembles a form of participation in someone's business that has a significant legal tradition, especially in civil law jurisdictions, since it comes from the mediaeval institution of the 'commenda': the Spanish contract of 'cuentas en participacion',[50] or the Italian 'associazione in partecipazione'.[51] In other jurisdictions this form of business participation is reflected in legal figures of a more associative nature, like the German 'stille Gesellschaft',[52] or the French 'société en participation'.[53] In any case, in all these legal systems the structure of this contract or partnership is similar to the underlying relationship between the promoter and the funder in this type of investment-based crowdfunding: it is a participation in the promoter's business or project, in the form of capital, in exchange for a share in the benefits derived from the venture, that is characterised

48 See for example in Germany L. Klöhn, L. Hornuf and T. Schilling: 'The Regulation of Crowdfunding in the German Small Investor Protection Act: Content, Consequences, Critique, Suggestions' (2016) 13 *European Company Law* 56, 58.

49 *ESMA Opinion*, above n. 18, p. 6.

50 Regulated in articles 239 to 243 of the Spanish Code of Commerce (*Código de Comercio*).

51 Articles 2549 to 2554 of the Italian Civil Code (*Codice Civile*).

52 Articles 230 to 236 of the German Code of Commerce (*Handelsgesetzbuch*).

53 Articles 1871 to 1873 of the French Civil Code (*Code Civil*).

by the flexibility in the terms of the agreement and the lack of legal personality of this association.

That being said, it must also be noted that investment-based crowdfunding models involving the issuance of securities (the so-called 'securities crowdfunding') are the most common types of investment-based crowdfunding in practice. From a legal perspective, securities crowdfunding is also more complex. In addition to the potential problems derived from the difficulties of determining the legal nature of the main transaction and the corresponding rights and duties of the parties in each case,[54] it also raises investor protection and market transparency issues. Connected to this, the role of contract platforms is also especially relevant in this crowdfunding model.

4.3. CONTRACT PLATFORMS AND SECURITIES CROWDFUNDING IN EUROPE – APPLICABLE RULES

Securities crowdfunding in Europe is affected by a wide range of rules, not only the bespoke national regulations passed recently in some Member States, but also European Union rules (and the national rules implementing them) on various aspects. The latter are especially important in those Member States that have not adopted a specific crowdfunding regime yet.

Most rules affect the contract platform as a professional intermediary operating in the field of financial markets but there are some, also very relevant for securities crowdfunding, that apply instead to the promoter that issues the securities, or alternatively to the third-party doing so. Therefore, this section starts by briefly analysing the latter – i.e. the rules on the Prospectus – and then turns to examine the rest of the rules potentially applicable to the contract platform.

4.3.1. *European Union Rules Potentially Applicable*

4.3.1.1. The Rules on the Prospectus

The first rules potentially applicable to securities crowdfunding are those related to the obligation to issue a Prospectus, i.e. the Prospectus Directive and the new Prospectus Regulation from the date of its application.[55] These rules require the

---

54 For an interesting and comprehensive study of the different contracts used in this type of crowdfunding, see L. Klöhn, L. Hornuf and T. Schilling: 'Crowdinvesting-Verträge. Inhalt, Entwicklung und praktische Bedeutung' 3/2016 *Zeitschrift für Bankrecht und Bankwirtschaft* 142 (this study focuses on the German experience but some of the identified trends can also be seen in other countries).

55 Directive 2003/71/EC of the European Parliament and of the Council of 4 November 2003 on the prospectus to be published when securities are offered to the public or admitted to

publication of a prospectus before the offer of securities to the public or the admission to trading of such securities on a regulated market, unless certain exclusions or exemptions apply. As mentioned above, these rules would affect the issuer, be that the promoter itself or another party issuing the securities once the crowdfunding campaign has ended successfully. It is unlikely that they would affect the contract platforms, since these usually do not directly issue the shares through which the crowdfunding is subsequently implemented. Nevertheless, since the business models are varied and still evolving this scenario cannot be completely excluded either.[56]

In any case, it must be remembered that these rules would only apply when this model of crowdfunding operates through the issuance of transferable securities and when the size of the offer is above the annual consideration fixed in the Directive or the Regulation.

According to the Directive offers with a total annual consideration below €5,000,000 fall outside its scope and those of less than €100,000 are exempted from the prospectus requirement.[57] These thresholds are relevant for securities crowdfunding since, even if these campaigns are usually below €5,000,000, offers between €100,000 and €5,000,00 can still be subject to national prospectus requirements.[58] And the drafting of a prospectus is a burdensome and costly task for the issuers, especially in the cases in which the securities are issued directly by the promoters, whose professional activity is most likely not connected with the financial markets. In this sense, the new Regulation sets a more positive framework for crowdfunding campaigns since it establishes that it shall not apply to offers of with a total consideration in the EU less than €1,000,000, and that Member States shall not extend the obligation to draw up a prospectus in accordance with the Regulation to these offers.[59]

The other exemptions stated in article 3 of the Directive or article 1.4 of the Regulation, namely those applying to offers addressed solely to 'qualified investors' or to offers addressed to a small amount of natural or legal persons per

---

trading and amending Directive 2001/34/EC (OJ L 345, 31.12.2003, p. 64). This Directive has been repealed by the Regulation (EU) 2017/1129 of the European Parliament and of the Council of 14 June 2017 on the prospectus to be published when securities are offered to the public or admitted to trading on a regulated market, and repealing Directive 2003/71/EC (OJ L 168/12, 30.06.2017). The Regulation shall apply from 21 July 2019, except for Article 1(3) and Article 3(2) which shall apply from 21 July 2018 and points (a), (b) and (c) of the first subparagraph of Article 1(5) and the second subparagraph of Article 1(5) which shall apply from 20 July 2017.

56 See for example business models described in *ESMA Opinion*, above n. 17, p. 3 (footnote 3).

57 Articles 1.2(h) and 3.2(e) of the Prospectus Directive (as modified by Directive 2010/73/EU). For offers between €100,000 and €5,000,00 Member States could apply their own national requirements, something that seventeen Member States have done with different results.

58 See sub-section 4.3.2.1 below.

59 Article 1(3) of the Prospectus Regulation.

Member State, may be relevant also, especially for small amount campaigns that can be covered with a relatively low number of investors.

4.3.1.2. The Markets in Financial Instruments Directive

A second piece of legislation potentially applicable is the Directive 2004/39/EC on markets in financial instruments (MiFID I),[60] and the MiFID II package in the future.[61] Unlike the rules about the Prospectus analysed above, these rules would affect the contract platform and not the issuer, if the former carries on MiFID services or activities in relation to MiFID financial instruments and it does not qualify for an exemption.[62] In this case, the platform will be subject to the obligations established in the Directive[63] and will get in exchange the benefit of the passport to undertake these activities across the EU without any further authorisation required.

In order to assess whether MiFID would be applicable to a specific case of securities crowdfunding, the types of financial instruments and financial services involved in the operation must be checked. As regards the former, most of the business models would include transferable securities such as shares or bonds, or other instruments like units in collective investment undertakings, which qualify as MiFID financial instruments according to Section C of Annex 1 of the Directive. If this were not the case, however, the contract platforms would not need to obtain an authorisation under MiFID and would instead only have to fulfil the corresponding national requirements.

As for the types of activities or services, the most common one provided by contract platforms is the reception and transmission of orders, which is included in Section A of Annex 1 of the Directive. Even if some contract platforms argue that the activity they perform is only the 'communication of expressions of interest' and not the reception and transmission of orders, the European

60 Directive 2004/39/EC of the European Parliament and of the Council of 21 April 2004 on markets in financial instruments amending Council Directives 85/611/EEC and 93/6/EEC and Directive 2000/12/EC of the European Parliament and of the Council and repealing Council Directive 93/22/EEC ([2004] OJ L 145, 30.04.2004, p. 1).

61 Directive 2014/65/EU of the European Parliament and of the Council of 15 May 2014 on markets in financial instruments and amending Directive 2002/92/EC and Directive 2011/61/EU ([2014] OJ L 173, 12.06.2014, p. 349); both its date of application and transposition into national laws have been extended, to 3 January 2018 and 3 July 2017 respectively. Regulation (EU) No 600/2014 of the European Parliament and of the Council of 15 May 2014 on markets in financial instruments and amending Regulation (EU) No 648/2012 ([2014] OJ L 173, 12.06.2014, p. 84).

62 Since the exemptions of article 2 of the Directive do not seem applicable, the relevant ones would be the optional exemptions for Member States established in article 3 (see section 4.3.2.2 below).

63 Capital requirements, organisational requirements and conduct of business requirements. Some of them vary according to the type of service or activity undertaken by the contract platform.

Securities and Markets Authority has taken the view that in order to operate outside MiFID on that basis there would have to be a real, substantive distinction between the expression of interest and something which could be considered as an order.[64] Other MiFID services or activities that could be relevant in some cases of securities crowdfunding are the 'execution of orders', as defined in article 4(4) of the Directive and, perhaps less frequently, 'investment advice'. This would have to be assessed on a case-by-case basis since the business models vary greatly and so do the activities performed by the contract platforms.[65]

Compliance under MiFID is costly. To start with, it includes significant capital requirements that depend on the type of activity performed by the contract platform. As for the initial capital requirements,[66] platforms considered to be investment firms carrying on MiFID services or activities on MiFID financial instruments must have an initial capital of €730,000[67] unless they meet the conditions for lower initial capital or an exemption.[68] In addition to this, there are also some on-going capital requirements but these are unlikely to apply to the platforms since they are connected to certain activities they usually do not perform, like dealing on their own account and the underwriting of financial instruments and/or the placing of financial instruments on a firm commitment basis.[69] Besides the capital requirements, MiFID establishes some organisational[70] and conduct of business requirements[71] that may be also costly to implement.

This regulatory burden on contract platforms that might be considered to fall under MiFID has prompted some of them to try to shape their activities in order to avoid such rules. In the same vein, some Member States that have enacted

64 *ESMA Opinion*, above n. 18, p. 16, detailing a non-exhaustive list of examples of factors that could be relevant to this aim.

65 On these activities, see *ESMA Opinion*, above n. 18, p. 16–17. The ESMA analyses also other types of MiFID services and activities which are much less likely to be performed by crowdfunding platforms, such as the underwriting of financial instruments and/or placing of financial instruments on a firm commitment basis, the placing of financial instruments without a firm commitment basis, or the operation of Multilateral Trading Facilities (*ESMA Opinion*, above n. 18, p. 17–18).

66 Article 12 of the Directive 2004/39/EC.

67 Article 28.2 of the Directive 2013/36/EU of the European Parliament and of the Council of 26 June 2013 on access to the activity of credit institutions and the prudential supervision of credit institutions and investment firms, amending Directive 2002/87/EC and repealing Directives 2006/48/EC and 2006/49/EC ([2013] OJ L 176, 27.06.2013, p. 338).

68 Article 29 of the Directive 2013/36/EU.

69 See article 128 *in fine* (referring to Section A of Annex I of Directive 2004/39/EC) and articles 129 to 134 of Directive 2013/36/EU.

70 Basically, article 13, article 18 on conflicts of interest and article 25 on record-keeping (eventually article 14 also, in the case of firms operating MTF) of the Directive 2004/39/EC.

71 Article 19 of Directive 2004/39/EC, which includes information and reporting obligations and the obligation to perform the suitability and appropriateness tests of the client in certain cases. (The possibility for the platforms to be exempted from conducting the appropriateness test if the conditions of article 19.6 of the Directive are met is a relevant issue: see *ESMA Opinion*, above n. 18, pp. 14–15).

specific regimes for investment-based crowdfunding have decided to authorise contract platforms using the exemption of article 3 of the Directive 2004/39/EC in order to lower those requirements and foster their activity.[72]

4.3.1.3. Other EU Rules

In addition to the two above-mentioned Directives, other EU rules could eventually apply also, depending on the activities undertaken by the contract platforms. Since securities crowdfunding is a quite recent phenomenon, the different types of related activities that contract platforms may decide to undertake will probably develop in the next few years so the potential applicability of the following EU rules cannot be discarded, even if some rules appear more likely to be triggered by platforms' activities than others.

For example, a set of rules that might be applicable to contract platforms is the Payment Services Directive.[73] The existing business models of securities crowdfunding differ in this respect, and the applicability of this Directive will therefore depend on the specific activities undertaken by the platform in relation to the payment of the funders' contributions to the promoters. In general terms, if the platform collects the funds in order to transfer them to the promoter if the campaign is successful or to return them to the funders if it is not, this Directive would probably apply, whereas if the platform does not intervene in the payment but instead leaves this activity to a third-party the Directive would not apply.[74]

Similarly, a relevant number of other EU rules could be potentially applicable, depending on the activities performed by the contract platforms, such as the Directive on investor-compensation schemes,[75] the Distance Marketing of Financial Services Directive,[76] the Alternative Investment Fund Managers

---

72 A different question is whether this result has been attained. For example, see a critical comment on the Italian regulation of crowdfunding in E. D'Ippolito, M. Musitelli and A. Sciarrone: 'Protecting Crowdfunders: Is a MiFID-Mimicking Approach Appropriate?' (2016) 13 *European Company Law* 27.

73 Directive 2007/64/EC of the European Parliament and of the Council of 13 November 2007 on payment services in the internal market, amending Directives 97/7/EC, 2002/65/EC, 2005/60/EC and 2006/48/EC and repealing Directive 97/5/EC ([2007] OJ L 319, 05.12.2007, p. 1), in force until 13 January 2018. From this date on, this Directive will be replaced by Directive 2015/2366/EU of the European Parliament and of the Council of 25 November 2015 on payment services in the internal market, amending Directives 2002/65/EC, 2009/110/EC and 2013/36/EU and Regulation (EU) No 1093/2010, and repealing Directive 2007/64/EC ([2015] OJ L 337, 23.12.2015, p. 35).

74 For a further and more detailed analysis on the applicability of Directive 2007/64/EC to contract platforms involved in investment-based crowdfunding, see *ESMA Opinion*, above n. 18, p. 34–37.

75 Directive 97/9/EC of the European Parliament and of the Council of 3 March 1997 on investor-compensation schemes ([1997] OJ L 84, 26.03.1997, p. 22).

76 Directive 2002/65/EC of the European Parliament and of the Council of 23 September 2002 concerning the distance marketing of consumer financial services and amending Council Directives 90/619/EEC and Directive 97/7/EC and 98/27/EC ([2002] OJ L 271, 09.10.2002, p. 16).

Directive,[77] the European Venture Capital Funds Regulation,[78] the European Social Entrepreneurship Funds Regulation,[79] the rules on Market Abuse,[80] the Fourth Anti-Money Laundering Directive,[81] the Unfair Commercial Practices Directive,[82] the Misleading and Comparative Advertising Directive,[83] the Unfair Terms in Consumer Contracts Directive,[84] the Consumer Alternative Dispute Resolution Directive,[85] the Consumer Credit Directive and Mortgage Credit Directive,[86] or the Directive on electronic commerce.[87, 88]

---

77 Directive 2011/61/EU of the European Parliament and of the Council of 8 June 2011 on Alternative Investment Fund Managers and amending Directives 2003/41/EC and 2009/65/EC and Regulations (EC) No 1060/2009 and (EU) No 1095/2010 ([2011] OJ L 174, 01.07.2011, p. 1).

78 Regulation (EU) No 345/2013 of the European Parliament and of the Council of 17 April 2013 on European venture capital funds ([2013] OJ L 115, 25.04.2013, p. 1).

79 Regulation (EU) No 346/2013 of the European Parliament and of the Council of 17 April 2013 on European social entrepreneurship funds ([2013] OJ L 115, 25.04.2013, p. 18).

80 Directive 2014/57/EU of the European Parliament and of the Council of 16 April 2014 on criminal sanctions for market abuse (market abuse directive) ([2014] OJ L 173, 12.06.2014, p. 179) and Regulation (EU) No 596/2014 of the European Parliament and of the Council of 16 April 2014 on market abuse (market abuse regulation) and repealing Directive 2003/6/EC of the European Parliament and of the Council and Commission Directives 2003/124/EC, 2003/125/EC and 2004/72/EC ([2014] OJ L 173, 12.06.2014, p. 1), both applicable from 3 July 2016.

81 Directive (EU) 2015/849 of the European Parliament and of the Council of 20 May 2015 on the prevention of the use of the financial system for the purposes of money laundering or terrorist financing, amending Regulation (EU) No 648/2012 of the European Parliament and of the Council, and repealing Directive 2005/60/EC of the European Parliament and of the Council and Commission Directive 2006/70/EC ([2015] OJ L 141, 05.06.2015, p. 73).

82 Directive 2005/29/EC of the European Parliament and of the Council of 11 May 2005 concerning unfair business-to-consumer commercial practices in the internal market and amending Council Directive 84/450/EEC, Directives 97/7/EC, 98/27/EC and 2002/65/EC of the European Parliament and of the Council and Regulation (EC) No 2006/2004 of the European Parliament and of the Council ('Unfair Commercial Practices Directive') ([2005] OJ L 149, 11.06.2005, p. 22).

83 Directive 2006/114/EC of the European Parliament and of the Council of 12 December 2006 concerning misleading and comparative advertising ([2006] OJ L 376, 27.12.2006, p. 21).

84 Council Directive 93/13/EEC of 5 April 1993 on unfair terms in consumer contracts ([1993] OJ L 95, 21.04.1993, p. 29).

85 Directive 2013/11/EU of the European Parliament and of the Council of 21 May 2013 on alternative dispute resolution for consumer disputes and amending Regulation (EC) No 2006/2004 and Directive 2009/22/EC ([2013] OJ L 165, 18.06.2013, p. 63).

86 Directive 2014/17/EU of the European Parliament and of the Council of 4 February 2014 on credit agreements for consumers relating to residential immovable property and amending Directives 2008/48/EC and 2013/36/EU and Regulation (EU) No 1093/2010 ([2014] OJ L 60, 28.02.2014, p. 34).

87 Directive 2000/31/EC of the European Parliament and of the Council of 8 June 2000 on certain legal aspects of information society services, in particular electronic commerce, in the Internal Market ('Directive on electronic commerce') ([2000] OJ L 178, 17.07.2000, p. 1).

88 For a general analysis of the applicability of these rules, see *ESMA Opinion*, above n. 18, pp. 12–27 and 34–40 and G.A. Gabison: 'Equity Crowdfunding: All Regulated but Not Equal' (2014–2015) 13 *De Paul Business and Commercial law Journal* 359, 376–386 (some of the comments refer to previous rules, recently replaced).

4.3.2. *National Rules on Crowdfunding*

In addition to the potential applicability of a significant number of EU rules, in some Member States securities crowdfunding can be affected by some specific national regimes recently implemented. In the last few years a growing number of countries have passed legislation in the field of financial-return crowdfunding. Some national regimes regulate both lending and investment models of crowdfunding and others only the latter.

As far as securities crowdfunding is concerned, even if all national regimes share the same regulatory concerns and have the same objectives in general terms, the ways to reach them are significantly different.[89] The regulations on securities crowdfunding enacted in Italy,[90] the United Kingdom,[91] France,[92] Germany,[93] Spain,[94] Portugal,[95] Austria,[96] and Finland[97] tackle basically the same issues and these can be grouped into two main areas. Certain rules relate basically to the offer and the corresponding investment made by the investors. Others are aimed at regulating the contract platforms, their activities, duties and responsibilities. Obviously, the two areas are closely related, since they all reflect an investor protection approach and some of the provisions related to the offer and the investment also have consequences for the regulation of contract platforms, but for the sake of clarity they will be analysed separately in the following two sub-sections.

4.3.2.1. Offer and Investment

A first aspect usually regulated by the national rules on crowdfunding is the type of financial instrument that can be offered. The options taken in the different countries vary in this respect. In some countries, like Portugal, all

---

89 This section is not intended to provide an in-depth comparative analysis of national regulations – a task that is beyond the scope of this chapter – but to highlight some of the most relevant regulatory issues and point out the significant differences among jurisdictions.

90 Decreto-legge 18 ottobre 2012, n. 179 (converted into Law by Legge 17 dicembre 2012, n. 221), implemented by the CONSOB Delibera n. 18592 of 23 June 2013. Some modifications were introduced in the Italian crowdfunding regime by Decreto-legge 24 gennaio 2015, n. 3 (converted into Law by Legge 24 marzo 2015, n. 33) and by the CONSOB Delibera 24 febbraio 2016.

91 FCA's Crowdfunding and the Promotion of Non-Readily Realisable Securities Instrument 2014, 27 February 2014.

92 Ordonnance n° 2014-559 du 30 mai 2014 relative au financement participatif.

93 Small Investor Protection Act (Kleinanlegerschutzgesetz), 23 April 2015.

94 Ley 15/2015, de 27 de abril de 2015, de fomento de la financiación empresarial.

95 Lei n.° 102/2015, de 24 de agosto, 'Regime jurídico do financiamento colaborativo', and Regulamento da CMVM n° 1/2016 'Financiamento Colaborativo de capital ou por empréstimo'.

96 Austrian Alternative Financing Act (Alternativfinanzierungsgesetz – AltFG), 19 May 2015.

97 Crowdfunding Act 734/2016, 21 June 2016.

types of financial instruments are allowed,[98] while in others only certain types of securities are permitted – sometimes only transferable securities like in Spain or in Finland; other times both transferable and non-transferable securities like in France, or those specifically defined by the lack of an acceptable secondary market such as the 'non-readily realisable security' of the British rules.[99] Finally, some countries establish more stringent limits, as is the case of Italy where there are limits not only as to the type of instruments that can be issued in this context but also as to the kind of company that may seek the funds. The Italian rules originally applied only to 'innovative start-ups', and since 2015 also to 'innovative small and medium enterprises (SMEs)' and to collective investment undertakings and companies that invest mainly in innovative start-ups and innovative SMEs.[100] Sometimes the type of instrument that can be issued is connected to the prospectus exemption or simplification, such as in Germany for example, where the exception from the prospectus requirement is available only for profit-participating loans, subordinated loans, and similar investments.[101]

Another important issue where regulatory differences among domestic regimes can be seen is the amounts that can be invested.[102] While some jurisdictions do not establish any limits, like France, Italy or Finland for example, in other countries maximum amounts per investor are fixed, in some cases at quite a low level. These maximum amounts are usually fixed for individuals only[103] and connected to their freely available assets or income.[104] This is the case in Germany, Spain, Portugal, Austria and the United Kingdom, even if the conditions and amounts differ. In Germany, investors having at least €100,000 of freely available assets can invest up to €10,000 in an issue; if not, they can only invest twice their monthly income (with a maximum of €10,000); and only €1,000 if they do not provide a statement on assets and income. In Spain and

---

98 The Portuguese Lei n.º 102/2015 has a broad scope, not only in respect of this question but also in general terms. It includes the four business models of crowdfunding analysed in this chapter (art. 3 Lei n.º 102/2015) and in the case of the investment-based model it admits not only the securities model but also the profit-sharing one (art. 3.c) Lei n.º 102/2015). The Law also includes a reference to the contractual rules applicable to the underlying legal relationship between the funder and the promoter (art. 10 Lei n.º 102/2015).

99 FCA's Policy Statement PS14/4, above n. 12, §1.16.

100 As a modified by Decreto-legge 24 gennaio 2015, n. 3. See E. D'Ippolito, M. Musitelli and A. Sciarrone, above n. 72, 27.

101 For a critical comment on this restriction see L. Klöhn, L. Hornuf and T. Schilling, above n. 48, pp. 61–62.

102 *European Commission Staff Working Document*, above n. 5, p. 40.

103 Not always though: for example in Spain small business that do not meet at least two of the following three conditions are also bound by those limits: €1,000,000 of assets; €2,000,000 of annual turnover; €300,000 of equity (see arts. 81 and 82 of Ley 15/2015, above n. 94).

104 This approach is modelled on the US regulation, the Crowdfund Act 2012 (Title III of the Jobs Act 2012). In the US this was one of issues that had been previously discussed by academics in the context of the drafting of a crowdfunding exemption (see C.S. Bradford, above n. 14, pp. 122–131).

Portugal the maximum amounts are fixed at €3,000 per project and €10,000 a year, for investors having an annual income of at least €50,000 or freely available assets of €100,000 (Spain), or an annual income of at least €70,000 (Portugal). In Austria the limit is €5,000 per investor each year or (exceptionally) no more than either twice their monthly net income or 10 per cent of their financial assets. In the United Kingdom the limit for certain non-sophisticated investors is also fixed at 10 per cent of the investor's net investable assets.

As can be seen from this brief description the regulatory options regarding the issue are significantly different, since some countries establish no limits at all, while others fix certain limits that are quite restrictive in some cases. Even when these limits exist, the specific rules differ in certain aspects of importance. For instance, while some countries establish limits only per issue and therefore the investors have in fact no real limit since they can invest in as many projects as they like, others have put in place more protective annual limits. Even in this last case the differences in the amounts are significant, as can be seen when comparing the Austrian annual limit of €5,000 to the Spanish and Portuguese ones of €10,000.

The maximum amount of the offer is another matter that is usually regulated at national level, connected with the prospectus exemption or simplification. Here again the national rules differ,[105] with amounts ranging from €1,000,000 to €5,000,000.[106] This is an extremely relevant issue given its connection with the prospectus exemption – the drafting and publishing of a prospectus being a costly burden on issuers. The different regulatory options may reflect the on-going debate about the appropriate amount to fix.[107] Investment-based crowdfunding campaigns are usually of a small amount since they are mainly launched by start-ups or SMEs in general. If the goal of the regulation were to foster this financing mechanism, it would seem appropriate to set the maximum amount for the offer to benefit from the prospectus exemption at a sensible level, taking into account the usual features of these campaigns. In general terms, the limits set in the national regimes – with most of the countries well above €1,000,000 – do not seem to coincide with the most usual amounts raised by crowdfunding campaigns, which are usually significantly lower.[108]

There are other issues also tackled by national rules, such as the information to be submitted by the issuer, where significant differences can also be seen.

105 There are also other national variations connected to other aspects of the offer, such as the type of investors to which the offer is made or the type of securities.

106 France is the only country having a €1,000,000 limit, followed by Austria with €1,500,000, Spain with €2,000,000, Germany with €2,500,000 and Italy, the UK and Finland with €5,000,000.

107 A question already discussed in the first academic studies on crowdfunding (see C.S. Bradford, above n.14, pp. 118–122).

108 See Proposal for a Prospectus Regulation, above n. 55, p. 13, stating that the offers of securities on crowdfunding platforms are typically below €500,000.

Typically this information refers to the investment and the risks associated with it, but some countries require the issuers to provide detailed information about them additionally.[109]

4.3.2.2. Regulation of the Contract Platform

Given that the presence of contract platforms as an intermediary between the promoters and the funders is a defining aspect of crowdfunding and that these platforms undertake very relevant activities in this context, most of the national regimes on crowdfunding regulate them to a greater or lesser extent.[110] The provisions targeting contract platforms include a number of issues, most of them related to the type of activities they perform and the corresponding need to get authorisation to do so, and also with other connected requirements such as minimum capital or professional requirements, regulation of potential conflicts of interests, due diligence to be performed by the contract platforms and information requirements and risk warnings to the investors.

A first important aspect is the authorisation of the platforms. Relating to this, four systems can be distinguished.[111] A first option is that the contract platforms be authorised under MiFID with all the obligations this entails, as discussed above. A second option is to get authorisation under the national crowdfunding regime according to the exemption established in article 3 of MiFID, which may imply lower requirements – depending on the country in question. In these two cases, the authorisation allows the contract platforms to provide investment services in relation to MiFID financial instruments, the difference being the acquisition or not of the EU passport. A third option is that the platforms be authorised under a national regime outside MiFID for activities not related to MiFID financial instruments – while they can still apply for MiFID authorisation for the rest. And finally, in those countries where the national regime considers that such platforms do not carry out any MiFID service or activity, they can be authorised outside MiFID completely. These different approaches have a very relevant impact on contract platforms since the need to get an authorisation implies a number of duties and obligations, whose specific content varies greatly depending on the type of authorisation required.

Obviously, the issue of the authorisation is connected to the kind of activities the platforms can provide under the different national rules, and this is a

---

109 This is the case in Spain (art. 78 Ley 5/2015) and Austria (art. 4 Alternativfinanzierungsgesetz – AltFG). In Italy, the platforms must verify some data about the promoters before publishing their offers on their websites (art. 24 'Regolamento sulla raccolta di capitali di rischio tramite portali on-line' of the CONSOB).

110 In the European context, Germany is probably the most striking exception in this matter since the Small Investor Protection Act leaves contact platforms almost unregulated (see L. Klöhn, L. Hornuf and T. Schilling, above n. 48, pp. 65–66).

111 *European Commission Staff Working Document*, above n. 5, pp. 18–20.

question that also varies from one jurisdiction to another. In some countries the platforms can only receive orders (like for instance in Italy), while in others they can also provide investment advice (for example in the United Kingdom, France and Germany). There are also other countries, like Spain, where the national crowdfunding regime only allows the platforms to perform 'technical activities' such as the reception, selection and publication of projects, and the development, establishment and exploitation of communication channels to facilitate the fundraising between investors and promoters, together with a number of ancillary services.[112]

It seems apparent from this that the approach taken as regards the role of the platforms differs greatly from one country to another – ranging from activities that can be considered as investment services and activities, to others that are more similar to technical assistance and representation. As a consequence, the national regimes differ not only in the requirement of getting some kind of authorisation – according to the types of activities that the platforms are allowed to perform – but also in other important connected aspects, such as the minimum capital or professional requirements, the regulation of potential conflicts of interests, the due diligence to be performed by the contract platforms and the information requirements and risk warnings to the investors.[113]

4.4. THE NEED FOR A LEVEL PLAYING-FIELD FOR SECURITIES CROWDFUNDING IN EUROPE

The previous sub-section has shown that securities crowdfunding in Europe is affected by a high number of rules, both European and national ones, and that the specific rules that may apply to a given case differ significantly from one country to another. It has also pointed out that these regulatory differences have an impact on certain aspects of the utmost relevance for the operation of contract platforms.

The decision to enact national bespoke regimes for financial-return crowdfunding in general and for securities crowdfunding in particular is a consolidated and growing trend in Europe. This is at least partially the consequence of the national legislators' and authorities' awareness of the increasing importance of this financing mechanism and the risks that an unregulated crowdfunding market may have for investors and markets. In contrast with this, the European Union does not seem preoccupied by the lack of European rules in this field, based on the argument that the crowdfunding market is still mostly local.[114]

112 Arts. 51.2 and 51.3 of Ley 15/2015, above n. 94.

113 See *European Commission Staff Working Document*, above n. 5, pp. 34–45.

114 *European Commission Staff Working Document*, above n. 5, p. 31.

This appears to be an unfortunate misunderstanding of the needs and potential of the crowdfunding industry in Europe. Surveys show that the industry is interested in developing more cross-border activity and that it is already doing it to some extent,[115] despite the legal uncertainty posed by the differences among national regimes and the lack of any harmonising intervention by the European Union. The logic is not that crowdfunding does not need regulation at European level because it is still mostly local, but just the opposite: crowdfunding is still mainly local, in spite of the interest of the industry to develop cross-border activity, (at least in part) because there is not a level playing-field across Europe for contract platforms. The legal uncertainty as to which rules would apply in cross-border campaigns and with foreign investors is a big part of the explanation for the underdevelopment of cross-border crowdfunding activity. In this context, if the development of a truly integrated market in this field is considered as positive – and it should appear to be, given the potential that crowdfunding has, as a mechanism to foster small businesses and start-ups – some degree of harmonisation appears to be desirable.

Crowdfunding in general belongs to the wider field of so-called 'collaborative economy' or 'sharing economy' and originated, at least partially, as a way out of the increasingly longer and more complex intermediation chains. In this sense, it can be perceived to a certain extent as a deregulation phenomenon. From the point of view of the legislative policy, this may still be appropriate to the non-financial models of crowdfunding – donation, reward and pre-purchase models – but not so much for the financial ones. The investment-based model analysed in this chapter poses concerns, especially from the viewpoint of investor protection but also more generally in the field of financial technologies,[116] that have being noticed by national legislators. The national crowdfunding regimes enacted until now seem a sensible response to tackle those concerns, but at the same time they act as entry barriers for platforms operating in this field of activity.[117] Harmonisation at EU level should therefore aim to establish a minimum level of investor protection across the European Union, while at the same time not deterring cross-border financing and keeping in line with the Capital Markets Union objectives.

---

115 *Communication 'Unleashing the potential of Crowdfunding in the European Union'*, above n. 19, p. 8: 38% of the European financial-return platforms operate cross-border and almost 50% would like to do so in the future.

116 See section 3.5, above.

117 As expressed by crowdfunding organisations themselves: see *Consultation on the Review of the Prospectus Directive 18/02/2015–13/05/2015 – Feedback statement on the public online consultation*, Bruselas, 10 de Marzo de 2016, p. 3 (available at <http://ec.europa.eu/finance/consultations/2015/prospectus-directive/docs/summary-of-responses_en.pdf>, accessed 25.11.2016).

This conclusion can be extrapolated to the other form of financial crowdfunding, loan-based crowdfunding, which is playing a huge role in financing small economic activities in the last few years. Given the already significant amounts raised through this model, its exponential growth and the increasing involvement of institutional investors and banks in this field, some level of EU regulatory intervention in this area would seem appropriate especially from the investor protection perspective.

5. CONCLUDING REMARKS

Crowdfunding is a very varied phenomenon. Economic agents have put in place a wide range of different business models based on the common philosophy of reaching out to the crowd through the Internet in order to get financing for their projects and business. These different business models respond to the different interests and needs of the involved parties, and they are very different from the legal point of view. While non-financial return models of crowdfunding are less relevant from the economic point of view and present fewer legal problems, financial-return models are very complex in their structure – and correspondingly in their legal nature – and they raise a wide range of problematic legal issues that have to be faced by regulators.

Having realised the need to regulate financial-return crowdfunding, several European countries have already passed domestic regimes, and others are working to do so in the near future. In most cases, the existing rules are applicable to securities crowdfunding but in some countries loan-based crowdfunding has also been regulated. In the case of securities crowdfunding – which has been chosen as a more specific subject of study in this chapter – even if in general terms the national regimes are consistent in their approaches and aims, there are some significant differences that might discourage the contract platforms of initiating or continuing with their cross-border activities. In this sense, it must be noted that contract platforms operating in this field are already trying to design their activities in order to escape regulation, because they perceive it as complex and costly.

Given that the interest in these cross-border activities is high among the crowdfunding industry and that its lack could affect market integration in the field of financial services, it seems advisable to initiate some work at EU level to at least harmonise national crowdfunding regimes. This is undoubtedly a complex issue, since crowdfunding is still a relatively new phenomenon and the specific business models put in place by economic agents are still evolving, especially in the field of investment-based crowdfunding. Nevertheless, a minimum harmonisation is possible, especially in the field of securities crowdfunding given the considerable amount of harmonised legislation in the field of financial services and the corresponding similarity of aims and approaches across Europe. Without any EU intervention in this area there is a risk that the national crowdfunding regimes that will very likely be put in place over the next years, even if they have similar underlying concerns and aims, will contain relevant differences in their specific provisions, a situation that can already be seen in the existing rules. And this might not only have the effect of hindering the development of the European crowdfunding market and industry, but it might also contribute to the fragmentation of the internal market.

TERMS OF SERVICE ARE NOT CONTRACTS – BEYOND CONTRACT LAW IN THE REGULATION OF ONLINE PLATFORMS

Przemysław Jacek Pałka

ABSTRACT

The chapter makes five claims. Firstly, on the descriptive level, terms of online services are not contracts for service in the traditional sense, since they often do not contain any obligations or promises on the side of the providers. Secondly, the question of whether these documents are contracts at all remains open. They always contain some contractual elements (licensing of software and/or content), but primarily set the rules specifying what users are (not) allowed to do, resembling more an exercise of property rights than contracts. Thirdly, the relations between online service providers and their users should be viewed through the lens of horizontal/vertical (private/public) relations. Online service providers might be *de lege* private entities, but the type of power they enjoy is public in nature. Fourthly, what should be noticed is their unilateral control of the code and algorithms behind their platforms. The unequal power position they enjoy towards the consumers comes not only from what is written in the terms, but most of all from the unconstrained control of the code. Finally, to mitigate this inequality, consumer law should concentrate not only on the substance of the terms, but predominantly on what the providers *do* with the code and the algorithms, and constrain the exercise of this power in a way that would benefit the consumers. The readers are encouraged to view the paper not as a doctrinal argument that the author would be defensive about, but rather as an invitation to critically reassess the concepts and preconceptions which inform lawyerly reflection about the new digital reality.

1. INTRODUCTION

The objects of inquiry of this chapter are online platforms, specifically Google, YouTube, Facebook and Twitter, and the terms of service of these platforms. The chapter's aim is to argue that terms of service of these platforms are not contracts for service and potentially not contracts at all (section 2). Rather, they should be seen as an exercise of property rights, similar to rules and regulations in physical proprietary spaces. The potential results of this finding, mostly regarding application of consumer law, are elaborated on (section 3). Further, the concepts of normative and factual (in)equality, which have informed the two major corrections of private law – i.e. labour law and consumer law – are used to operationalise the concept of the 'code'[1] in the context of online platforms. It is argued that the owners of an online platform remain in a position of power towards the platform users not only as a result of their unilateral control of the terms of service, but largely because they are currently allowed to unilaterally control the code. If one chooses to regulate this sphere, the regulation should not only take place within the realm of contract law, but rather should be directed at limitations of property rights and freedom of the design and usage of the code (section 4). Finally, potential solutions to the dangers faced by consumers and society at large are sketched out (section 5). Conclusions follow.

This argument might seem surprising, given that the chapter is published in a book concerned with contract law in the digital era. However, the choice is conscious, and to explain it, two remarks should be made. Firstly, the claim 'terms of service are not contracts, but an exercise of property rights' is not

[1] The concept of 'code' is understood throughout the chapter as in: L. Lessig, 'The Law of the Horse: What Cyber Law Might Teach' (1999) 113 *HLR (Harvard Law Review)* 501, 546. Hereafter, the word 'code' is used without quotation marks.

meant to be prescriptive, but descriptive. It is not argued that they should be regulated as such, nor that such a state of affairs should be evaluated positively. Rather, given the current socio-economic practice and the contents of terms of service under study, such a legal classification seems to be the most accurate. In other words, the aim of the chapter is not to advocate for such a proprietary solution, but to facilitate understanding of the current situation.

The problem of understanding leads to the second remark. There is an agreement in law and technology scholarship that when regulating new technologies, one should do so in a way that minimises the dangers caused by them, without impeding the advantages they offer.[2] What exactly should be seen as a danger and what as an advantage is a political evaluation to be made, but such an evaluation, as well as any concrete prescriptive proposals following it, always presupposes an understanding of the phenomenon. And understanding is not merely knowing facts and data, but is a result of the application of a conceptual framework, a theory, to the facts under consideration. *A contrario*, a lack of understanding might result not only from insufficient data, but also from the application of an inadequate framework to a factual situation. The difference between traditional legal scholarship and law and technology scholarship is that the former had the law as its object of study, while the latter studies socio-technological phenomena from the perspective of the law. Needless to say, the methods of each differ.

New technologies confront lawyers with two types of problems: regulatory and theoretical. The first are specifications of the question: what should be done with the phenomenon under study? The second are one step before: what is it precisely that one is dealing with? Lawyers like order. Lawyers tend to place new phenomena under known categories. Lawyers often 'rush to conclusions', wishing to solve theoretical problems quickly, to be able to move to the regulatory ones. Constitutional lawyers will see constitutional problems wherever they look; law and economics lawyers will see economic relations wherever they look; and contract lawyers will see contracts wherever they look. And that is good. This enriches legal academia. The aim of this piece is not to criticise this. The aim of this piece is to simply offer an alternative view.

2. CONTRACTS FOR SERVICE vs. TERMS OF SERVICE

The purpose of this section is to argue that the terms of service[3] of online platforms are not contracts for service as understood by contract law. Firstly,

---

2 See for example: J. Zittrain, *The Future of the Internet and How to Stop It*, Yale University Press, New Haven CT 2008.

3 These documents occur under different names: 'Terms of Service', 'Terms and Conditions', or simply 'Terms'. However, their contents resemble one another, and they serve similar

the notions of a 'contract for service' and a 'service' are defined. Secondly, ToS of four internet platforms: Google, YouTube, Facebook and Twitter, are analysed. In short, the argument is that the *essentialia negotii* of a contract for service encompass one party's obligation to supply a service to another party, whereas no clause stipulating such an obligation (or any corresponding right) is present in the ToS under study. Having demonstrated this absence, and in fact an absence of any obligations regarding the service on the side of the service providers, the argument moves to questioning whether terms of service are contracts at all.

2.1. DEFINITIONS – 'CONTRACT FOR SERVICE' AND 'SERVICE'

The Draft Common Frame of Reference[4] defines a contract for service as:

> a contract under which one party, the service provider, undertakes to supply a service to the other party, the client.[5]

Examples contained in the DCFR include: construction, processing, storage, design, information or advice, and treatment. The known distinction between obligations of skill and care, and obligations to achieve a result, are introduced.[6] Despite the lack of a legal definition of a 'service' itself, the general meaning of the word is clear.

Services are about doing something, about performing an action. Unlike in the case of sale, which is about the transfer of an ownership right of goods, a service is not about a transfer of rights, but about one party doing something for another. In providing a construction service one builds something for a client, in providing legal services one gives another person advice, drafts documents and represents him or her in court, in operating a hairdressing service one would cut another person's hair, etc. A contract for service gives rise to an obligation for one party to undertake such an action, and a claim on the side of the other party to have an action performed.

---

functions. For this reason, I use the original titles when speaking about particular documents, while when speaking about the phenomenon in general I always use the notion 'terms of service', sometimes abbreviated as 'ToS', for the sake of consistency.

4 Acknowledging that DCFR is politically and academically dormant, I still believe that it serves as a good source of common sense, acceptable for all, legal definitions. Since the purpose of this piece is not to study the law of any particular country, nor is it an exercise in comparative law, but rather to study a social and technological phenomenon through the lens of private law, I find DCFR a compelling choice. However, should there exist a legal system defining a contract for service in a way that undermines the argument of this chapter, I would be more than happy to learn about it.

5 DFCR IV. C.–1:101.

6 DCFR IV. C.–2.

Moving one's focus from the law books to a smartphone screen, what is it that the online platforms studied here do? Google provides a search engine, which allows the user to search for information on the web. YouTube allows one to upload videos, as well as to watch and comment on videos uploaded by other users. Facebook hosts one's information, provides a means for expression, links people with their friends and facilitates communication. Similarly, Twitter. All four perform functions of high importance for the digital society we currently live in.[7]

However, the first potential terminological confusion should be visible right now. Are Google, YouTube, Facebook and Twitter services in themselves? There is a tendency to call them so, but *de lege* they are not. Ontologically speaking, what one can see is three different types of entity: the platforms,[8] i.e. 'facilities' used to perform the service; services, i.e. the actions performed; and companies owning the platforms and performing the services. As a result, if there is a legal relationship between Facebook Inc. and a particular user, the party to the relationship is Facebook Inc., but the service itself is provided by an automatized platform, the software agent(s) to be precise.[9] There is no actual person – no employee of Facebook Inc. or Google Inc. – placing a photo on one's timeline, or sending one the results of a search request. All this is done by computer programs, owned by those companies. In consequence, the companies can be labelled 'platform owners' where the facilities are concerned (they have proprietary rights over the components of the platforms: servers, software, databases, graphic interfaces etc.), and 'service providers' where the actions performed for the users are concerned.

The substance of the relationship between the platform owners and the platform users is defined by the terms of service. Despite the fact that 'I have read the terms of service …', as the joke has it, happens to be the most often repeated lie on the planet, it is worthwhile to actually study them in detail.

---

7 For a good overview of the social and political functions served by the online platforms under study, see the collection: D. Trottier and C. Fuchs (eds.), *Social media, politics and the state: protests, revolutions, riots, crime and policing in the age of Facebook, Twitter and YouTube*, Routledge, New York 2015.

8 Platforms themselves are made up of different types of entity: websites, algorithms, servers, databases etc. Note that the word 'platform' is not a legal concept. Just like a 'user', it is used to refer to particular factual phenomena, but carries no legal meaning, unlike for example a 'service' or a 'consumer'.

9 For a legal conceptualisation of a software agent, see: G. Sartor, 'Cognitive automata and the law: electronic contracting and the intentionality of software agents' (2009) 17 *AI&L (Artificial Intelligence and Law)* 253, 290.

2.2. TERMS OF SERVICE – GOOGLE, YOUTUBE, FACEBOOK AND TWITTER

Google's Terms of Service open with an assertion:

> Thanks for using our products and services ('Services'). ... By using our Services, you are agreeing to these terms.[10]

Right afterwards, they set forward rules clarifying what a user is not allowed to do while using the platform,[11] as well as stipulate the sanction for breaking these rules:

> Don't misuse our Services. For example, don't interfere with our Services or try to access them using a method other than the interface and the instructions that we provide ... We may suspend or stop providing our Services to you if you do not comply with our terms or policies or if we are investigating suspected misconduct.

Notably, the sanction is exclusion from the platform. If Google wishes to do so, on the factual level, it will not mean that someone stops doing something for a user, but that a particular user is denied access to the platform.

Further sections clarify the matters of:

- Copyright: not everything displayed by Google is its property; the user obtains no copyright by using the service; the user retains the ownership of his or her content, but grants Google a lucrative licence to use it. This is the first contractual obligation occurring in the ToS, obliging the user.
- Privacy, or in European terminology: personal data protection. The user agrees to Google processing her or his data under specific conditions.[12] The question remains open whether a data subject agreeing to data processing remains in a contractual or administrative legal relationship with the data controller. However, there is no need to dwell on this problem here, given that even if this is a contractual obligation, the obliged party is again the user.

---

10 This and further quotations from: 'Google Terms of Service', last modified 14.04.2014, in force as of 21.08.2016: http://www.google.com/intl/en/policies/terms/.

11 'Services', in their terminology. It is interesting to see that the ToS speak of 'using' the services, which is not an expression one would use in case of services typically in law. One does not 'use' the service of a lawyer giving him or her advice, or 'use' a service of a hairdresser. One receives them. What Google's ToS label 'Services' is what has been defined as a 'platform' in section 2.1 above, in order to avoid terminological confusion.

12 Google, just as all the other platforms under study, places a very general clause in the ToS and further specifies the privacy policy in a separate document, which a user also accepts by using the service. 'Google Privacy Policy', last modified 28.06.2016, in force as of 21.08.2016, http://www.google.com/intl/en/policies/privacy/.

- Software licence: Google grants the user a limited licence to install the software necessary to use the platform. This is the first, and only, right granted to the user in the Terms.

These three subject-matters are regulated in all ToS under analysis here. The reason behind this is the binding nature of copyright law and personal data protection law. In other words, they must be clarified for the best interest of the platform owner (service provider). However, they do not say anything about the service itself.

The most interesting part comes next. In the section 'Our Warranties and Disclaimers', Google's ToS state:

> Other than as expressly set out in these terms or additional terms, neither Google nor its suppliers or distributors make any specific promises about the services. For example, we don't make any commitments about the content within the services, the specific functions of the services, or their reliability, availability, or ability to meet your needs. We provide the services 'as is'.

Interestingly, no specific promises are set out in these terms. This section is followed by a series of clauses that make a red light appear in a mind of any consumer lawyer. There is a full exclusion of any liability, an assertion of Google's right to modify the ToS, as well as the service (platform) itself, followed by choice of law (California) and jurisdiction clause (Santa Clara County, California).[13]

Given that the only right conferred to a consumer in the terms of service is a revocable licence to use the software, whatever would be the object of the legal dispute against Google in Santa Clara, it would not arise from contractual obligations, because there are no such contractual obligations.

The terms of service of YouTube,[14] Twitter[15] and Facebook[16] resemble Google's in several ways. They all state that one agrees to the ToS by simply

---

13 For a general, but marvellous analysis of the unfair terms regulation, in its historical and comparative context, see: H. Micklitz, 'Unfair Terms in Consumer Contracts' in N. Reich, H.W. Micklitz, P. Rott and K. Tonner, *European Consumer Law*, 2nd edn., Intersentia, Antwerp 2014, pp. 125–164. For a specific study of online platforms' terms of service from the unfair terms regulation perspective, see: M. Loos and J. Luzak, 'Wanted: A Bigger Stick. On Unfair Terms in Consumer Contracts with Online Service Providers' (2016) 39 *JCP (Journal of Consumer Policy)* 63, 90.

14 YouTube's 'Terms of Service', last modified 09.06.2010, in force as of 21.08.2016: https://www.youtube.com/static?gl=GB&template=terms.

15 'Twitter Terms of Service', last modified 27.01.2016, in force as of 21.08.2016: https://twitter.com/tos?lang=en.

16 Facebook's 'Statement of Rights and Responsibilities', last modified 30.01.2015, in force as of 21.08.2016: https://www.facebook.com/legal/terms.

using the platform, contain no promises on what the services will actually be, clarify matters of copyright on content (the user keeps it, but gives the providers a licence), software (user receives a limited licence to use the software necessary to use the platform) and privacy matters, exclude liability, and specify the governing law and jurisdiction.

What distinguishes these three platforms from Google, due to their 'expressive' nature (user is enabled to share content, express himself or herself), is the robust regulation of what their users are not allowed to do while using the platforms. The ToS contain some prohibitions themselves (not to spam, not to offend others, not to harass others etc.), but also refer to the 'rules' (in the case of Twitter)[17] and 'community guidelines/standards' (in the cases of YouTube[18] and Facebook)[19], being separate documents containing codes of behaviour for the platforms' users. Violation of these rules results in a user being excluded from a platform and their account being deleted.

'Twitter Rules' forbid violation of intellectual property rights, hate speech, harassment and threats, namely actions that would be illegal regardless of this prohibition. However, Twitter decides to police such actions itself, by removing the content and blocking the user, which is not in all cases required by law. On the other hand, there are also actions that would not be illegal in themselves (like impersonating someone for the purpose of parody, sharing with the public personal information) which Twitter forbids anyhow. Rules of Facebook and YouTube are similar to this extent. They always contain the double-move: the warning to engage in 'private-policing' of illegal behaviour (be it private or public offence, like shaming someone or making threats, respectively); and limitations of acceptable behaviour within the realm of still-legal, but undesirable (by the company) behaviour.

All the ToS, if one includes the other documents they refer to, speak a lot about what one is not allowed to do while using the platforms, and stipulate a sanction (exclusion from a platform), but confer no rights to actually use the platform, or any promises about what the platform will look like or the services will be like. If one compares this to the definition of a contract for service, one should conclude that the ToS, whatever they are, are not contracts for service. Neither Google, nor YouTube, nor Facebook, nor Twitter 'undertakes to supply a service to the other party, the client'. On the contrary, they are quite explicit about the fact that they actually do not consider themselves obliged to do anything.

---

17 'Twitter Rules', https://support.twitter.com/articles/18311. Unlike terms of service, these documents do not have a date. Last accessed 21.08.2016.

18 Youtube's 'Community Guidelines': https://www.youtube.com/yt/policyandsafety/en-GB/communityguidelines.html. Last accessed 21.08.2016.

19 Facebook's 'Community Standards': https://www.facebook.com/communitystandards. Last accessed 21.08.2016.

That terms of service are not contracts for service has been established. However, if the only right conferred is the licence to use the software, and yet ToS are about many more things than just granting the licence on the software, are they contracts at all? What else would they be?

Twitter's ToS contain a clause:

> All right, title, and interest in and to the Services (excluding Content provided by users) are and will remain the exclusive property of Twitter and its licensors.[20]

Twitter claims that 'the Services' are its property. Obviously, this does not yet mean this is the case; it only means that Twitter believes so. However, the proposition is an interesting one. Are terms of service an exercise of a property right?

3. ONLINE PLATFORMS AS PROPRIETARY SPACES

The purpose of this section is to argue that online platforms should be viewed as proprietary spaces and that their terms of service should be treated as an exercise of a property right on them, rather than contracts. Firstly, the parallel between using a platform and entering a private space is drawn, in order to demonstrate that by merely using one's property or benefiting from an action that could potentially be considered a service one does not become a party to any contract. Secondly, the consequences of these findings are elaborated, mostly regarding legal limitations on the discretionary power of platform owners (service providers), application of consumer law and private international law. Having demonstrated all this, the argument moves to the claim that just as much as it would be easy to bring terms of service under the consumer law regulation (by e.g. amending the directives' text), the real inequality of power between platform owners and platform users lies not within the realm of contract law, but in the unilateral power to control the code, currently unregulated, enjoyed by the platform owners.

An immediate qualification of the claim 'online platforms should be viewed as property and ToS as an exercise of a property right' is needed. As stated already in the Introduction, it is claimed neither that online platforms should be declared a type of property by binding law, nor that it would be beneficial from a regulatory point of view to treat them as property. The claim is of a theoretical, positive nature, seeking understanding: given the current practice of the platform owners, the current contents of terms of service and the normative

20 'Twitter Terms of Service', last modified 27.01.2016, in force as of 21.06.2016: https://twitter.com/tos?lang=en.

background of both, if one wishes to understand what is going on and why, one should adopt this proprietary perspective.

3.1. 'NO ICE CREAM IN THE BOOKSTORE' – TERMS OF SERVICE AS AN EXERCISE OF PROPERTY RIGHTS

Every student of jurisprudence should be able to answer the question why the 'no vehicles in the park' rule in the H.L.A. Hart's *Concept of Law*,[21] despite its vagueness, was binding and had a normative power. The rule was enacted by a public body, properly authorised to do so by a legal act of a higher rank, again properly enacted by an authorised public body, elected in accordance with yet higher procedural rules … all the way up to the rule of recognition. However, the question would become more complicated if this park were a private park.

Imagine a person enters a bookstore, with a clear 'no ice cream' sign at the entrance. Yet, he holds an ice cream in his hand. The shop owner approaches him and asks the person to leave, which that person agrees to and complies with the request. Should one accept that the shop owner had a right to ask the person to leave her store (though not a right to forcefully remove him, which will be studied in section 4 below), the question is: what was the legal basis of this right? Was it a contractual right or a property right?

To claim the former would be to claim that whenever one enters a private space under some condition, or even without it, or actually whenever one uses someone else's property with the owner's consent, there is a contractual relationship between the user and the owner. This would mean that every time someone lends a pen to a friend, or invites a guest to their house for a beer, there is a contract. However, there is no legal, statutory, judicial or doctrinal, reason to believe that this is a case. The owner of a thing, movable or immovable, may use it as he or she wishes, and exclude others from using it,[22] obviously subject to certain limitations. 'May' is telling here, as opposed to 'must'. It is the owner's right, not an obligation, to allow or exclude others. Similarly, just because an owner does not oppose someone else's usage of his or her property, it would be a mistake to claim that this person has a right to use it, a right arising from a contract. He or she is simply left undisturbed, but has no claim to be left undisturbed. There is no contract.

---

21 H.L.A. Hart, *The Concept of Law*, 2nd edn., Oxford University Press, Oxford 1994, pp. 126–130.

22 Exclusion is not always a necessary feature of a property right, as an example of Scandinavian land law demonstrates. However, it is one in a vast majority of cases. For an interesting discussion of the problem, see: G.S. Alexander and E.M. Peñalver, *An Introduction to Property Theory*, Cambridge University Press, Cambridge 2012, p. 4.

There can be a contract, needless to say. Social-economic practice knows of numerous examples. There are contracts for exclusive use of someone's real estate, think of hotels or short-term lending.[23] More importantly, there are contracts allowing access to someone's proprietary space, for example private theme parks, zoos, swimming pools or discos, where one needs to buy a ticket to enter. These spaces would usually have rules and regulations stipulating what one cannot do while being inside the space, as well as specifying a sanction, like a monetary fine or an obligation to leave the space. When one buys a ticket, a mutual legal relationship arises, and its substance would be: 'you can enter my space, stay there for the agreed period of time and use the facilities you find there, and I cannot make you leave (so I grant you a right to be there), as long as you do not violate the rules regulating the space, which you now accept'. Moreover, it can be argued that on the side of the space owner, apart from granting a right to access and stay, there is a certain promise about what the customers (users of the space) will find inside. If the space owner claims that there is a rollercoaster inside the theme park, or a sauna at the swimming pool, or a gorilla in the zoo, and, having purchased a ticket, a customer realises that these entities are missing, one can imagine the customer successfully claiming a refund of the money, simply based on non-conformity with the contract. In short, social-economic practice knows of contracts where the owner of real estate would grant someone a right to access it and stay there for an agreed period of time, as well as make certain promises about what is inside the space, while the consumer would agree to pay the price and abide by the rules, under a sanction of losing the right to be in the space.[24]

The question then arises: when is there a contract and when is there no contract? The easy answer would be: when parties actually conclude one there is one, while when parties do not, there is not. Easy cases are easy to find. When one invites neighbours over for a garden party or allows a friend to sleep at one's home, there is no contract. When one charges a fee for entering an open-air party, or rents out a room at Airbnb, there is a contract. In the former situations the guests have no right to stay when the owner asks them to leave for no reason, in the latter they do. What is the difference between these two situations? One could point to remuneration, or to the economic context, but what actually seems to be decisive is the mutual intention of the parties for a right to access and stay to be granted.

---

23 The currently most relevant example is Airbnb, studied in detail above by V. Mak, in this volume.

24 However, just because it is possible, it does not yet mean that there always is a contract. And even if one really wanted to see a contract in ToS, the analysis of their content has demonstrated that there is no description to be treated as a standard for conformity or non-conformity.

The qualified question arises: does the existence of rules and regulations 'enacted' by the owner automatically give rise to a contractual obligation? The answer seems to be no. Think of a less obvious example, like a shopping mall. A shopping mall is a space where someone would enter in order to potentially conclude a contract of sale or for a service, but it is possible to enter it and stay there just in order to be there (there are people who nowadays seem to enjoy this way of spending their free time). Shopping malls may have rules, for example 'no biking', 'no listening to loud music', 'no shouting'; but the mere fact that these rules are there does not yet mean that as long as someone does not violate any of them, one has a right to stay there. Imagine a group of friends entering a shopping mall and drinking alcohol there. Imagine there is no rule in the regulations prohibiting consumption of the alcohol. However, the owner finds it undesirable and asks them the leave.[25] The reason the owner has a right to do so is because the mall is her property, while the people she speaks to have at no point acquired a right to be undisturbed there.

The final question is: what is the normative status of the rules and regulations? To be specific: is their 'enactment' necessary for the owner to exclude someone from her property? The answer is no (no property law knows of such a limitation), and as a result, one should conclude that the rules and regulations in themselves have no normative value.[26] They are simply an announcement of how the owner plans to exercise her property right. However, as long as there was no contract concluded – which, as was shown, is possible, but not necessary – the owner is not bound by them, either in the negative and positive sense. She does not have to ask someone who violates the rules to leave. And she can still ask someone to leave even if the person does not violate any of the rules. Obviously, her right, as every property right, is not unlimited. There are rules, especially of anti-discrimination law, serving as a limitation of her freedom to exercise the property right. However, she still enjoys a freedom to do whatever the law does not forbid her from doing, and not merely a competence to do only what the law allows her to do. This is still, despite public law limitations, a realm of private law.

Which leads one to the remark: the space owner has a right to ask someone to leave, but has no right to forcefully remove a person.[27] This is a fundamental distinction in the contemporary world. Private persons are given freedom to

---

25 This would most probably not be done by the owner, but by a security guard or a manager. The simple example of the actual owner doing so is used to avoid complex considerations which are not central to this chapter's argument.

26 The author of the chapter would like to thank Filipe Brito Bastos for pointing this out to him.

27 There are exceptions. Should a person pose an immediate danger to others' life, health or property, the owner, or actually any person witnessing it, would have a right to use a proportional physical force. But if an owner simply does not like the fact that someone does something disturbing in her subjective opinion, she has no right to use force.

exercise their subjective rights, but the state has a monopoly on executing them. This fundamental distinction is blurred in case of internet platforms, since the use of 'force' in their case does not mean physically interfering with someone's bodily integrity, but simply operations over the code. To give an example: to remove a customer from a tangible shop, the owner would need to physically displace him or her; to remove a customer from an online platform, it is sufficient for the platform owner to click a button within the IT system. This will be studied in more detail in the section 4 below.

If one merges the analysis above with the analysis of the internet platforms, one will observe a similarity. It is possible that to enter and use a platform, one would conclude a contract. This is so, for example, in the case of Netflix or Spotify, who write in their terms of use, respectively:

> During your Netflix membership we grant you a limited, non-exclusive, non-transferable, license to access the Netflix service and view movies and TV shows on a streaming-only basis.[28]

And:

> The Spotify Service and the Content are the property of Spotify or Spotify's licensors. We grant you a limited, non-exclusive, revocable licence to make use of the Spotify Service, and a limited, non-exclusive, revocable licence to make personal, non-commercial, entertainment use of the Content (the 'Licence').[29]

However, from the fact that it is possible that a contract must be concluded before one can enter and use the platform, it does not follow that whenever one enters and uses one, there is a contract.

Two observations should be made. Firstly, the way Netflix and Spotify speak about their platforms is property talk. The latter explicitly claims as much; the former does so implicitly, by granting a user a 'licence'. To grant a licence to use something, one needs to own that something in a first place.[30] This, as has already been said, does not mean that platforms are these companies' property *de lege lata* (though many of their necessary components are: servers, databases, graphic interfaces, software etc.), but it does express how these companies perceive the platforms they operate. Secondly, when a right to access and use is granted in terms of service, these ToS will be treated as a contract (albeit not a

---

28 Netflix's 'Terms of Use', last updated 05.05.2016, in force as of 21.08.2016: https://help.netflix.com/legal/termsofuse?locale=en&docType=termsofuse.

29 'Spotify Terms and Conditions of Use', last updated 09.09.2015, in force as of 21.08.2016, https://www.spotify.com/ie/legal/end-user-agreement/.

30 Or have a sub-licensable licence. One way or another, a licence always presupposes an original property right.

contract for service), while if there are no rights granted, the ToS will be just an announcement of how the platform owner plans to exercise her property right. No more, no less.

One last remark in this subsection should be made about the contractual elements that happen to occur in almost all ToS, those being contracts and those being not, namely: a licence to use the content, a licence to use a software, and privacy agreement (if one sees it as a contract). Should one consider again the bookstore example, one will notice that a customer entering it sees the store and what is inside, while the store's owner sees the customer. Metaphorically speaking: the layout of the store is the 'content', the customer's brain is the 'software', and the shop owner's oversight is the 'privacy'. There need not be any contract, because the whole situation is material, tangible. An internet platform, on the other hand, is highly technologically mediated, in the presence of data protection laws and copyright laws, hence a need for these 'contracts' in terms of service. Their presence, however, does not make these terms contracts themselves.

3.2. CONSEQUENCES OF TERMS OF SERVICE NOT BEING CONTRACTS

Three major consequences follow from the proposition advocated above. Firstly, the limitation on the contents of terms or services will not be equal to limitations on contractual freedom in a given legal order, but to limitations on an exercise of property rights, arguably of a different nature and substance. Secondly, a significant part of consumer law, including the Unfair Contract Terms Directive 93/13[31] and the currently worked on Digital Content Directive,[32] will not apply to them. Thirdly, there are consequences from the point of view of private international law.

Starting with the last consequence, the author of this piece can hardly call himself an expert in private international law. Despite having studied the subject while preparing this chapter, he still does not feel comfortable drawing substantive conclusions.[33] For this reason, he would just like to draw the reader's

[31] Council Directive 93/13/EEC of 5 April 1993 on unfair terms in consumer contracts [1993] OJ L95.

[32] Proposal for a Directive of the European Parliament and of the Council on certain aspects concerning contracts for the supply of digital content, COM/2015/0634 final – 2015/0287 (COD).

[33] He can, however, recommend a fascinating book on the matter, dealing precisely with private international law and internet, see: D. SVANTESSON, *Private international law and the Internet*, 3rd edn., Kluwer Law International 2016. See also, D. SVANTESSON in Part II of this volume.

attention to the fact that depending on whether an obligation is of contractual or non-contractual nature, different rules of private international law, concerning both choice of law and jurisdiction, will apply. However, what precisely would the difference be, is the question that will remain asked, but unanswered.

Moving to the second consequence, there is a question of the directives' applicability. In their remarkable study on the terms of service of Facebook, Google, Twitter and Dropbox through the lens of the Unfair Contract Terms Directive, Marco Loos and Joasia Luzak, when confronting the question of the Directive's applicability to the terms of service of online platforms, observe:

> The Unfair Contract Terms Directive only applies to contractual terms: Article 2 under (a) of the Directive defines 'unfair terms' as 'the contractual terms defined in Article 3.' The Directive does not elaborate on the notion of a 'contractual term.' … In our view, 'contractual terms' are terms that confer a right or an obligation to one of the parties or otherwise regulate the required behaviour of a party in her contractual relationship with the other party.[34]

Even if one accepts this broad definition as valid, one puzzle remains. Does a term need to be a part of a contractual relationship to be considered contractual within the meaning of the Directive? If so, then one should conclude that the Directive does not apply to terms of service. However, a more favourable reading of this claim is possible, according to which even if the entire relationship is not of a contractual nature, particular terms might still be considered contractual within the meaning of the Directive. If this were the case, liability clauses, jurisdiction and governing law clauses would potentially be under the scrutiny of the Directive. This does seem peculiar, given that the dispute between a user and a platform owner cannot have as its object the non-performance of the contract, since there is no contract.[35] The Directive could potentially be applicable, though. In the end, this is a rather theoretical problem, and as signalled above, a simple amendment of the Unfair Contract Terms Directive, or a new directive, or an ECJ judgment would suffice, if only it would contain the norm 'the Unfair Contract Terms Directive applies to the terms of service of internet platforms'. However, even if the directive applies, either as a result of a favourable interpretation, or as a result of the law's amendment, the most fundamental problem remains, and that is unilateral control of what the platform actually is and does, and in the broadest sense possible, what is happening there.

---

34 M. Loos and J. Luzak, above n. 13, 65.

35 Let me once again stress that there *might* be a contract, as is the case regarding Netflix and Spotify. But in the case of the platforms analysed in this chapter, namely Google, YouTube, Facebook and Twitter, as was shown in sections 2 and 3.1., there is no reason to treat them as contracts.

Loos and Luzak, among the categories of potentially unfair terms in ToS, list 'Unilateral Changes to the Service Itself', stating:

> When consumers conclude a contract with an online service provider, they expect to receive a certain service. If the service provider could unilaterally decide to change this service's scope or nature that could leave a consumer bound to a contract she might not have wanted.[36]

The key phrase here is 'when consumers conclude a contract'. But in the case of Google, Facebook, YouTube and Twitter consumers do not conclude a contract. Platform owners specifically state that they make no promises and come under no obligation as regards the particular functionalities, or even very existence, of their platforms. And the truth is that they do modify their services constantly, which any user of any of these platforms knows more than well. Such a practice is not unfair or unlawful, as long as there is no contract and the legal relationship is simply about allowing others to use one's property. For the very same reason, one should question whether the Digital Content Directive would apply to terms of service, which in article 3.1. states:

> This Directive shall apply to any contract where the supplier supplies digital content to the consumer or undertakes to do so and, in exchange, a price is to be paid or the consumer actively provides counter-performance other than money in the form of personal data or any other data.[37]

The decision to finally start treating personal data as a form of remuneration should be applauded, but the main problem remains. If ToS are not contracts, the Digital Content Directive does not apply. And even if also this were changed in the Directive, so that it would apply as consequence of some rephrasing, in order to achieve the aims stated in article 1:

> This Directive lays down certain requirements concerning contracts for the supply of digital content to consumers, in particular rules on conformity of digital content with the contract, remedies in case of the lack of such conformity and the modalities for the exercise of those remedies as well as on modification and termination of such contracts ...[38]

The question that remains unresolved is: conformity with what would be ensured, since not only are no promises made, but also no description is given anywhere in the ToS? And to correct this, something much more fundamental than simply

---

36 M. Loos and J. Luzak, above n. 13, 72.
37 Proposal for a Directive ... above n. 32.
38 Ibid.

clearing up the applicability of the directives is needed. Platform owners would need to be legally obliged to conclude an actual contract, conferring rights and obligations, with every user, and in this contract specify what the platform will be and do. The consequences of such a legislative move, ranging from freezing innovation to an enormous rise in the cost of running internet platforms, will be left for the reader to contemplate. What seems clear is that this is not an option.

There is a problem, though. The fact that platform owners can essentially do whatever they wish, modify their platforms, exclude people from them, given the social and almost political roles that these platforms play in our society, is troubling. Not only consumers' interest, but the interest of society as a whole is at stake. There is really a lot of uncontrolled power gathered in quite few hands. The solution, however, lies not within the realm of contract law. The solution lies in putting boundaries on the unilateral control of the code. Before one moves in that direction, however, it might be beneficial to refresh an old and dusty concept of horizontal and vertical relations.

4. HORIZONTAL RELATIONS, VERTICAL RELATIONS, AND THE CODE

The purpose of this section is to argue that in order to understand the relationship between platform owners and platform users, as well as potential dangers that consumers and the societies face in the current state of law and practice, one should employ the analytical tool of horizontal and vertical relations. In short, it is argued that these tools can be used to analyse many more spheres of social life than just law; that the difference between legal and factual inequality blurs when the code is concerned; and that this blurring is where the relationship under study dwells. Having introduced the distinction, the argument moves to claiming that a potential regulatory response lies not within the realm of contract law, but in the regulation of the code. Code, being a part of the wider phenomenon of digitalisation, blurs the boundary between normative and factual, and gives platform owners a significantly powerful position towards their users.

4.1. LEGAL AND FACTUAL INEQUALITY

It has become a commonplace in legal academia to claim that the private/public law divide cannot be upheld. There are different arguments for why exactly this is the case – not necessarily consistent with each other – based on divisions according to subject, object or method. There are claims that the law has changed and is no longer private, as well as claims that there cannot possibly be such thing as a state-made private law.[39] The view of the author of this chapter is that if it is a common wish to abolish the distinction, it might just as well be abolished, but it should be abolished carefully. When throwing 2000-year-old concepts into the garbage of history, one risks throwing away too much. And the concept that should be saved, given its analytical usefulness, is the concept of horizontal and vertical relations.

Whether a relation is vertical or horizontal depends on the parties' equality or inequality towards one another. A vertical relationship occurs when one party remains in a power position towards the other, while a horizontal relation occurs when the parties' positions are equal. These are, obviously, ideal types, and the social practice will know of more nuanced situations, but defining the ideal types is a necessary first step. There are two types of inequality and equality, and as a result two types of verticality and horizontality, first depending on competences, and the other depending on force. There is a normative[40] (in)equality and a factual (in)equality.

The parties would be normatively unequal if one of them had a competence to unilaterally administer the rules governing the relationship and the rights forming its substance. 'Administer' here means both creating and modifying the rules, as well as adjudicating based on them or enforcing them. In such a vertical relation, the party having the competence to unilaterally administer the rules would be in a power position towards the other one. Examples here, for the moment just from the domain of law, encompass a policemen giving someone a ticket, a tax officer issuing a decision, a judge deciding a case, but also a parliament changing a civil code or a city council enacting local laws.

Normative equality, on the other hand, and so a situation labelled a 'horizontal relation', occurs when none of the parties has a competence to unilaterally administer the rules governing it. Examples here are situations of contract, tort, property and inheritance, so the actions regulated by the branches of law that used to be, traditionally, labelled private law. Note the difference, introduced in the previous section, between exercising a right and executing the right. Clearly, one could argue that in cases of tort law, or *negotiorum gestio*, or property, it is for one party to unilaterally decide on the substance of the relationship via her actions (give rise to rights and obligations). However, horizontality is not defined based on this, but based on administering the rules governing the relationship. In a horizontal normative (here, legal) relation parties cannot change the rules of property law, tort law or inheritance law, nor can they execute a right they wish

[39] For a refreshing and rigorous take on the matter, see: H.W. Micklitz, 'Rethinking Public/Private Divide' in M. Maduro, K. Tuori and S. Sankari, *Transnational Law: Rethinking European Law and Legal Thinking*, Cambridge University Press, Cambridge 2014, pp. 271–306.

[40] Why 'normative' and not 'legal'? For, as will be shown shortly, this concept can be used to study many more types of normative systems than just law.

to exercise. They need the legislature and courts (police) to do that, respectively. And both legislature and courts remain in a vertical relation towards the parties to a horizontal relation, which is the reason why procedural law, even civil procedural law, has traditionally been classified as public law.[41]

Normative (in)equality should be distinguished from factual (in)equality. Arguably, the classic legal scholarship[42] of the beginnings of the nineteenth century would take a position according to which normative equality is sufficient to achieve the factual one. In other words, one assumed the other. However, as history soon showed, this is not the case. The reactions to factual inequality occurring within legally horizontal relations were the two major 'corrections' of private law: labour law and consumer law.

The parties would be factually unequal, if due to any extra-legal reasons one of them has a higher chance of influencing the content of the relation (content, not the rules governing it) that is being established between them. Labour law and consumer law know of numerous examples: necessity caused by the life situation of the worker may lead him or her to accept low wages and poor working conditions; information asymmetry, imbalance in bargaining power and a weaker economic position may lead consumers to accept contracts placing them in a clearly disadvantageous position. Hence the need for limitations on the freedom of contract, *ius cogens* norms, pre-contractual information duties, more rights for workers and consumers, work conditions safety and product safety law, etc. The idea, in short, was that modifying legal equality, by essentially creating legal inequality where the factually weaker party is legally stronger, would lead to overall equality of the relations.

Before moving back to the internet platforms, the above-mentioned remark that this tool can be used to analyse many more types of relations than just legal ones, should be elaborated. Consider an example from sport. In a professional football game, players remain in a horizontal 'game-rules' relation towards one another (none of them can change them or enforce them), while they remain in a vertical 'game-rules' relation towards the referee, who can decide on fouls, yellow and red cards, penalties etc. Similarly, in religious situations, if one person lies to another, he or she commits a sin in a horizontal relation towards that person, while he or she remains in a vertical relation towards the priest who can absolve

---

41 Note that according to this view, the law that governs (establishes and gives substance to) horizontal (private) relations is the private law, while the law that governs vertical (public) relations is the public law. Not the other way round, as would be tempting to claim. In consequence, a relation is not private because it is regulated by private law, but rather because the relation gets established as a private one, the law that regulates it is private law. Personally, the author of this chapter has not ever encountered a good argument against this distinction. However, this problem in itself is not a subject of this chapter.

42 Understood as in: D. Kennedy, 'Three globalizations of law and legal thought: 1850–2000' in D.M. Trubek (ed.), *The new law and economic development: a critical appraisal*, Cambridge University Press, Cambridge 2006, pp. 19, 73.

him or her from that sin. Students remain in horizontal 'school-rules' relations towards one another, while they remain in a vertical relation towards the teacher or a principal. However, all these are examples of normative (in)equality, where there is no need to use force.

Should one look through these lenses at the phenomenon of internet platforms, one would see two issues, an easy one and a complicated one. Easy is the contract law situation. A starting point it is the legal equality between the persons, the platform owner and the platform user. However, since platform owners are entrepreneurs, have much better information, and in case of Google, YouTube, Facebook and Twitter occupy an almost-monopolistic position, should they wish to conclude contracts with their users, they would be bound by consumer law (obviously, only if the user is a consumer). Hence, the legal position is corrected in order to balance the factual inequality. As was shown above, however, these platforms do not conclude contracts with consumers that often.

A much more complicated issue is what Google, YouTube, Facebook and Twitter do outside of the realm of contract law, and within the realm of the code, where vertical and horizontal 'digital' relations occur. To physically remove someone from one's land, one needs to use force, which power is limited to public bodies. Hence, one needs a party with vertical position to execute the right. In case of internet platforms, platform owners can 'remove' users by simply deleting an account. 'Can' signifies here the factual position (since they control the code) and legal position (since no law forbids them from doing so, and they are still 'private' parties). Digital relations cannot easily be labelled normative or factual, due to very peculiar characteristics of the code itself. It is time to take a closer look at it.

4.2. CODE IS LAW AND ENVIRONMENT – THE BLURRING LINE BETWEEN VERTICALITY AND HORIZONTALITY

The 'discovery' of the code for legal academia, i.e. the description and the conceptualisation of the phenomenon in question, should be attributed to Lawrence Lessig, who distinguished four 'modalities of regulation': law, social norms, market and 'architecture', whereas the code belongs to the last modality.[43] Lessig's argument, in short, was that each of these modalities regulates individuals' behaviour, but also that each of these modalities can be used to regulate another modality. Particularly, law can regulate the behaviour of individuals directly, or indirectly through influencing social norms, or

43 L. Lessig, above n. 1.

markets, or the code. The concept has been further elaborated by other scholars, particularly by Roger Brownsword, who in his remarkable work brought the concept into the discourse of private law, as well as highlighting the moral and democratic considerations that should be given to the code, and more generally, technology, as a part of what he calls 'regulatory environment', especially given the move from prescription to (im)possibility as a mode of regulation.[44]

It is not the aim of the author of this piece to summarise the work of these great scholars – the originals serve the purpose better – but rather to make a little contribution to the legal scholarship concerned with the code. It is, on one hand, suggested that legal scholars might benefit from studying code not only as a mode of regulating the behaviour of individuals, but also as a phenomenon shaping the substance of socio-economic relations (which might be vertical or horizontal), and on the other hand it is highlighted that the code is not only a part of the regulatory environment, but also itself forms subjects (software agents) and objects (digital content) to be regulated.

To best understand what is the significance of the emergence of the code for law and legal thought, one should first see what was the conception of the reality assumed by private law before the phenomenon of digitalisation[45] occurred. In short, human beings would get into relations with one another, relations concerning objects (material, made up of atoms; and immaterial, social constructions), and these relations were regulated by the laws of nature (physics, chemistry and biology) as well as social norms (legal, moral and many other types). So there is one layer of 'brute facts',[46] describable by natural sciences: human beings as biological systems, different types of entities made up of matter, and the laws of nature. Then, there is a second layer, of social facts, where human beings would be given statuses (natural person, a corporate body, a judge), create socially constructed entities (rights, money, a company) and regulate their own behaviour through social normative systems (most significantly, but not only, the law).

If one compares the laws of nature to social norms (including law) one will see two differences. Firstly, laws of nature are human-independent.

---

44 See in particular: R. Brownsword, 'Whither the Law and the Law Books? From Prescription to Possibility' (2012) 39 *JL&S (Journal of Law and Society)* 296, 308; R. Brownsword, 'The shaping of our on-line worlds: getting the regulatory environment right' (2012) 20 *IJLIT (International Journal of Law and Information Technology)* 249, 272; R. Brownsword, 'In the year 2061: from law to technological management' (2015) 7 *LIT (Law, Innovation and Technology)* 1–51; R. Brownsword, 'Technological management and the Rule of Law' (2016) 8 *LIT* 100, 140.

45 Digitalisation is understood broadly here, as a social and technological phenomenon, caused by rapid development and widespread of information technologies, including personal computers and smart devices, and connecting of these devices through the global internet network, a phenomenon that occurred throughout last two decades.

46 As in: J.R. Searle, *The Construction of Social Reality*, Allen Lane, London 1995, pp. 1–30.

Humans cannot create them; humans cannot change them. They are necessary properties of the world that humans inhabit. Humans might master them, discover them, learn how to use them, but that is all. Social norms, on the other hand, are fully human-made. They are contingent and human-independent. They can be whatever humanity decides them to be.[47] They can be changed.

Secondly, the laws of nature not only cannot be changed, but they also cannot be broken. Social norms, on the contrary, can. Social norms, including law, result in prescription. They state what one *should* do. But they do not make it impossible to undertake an action.[48] One could risk a statement that the reason humans enact laws is because there are some realisations of the physical possibilities that they collectively find undesirable, and so prohibit them or at least regulate them. There are tort rules precisely because it is physically possible for someone to hurt someone else; there are ownership rules because it is possible to take a thing from someone else etc. The positive laws are supposed to inform relations between humans, but they can be broken.

In short, the laws of nature are human-independent and necessary, and result in the possibility/impossibility of an action; social laws are fully man made and contingent (designable), and result in the prescription/prohibition of action, though they do not make an action physically impossible. The code is a mix of these two: it is human-made and contingent (it does not have to be the way it is), though it results in possibility/impossibility of a certain action.

An example well-known to scholars is reading books. Imagine that a library has only one copy of a book one wants to read. However, someone else has checked it out and is reading it right now. It is physically impossible to 'double' the book, so that both persons can read it on the same time. What is possible is for one to borrow the book for half an hour and copy it using the copying machine. Now, whether it is allowed to copy the entire book is a result of the content of the copyright law in the given country (let us, for the sake of simplicity, assume that the law says that it is allowed to copy just one chapter of a book). That is a human-made rule, paired with some sanction, though one is free to break it.

Now, assume that a library purchased access to an online-library, containing that book as an e-book. Currently, numerous people can read it at the same time, but only when connected to the internet, and only on the premises of the library. If one wants to, one can download one chapter of that book to print it. If one goes to a conference and would like to take that book along, one cannot access

47 This is not a positivistic view aimed at criticising natural law legal philosophy. On the contrary, even if one believes there are objective moral standards, as the author of this piece does, and that the law that does not meet the minimum requirements does not deserve to be called law, or even simply is not law, one should note that such 'legal' norms have been enacted and enforced throughout the history. Ergo, it is possible, even if morally wrong.

48 R. Brownsword, 'Whither ...' above n. 44.

the book online from outside of the library, and cannot download and print the whole thing, only one chapter. It is not that this is merely not allowed, it is physically impossible. But it is not impossible out of necessity, it is impossible because someone had designed it this way. It could just as well be designed differently. It could be possible to access the book from wherever (after e.g. providing a password), it could be possible to download the whole book; it was just a decision of the service provider to design it the way it is. And this decision, even if there is a contract, does not need to be written there. It is sufficient that it is incorporated into the code.

This is just one example, but the moment one adopts this perspective, one begins to notice examples basically everywhere in the online platforms. On Facebook: what is displayed on one's timeline, what pages are suggested for one to 'like', the very fact that one can 'like' something or comment on something; all this is just designed this way. On Google: what pops up as a result of a search, what commercials are being displayed, what data Google gathers about its users, none of this is the way it has to be, it is just designed this way. One might dislike it, but one cannot 'infringe it' in the way one could infringe the law or any other social norm.

This might sound trivial, but much more serious examples are not hard to find. Imagine that Google decides not to display a particular type of content (e.g. supporting a particular political party). Or that Twitter decides to block users making some type of claims that are lawful, but inconsistent with the company's policy. Or that YouTube will allow one to upload, but then will not display in search results a particular type of content. Or that Google scans one's emails to know what one is interested in. Or that Facebook scans one's conversations, or keeps one's photos on some server, even after one 'deletes' them. All these actions are not actions that anyone agreed to in any contract for a service, because there is no contract for a service. And so it cannot be regulated by contract law.

At this point one can see what is meant by digital relations. If one person searches another using Google, or comments on someone's video on YouTube, or communicates with someone using Facebook, or argues with someone on Twitter, they remain in horizontal digital relations to each other. What they can do depends on the platform owners, regulating the code. For this reason, platform owners remain in a vertical relation to their users. Additionally, as signalled in the first section, the 'execution' of policies adopted by these companies is not undertaken by human beings, but by artificial intelligence agents, which themselves are 'made of code'.

As a result of all these transformations, the actual ontology of the universe has changed. It is no longer made only of matter 'regulated' by the laws of nature and 'social entities' regulated by social laws. It is now also made of digital entities, and also regulated by the code. However, the freedom that platform owners enjoy while designing the code is hardly limited.

Apart from the freedom in design of the code, which to a certain extent resembles the 'normative' verticality in which they stand towards their users, platform owners can also 'execute' the code, by for example deleting one's account or blocking access to someone, which resembles rather the 'factual' verticality. Since removing someone from the platform does not require a use of 'physical' force, but of 'digital' force, and the latter is not monopolised by the state, platform owners find themselves in a position that in many ways shares the features that traditionally would be attributed to public power.[49]

5. REGULATING ONLINE PLATFORMS – BEYOND CONTRACT LAW IN CONSUMER PROTECTION

The purpose of this section is to argue that since the dangers for consumers, and for society at large, created by the online platforms owners, result not from potential unfairness of contractual terms or non-conformity with the contracts – since there are often no contracts – but from the unilateral control of the code by the service providers, the potential regulation of online platforms should go not only in the direction of contract law, but primarily towards the regulation of their policies and the control of the code. Firstly, the 'public' concerns, resulting from potential violations of fundamental rights and freedoms are highlighted. Secondly, the potential means of regulating the control of the code are suggested.

5.1. ONLINE PLATFROMS AS PUBLIC PRIVATE SPACES

In the first section it was suggested to look at online platforms as proprietary spaces. Should one think about it, almost all these 'spaces' are privately owned. Yet, very often they serve a 'public' function.[50] Facebook, Twitter and YouTube are spaces of public discourse, with the classic examples of the Arab Spring and current political campaigns.[51] They are forums where people discuss, and sources of information about the world. Similarly, Google, whether one likes it or not, has become a major source of information for a large part of society.

If one broadens the perspective for a while, and thinks of internet platforms not as property, but as mini quasi-jurisdictions, one will see a parallel between the human rights movement that occurred in the nineteenth and twentieth centuries,

---

49 For an elaboration of this statement, including more recent examples, see: https://przemyslaw.technology/2016/11/03/facebooks-exercise-of-public-power/.

50 An interesting treatment of the phenomenon, from the constitutional law perspective, is G. Teubner, *Constitutional fragments: societal constitutionalism and globalization*, Oxford University Press, Oxford 2012.

51 D. Trottier and C. Fuchs, above n. 7.

aimed at securing the freedom of speech and association from the intervention of the state, and the current power held by the online platform owners, who also happen to be multinational corporations. As was demonstrated in the first section of the chapter, platform owners not only police actions that are contrary to valid law (like users making threats), but also many actions that arguably would be legal in public spaces. For example, the limitation of free speech or a right to information that goes beyond what was agreed as a result of public political deliberation might be undesirable. The line is not clear. If YouTube or Facebook decide not to allow display of any nudity at their platforms, even for artistic reasons, this might feel legitimate, proportional. However, if they decide not to display some types of political content, this choice might be questionable. Note that even the vocabulary just used: 'legitimate' and 'proportional' echoes the public law way of thinking.

Such policies might be made explicit in the rules (those separate documents referred to by terms of service) and easy to detect, but they might just as well be 'hidden' in the code. This problem will be addressed in the subsection below.

In short, one could argue that some sort of 'proportionality test' for the policies of online platforms is needed. They could be allowed to prohibit more than is prohibited in the public space, but only as long as this does not interfere with the nature of liberties being exercised on these platforms. This is, ultimately, a constitutional law question.[52]

As a result, the question of blocking users from access and deleting their accounts emerges. Currently, online platform owners can do so at their discretion, as an exercise of their property right. However, this property right should not be unlimited. Just as much as there are good reasons to do so (e.g. to prevent hacking, spamming, violating laws), the discretion should be controllable by the same test as signalled above.

5.2. LIMITING THE UNILATERAL CONTROL OF THE CODE

The previous subsection's analysis could be compared to substantive law, while this subsection is concerned with the digital equivalent of procedural law. Just as public bodies are limited not only in their enacting of substantive law, but also in the way they use their monopolised physical force, regulation of internet platforms should concentrate as well on the exercise of the 'digital force'. In other words, if one tried to distinguish normative and factual verticality and horizontality in the control of the code, the previous subsection would be concerned with the former, while this would be concerned with the latter.

---

52 G. Teubner, above n. 50.

The major difficulty here results from the fact that the code is 'hidden'. One can study the 'behaviour', but one cannot study the reasons of it. However, regulation on both levels is possible.

One could argue that it is sufficient to monitor the results of the code's functioning. As long as there are no complaints, as long as everyone seems to be content, there is no reason to control how exactly the 'digital force' is used. However, this is based on the assumption that such complaints would be made in the times when the public would generally perceive them as desirable. Another possibility is to actually ask for the disclosure of the source code. This results in numerous problems, ranging from the fact that the code is proprietary (which still could be taken care of by administrative control being obliged to keep it secret), to a much more fundamental problem, that is: the amount of code is enormous, and it is not that easily understandable for humans. Third possibility is to regulate the design of the code *ex ante*, either by creating some standards in the most vulnerable spheres, or by requiring some normative components to be built into the software.

However, this is when the legal analysis reaches its limits and help from political science on one hand, and information technology on the other, are necessary. The first step is to realise that there are new types of dangers, and to understand from the general nature of these dangers a potential way of addressing them. To begin this process was the ambition of this piece. How exactly to solve this problem, is a question for a separate inquiry.

6. CONCLUSIONS

Online platforms might be a relatively recent development, but in one form or another, they are here to stay. The difficulties signalled above will not disappear. They require a careful legal response, based on a good understanding of the phenomenon in question. And it was to slightly improve this understanding that this chapter aimed at.

It has been demonstrated that terms of service of Google, YouTube, Facebook and Twitter are not contracts for service, and that it is possible to argue that they are not contracts at all. Not all terms of service of internet platforms are non-contracts, one can find counter examples; but these platforms show that a contractual relationship between a platform owner and a platform user is not the only possible option. More importantly, even if they were treated as contracts, what could be achieved by amending the existing laws, the most fundamental problems would remain unsolved. These problems result from the fact that the owners of platforms under study do not offer any descriptions and make no promises about these platforms, and so there is nothing they can possibly conform or not conform with. What they do, however, is to treat these platforms as their property, what they can do not only *de lege*, but also *de facto*, given their unilateral control of the code and the lack of regulation of the usage of the 'digital force'.

How exactly such a regulation could look like is a question beyond the limits of simply legal analysis. This chapter started with a plea for adopting critical perspective on the analytical framework one uses in order to interpret the reality; and it hereby finishes with a plea for more interdisciplinary dialogue between legal scholars, political scientists and engineers. As stated above, the code is fully designable. One can make it what one wants. However, understanding should always come first. And now it lies on the intersection of several disciplines.

PART III

DIGITAL FORMATION OF CONTRACT – MORE VIRTUAL AND MORE FORMALISED

THE E-COMMERCE DIRECTIVE, CONSUMER TRANSACTIONS, AND THE DIGITAL SINGLE MARKET – QUESTIONS OF REGULATORY FITNESS, REGULATORY DISCONNECTION AND RULE REDIRECTION

Roger BROWNSWORD

ABSTRACT

This chapter poses two principal questions. First, even if, at the time of its enactment, Directive 2000/31/EC (the E-Commerce Directive) was right to treat off-line and on-line transactions as functionally, contextually, and normatively equivalent, does that continue to be the appropriate regulatory view? Secondly, how should regulators view the distinction between on the one hand transactions that are made (off-line or on-line) between business suppliers and consumer contractors and on the other, automated transactions for the supply of goods or services to consumers?

Responding to the first of these questions, it is suggested that there are reasons for thinking that the context for on-line transactions is materially different from that for off-line transactions, as a result of which the balance of contracting power and influence in on-line transactional environments has changed, to the detriment of consumers. Accordingly, for the sake of consumer protection, the time is right to review the prevailing regulatory view.

Responding to the second question, it is suggested that where transactions for routine consumption of goods and services are fully automated, consumer *contractors* seem to be reduced to *mere consumers*. Arguably, this represents a radically new context for consumption that invites a bespoke regulatory response. Moreover, to the extent that consumer transactions are technologically mediated or managed, this implies that the guidance provided by rules will not be directed at those who supply consumer goods or services or at those who consume such goods and services so much as at those who design and supply the systems that manage those transactions.

1. INTRODUCTION

Twenty years ago, when UNCITRAL published its Model Law on Electronic Commerce,[1] there was felt to be an urgent need to set out 'internationally acceptable rules aimed at removing legal obstacles and increasing legal predictability for electronic commerce.'[2] In particular, it was thought to be important to provide 'equal treatment to paper-based and electronic information'.[3] In Europe, too, this sense of urgency and importance was shared. If small businesses in Europe were to take advantage of the opportunity afforded by emerging Information and Communication Technologies to access new markets, and if consumers were to be sufficiently confident to order goods and services on-line, it needed to be absolutely clear that e-transactions (no less than 'traditional' contracts) were recognised as legally valid and enforceable.[4] Accordingly, at the time of the enactment of Directive 2000/31/EC (the E-Commerce Directive), the regulatory priority was to remove any uncertainty about the legal status of 'on-line' transactions, Article 9(1) of the Directive duly requiring Member States to ensure that, in effect, their national legal frameworks for 'off-line' transactions (paradigmatically, for the supply of goods and services) apply also to e-transactions.[5]

---

1 Available at: http://www.uncitral.org/uncitral/en/uncitral_texts/electronic_commerce/1996Model.html (last accessed 3 May 2016).

2 Ibid. (expressing the purpose of the Model Law).

3 Ibid.

4 R. Brownsword and G. Howells, 'When Surfers Start to Shop: Internet Commerce and Contract Law' (1999) 19 *Legal Studies* 287.

5 It was in this context that the idea crystallised that regulators should act on the principle that 'what holds off-line, must hold on-line': see B.-J. Koops, M. Lips, C. Prins, and M. Schellekens (eds.), *Starting Points for ICT Regulation – Deconstructing Prevalent Policy One-Liners*, T.C.M. Asser, The Hague 2006.

Today, in Europe, against the background of the Digital Single Market Strategy,[6] there is a renewed sense of urgency. If the participation (especially, the cross-border participation) of small businesses and consumers in e-commerce is to increase and, with that, if the European economy is to grow, further legal action is required: there are obstacles to be removed and legal predictability needs to be improved. As the Commission puts it, if the potential of e-commerce is to be 'unleashed', there is a '*need to act now on the digital dimension*.'[7] Elaborating on this imperative, the Commission states:

> The pace of commercial and technological change due to digitalisation is very fast, not only in the EU, but worldwide. The EU needs to act now to ensure that business standards and consumer rights will be set according to common EU rules respecting a high-level of consumer protection and providing for a modern business friendly environment. It is of utmost necessity to create the framework allowing the benefits of digitalisation to materialise, so that EU businesses can become more competitive and consumers can have trust in high-level EU consumer protection standards. By acting now, the EU will set the policy trend and the standards according to which this important part of digitalisation will happen.[8]

It is in this setting that the Commission has proposed two new Directives – one on contracts for the supply of digital content,[9] the other on on-line and distance sale of goods contracts[10] – which, together with a proposed Regulation on the cross-border portability of on-line content services, mark the first new legislative initiatives under the Digital Single Market Strategy.[11]

As the Commission recognises – notably, by bringing forward the proposed Directive on contracts for the supply of on-line digital content (including not only video, audio, and games, but also digital content for upcoming 3D printing applications)[12] – there are some glaring gaps in the current

---

6 European Commission, Communication from the Commission to the European Parliament, the Council, the European Economic and Social Committee and the Committee of the Regions, 'A Digital Single Market Strategy for Europe' COM(2015) 192 final (Brussels, 06.05.2015).

7 European Commission, Communication from the Commission to the European Parliament, the Council and the European Economic and Social Committee, 'Digital contracts for Europe – Unleashing the potential of e-commerce' COM(2015) 633 final (Brussels, 09.12.2015), 7.

8 European Commission, above n. 7, 7.

9 European Commission, Proposal for a Directive of the European Parliament and of the Council on certain aspects concerning contracts for the supply of digital content, COM(2015) 634 final (Brussels, 09.12.2015).

10 European Commission, Proposal for a Directive of the European Parliament and of the Council on certain aspects concerning contracts for the online and other distance sales of goods, COM(2015) 635 final (Brussels, 09.12.2015).

11 European Commission, above n. 7, 3.

12 Proposal for a Directive, above n. 9.

legislative framework for e-commerce in Europe, much of which pre-dates even the earliest on-line consumer transactions, let alone e-commerce as it has now developed.[13] The focus of this chapter, however, is not on the self-evident shortcomings of the legislative framework but on the assumptions that underlie it. In particular, it is about the appropriateness of those assumptions in a context that the Commission rightly characterises as one of rapid technological and commercial change – a context that, so far as consumers are concerned, includes not only changes in the way that goods and services are purchased but also changes in the products themselves as devices become smarter by virtue of being digitally enabled.

To state the obvious, in those legislative instruments that pre-date the development of e-commerce, there was no reason or need to consider whether (then non-existent) on-line environments were comparable to off-line environments for consumer transactions. However, by the time of the E-Commerce Directive, this had become one of the central regulatory questions. In some respects, notably in relation to the potential liability of Internet Service Providers for the transmission, caching, and hosting of information,[14] the Directive recognises that on-line environments are different and that some adjustment of off-line law is required. However, so far as contracts are concerned, the Directive reflects an approach that David Post describes as that of the 'unexceptionalists',[15] this being the view that on-line transactions require no special regulatory treatment (other than to confirm their legal enforceability in principle).

The Directive's unexceptionalist view of contracts is underpinned by three key assumptions. First, it is assumed that on-line contracts are *functionally* equivalent to off-line contracts – for example, the sale of a book at Amazon

---

13 As is well-known, the so-called legislative framework for e-commerce is not found in one comprehensive Directive; and the E-Commerce Directive itself is but one element in a group of legal instruments that have been pressed into regulatory service as e-commerce has developed. This group currently comprises: Directive 2011/83/EU on consumer rights (amending earlier Directives and regulating, in particular, consumers' information rights and the right of termination at will (cooling-off period)); Directive 1999/44/EC on consumer sales and guarantees (regulating, in particular, the seller's liability for non-conformity of the object sold as well as guarantees); Directive 93/13/EEC on unfair terms in consumer contracts; and Directive 2000/31/EC on e-commerce. See, further, European Parliament, 'Contract law and the Digital Single Market – Towards a new EU online consumer sales law?' (September 2015, PE 568.322).

14 See, Articles 12, 13, and 14 of the Directive. The fact that the Directive treats the Internet as 'exceptional' relative to, say, the law of defamation and copyright but as 'unexceptional' relative to contract law is not necessarily contradictory: compare M.E. Kaminski, 'Robots in the Home: What Will We Have Agreed To?' (2015) 15 *Idaho Law Review* 661, 663; and R. Calo, 'Robotics and the Lessons of Cyberlaw' (2015) 103 *California Law Review* 513, 550–553.

15 D.G. Post, *In Search of Jefferson's Moose*, Oxford University Press, Oxford 2009, 186.

on-line is no different functionally to the sale of a book off-line at a bricks-and-mortar bookshop. Secondly, it is assumed that the *context* for on-line transactions is not materially different from the context for off-line transactions: to the contrary, there is a relevant similarity between off-line and on-line shops. Granted, the architecture of on-line shopping environments is different to the architecture of off-line shopping environments and it affects the options available to consumers – for example, as Eliza Mik remarks, one is rarely 'teleported' into a bricks-and-mortar shop but, in the web world, 'a person browsing recipes can easily [click into] an on-line book shop'.[16] However, it was assumed that the differences would not operate in ways that would be prejudicial to on-line shoppers. Indeed, there was even reason to think that the on-line architecture – at any rate, 'click wrap' assent rather than 'browse wrap' notice – might prove to be more protective of consumers' interests because it would make it possible to encourage consumers to read the supplier's terms and conditions carefully before proceeding with the purchase.[17] Thirdly, building on the first two assumptions, we have the idea of *normative* equivalence, the assumption being that those laws that apply to off-line transactions should also apply to on-line transactions. In Europe, this means that the general law of contract, in conjunction with a special body of regulation for consumer transactions, should be copied across from off-line transactions to on-line transactions. Insofar as the Directive was criticised, it was mainly to regret that, in the final version of Article 11 (dealing with the placing of the customer's 'order'), an opportunity had been missed to clean up some inconsistencies in the general law on the formation of contracts. If anyone thought that on-line transactions might need some special regulatory attention, this was something to be revisited in the uncertain future.

In fact, at the time of the Directive, there were a few speculative thoughts about where we might be going with e-commerce, notably a prescient article by Richard T. Ford in the *Stanford Law Review*.[18] Amongst the developments anticipated by Ford were the profiling of consumer preferences (which, aided by machine learning, gets better and better) and the servicing of one's consumption needs by automated processes, or by something akin to what Ford called a 'cyberbutler'. Imagining such a future, Ford foresaw that a consumer would

---

16 E. Mik, 'The *Un*importance of being "electronic" or – popular misconceptions about "Internet contracting"' (2011) 19 *International Journal of Law and Information Technology* 324, 340.

17 Moreover, with burgeoning *ex post* consumer reviews, one might have expected this information to have some corrective effect on conspicuously unfair terms: see, e.g., S.I. Becher and T.Z. Zarsky, 'E-Contract Doctrine 2.0: Standard Form Contracting in an Age of Online User Participation' (2008) 14 *Michigan Telecommunications and Technology Law Review* 303.

18 R.T. Ford, 'Save the Robots: Cyber Profiling and Your So-Called Life' (2000) 52 *Stanford Law Review* 1572.

sign over their pay cheque to the cyberbutler who would hold it in trust for the consumer's benefit; then, guided by the consumer's profile, the cyberbutler would place appropriate orders so that, each day, the consumer would 'come home to a selection of healthy and nutritious groceries from webvan.com or a Paul Smith shirt from boo.com or the latest Chemical Brothers CD from cdnow.com'.[19] By 2017, the cyberbutler would have changed to different suppliers of groceries, shirts, and CDs (webvan.com and boo.com being spectacular dot.com failures, and a declining cdnow.com being purchased by Amazon); and, while groceries and shirts would still be required, many consumers, rather than buying CDs, would subscribe to streaming services such as Spotify or Apple Music or even revert to vinyls.[20] Nevertheless, Ford's sense of the bigger picture is sound. Moreover, Ford's view chimes in with what, much more recently, Mireille Hildebrandt terms a 'new animism'[21] that characterises a transformative 'onli*fe*' world that is 'situated beyond the increasingly artificial distinction between online and offline.'[22] What the new animism signifies is

> the fact that our life world is increasingly populated with things that are trained to foresee our behaviours and pre-empt our intent. These things are no longer stand-alone devices; they are progressively becoming interconnected via the cloud, which enables them to share their 'experience' of us to improve their functionality We are in fact surrounded by adaptive systems that display a new kind of mindless agency … The environment is thus becoming ever more animated. At the same time we are learning slowly but steadily to foresee that we are being foreseen, accepting that things know our moods, our purchasing habits, our mobility patterns, our political and sexual preferences and our sweet spots. We are on the verge of shifting from using technologies to interacting with them, negotiating their defaults, pre-empting their intent while they do the same to us.[23]

In this onli*fe* world, the consumption of goods and services becomes more personalised, more profiled, more anticipatory and more automated;[24] and, while we can assume that, at some originating point, a human consumer signs up for the service, from that moment on humans play little or no active part in the world of transactions.[25] As with smart technologies generally, the consumer

---

19 R.T. Ford, above n. 18, 1578.

20 See the report for 2015 issued by the International Federation of the Phonographic Industry: available at: http://www.ifpi.org/news/Global-digital-music-revenues-match-physical-format-sales-for-first-time (last accessed 14 April 2016).

21 M. Hildebrandt, *Smart Technologies and the End(s) of Law*, Edward Elgar, Cheltenham 2015, viii.

22 M. Hildebrandt, above n. 21, 8.

23 M. Hildebrandt, above n. 21, viii–ix.

24 Generally, see C. Steiner, *Automate This*, Penguin, New York, 2012.

25 I make no predictions about the precise array of technologies that will be employed to ensure that consumer orders are seamlessly processed and delivered. For one possibility, see J. Dean, 'Roboshop: now drones really deliver the goods', *The Times*, 26 April 2016, p. 1. Similarly,

signs up for a device that comes with a package of services and then 'sets and forgets'.

It follows that the distinction between a mature off-line consumer marketplace and an embryonic on-line marketplace – a distinction that is implicit in but central to the E-Commerce Directive – is not only the precursor to an onl*ife* marketplace that blurs the on-line/off-line distinction but also to a quite different distinction between consumer transactions that are actively negotiated and performed by human agents, and transactions for the supply of consumer goods and services that are processed automatically (by 'mindless' agents) with at best the passive involvement of human agents. Framing e-commerce in this way, two questions arise. First, even if, at the time of its enactment, the E-Commerce Directive was right to treat off-line and on-line transactions as functionally, contextually, and normatively equivalent, does that continue to be the appropriate regulatory view? Or, should some special regulatory allowance be made for what now seem to be material contextual differences between the two transactional environments? Secondly, how should regulators view the distinction between transactions that are made (off-line or on-line) between business suppliers and consumer contractors, and automated transactions for the supply of goods or services to consumers? Should regulators treat this distinction as immaterial and regard anticipatory and automated transactions as equivalent to non-automated transactions? What is the significance of the onl*ife* world for transactions? If, instead of regulating the consumer marketplace by specifying the transactional ground rules for sellers and purchasers, the technological management of transactions takes the regulatory strain, what should we make of this?[26] Rather than asking whether the E-Commerce Directive (or the regulatory environment of which the Directive is a part) needs some modification, should we be asking whether the assumptions that the Directive made about how to regulate the routine consumption of goods and services need to be fundamentally reconsidered?

There are too many questions here for me to answer – and, anyway, I am not sure that I can answer all of them. Some of these questions ask whether the E-Commerce Directive, or the Directive in conjunction with other laws, is

---

I take a technology-neutral view of how payment of the price will be automated. However, for an example of a smart contract, employing GPS tracking of a package and payment by Bitcoins, that covers both the risk of non-delivery and non-payment, see R.H. Weber, 'Contractual Duties and Allocation of Liability in Automated Digital Contracts' in R. Schulze and D. Staudenmayer (eds.), *Digital Revolution: Challenges for Contract Law in Practice*, Nomos, Baden-Baden 2016, 163, at 180. Generally, on 'smart contracts' see D. Tapscott and A. Tapscott, *Blockchain Revolution*, Portfolio Penguin, London 2016, 101–103; and, for an excellent discussion, see K.E.C. Levy, 'Book-Smart, Not Street-Smart: Blockchain-Based Smart Contracts and The Social Workings of Law' (2017) 3 *Engaging Science, Technology, and Society* 1.

26 See R. Brownsword, 'In the Year 2061: From Law to Technological Management' (2015) 7 *Law, Innovation and Technology* 1.

now 'disconnected' from the technological state of the art, from the purposes for which the technology is applied (for example, to facilitate peer-to-peer transactions), or from the business models and associated assumptions made by the legislators.[27] If so, we should ask whether regulatory re-connection is required; and, if so, how that re-connection is to be best achieved. Other questions concern the displacement of the rules that regulate consumer transactions and prompt thoughts about the redirection of rules towards the technological designs that will structure the automated processes that service consumer needs. Yet other questions concern the future of the Rule of Law itself: to the extent that technological management does the regulatory work, will it be possible to draw on rule-based notions of legality in order to check and correct regulatory use and abuse of power?

Briefly, what I will suggest is the following. First, there are reasons for thinking that there are a number of features of on-line transactional environments that have an impact on the balance of interests (between business suppliers and consumers) that we judge to be 'acceptable' in off-line transactional environments. Arguably, the cumulative effect of these features materially changes the balance of contracting power and influence in on-line transactional environments; and, it does so to the detriment of consumers. This undermines the unexceptionalist claim that the context of on-line transactions is not materially different from the context of off-line transactions; and, once that claim is undermined, the assumption that it suffices simply to apply the off-line law to on-line transactions is thrown into serious doubt. Secondly, when routine consumption needs are served by the equivalents of Ford's cyberbutler, or by cyberchaffeurs in driverless cars, consumer *contractors* seem to be reduced to *mere consumers*. Although there is a sense in which cyberbutlers or cyberchaffeurs act as agents on behalf of their consumer principals, this is a radically new context for consumption that invites a bespoke regulatory response. Thirdly, the extent to which consumer transactions are technologically mediated or managed has important implications for the way in which they are regulated. To the extent that rules are employed to guide the conduct of the regulated, they will not be directed at those who supply consumer goods or services or at those who consume such goods and services so much as at those who design and supply the systems that manage those transactions.[28]

---

27 See R. Brownsword and M. Goodwin, *Law and the Technologies of the Twenty-First Century*, Cambridge University Press, Cambridge 2012 chs. 15–16; and, for critical analysis of disconnection in the case of e-signatures and e-money, see C. Reed, 'The Law of Unintended Consequences – embedded business models in IT regulation' (2007) (2) *The Journal of Information and Technology Law* (*JILT*), part 3.1: http://www2.warwick.ac.uk/fac/soc/law/elj/jilt/. However, see now, Regulation (EU) No. 910/2014 (on electronic identification and trust services for electronic transactions in the internal market).

28 Compare, R. Brownsword, 'Technological Management and the Rule of Law' (2016) 8 *Law, Innovation and Technology* 100.

The chapter is in four principal parts. First, starting on relatively familiar ground, I consider whether the regulation of unfair terms in business-to-consumer e-transactions is fit for purpose. Secondly, I ask whether consumers need to be protected against the profiling, personalising, and nudging techniques employed by on-line suppliers; and, if so, how that protection might be implemented. Thirdly, I consider whether the automated processing of transactions is a cause for concern and, if so, whether revising the E-Commerce Directive is the appropriate response. Finally, in the light of the foregoing, I comment briefly on the relevance of the Commission's recently announced two proposed Directives (on digital content and on-line sale of goods).[29] Once again, these Directives raise questions about the appropriateness of their underpinning assumptions – not least, the assumption that, digitally-enabled smart devices notwithstanding, the supply of digital content can be cleanly separated from on-line sale of goods. However, so far as the cornerstone assumption of unexceptionalism is concerned, the Directives suggest a change of direction: the Commission's current thinking is not so much that the regulation of on-line transactions needs special treatment because consumers are especially vulnerable in these environments but because this is required by the digital economic strategy. To this extent, it is the legislative framework for e-commerce, rather than the general law of contract, that shapes the regulatory environment for transactions.

2. UNFAIR CONTRACT TERMS

The E-Commerce Directive says nothing about unfair terms in on-line consumer contracts. However, protective measures relating to off-line transactions apply; and, if a term will pass muster in an off-line contract, the implication is that it will also be treated as 'not unfair' in an on-line contract. Yet, even if the off-line tests are fit for purpose, is it right to apply the same tests to on-line transactions? Are there not material differences between off-line and on-line contracting environments?

Let us start by noting a couple of almost too-obvious-to-record, yet highly significant and distinctive, features of on-line contracting. First, there is the striking fact, noted by Mark Lemley, that consumers who make their purchases

[29] European Commission, Proposal for a Directive of the European Parliament and of the Council on certain aspects concerning contracts for the supply of digital content, COM(2015) 634 final (Brussels, 09.12.2015); and European Commission, Proposal for a Directive of the European Parliament and of the Council on certain aspects concerning contracts for the online and other distance sales of goods, COM(2015) 635 final (Brussels, 09.12.2015).

in off-line stores are rarely required to sign up to the suppliers' terms and conditions in the way that is characteristic of on-line shopping.[30] Thus,

> Merchants and consumers at grocery stores, restaurants, bookstores, clothing stores, and countless other retail outlets seem perfectly able to enter into contracts without a written agreement specifying their rights and obligations. Nonetheless, many of those same retail outlets impose standard form contracts on their online users, probably because it is easier to get someone to click 'I agree' as part of an online transaction than it is to have a clerk obtain a signature on a written form.[31]

Secondly, on-line transactions are technologically mediated in a way that is quite different to the paradigmatic off-line transaction. Consumers are, so to speak, technologically 'mediated consumers', approaching 'the marketplace through technology designed by someone else'[32] – note, first the technological mediation and, secondly, the fact that it is not designed by the consumer. As Ryan Calo memorably puts it, in these environments, an offer is 'always an algorithm away'.[33] If, in these new transactional settings, on-line suppliers are opportunistically loading their standard forms to the detriment of consumers in a way that does not happen in off-line contracting, this immediately raises questions not only about the equivalence of off-line and on-line contracts but also about whether on-line suppliers are taking unfair advantage of the on-line environments in which they can now sell to consumers.

Although some commentators believe that the off-line controls are perfectly adequate to regulate on-line business practice,[34] and although a survey of the websites of 500 leading Internet retailers has suggested that on-line sellers are not actually taking advantage of consumers and that 'the contract terms and contracting interfaces of internet retailers are surprisingly benign',[35] the view persists that on-line suppliers are taking advantage of consumers; that, as a result, consumers are exposed to new vulnerabilities and new kinds of unfairness; and that a new approach is called for.

According to Nancy Kim, for example, efforts to create a 'smooth website experience' for consumers militate against consumers reading terms; and this is compounded by companies who take advantage of consumer behaviour by including 'ever more aggressive and oppressive terms.'[36] Kim argues that

---

30 M.A. Lemley, 'Terms of Use' (2006) 91 *Minnesota Law Review* 459.

31 M.A. Lemley, above n. 30, 466.

32 R. Calo, 'Digital Market Manipulation' (2014) 82 *George Washington Law Review* 995, 1002.

33 R. Calo, above n. 32, 1004.

34 See, e.g., R.A. Hillman and J.J. Rachlinski, 'Standard-Form Contracts in the Electronic Age' (2002) 77 *New York University Law Review* 429.

35 R.J. Mann and T. Siebneicher, 'Just One Click: The Reality of Internet Retail Contracting' (2008) 108 *Columbia Law Review* 984, 1000.

36 N.S. Kim, 'Situational Duress and the Aberrance of Electronic Contracts' (2014) 89 *Chicago-Kent Law Review* 265, 265–266.

the courts should respond, inter alia, by reinvigorating 'reasonable notice' requirements in a way that encourages the design of on-line environments that force consumers to slow down, and that employs both visual (e.g. traffic light) and sensory signals to aid consumer navigation of sites.[37] While there has been a tendency to assimilate e-contracts to paper contracts, Kim emphasises that the focus should be on their differences rather than their similarities.[38] In a similar vein, Stephen Waddams has argued that on-line environments tend to exacerbate familiar off-line problems with standard forms and unfair terms in consumer contracts – for example, the presentation of electronic documents makes it difficult to evaluate the terms and conditions; and, anyway, users know that the terms are not negotiable; all of which means that, in practice, it is relatively easy for businesses to include burdensome terms.[39] However, in Europe, consumers have the protection of Directive 93/13/EEC as well as the protection subsequently afforded by Directive 2011/83/EC on Consumer Rights.[40] Should we assume, therefore, that no further action is required?

To a considerable extent, the fitness for purpose of the Directive on unfair terms in consumer contracts hinges on the guidance given by the CJEU and then the implementation of that guidance by Member States. In the leading case of *Aziz*,[41] both Advocate General Kokott and the First Chamber of the Court emphasise that the test of unfairness (in Article 3.1 of the Directive) is very general in nature and leaves much to the national courts who are in a position to provide the context and particular circumstances for the test's application. What *Aziz* suggests is that national courts might apply the test in two stages. First, there is the question of whether the term at issue causes a significant imbalance

---

37 N.S. Kim, 'The Duty to Draft Reasonably and Online Contracts' in L.A. DiMatteo et al. (eds.), *Commercial Contract Law: Transatlantic Perspectives*, Cambridge University Press, Cambridge 2012, 181, 190–200. She also suggests, in Kim, above n. 36, a limited extension of duress – 'situational duress' as she calls it – to regulate those practices where consumers are given no reasonable alternative other than to agree to certain terms and conditions. The use of such design features is important not only for the incorporation of terms but also for the formation of contracts: see E. Macdonald, 'When is a Contract Formed by the Browse-Wrap Process?' (2011) 19 *International Journal of Law and Information Technology* 285.

38 N.S. Kim, above n. 36, 286.

39 S. Waddams, 'Contract Law and the Challenges of Computer Technology' in R. Brownsword, E. Scotford and K. Yeung (eds.), *The Oxford Handbook of Law, Regulation and Technology*, Oxford University Press, Oxford 2017, Ch. 13. These difficulties are even more pronounced in relation to the terms and conditions that come with smart devices (such as smartphones, cars, homes, fitness monitors, and so on): see S.R. Peppet, 'Regulating the Internet of Things: First Steps Toward Managing Discrimination, Privacy, Security and Consent' (2014) 93 *Texas Law Review* 85, 139–147.

40 For the principal protections of the latter, see 'Consumer Rights: 10 ways the new Consumer Rights Directive will give people stronger rights when they shop online' Memo/11/450 (Brussels, 23 June 2010).

41 Case C-415/11 *Mohamed Aziz v. Caixa d'Estalvis de Catalunya, Tarragona i Manresa (Catalunyacaixa)* CJEU judgment, 14 March 2013, ECLI:EU:C:2013:164; Opinion of Advocate General Kokott, 8 November 2012, ECLI:EU:C:2012:700.

in power, to the detriment of the consumer. This is to be assessed relative to the legal position of the consumer the contractual term apart. Following the Advocate General, the Court says that regard must be had to 'what rules of national law would apply in the absence of an agreement by the parties'.[42] Then,

> [s]uch a comparative analysis will enable the national court to evaluate whether and, as the case may be, to what extent, the contract places the consumer in a legal situation less favourable than that provided for by the national law in force.[43]

If this comparative analysis shows that there is a significant imbalance to the detriment of the consumer, then there is a second question to be asked, namely, whether this is an imbalance that arises contrary to the requirement of good faith. For the purposes of answering this second question, *Aziz* suggests that the national court should assess 'whether the seller or supplier, dealing fairly and equitably with the consumer, could reasonably assume that the consumer would have agreed to such a term in individual contract negotiations.'[44]

These articulations of Article 3.1 in *Aziz* are made by a court that is very sensitive to the imbalance in both bargaining power and information that typically characterises dealings between business suppliers and their consumer customers.[45] It follows that it is for the national courts to employ the Directive in a way that compensates for this imbalance.[46] Nevertheless, in a recent decision, *ParkingEye Limited*,[47] the majority of the UK Supreme Court has seized on a remark made by Advocate General Kokott to weaken the protection of consumers. The context for the Advocate General's remark is that it is not enough that the effect of the term is to treat the consumer less favourably than the background legal position; a significant imbalance to the detriment of the consumer is not the whole test; if the term is to be treated as unfair, there must also be a failure to meet the good faith requirement. At which point, the Advocate General continues:

> Consequently, the principle of contractual freedom is observed and it is recognised that in many cases parties have a legitimate interest in organising their contractual relations in a manner which derogates from the statutory provisions.[48]

---

42 *Aziz*, CJEU judgment, para. 68.
43 Ibid.
44 Para. 69.
45 Paras. 44–45. For a sense of how *Aziz* fits into the broader landscape of justice in European private law, see C. Mak, 'Justice through European Private Law' (inaugural lecture at the University of Amsterdam, 19 February 2016).
46 Para. 46.
47 *Cavendish Square Holding BV v. Talal El Makdessi; ParkingEye Limited v. Beavis* [2015] UKSC 67.
48 *Aziz*, para. 73 of the Advocate General's Opinion (delivered 8 November 2012).

However, these remarks can be read as an invitation to focus less on whether the supplier could reasonably assume that the consumer would have agreed to such a term in individual contract negotiations and more on whether the supplier has a legitimate interest in the term relative to a reasonable business model.

In *ParkingEye*, the question was about the fairness of a particular term at a retail shopping car park. Notices at the car park clearly indicated that parking, although free, was limited to a maximum of two hours, and that parking for more than the permitted time would result in a charge of £85. In the test-case, the motorist left his car parked for 56 minutes more than the permitted time. Six members of the UK Supreme Court, relying on *Aziz*, held that the term was not unfair. One member of the Court disagreed, taking the view that the car park company had not discharged the burden of showing the reasonableness of this term. While the majority highlight the legitimate interest of the company, the one minority judge, Lord Toulson, highlights the viewpoint of the consumer.

The principal majority judgment is given by Lords Neuberger and Sumption, with Lord Carnwath agreeing; Lord Mance writes his own judgment on the point at issue; and Lords Hodge and Clarke agree that the term imposing the £85 charge is not unfair. Against the background of the Advocate General's opinion in *Aziz*, the majority reasoning runs as follows. First, the charge did operate to the detriment of the consumer because, under the ordinary law, the unlicensed parking of the car would have amounted to a trespass, and damages for the trespass (if the landowners had pursued the matter) would have been limited to the occupation value of the space. Secondly, with regard to the question of the parking operators' good faith, the question is not whether the particular motorist 'would in fact have agreed to the term imposing the £85 charge in a negotiation, but whether a reasonable motorist in his position would have done so.'[49] Thirdly, having taken into account the importance to both the freeholders and the lessees of the retail outlets as well as to the shoppers of ensuring that parking space is available (and not clogged up by commuters using the adjacent railway station or by other long-term users), the majority were satisfied that 'a hypothetical reasonable motorist would have agreed to objectively reasonable terms, and these terms are objectively reasonable.'[50] Given that, on this analysis, terms are only objectively reasonable if a hypothetical reasonable motorist would have agreed to them, then this amounts to saying that the terms will not be unfair if a hypothetical reasonable motorist would agree to them. Or, translating the language of *Aziz*, it is for national courts to assess whether the seller or supplier, dealing fairly and equitably with the consumer, could reasonably assume that a hypothetical reasonable consumer would agree to the term.

---

49 *Cavendish Square Holding BV v. Talal El Makdessi; ParkingEye Limited v. Beavis* [2015] UKSC 67, para. 108.

50 Ibid., at para. 109.

If this is the question, then not only the individual consumer but also individual contract negotiation is relegated to the background. Instead, it is the hypothetical reasonable consumer who is promoted to the foreground, prompting the obvious question: relative to whose or which viewpoint is the hypothetical consumer to be judged reasonable or unreasonable in accepting the term at issue? In *ParkingEye*, the critical question for the majority is whether such a hypothetical party would accept that the car park operators' business model is reasonable and, concomitantly, whether this underpins legitimate business interests that suffice to displace any residual reservations about contract or consent. Addressing this question, Lord Mance accepts that the particular motorist would probably have argued for a form of graded payment, rather than the £85 charge, in the event of exceeding the two-hour limit. However,

> [c]onfronted with the other interests involved and the considerations making that [i.e. the graded payment proposal] unacceptable from [the providers'] viewpoint, I am not at all confident that he or she would have refused to accept the risk of having to pay £85 ... in the event of overstaying.[51]

In other words, the car park operators have a legitimate interest in regulating parking in the way that they do; they can reasonably decline to accept counter-proposals from motorists; and they can reasonably suppose that a hypothetical reasonable consumer (understanding the business case for, coupled with the general utility of, the charge) would agree to the term and might even take the risk of using the car park.

Like the majority, Lord Toulson follows the guidelines in *Aziz* but he arrives at a different view. First, in agreement with the majority, Lord Toulson holds that the term imposing the £85 charge 'created a significant imbalance ... because it far exceeded any amount which was otherwise likely to be recoverable as damages for breach of contract or trespass.'[52] Secondly, unlike the majority, Lord Toulson takes Advocate General Kokott to be setting out a protective test of good faith such that the burden is on the supplier to show that it could be fairly assumed 'that the consumer would have agreed [to the term] in individual negotiations on level terms.'[53] For a number of reasons – largely, common sense reasons why, in special circumstances, an £85 charge should not be applied – Lord Toulson declares himself not satisfied that the car park operators had discharged the burden of showing that they could reasonably assume that 'a party who was in a position to bargain individually, and who was advised by a competent lawyer, would have agreed to the [term that imposed the charge]'.[54]

51 Ibid., at para. 209.
52 Ibid., at para. 307.
53 Ibid., at para. 309.
54 Ibid., at para. 314.

Or, to put this more directly, if Lord Toulson himself had been the hypothetical consumer, taking his own viewpoint as the reference point for reasonableness, he would have had more questions for the parking operators before he would have treated the term as acceptable.

What should we make of this? The obvious criticism of Lord Toulson's approach is that, as he concedes, there is a certain 'artificiality' in hypothesising individual negotiation of such terms.[55] The reality is that motorist-shoppers do not individually negotiate the terms and conditions for what, for the vast majority, is two hours free parking at their local supermarket or retail outlet. The idea that consumers have any choice as to the terms on which they use these car parks is absurd; if they want to park their cars, customers have to do so on the terms that are dictated by the car park operators. Parking (for up to two hours) is free; but the terms and conditions are displayed on a take-it-or-leave-it basis. Nevertheless, mindful of the majority's approach, Lord Toulson is anxious to emphasise that the test is whether a supplier would be able to sell the term as reasonable to a *consumer*, not to others who have a stake in the business success of the retail outlet. Moreover, what has to be sold is the reasonableness of a term that, relative to the ordinary legal position, leaves the consumer worse off. Hence, for Lord Toulson, this is why the law requires a supplier who seeks to rely on such a term 'to put itself in the customer's shoes and consider whether it "can reasonably assume that the customer would have agreed" to it.'[56]

Returning to on-line consumer environments, there will be many examples of sites (like the off-line car park) that are free to access (in the sense that no fee has to be paid) but that make entry and use subject to non-negotiable terms and conditions.[57] If a consumer wishes to challenge one of those terms as unfair, *Aziz* suggests a reasonably high-level of protection. However, if national courts, as Lord Toulson puts it, apply *Aziz* in a way that 'waters down the test'[58] – for example, by prioritising a 'not unreasonable' business perspective over a 'not unreasonable' consumer perspective, or even by recalling a notion of 'freedom of contract' that treats consumers as bound by terms of which they have been made aware despite having no freedom to negotiate them – then the application of the off-line rules to on-line environments leaves consumers vulnerable.

Occasionally, even in relation to consumer transactions, we hear echoes of classical contractual thinking. However, so far as unfair terms in consumer contracts are concerned, the governing approach is, and has been for a

---

55 Ibid., at para. 313.

56 Ibid.

57 For discussion of the fairness of 'give data to get service' deals, see N. Helberger, 'Profiling and Targeting Consumers in the Internet of Things – A New Challenge for Consumer Law' in R. Schulze and D. Staudenmayer, above n. 25, 135, 142–151.

58 *Cavendish Square Holding BV v. Talal El Makdessi; ParkingEye Limited v Beavis* [2015] UKSC 67, at para. 315.

considerable time, 'regulatory'.[59] The fairness of terms does not depend upon whether the consumer agreed to them on a free and informed basis, but on their compatibility with the relevant regulatory objectives. In the years before the platforms for e-commerce had been developed, the making of the Single Market in Europe required not just a harmonisation of consumer protection laws but also a sufficiently high level of protection to engender trust and confidence on the part of consumers. With the arrival of e-commerce, it became important to ensure that consumers enjoyed the equivalent level of protection and displayed the same degree of trust and confidence to engage in on-line transactions. The steps taken to achieve this equivalence were minimal. The question raised by the foregoing discussion is whether further regulatory action is required.

Where the design of an on-line environment is akin to a maze or a trap (as with 'browse-wrap' contracts), and where the consumer's principal protection against unfair terms and conditions is a requirement of reasonable notice, it is imperative that this requirement is strictly applied.[60] In Europe, where the provisions of the Directive on unfair terms in consumer contracts are the principal protection, we might think that there is less cause for concern. Nevertheless, there are reasons at least to query the fitness for purpose of the E-Commerce Directive in conjunction with the Directive on unfair terms in consumer contracts. First, the latter Directive predates e-commerce. The question here is whether we are satisfied that the somewhat general (and potentially flexible) test of unfair terms in consumer contracts can be satisfactorily applied to on-line transactions. Secondly, the leading cases on the test, such as *Aziz*, concern off-line transactions. The question is whether it is appropriate to apply off-line jurisprudence to on-line transactions – particularly where, as in *ParkingEye*, we find a court arguably rebalancing the interests of businesses and consumers in favour of the former. Thirdly, the E-Commerce Directive assumes an equivalence between off-line and on-line transactions: normatively, the same rules should apply; and, functionally, a deal is a deal, a purchase is a purchase, whether made off-line or on-line. If these assumptions are sound, this should assuage the first two concerns. However, if as some commentators suggest, the features of on-line environments for consumer transactions stack up to make them cumulatively different from off-line environments, and if as a consequence some de facto power is returned to suppliers, then there might be new vulnerabilities for consumers of just the kind that, in the first place, prompted the Directive on unfair terms in consumer contracts. If so, then consideration needs to be given

---

59 See, R. Brownsword, 'Regulating Transactions: Good Faith and Fair Dealing' in G. Howells and R. Schulze (eds.), *Modernising and Harmonising Consumer Contract Law*, Sellier, Munich 2009, 87.

60 Compare, e.g., M. Lemley, above n. 30. N.S. Kim, above n. 36 and 37.

to whether there should be a more intense scrutiny of those terms in on-line consumer transactions that are alleged to be unfair.[61]

Summing up, there are several questions, both of principle and of an empirical nature, threaded together in these remarks about potentially unfair terms in on-line consumer contracts. Perhaps the first question is whether there is evidence of significant use of unfair terms in on-line consumer transactions – that is to say, terms that either would not appear in equivalent off-line consumer contracts or that would not be used in any off-line contracts.[62] If so, the next question is whether consumers can be plausibly said, at best, to be consenting to these terms or, at least, to be proceeding with reasonable notice of such terms. If not, the question then is whether the Directive on unfair terms in consumer contracts is fit to correct such unfairness. If not, the question is what kind of further protective law is required.

3. PROFILING AND PERSONALISATION

Richard Ford imagines an on-line environment in which my data is used by suppliers and others to develop a profile of the-consumer-that-is-me to the point that they 'will suggest books I'll enjoy reading, recordings I'll like to listen to, restaurants I'll be glad I tried, even if I wouldn't have chosen any of them on my own.'[63] While some of these suggestions will coincide with my likes, others will not. However, the more that my preferences are revealed and used to refine the profile, the more that I will like them and the more reliant on them I will become. Before too long, there is little or no distance between me and my profile and the profilers seem to know me better than I know myself.

---

61 Some support for the view that the CJEU already has sufficient legal resources to protect on-line consumers against unfair contract terms might be derived from the recent decision of the Third Chamber of the Court in Case C-191/15, *Verein für Konsumenteninformation v. Amazon EU Sàrl*, judgment of 28 July 2016, ECLI:EU:C:2016:612. There, the Court held that, while there is no rule against Amazon or other on-line suppliers putting choice of law clauses in their standard terms and conditions, such a term will be unfair 'in so far as it leads the consumer into error by giving him the impression that only [the chosen law] applies to the contract, without informing him that under Article 6(2) of the Rome I Regulation he also enjoys the protection of the mandatory provisions of the law that would be applicable in the absence of that term …' (para. 71).

62 Compare, too, European Commission, Communication from the Commission to the European Parliament, the Council, the European Economic and Social Committee and the Committee of the Regions, 'Online Platforms and the Digital Single Market: Opportunities and Challenges for Europe' COM(2016) 288/2, Brussels, 25 May 2016, at 12–13, where the Commission recognises that there needs to be further investigation into whether, in B2B relations, on-line platforms are imposing unfair terms and conditions on SMEs and micro-enterprises.

63 R.T. Ford (n. 18), 1576.

Yet, if on-line suppliers know me better than I know myself, how far does this depart from the world of off-line consumption? Possibly, there will be some marketplaces in which traders really do know their customers but, in many off-line environments, each consumer is simply another number to add to the footfall. Where the latter is the case, does this give rise to regulatory concern with regard to the balance of power, to the transparency of the dealing, and to the autonomy of consumers? As with the concern about unfair terms, are there features of on-line consumer environments that cumulatively differentiate them in a material way from off-line marketplaces?

It is in the nature of consumer profiling, particularly when powered by machine-learning, that it will become more 'discriminating' as more data is acquired relating to the preferences of individual consumers or groups of consumers. For the purposes of this chapter, however, let me assume that whatever discrimination is exercised it is used in a way that is lawful.[64] Nevertheless, this does not exhaust concerns about the vulnerabilities of consumers in on-line environments.

Articulating concerns of this kind, Eliza Mik has recently written:

> Online businesses influence consumer behaviour by means of a wide range of technologies that determine *what* information is displayed and *how* and *when* it is displayed. This creates an unprecedented power imbalance between the transacting parties, raising questions not only about the permissible levels of procedural exploitation in contract law, together with the adequacy of existing consumer protections but also, on a broader level, about the impact of technology on the autonomy of the consumer.[65]

Mik does not claim that on-line consumer environments are wholly different in kind to their off-line equivalents; but she does argue that there are elements in the former that render them significantly different. Thus:

> We can concede that we have always been manipulated by advertisers and sales people, and that our choices have always been limited to what owners of malls or supermarkets decided to display. Malls, shops and the packaging of goods have always been designed to influence our purchasing decisions. Malls, shops and vending machines do not, however, change their layout and contents in real-time to match specific individuals at crucial moments related to their psychological or physiological states. Traditional transacting environments cannot detect and exploit

---

[64] Compare the protective decision in *CCN Systems Ltd v. Data Protection Registrar* (Case DA/90 25/4/9, judgment delivered 25 February 1991), where the question was whether it was fair to use 'third-party' address-based information to make a decision where a first-party (who might have no relationship with the third-party) applies for credit. Even though it was accepted that such third-party information might have general predictive value and utility, its use was held to be unfair to the individual.

[65] E. Mik, 'The Erosion of Autonomy in Online Consumer Transactions' (2016) 8 *Law, Innovation and Technology* 1, at 2.

individual vulnerabilities. There is fairness in the fact that everybody is presented with the same range of choices in the same way. Every sales person faces limits as to what she can directly observe from the interaction with the consumer. She does not know the consumer's prior purchasing history with *other* shops, his circle of friends, his medical correspondence and his cognitive preferences. She can adapt the sales strategy to a limited range of consumer characteristics but, leaving aside extreme examples, is unable to detect idiosyncratic vulnerabilities. In recommending specific products, the sales person relies on her intuition and experience – not on the combined experience derived from billions of transactions. Some shops pay higher rent for space in high-traffic areas, but once the spaces have been allocated mall operators cannot promote certain shops by making others more difficult to access.

... Unquestionably, commercial websites can be compared to shops or malls. We can focus on the similarities: in both instances a range of goods is presented for sale. We can also focus on the differences. Apart from the obvious ones, such as automation and lack of direct human contact, the cognitive and sensory experience of navigating web interfaces differs from walking around supermarkets. Browsing the Amazon app differs from browsing a physical bookstore. Amazon is not a shop but a symbolic abstraction of a shop ... The web must be recognized as a discrete transacting environment, where consumers process and interact with information differently than offline, and where they are subject to different, more powerful influences.

... In sum, there is nothing new in the fact that businesses try to influence consumption choices. It is the differences in the available tools and in the characteristics of the online environment that warrant legal attention.[66]

How, then, should we respond to these different tools and characteristics? Should we have recourse to the protective principles of the general law of contract, or should we rely on a more regulatory approach?

Within each legal system, there will be doctrines (such as, in English law, the doctrine of undue influence) that seek to protect parties whose transactional autonomy is compromised.[67] Typically, the context is one in which A is so reliant on B for advice and assistance that A routinely follows B's advice. This does not presuppose any active or conscious wrongdoing on B's part; the problem is that A no longer exercises any independent transactional judgement. In many ways, we might find such a relationship of dependence in the dealings between consumers and their on-line suppliers. However, the kind of profiling and personalised service that is under question is not only widespread in on-line consumer

---

66 E. Mik, above n. 65, 22–24. In similar terms, see R. Calo, above n. 32.

67 In the leading case of *Royal Bank of Scotland plc v. Etridge (No. 2)* [2001] UKHL 44, at para. 11, Lord Nicholls remarked that 'there is no single touchstone for determining whether the principle [of undue influence] is applicable. Several expressions have been used in an endeavour to encapsulate the essence: trust and confidence, reliance, dependence or vulnerability on the one hand and ascendancy, domination or control on the other. None of these descriptions is perfect. None is all embracing. Each has its proper place.'

environments; it is presented as a service to better inform consumers. As Ford notes, the suggestions that come in might be for goods or services that we have not thought about buying, and which, having acted on the recommendations, we found we liked. There does not seem to be too much to object to in that. However, if particular consumers find that they are unable to put any distance between such recommendations and their shopping choices, they might argue that the on-line transactions into which they enter are no longer 'their own'; and it might be possible to invoke protective general doctrines. That said, because recommending practices of this kind are pervasive – and because, as Natali Helberger rightly remarks, there is a 'fine line between informing, nudging and outright manipulation', all this presenting 'one of the main challenges for consumer law and policy in the context of profiling and targeting in the Internet of Things'[68] – perhaps a regulatory response is more appropriate. This, indeed, is the route that Mik takes and her view is that the best regulatory resources currently in place in Europe are in Directive 2005/29/EC on unfair commercial practices (the UCPD).

As is well-known, the UCPD prohibits unfair commercial practices – particularly misleading and aggressive commercial practices – that distort the economic behaviour of consumers. At the time of the UCPD's enactment, the notions of 'nudging' and of the 'choice architecture' were not yet part of everyday regulatory discourse. Today, it is a very different story. For example, Article 22 of the Consumer Rights Directive recognises that there is a problem where the choice architecture of a web-site is such that pre-ticked boxes default the consumer to additional 'options', such as insurance. Here, the regulatory response is to require an express opt-in by the consumer, failing which any payment for such additional services is to be reimbursed. Hence, if we think that the problem with profiling and personalisation is that it involves an unacceptable 'nudge' – the supplier nudging the consumer towards a purchase that (i) is in the economic interest of the supplier but (ii) is not necessarily in the economic interest of the consumer (even though the supplier can plead in good faith that it reasonably believes that the subject-matter of the purchase might be one in which the consumer is interested) – the question is whether the spirit and intent of the UCPD can be brought to bear on these on-line commercial practices.

The general test of unfairness, in Article 5(2) of the UCPD, provides that a commercial practice is unfair if (a) it is contrary to the requirements of professional diligence and (b)

> it materially distorts or is likely to materially distort the economic behaviour with regard to the product of the average consumer whom it reaches or to whom it is addressed, or of the average member of the group when a commercial practice is directed to a particular group of consumers.

---

[68] N. Helberger, above n 57, 152.

According to Article 2(e), a practice materially distorts the economic behaviour of consumers if its use is such as 'to appreciably impair the consumer's ability to make an informed decision, thereby causing the consumer to take a transactional decision that he would not have taken otherwise.' Given that the two classes of unfair commercial practices at which the Directive is principally aimed are those that are (i) misleading and (ii) aggressive, we need to read the definition of material distortion in Article 2(e) as saying 'to appreciably impair the consumer's ability to make a decision *that is both free and informed*, thereby causing the consumer to take a transactional decision that he would not have taken otherwise.' Employing this definition, we can then treat material distortion as occurring where, because of misleading commercial practices, the consumer's decision is not properly *informed* but also where, because of aggressive commercial practices, the consumer's decision is not *free*.

Applying this test to the use of nudges by on-line sellers, there are two senses in which we might suggest that this practice materially distorts the transactional decisions made by the average consumer. First, we might suggest that nudged transactional decisions are not free; secondly, we might suggest that they are under-informed or misinformed – and, in both cases, we would argue that consumers make a decision to purchase that they otherwise would not have made.

In response to the first suggestion, it might be objected that transactional decisions are never free; and that, insofar as the Directive prohibits aggressive commercial practices, it is contemplating a much more overt impingement on the freedom of consumers. That said, those who advocate nudges do not shrink from the first kind of objection. To the contrary, such advocates regard it as a virtue of nudging that it is fully compatible with the autonomy of those who are nudged because there is always the opportunity to opt-out.[69] In practice, of course, where the norm is to go with the nudge, the defaults might become somewhat 'sticky' and the opportunity to opt-out is more formal than real; but where a supplier is simply recommending a product that seems to fit well with the consumer's profile, the choice architecture requires the latter to opt-in – the nudge is a gentle one. Moreover, even if one accepts the nudge, the consumer has the right to withdraw within 14 days.[70] By contrast, if the default were set for 'buy' and, in order to avoid the purchase, it required the consumer to opt-out, this would be a much more questionable – perhaps even 'aggressive' – nudge, analogous to off-line 'inertia selling' that has long been regulated.[71]

---

69 R.H. Thaler and C.R. Sunstein, *Nudge: Improving Decisions About Health, Wealth and Happiness*, Yale University Press, New Haven CT 2008.

70 See Article 9(1) of Directive 2011/83/EU on consumer rights.

71 Compare, too, L.A. DiMatteo, 'Regulation of Share Economy: A Consistently Changing Environment' in R. Schulze and D. Staudenmayer, above n. 25, 100 (for a non-existent 'unsubscribe option' in Lyft's terms of service with customers).

With regard to the second suggestion, the obvious response is that suppliers are endeavouring to ensure that their consumer customers are fully informed. Again, advocates of on-line selling will claim that there is much more information available to consumers than in off-line shopping environments. However, this might be thought to miss the point. The objection is not that the consumer was misled in relation to the characteristics of the products that were purchased or recommended, but that the supplier 'manipulated' the consumer without disclosing the process that enabled such targeted and 'accurate' recommendations to be made. While such an objection would seem to point to an example of a failure to meet the requirements of 'professional diligence' (specifically by being contrary to good faith), it is not so clear how this practice results in a material distortion of the average consumer's transactional decisions.

Within the Directive, there might be a peg for this kind of objection in the notion of 'undue influence', which is defined in Article 2(j) as follows:

> 'undue influence' means exploiting a position of power in relation to the consumer so as to apply pressure, even without using or threatening to use physical force, in a way which significantly limits the consumer's ability to make an informed decision.

As with the general definition of material distortion, we surely have to read this definition as saying 'in a way which significantly limits the consumer's ability to make a decision *that is both free and informed*' – not least because, within the overall scheme of the Directive, the idea of undue influence is given, alongside harassment, coercion and the use of physical force as a feature of aggressive commercial practices. Reading the Directive this way, it might be argued that a personalised and profiled nudge amounts to aggression by undue influence: because the nature of the nudge is not disclosed, there is a lack of information about the extent to which the transactional decision of the consumer is being influenced. Or, to put this more straightforwardly, there is a lack of transparency. Indeed, here, we should note the Commission's recent recognition that '[g]reater transparency is … needed for users [of on-line platforms] to understand how the information presented to them is filtered, shaped or personalised, especially when this information forms the basis for purchasing decisions …'[72] That said, the benchmark in the Directive is the average consumer, this being a consumer 'who is reasonably well-informed and reasonably observant and circumspect, taking into account social, cultural and linguistic factors'.[73] No doubt, there will be a good deal of variation in the understanding of consumers about how the choice architecture of their on-line shopping environments structures and influences their transactional decisions; and it is not clear that the off-line benchmark

72 European Commission, above n. 62, 10–11.
73 Recital (18) of the Directive.

works so well in on-line environments. However, the more that consumers understand about the way that on-line environments manage and channel their behaviour, the less plausible it will be to plead that nudging amounts to undue influence and an unfair commercial practice.[74] At this stage, if there is to be an objection to nudging, it might be (as Cass Sunstein now recognises) that there is an argument to be made for active choosing when 'learning, authenticity, responsibility, and the development of values and preferences are important.'[75] However, the idea that routine consumer choices fall into this special category is not terribly plausible.

There are two other points to make in relation to the Directive. The first is that the Directive lists (in Annex 1) some 31 commercial practices, some misleading in nature, others aggressive, that are to be treated as unfair in all circumstances. Some of these practices (for example, 'bait and switch') assume off-line environments but many are, in principle, relevant to on-line environments. The first three listed cases, for instance, where misleading claims are made about being a signatory to a code of practice, or about the credentials of the code, or about having a trust mark, and so on, might be relevant if codes or trust marks dealing with on-line nudging and profiling were to be developed. However, there is nothing in the list that supports the idea that nudging itself should be categorically considered unfair.

Nevertheless, at some time in the future, one might imagine an argument against nudging and profiling that raises the question of whether there is a risk that consumers might become trapped in their own (machine-learning-assisted) personal 'echo-chambers', and whether this risk needs to be managed.[76] The thought is that those consumers who simply want to experiment or change their profiles might find it difficult to do so. Might it be that consumers of this kind – consumers, of course, who are not in this case assisted by their right to withdraw within the cooling off period – are 'vulnerable' in a sense recognised by the Directive?

This takes us to the second point. Article 5(3) of the Directive does indeed make special allowance for 'consumers who are particularly vulnerable to the

74 Compare N. Helberger, above n. 57, 157: 'One important factor in this context could be the knowledge of the user of the fact that she is being persuaded, based on her persuasion profile. This is because only with such knowledge is she actually able to mobilise her defence strategy, should she wish to do so. Another important factor could be her ability to opt out of targeted messages, as a means to restore the imbalance in control power between user and trader.'

75 C.R. Sunstein, *Choosing Not To Choose*, Oxford University Press, Oxford 2015, at 119–120.

76 See, e.g., European Data Protection Supervisor, *Towards a New Digital Ethics* (Opinion 4/2015) 11 September, 2015, at 13: 'Profiles used to predict people's behaviour risk stigmatisation, reinforcing collective stereotypes, social and cultural segregation and exclusion, with such "collective intelligence" subverting individual choice and equal opportunities. Such "filter bubbles" or "personal echo-chambers" could end up stifling the very creativity, innovation and freedoms of expression and association which have enabled digital technologies to flourish.'

practice or the underlying product because of their mental or physical infirmity, age or credulity in a way which the trader could reasonably be expected to foresee.' Where a consumer is within such an identifiable group, the benchmark is adjusted to that of the average member of that group. However, if we try to align this with the complaint that a group of consumers find themselves trapped in their own profiles, there is an obvious difficulty in saying that the reason for their alleged vulnerability is their mental or physical infirmity, or their age or credulity. There might also be a difficulty in treating a practice that steers a consumer away from trying new and different kinds of product options as a material distortion of the consumer's transactional decision. To be sure, informal guidance on the Directive suggests that the concept of a 'transactional decision' should be read broadly to include decisions both to purchase and not to purchase.[77] However, the example that is given in the guidance is an off-line one: a consumer sees a promotional offer for a digital camera; the consumer goes to the shop intending to buy the camera; but, the consumer then learns that the price advertised applies only if the purchaser also subscribes to a photography course; so, the consumer decides not to buy the camera.[78] Although this sequence of events ends with a decision not to purchase, it is a long way from the kind of situation that we are discussing; and, even if these difficulties can be overcome, it is far from clear whether a creative interpretation of the Directive, or a bespoke regulatory response, is the smarter way of handling this question.

There is one other radical thought: Ryan Calo suggests that there is a sense in which the power of profiling is such that even average consumers are vulnerable – there will be times and places when their defences or levels of resistance are lowered.[79] Thus:

> In its purest form, digital market manipulation recognizes that vulnerability is contextual and a matter of degree and specifically aims to render all consumers as vulnerable as possible at the time of purchase. A given consumer may not be vulnerable most of the time and will act rationally in her own interest. But under very specific conditions ... she may prove vulnerable for a short window.[80]

Not only does this analysis collapse the distinction between average and vulnerable consumers on which European consumer law is predicated, it challenges in the starkest way the unexceptionalist credo that on-line trading is business as usual. For Calo, 'digital market manipulation combines, for the

---

77 European Commission, *Guidance on the Implementation/Application of Directive 2005/29/EC on Unfair Commercial Practices* (Commission Staff Working Document) Brussels, 3 December 2009 SEC(2009) 1666.

78 European Commission *Guidance* (above n. 77) 22–23.

79 R. Calo, above n. 32, 1033. For the relevance of the ease with which a nudge can be resisted, see Y. Saghai, 'Salvaging the Concept of Nudge' (2013) 39 *Journal of Medical Ethics* 487.

80 R. Calo, above n. 32, 1033.

first time, a certain kind of personalization with the intense systemization made possible by mediated consumption.'[81] In other words, consumers are more vulnerable in on-line environments and suppliers take advantage of their position systematically to target consumers at their most vulnerable moments.

Returning to Mik – for whom 'the main weaknesses of the UCPD lie in the definitions and assumptions underlying the concepts of "average" and "vulnerable" consumers as well as the narrow definition of "undue influence"'; and, for whom there is a problem with the Directive's failure to appreciate and address 'the problems inherent in misleading rankings and recommendations'[82] – unfair manipulative practices are better dealt with under the Directive rather than by resorting to a targeted regulatory response. If so, as with concerns about unfair terms, the answer is not to rewrite the E-Commerce Directive itself (which is largely irrelevant) but to ensure that a linked relevant Directive is purposively interpreted and applied to cases of unfair exploitation of on-line environments for consumer transactions. As for a precision-targeted regulatory response, not only is the rationale for targeting nudging unclear, we can be certain that today's targeted response will soon be outrun by tomorrow's technologies. With this thought, we can move on to a radical transformation of our routine consumption practices as humans are pretty much taken out of the transactional equation, consumer contractors becoming mere consumers.

4. AUTOMATED PROCESSING

While today's virtual assistants have impressive but limited functionality – 'informing their owners of important diary events' or 'booking tables and tickets' – it seems that 'Microsoft, Amazon and other technology giants are competing to create virtual assistants that may one day take over the running of our lives.'[83] With such a heavy investment in artificial intelligence, we surely must take seriously Ford's 'cyberbutlers' and Hildebrandt's onli*fe* world; but what does this signify for the E-Commerce Directive – the sparse provisions of which make no explicit reference to electronic agents[84] – and, more generally, for contract law?

Immediately, a host of questions present themselves. For example, should we try to find analogies for these new on-line or onli*fe* transactions in familiar

81 R. Calo, above n. 32, 1021.

82 E. Mik, above n. 65, 35.

83 J. Dean, 'Poets and playwrights give robots a dash of humanity' *The Times* (11 April 2016) p 17.

84 As noted in E.M. Weitzenboeck, 'Electronic Agents and the Formation of Contracts' (2001) 9 *International Journal of Law and Information Technology* 204 (comparing the Directive with early attempts, particularly in North America, to create explicit legal frameworks for electronic agents).

off-line contractual concepts? If so, should the consumer be treated as a principal, with the transactional technology as an agent; or, where the consumer's regular needs are automatically met, should we treat the consumer as being a third-party beneficiary of the transactions? In a world of (self-executing) smart contracts, does it make sense to persist with the idea that the law needs to correct for the historic off-line asymmetry between suppliers and their consumer customers, for the vulnerability of consumers, for differentials in bargaining power, for a lack of good faith, and so on? Granted, it might remain relevant to protect the reasonable expectations of consumers, but is this best done by trying to apply a repertoire of ideas developed for off-line consumer transactions or by thinking afresh about the fair distribution of risks associated with the use of technologies that service our basic requirements? Just as we need to address the right kind of regulatory approach to autonomous vehicles (where human drivers are taken out of the equation) should we also address automated transactions (where human suppliers and purchasers are taken out of the equation) in a similar way?

Reflecting on early indications of this kind of development, Ian Kerr doubted that we could refer to such automated transactions as being in any meaningful sense contractual. Thus:

> Having migrated into electronic environments, commercial transactions are no longer entered into and carried out exclusively by humans. Many such transactions are initiated and completed by avatars, vReps, digital buddies, and various kinds of shopping bots. These technologies remove human beings from at least one side of the transaction. As a result, it has become disingenuous to characterize many online transactions as giving rise to contracts in the traditional sense – namely, a 'jural relation that is founded upon agreement.' Computer generated transactions no longer fit within the traditional paradigm of contract doctrine. Properly speaking, they are not the 'manifestation of a mutual concordance between [two] parties as to the existence, nature and scope of their rights and duties.'[85]

In a similar vein, Shoshana Zuboff offers a view of the way in which, in a world of technological management, a new form of (surveillance) capitalism may install a new kind of sovereign power.[86] In such a world, a big data corporation

> may sell access to an insurance company, and this company purchases the right to intervene in an information loop in your car or your kitchen in order to increase its revenues or reduce its costs. It may shut off your car, because you are driving too fast.

---

85 I.R. Kerr, 'Bots, Babes and the Californication of Commerce' (2004) 1 *University of Ottawa Law and Technology Journal* 284, at 288–289. To similar effect, see M.J. Radin, 'Humans, Computers, and Binding Commitments' (2000) 75 *Industrial Law Journal* 1125.

86 S. Zuboff, 'Big Other: Surveillance Capitalism and the Prospects of an Information Civilization' (2015) 30 *Journal of Information Technology* 75.

> It may lock your fridge when you put yourself at risk of heart disease or diabetes by eating too much ice cream. You might then face the prospect of either higher premiums or loss of coverage … [S]uch possibilities … represent *the end of contracts* … [They replace] the rule of law and the necessity of social trust as the basis for human communities with a new life-world of rewards and punishments, stimulus and response (emphasis added).[87]

If autonomous cars find their way on to our roads as quickly as smart fridges find their way into our homes, at least one of these risks will not materialise – because we will not be driving cars they will not be disabled when we are driving too fast; and, the premium for any motoring insurance that we might need will not be fixed by reference to what we have in our fridge. Yet, is the general point made by Zuboff right? When transactions are technologically managed, when performance and compliance are technologically guaranteed, does this represent the end of *contracts*? Are smart contracts no longer 'contracts'? And, how should regulators respond?

First, we can agree with Kerr that automated transactions depart from the traditional idea of a contract. However, many consumer transactions departed from this idea long before there was any migration to on-line environments. The notional link between suppliers and consumers is one of a contract, and the interaction assumes a transactional form but it is a heavily regulated exchange. If automated transactions mean that there is no longer a credible contractual link, what we are left with is regulated consumption – which is not so different to what we already have, both off-line and on-line. Secondly, we can also agree with Zuboff that the collection, commercialisation and use of personal data could run out of control;[88] but, in Europe, we have to see whether the new General Data Protection Regulation is able to check the actions of big data corporations. So far as automated decisions are concerned, the Regulation updates the original provision in Article 15(1) of Directive 95/46/EC (the Data Protection Directive), this provision being designed to protect a person against automated decisions that produce legal effects concerning him or that significantly affect him and which are intended to evaluate certain personal aspects relating to him, such as his performance at work, creditworthiness, reliability, or conduct, and so on. Where such processing takes place in a contractual context – at any rate, 'provided the request for the entering into or performance of the contract, lodged by the data subject, has been satisfied' – or where the data subject's legitimate interests are suitably safeguarded,

---

87 S. Zuboff, above n. 86, 85–86.

88 Arguably, it is already out of control. For an insight into the present and a vision of the future, see V. Mayer-Schönberger and K. Cukier, *Big Data*, John Murray, London 2013; and for some evidence of the way that data protection restrictions are routinely breached in e-commerce, see M. Borghi, F. Ferretti and S. Karapapa, 'Online Data Processing Consent under EU Law: A Theoretical Framework and Empirical Evidence from the UK' (2013) 21 *International Journal of Law and Information Technology* 109.

Article 15(2) permits Member States to allow such automated decision-making to take place. Thirdly, however, it is not so clear that this is the end of contract. Indeed, to the extent that consumers subscribe to a suite of cyberbutler services, these original authorising transactions are critical. Granted, once a consumer's PDA (personal digital assistant) is licensed to take care of their routine needs, and once it is 'transacting' with other smart devices as and when required for that purpose, there will be little sign of the consumer as a contracting party; but the act of licensing (just like a principal's authorisation of an agent) is critical.[89] Fourthly, when routine consumption is fully automated, it should be possible to design into the technologies that manage the supply of goods and services to consumers for payment those performance requirements that would otherwise be prescribed by rules addressed to the suppliers and the purchasers. In this respect, the first priority for the E-Commerce Directive will look somewhat anachronistic: in future, parties to on-line contracts will not need an assurance that the rules for off-line transactions apply because those contracts will be technologically managed in a way that secures the parties' rights and responsibilities. But, as Zuboff implies, does this signify the replacement of the rule of law?

We can defer discussion of the data protection issues to another occasion, but we can say a little more about each of the other points, starting with the regulation of consumer transactions, that is to say, with 'regulated consumption'.

4.1. REGULATED CONSUMPTION

In many legal systems, there will be a well-known story of the transformation of contract law – much of this taking place in the middle decades of the twentieth century – from a general law of transactions to a bifurcated approach that distinguishes sharply between commercial contracts and consumer contracts. Thus, in English law, a special set of rules has been crafted to accommodate what are seen as the reasonable expectations of consumers. For example, there is a high level of control over allegedly unfair terms and unfair commercial practices,[90] a high threshold for the incorporation of terms,[91] a non-excludable right of rejection where goods are not of satisfactory quality or reasonably

[89] Compare E.M. Weitzenboeck, above n. 84; and, for matters arising in relation to consumer contracts, see S. Feliu, 'Intelligent Agents and Consumer Protection' (2001) 9 *International Journal of Law and Information Technology* 235.

[90] See, e.g., the Unfair Contract Terms Act 1977; the Directive on Unfair Terms in Consumer Contracts 1993/13/EC; and the Unfair Commercial Practices Directive 2005/29/ EC.

[91] In English law, the best example from a clutch of cases is *Thornton v. Shoe Lane Parking Ltd* [1971] 2 QB 163.

fit for purpose,[92] and the recognition of consumer surplus in making awards of damages.[93] With the enactment of the Consumer Rights Act 2015, this evolutionary stage is almost complete.

However, this is only part of the story. In Europe, from the mid-1980s onwards, the rule framework for the consumer marketplace became increasingly 'regulatory'.[94] The raft of Directives (listed in recital (11) of the E-Commerce Directive) that instate a high level of consumer protection are not designed to render the general law of contract more coherent or consistent; these are interventions that are specifically intended to lay the foundations for a vibrant European marketplace.[95] These are not adjustments that are designed to maintain the integrity of a body of private law; these are instruments of economic growth. Again, I take it that this is a familiar story.[96]

Although both parts of this story have tended to converge, the contractual basis of the former and the regulatory basis of the latter might one day pull in different directions. For example, while those with a 'contractual' mind-set might reason that agency is the analogue for automated transactions, those with a regulatory approach might reason in a way that is more akin to risk management. Similarly, while for 'contractualists', obligations are always rooted in private ordering, albeit highly attenuated in the consumer markets, for regulatory folk, ordering and obligations are driven by the particular regulatory purposes. So long as consumer protection is high on the list of regulatory priorities, there should continue to be a convergence; but, if general utility becomes the key priority, a quite different dynamic takes over.

4.2. CYBERBUTLERS AND THE ORIGINAL CONTRACT

In the onl*ife* world, our routine needs are taken care of by cyberbutlers and by a succession of smart environments that are technologically managed. In such a world, let us assume that consumers are faced with a choice of cyberbutler service providers, each provider offering a package of terms and conditions.

---

92 In English law, see section 14 of the Sale of Goods Act 1979, reinforced by section 6(2) of the Unfair Contract Terms Act 1977.

93 Seminally, see *Jarvis v. Swan's Tours Ltd* [1973] QB 233 and Case C-168/00 *Simone Leitner v. TUI Deutschland* [2002] ECR I-2631.

94 See R. Brownsword, 'The Law of Contract: Doctrinal Impulses, External Pressures, Future Directions' (2014) 31 *Journal of Contract Law* 73.

95 See, e.g., R. Brownsword, 'The Theoretical Foundations of European Private Law: A Time to Stand and Stare' in R. Brownsword, H.-W. Micklitz, L. Niglia, and S. Weatherill (eds.), *The Foundations of European Private Law*, Hart Publishing, Oxford 2011, 159, 164–166.

96 See, further, H.-W. Micklitz, 'The Visible Hand of European Regulatory Private Law: The Transformation of European Private Law from Autonomy to Functionalism in Competition and Regulation', EUI Working Papers, Law 2008/14.

Some of these packages will be relatively narrow and specialised, others will be far broader. Within these broader packages, defaults will be set for supplying needs that are widely regarded as basic, repeat, and routine; but then there will be goods and services that some individuals will choose to treat as routine while others will want to treat them as non-routine (meaning that they will be ordered only as and when they are specifically requested); and, perhaps, there will be some goods and services which will never be ordered without the specific request of the consumer. So, contract is the basis on which consumers sign up to a particular package; and, within the package, specific authorisation is sometimes required for non-routine purchases. The critical point is that, so far as the package contract is concerned, the ideal-typical contractual conditions must be satisfied; or, as Margaret Radin says,

> If the future of contract makes it ever more clear that the only point of choice is whether or not to buy the product-plus-terms, we could [on my analysis, we '*should*'] focus our attention on making that choice really a choice.[97]

However, so far as consent and authorisation within the package are concerned, the requirements may be specified by the package or by background regulation.

If the anchoring point for the package is to be a founding contract, then this is where we need to find Kerr's 'jural relation that is founded upon agreement' and the 'manifestation of a mutual concordance between [two] parties as to the existence, nature and scope of their rights and duties';[98] this is where the consumer has to give a free and informed consent to the package and its terms. While everyone can agree that coercive and fraudulent actions by the supplier are incompatible with the consumer giving a free and informed consent, beyond this as we consider duress, pressure and influence, or notice of terms, we enter into deeply contested territory where more and less protective conceptions of 'being free' and 'being informed' are articulated. Still, until automated supply is the norm, the significance of entering into a package needs to be highlighted: the context in which packages are offered needs to be such that the consumer is free to say 'no' to *any* package (not just 'no' to some packages but eventually 'yes' to one); and the consumer needs to understand that declining any package is an option. Moreover, the consumer needs to understand that, if he signs up for a package, many of his routine needs will be automatically serviced. This invites a regulatory framework that takes this one transaction out of the background and

---

97 M.J. Radin, above n. 85, 1161. If the choice is simply too complex for consumers, the alternative is to leave it to regulators to black-list some terms, to require others to be set aside for separate explicit agreement, and to require others to be conspicuously displayed.

98 I.R. Kerr, above n. 85.

puts it into the spotlight – and all this *a fortiori* if the founding contract is itself presented in an on-line environment.

That said, such a precautionary and consumer protective regulatory intervention might soon seem anachronistic. As the balance changes between fully automated and non-automated consumption, there will probably be defaults and nudges towards automated packages; and this might well be viewed as acceptable when it is reasonable to assume that this is what most consumers want. In time, consumers who want to consume in the old-fashioned way might find that this is no longer a practical option. In time, the justification for what is in effect imposed automation will not be that it rests on consensually-agreed packages but that it serves the general welfare. Instead of contract, the justification is utility, qualified perhaps by the need for an acceptable distribution of benefit and risk.[99]

In the onl*ife* world of automated consumption, as I have said, there might well be a significant number and range of transactions that require the authorisation of the consumer. However, the degree of delegated authority enjoyed by cyberbutlers might vary from one consumer to another.[100] Suppose, for example, that consumer X, having contracted for a package that promises automated provision of his basic needs, decides that it is time to take a holiday. Under the terms of the package, holidays are not classified as basic needs; the booking of a holiday has to be initiated by X. Accordingly, X informs his cyberbutler, CB, that he plans to take a holiday. How much authority is to be delegated to CB? In principle, relative to the booking of a holiday, the delegation by X to CB might be (i) advisory or executory, and (ii) closed or open. The permutations are as follows:

(i) Advisory/closed (e.g., X instructs CB to identify, but not book, the best value 7-day beach holiday at a Mediterranean resort, with 4 star hotel accommodation, that costs in the range of 900–1,000 euros);
(ii) Executory/closed (e.g., X instructs CB to identify *and to book* the best value 7-day beach holiday at a Mediterranean resort, with 4 star hotel accommodation, that costs in the range of 900–1,000 euros);
(iii) Advisory/open (e.g., X instructs CB to identify, but not book, the best value and suitable holiday option for him); and
(iv) Executory/open (e.g., X instructs CB to identify *and to book* the best value and suitable holiday option for him).

---

99 See R. Brownsword, above n. 95, 161–164.

100 Compare R. Brownsword, 'Autonomy, Delegation, and Responsibility: Agents in Autonomic Computing Environments' in M. Hildebrandt and Antoinette Rouvroy (eds.), *Autonomic Computing and Transformations of Human Agency*, Routledge, London 2011, 64.

If X uses CB only in an advisory capacity, this seems unproblematic; X makes the final choice. If X uses CB in an executory/closed capacity, this still seems relatively unproblematic from X's perspective. For X, the 'riskiest' delegation to CB is the executory/open option; but, if X is confident that CB knows X's preferences, this too might be a delegation that X is happy to make.

So long as CB acts on X's instructions and does not exceed the terms of the delegation, the holiday providers, like X, seem to be at little risk. As with off-line bookings, the technological management of the transaction can ensure that the price of the holiday is paid 'up front'. However, should CB exceed its authority – whether because CB overrides X's instructions as being less than optimal relative to X's interests, or simply because there is a malfunction – there will need to be compensatory arrangements. While contractualists will probably look for guidance to traditional (or modified) off-line agency rules (with the acts of the 'agent' being 'attributed' to the consumer), those with a regulatory mind-set will more likely favour a prescribed scheme of insurance or indemnity[101] There is also, of course, the possibility that the design of the technology is so smart that, even if a malfunction occurs, it is detected and corrected before any loss occurs.

Whether or not technological design and management can guarantee performance and compliance on both sides of a consumer transaction remains to be seen. Certainly, we can be assured that technology (particularly, that designed for pre-payment) will guarantee that providers will be paid. Similarly, we can surely assume that cyberbutlers will be designed to spot non-conforming goods or services that are manifestly not as ordered or that are patently of unacceptable quality – but there might still be some latent quality issues that do not show until the goods are used.

4.3. TECHNOLOGICAL MANAGEMENT, RULES AND THE RULE OF LAW

When rules of law that are intended to guide human behaviour are displaced by technological management that takes humans out of the equation, we might wonder what happens to the rules that are displaced and how the ideals of the Rule of Law are satisfied.[102]

To respond to the first of these questions, imagine that there is a rule that requires x (such as the supply of goods of satisfactory quality and the payment of the price) but, because the rule is ineffective, regulators resort to technological management to eliminate the possibility of not-x (supplying goods that are not of

[101] Compare E.M. Weitzenboeck, above n. 84; and, S. Feliu, above n. 89.

[102] For an extended discussion of these issues, see R. Brownsword, above n. 28.

satisfactory quality or non-payment of the price). Even if the rule that requires x is superseded by technological management it is not entirely redundant because it expresses the regulators' normative view (namely, that 'regulatees' ought to do x).

Accordingly, where technological management is linked in this way to an implicit normative view, the regulatory position is as follows:

- a regulator, R, has a view about whether regulatees should be required to, permitted to, or prohibited from doing x (the underlying normative view);
- R's view could be expressed in the form of a rule that requires, permits, or prohibits the doing of x (the underlying rule);
- but, R uses (or directs others to use) technological management rather than a rule;
- and R's intention in doing so is to translate the underlying normative view into a practical design that ensures that regulatees do or do not do x (according to the underlying rule);
- the ensuing outcome being that regulatees find themselves in environments where the immediate signals relate to what can and cannot be done, to possibilities and impossibilities, rather than to the underlying normative pattern of what ought or ought not to be done.

This means that, where technological management is employed, there is some redirection of the rules. Before the particular measures of technological management that have been authorised actually take their place in the regulatory environment, before regulatees find that their practical options and possibilities have been altered, there is an important step of direction (to use technological management) and compliance. Indeed, the direction might take the form of a *rule* that requires, say, providers of products or services to adopt some form of technological management; and, to this extent, rules are still being used to channel conduct (in this case, the conduct of producers and providers of goods and services). However, for end users of such products or services, it is technological management rather than a rule that both channels their conduct and grounds their expectations in relation to such products or services.

Does this redirection of rules, away from suppliers of consumer goods and services and their customers to the providers of the technologies that enable such goods and services to be supplied, signal a challenge for the Rule of Law? In general, the automation of processes together with the technological management of transactions and interactions does raise important challenges for our ideals of legality (ideals that are predicated on regulation by rules rather than regulation by technological fixes). However, in a working democracy with developed public institutions for policy-making and regulation, it should be possible to maintain public scrutiny of both the *purposes* for which the technology is to be deployed and the acceptability of using particular *technologies* for regulatory purposes.

Yet, is this not too sanguine a view? Technologies with regulatory effects are commonly developed in the private sector – digital rights management technologies are one such example. Where the purposes for which such technologies are employed (such as the protection of IP rights) are not clearly unlawful, it is easy to assume that they are compatible with the Rule of Law. However, this allows technological management, so to speak, to sail close to the wind (at the margins of legality) and it omits to scrutinise the creeping use of technological management itself. Accordingly, there needs to be some public oversight of technologies that feature in the provision of consumer needs and do so in ways that have regulatory effects.[103]

5. THE TWO PROPOSED DIRECTIVES – A NEW EXCEPTIONALISM?

In December 2015, the Commission published a Communication announcing two proposed new Directives (one on contracts for the supply of digital content,[104] the other on on-line and distance sale of goods contracts)[105] which, together with a proposed Regulation on the cross-border portability of on-line content services, mark the first new legislative initiatives adopted under the Digital Single Market Strategy.[106]

The outstanding feature of both proposed Directives, which are maximum harmonisation measures, is that they are presented as win-win – i.e. win for

[103] In this context, we should note the concluding remarks of the European Data Protection Supervisor (above n. 76) at 14 highlighting the significance of respect for human dignity: 'Privacy and data protection are part of the solution, not the problem. For the time being, technology is controlled by humans. It is not easy to classify neatly these potential developments [such as big data, the Internet of Things, ambient and cloud computing, and so on] as good or bad, desirable or harmful, advantageous or detrimental, even less so when a number of potential trends have to be seen in context. Policy makers, technology developers, business developers and all of us must seriously consider if and how we want to influence the development of technology and its application. But equally important is that the EU consider urgently the ethics and place for human dignity in the technologies of the future.'

On this general issue, see M. Duwell, 'Human Dignity and the Ethics and Regulation of Technology' in R. Brownsword, E. Scotford and K. Yeung (eds.), *Oxford Handbook on Law, Regulation and Technology*, Oxford University Press, Oxford 2017.

[104] European Commission, Proposal for a Directive of the European Parliament and of the Council on certain aspects concerning contracts for the supply of digital content, COM(2015) 634 final (Brussels, 09.12.2015).

[105] European Commission, Proposal for a Directive of the European Parliament and of the Council on certain aspects concerning contracts for the online and other distance sales of goods, COM(2015) 635 final (Brussels, 09.12.2015).

[106] European Commission, Communication from the Commission to the European Parliament, the Council and the European Economic and Social Committee, 'Digital contracts for Europe – Unleashing the potential of e-commerce' COM(2015) 633 final (Brussels, 09.12.2015), at 3.

small businesses, and win for consumers; and, indeed, a win for everyone who benefits from the anticipated growth of the European economy. So far as businesses are concerned the gains are clear: fully harmonised cross-border rules with regard to on-line sale of goods contracts as well as to contracts for the supply of digital content should mean that the business environment is more predictable. So far as consumers are concerned, there are certainly gains in relation to digital content (although, where Member States such as the UK have already legislated for conformity in relation to such content, there would need to be a close analysis of the detail)[107] but it is much less clear that consumers gain by the mandatory imposition of the hierarchical remedial regime for sales. For example, following the enactment of the Consumer Rights Act 2015, in the United Kingdom, consumers have at least 30 days within which to exercise a so-called 'short-term right to reject' faulty goods and to obtain a full refund. If the proposed Directive were to be enacted, this right would have to be repealed, leaving consumers unable to obtain a refund

> until they had first pursued other remedies (repair; replacement; full or partial refund if a repair or replacement cannot be provided within a reasonable time and without significant inconvenience to the buyer) unless the retailer decides to provide more generous conditions.[108]

Somewhat unconvincingly, in the Explanatory Memorandum that accompanies the proposal, we read that although 'Member States will not be able to adopt or maintain more protective consumer protection rules, overall a high level of consumer protection will be ensured, and cross-border enforcement of the rules will be enhanced.'[109] More accurately, then, the proposed Directives probably amount to a win for small businesses with a win for some consumers but a loss for others. Whether or not this will have any negative impact on the consumer confidence that is required if the on-line market is to realise its potential remains to be seen.[110]

My purpose in this part of the chapter, however, is not to assess whether these latest initiatives from the Commission – 'a new chapter in the process of Europeanisation of contract law' as it has been described[111] – will achieve their

---

107 For an initial analysis of the relevant differences between the digital content provisions of the UK Consumer Rights Act 2015 and the proposed Directive, see Department for Business Innovation and Skills, *Draft Directives on the Online Sale of Digital Content and Tangible Goods: UK Government Call for Views* (January 2016) 5–8: available at https://www.gov.uk/government/uploads/system/uploads/attachment_data/file/496345/bis-16–73-online-sales-call-for-evidence.pdf (last accessed 7 May 2016).

108 Department for Business Innovation and Skills, above n. 107, 9.

109 European Commission, above n. 104, 11.

110 We should take into account, too, any interpretive 'slack' left in the details of the remedial regime: compare, e.g., *Weber and Putz*, Joined Cases C-65/09 and C-87/09.

111 European Parliament, above n. 13, 27.

regulatory objectives. Nor is it to pursue the very important questions raised by Christiane Wendehorst[112] as to whether, with the proliferation of smart digitally enabled devices, the proposed Directives are already making a fundamental mistake by assuming that a clean distinction can be drawn between the supply of digital content and the on-line sale of goods, whether the sales proposal 'fails to reflect the ongoing transition from the sales paradigm based on ownership to the service paradigm of continuous access and supply',[113] and whether a more holistic approach is needed 'which not only focuses on the relationship between the buyer and the seller but equally on the relationship between the end user and the producer or the supplier of necessary digital infrastructure.'[114] Rather, my purpose is simply to consider whether the Commission has abandoned the unexceptionalist assumptions of the E-Commerce Directive as well as whether the proposed Directives engage with the particular questions raised in the foregoing discussion.

First, the Directives do not engage with the kind of automated supply of consumer needs that I anticipate. Indeed, in both proposals, consumers are defined as 'natural persons', implying that the agents involved in on-line transactions are at least natural humans on the side of the consumer. However, recital (17) of the digital content proposal says the following:

> Digital content is highly relevant in the context of the Internet of Things. However, it is opportune to address specific issues of liability related to the Internet of Things, including the liability for data and machine-to-machine contracts, in a separate way.

I take it that this is a promise of a focused regulatory assessment of machine-to-machine transactions in future, in which case, this is an important space to be watched.[115]

Secondly, the proposed Directives indicate no concern about the imbalance of power in on-line environments. However, both the Directive on unfair terms in consumer contracts and the unfair commercial practices Directive are due to be reviewed as part of the Regulatory Fitness and Performance programme.[116] Amongst the questions for the review should be whether the vulnerability of consumers in on-line environments is actually being exploited, whether corrective action needs to be taken, and if so what form such corrective measures might assume.

Thirdly, the proposed Directives indicate no concern about the kind of nudging and influence that suppliers can exert in on-line environments.

---

112 C. Wendehorst, 'Consumer Contracts and the Internet of Things' in R. Schulze and D. Staudenmayer, above n. 25, 189.
113 C. Wendehorst, above n. 112, 222.
114 Ibid.
115 Generally, see S.R. Peppet, above n. 39.
116 European Commission, above n. 106, 8.

I have conceded that it is not entirely clear what the problem (if, indeed, there is one) is in this respect.[117] Again, though, this merits the Commission's attention.

Fourthly, do these proposed Directives indicate that the Commission is revising the unexceptionalist assumptions that have so far underpinned its thinking? In its Communication, the Commission underlines the importance of ensuring consistency between on-line and off-line rules. Thus:

> Given the increasing importance of the omni-channel distribution model (i.e. selling at the same time online and offline), the Commission will take all necessary steps to align the rules for online and offline sales of goods. It will ensure that consumers and businesses will be able to rely on a coherent legal framework which is simple to apply everywhere in Europe.[118]

Yet, one of the first points highlighted by the Department for Business Innovation and Skills' consultation paper on the proposed Directives is that:

> The proposals could see two sets of rules existing for online and other distance sale of goods and for offline, or face-to-face purchasers. This could create differences in the rights enjoyed by consumers depending on whether they bought their goods online or off-line (face to face, in a shop, for example).[119]

Such a two-track rule regime (especially concerning such an important aspect as remedial rights) might impede the Commission's regulatory objectives. On the one side, consumers might shy away from the on-line remedial regime in favour of more attractive off-line rights – or, where off-line sellers are anxious to retain their customers, even more attractive customs and practices found in some off-line retail outlets. On the other side, while the consultation on the proposed sales Directive indicated that 'omni-channel businesses could actually cope with possible transitional differences between the online and face-to-face sales regimes for goods',[120] we can take it that some suppliers might have difficulty in operating two remedial regimes.

Reading between the lines of the proposals and taking into account the recent history of which they are a part, we might detect two impulses for the Commission. One impulse is to salvage something from the considerable investment made in the CFR and the proposed (but now abandoned) CESL. Imposing a common remedial regime, derived from the CFR and CESL, for on-line consumer sales – and, *a fortiori* for consumer sales, whether on-line or off-line – would be one way of justifying the investment. The other impulse

---

117 But, see above n. 103, for the European Data Protection Supervisor's remarks about the importance of human dignity.

118 European Commission, above n. 106, 8.

119 Department for Business Innovation and Skills, above n. 107, 9.

120 European Commission, above n. 105, 12.

is to prioritise the needs of prospective on-line suppliers lest they should decline to participate in the on-line market and, thereby, fail to contribute to economic growth in Europe. Applying this thinking, concerns about coherence, consistency, and non-fragmentation notwithstanding, the effective pursuit of the regulatory objectives might necessitate (at any rate, initially) a two-track remedial regime, where 'exceptionalism' is conceded for the sake of on-line growth. Indeed, there might even come a time when the needs of prospective on-line suppliers drive whatever changes are required in relation to the legal framework to such an extent that this requires the rules for *off-line* consumer transactions to be brought into line with those for on-line transactions. If this reading is correct, if such a harmonised 'unexceptionalism' were to be adopted, this would represent a striking inversion of the Commission's approach at the time of the E-Commerce Directive: instead of the rules for off-line contracts dominating the rules for on-line contracts, and instead of the interests of consumers taking priority over those of suppliers, we would have the rules for on-line contracts dominating, together with a prioritisation of the interest of businesses.

This last point is worth spelling out because it is of general relevance for the balance of interests between on-line suppliers and consumers. At the time of the E-Commerce Directive, the starting point was the need to align the *enforceability* of off-line and on-line transactions (not just for the sake of consumer confidence but also for business certainty). Consumers were already treated in an exceptionalist way relative to the traditional principles of contract law and that exceptionalist treatment of off-line consumer transactions was carried across, under unexceptionalist assumptions, to on-line consumer transactions. While it continues to be important to secure the enforceability of both off-line and on-line transactions, what might now be taking shape is the assumption that there should be a common legal framework (concerning remedies and the like) for off-line and on-line contracts; but, within that common framework, the impetus comes not from the off-line vulnerability of consumers, but from the on-line convenience and needs of suppliers in conjunction with the perception that channelling more consumption on-line is the way to grow the economy. To this extent, consumers are treated as mere market functionaries. Needless to say, such an approach could be damaging to consumers if it is applied in relation not only to remedies, but also to the control of unfair terms or unfair commercial practices.

6. CONCLUSION

Starting with the E-Commerce Directive, and taking in the satellite Directives on unfair terms in consumer contracts and on unfair commercial practices, this chapter raises questions about regulatory disconnection and regulatory redirection.

The first question is whether the constellation of laws that constitutes the regulatory environment for consumer on-line transactions is disconnected and in need of some re-connection. The second question is whether, with the automated provision of routine and repeat consumer goods and services, there needs to be some regulatory redirection – in short, whether technological management should bear the regulatory burden as between providers and purchasers of consumer goods and services, leaving rules to be re-directed at those who design the technological infrastructures.

With regard to the first question, there are reasons for thinking that the context for on-line consumer transactions is materially different to that for off-line transactions in a way that invites a more intense protection against unfair terms. Although the Directive on unfair terms in consumer contracts is flexible enough to serve this purpose, it is predicated on the same questionable unexceptionalist assumptions that underpin the E-Commerce Directive; and, if national courts (as in *ParkingEye*) might be inclined to water down the protection of consumers in off-line contexts, then there are obvious dangers in using this as the benchmark for on-line transactions. Moreover, the Commission's most recent thinking in the two proposed Directives suggests that it might be more interested in improving the regulatory environment for small businesses than in improving it for consumers.

Beyond unfair terms, there are reasons for thinking that consumers in on-line environments are vulnerable to defaults and nudges that might compromise their autonomy. There might be resources in both the general law of contract and the Directive on unfair commercial practices that can provide some response to this concern. However, the concerns themselves probably need some clarification before an appropriate regulatory response can be made. Beyond all this, however, the rapid development of technologies that initiate, support, and manage transactions suggests that the servicing of consumer needs will take place, to a significant extent, neither off-line nor on-line but in an on-*life* environment – an environment in which consumers are barely even cogs in the machine. With the emergence of such environments, the most fundamental assumptions of the E-Commerce Directive are brought into question: in future, it will not suffice to ask whether a transaction is off-line or on-line; it will not suffice to regulate consumer transactions by reference to either the off-line (traditional) rules or the on-line rules; we will need also to recognise and regulate 'transactions' that are neither off-line nor on-line but on-*life*.

This last remark cues in the second question. The Data Protection Directive, and now the GDPR, recognises the need to regulate automated decisions. However, the constellation of e-commerce law does not really anticipate a world of automated supply, where the performance by both provider and purchaser is technologically managed. As we step into this world of smart contracts, there is a case for adopting a regulatory framework that highlights the significance of signing up for a package, that ensures that consumers know what they are getting into, and that gives them an easy exit if they so wish. Quite quickly, we might find that these packages are so commonplace and consumers are so comfortable with their cyberbutlering services that regulatory oversight might be eased. At the same time, we need to get to grips with the idea that the regulatory environment for consumption of goods and services involves rules that are no longer directed at the 'contracting parties' but rather at those who are suppliers of the technological infrastructure together with measures of technological management that displace the rules.[121]

Finally, what is the 'take home' message from this chapter? Essentially, it is that the E-Commerce Directive, being hobbled by 'unexceptionalist' assumptions, offers no response to the concerns that we might have about the acceptability of the balance of interests in on-line consumer environments. If the current regulatory environment has responses, they are to be found in the provisions of other Directives which might or might not be adequate. Although the fitness of those Directives is to be reviewed, there is no guarantee that protection of consumer interests is now the most important regulatory priority for a Commission that has pinned its hopes on growth in on-line supply and consumption. More seriously, neither the E-Commerce Directive nor other Directives are drafted to regulate the next phase in the evolution of the consumer marketplace – the development of 'smart' shopping, where we have fully automated supply of consumer goods and services, where humans are largely taken out of the transactional equation, and where technological management takes over securing compliant performance. Finally, for the avoidance of misunderstanding, let me emphasise that I am not anticipating that, any time soon, humans will cease to transact as consumers any more than that they will cease to drive their cars – for some time, humans will surely continue to enjoy the shopping experience just as they enjoy the driving experience. However, a niche will be found for automated consumption exactly as a niche will be found for driverless cars; and even if this is not the thick end of a wedge, it is a thin end that will make it increasingly difficult to maintain an unexceptionalist view.

---

121 Compare, too, R. Brownsword, 'The Shaping of Our On-Line Worlds: Getting the Regulatory Environment Right' (2012) 20 *International Journal of Law and Information Technology* 249; and A. Ezrachi and M.E. Stucke, *Virtual Competition*, Harvard University Press, Cambridge, Mass. 2016, echoing, in relation to competition law, many of the themes of this chapter (e.g. at 32–33 where the authors anticipate the creation of 'an economy which, for all purposes, is planned not by bureaucrats or CEOs but by the technostructure').

CONNECTED CONTRACTS RELOADED – SMART CONTRACTS AS CONTRACTUAL NETWORKS

Florian IDELBERGER

ABSTRACT

Blockchain technology and 'smart contracts' are widely debated in many industries, but especially among legal professionals and academics. Some practical legal questions can be answered relatively quickly or have to be postponed by 'we do not know' or 'it depends'.

More interesting than those considerations, however, is whether the emergence of smart contracts based on blockchain technology as a technological materialisation of connected contracts raises issues for the conceptualisation of transnational contract law and what a new conceptualisation, taking into account these issues, could look like.

To this end, this contribution tries to acknowledge or incorporate existing work in the area of technology and law such as ontologies, legal reasoning and simple markup languages, but then goes beyond that and tries to explore a socio-legal concept of smart contracts that incorporates the sociological concept of networks by Latour and the system-theoretical approaches of Luhmann with the descriptions of 'connected contracts' by Teubner, ultimately incorporating them into the aforementioned 'technological materialisation' of the network structure of law generally and connected contracts specifically.

This then can serve as an important methodological tool for the future, to research and describe 'smart contracts' at a higher level of abstraction.

1. INTRODUCTION

Certain contractual agents, also called 'smart contracts', running on blockchain technology have gained increasing importance due to promising increased automation and assurance for digital contracting, aiming to bridge law and software code. Thus, this contribution investigates these phenomena, recognising that these developments are potentially game-changing for commerce and further digitalisation of contract law.

To this end, 'smart contracts' and the systems they are running on are analysed with regard to developments of 'connected contracts' and a network(ed) understanding of contract law already developed for newer contractual and company law constructs such as just-in-time production. In order not to limit the examination to 'traditional' manufacturing networks but to re-investigate the phenomenon of networks in law more generally, this is complemented by taking account of socio-legal descriptions of networks and law, as well as providing a brief account of current or past alternative approaches to bridge law and technology that are relevant for context and understanding.

This topic is very timely, as blockchain technology and 'smart contract' agents running on them are developing in many directions, with potential uses in everything from ordinary sales contracts and licensing to auditing and providing identity services, where in many cases the use case is accompanied by legal relations. The most prominent technologies (Bitcoin, Ethereum) in development are used in this chapter to describe the technological systems and what they can do. This description is then contrasted with existing research from Artificial Intelligence and Law, Rule Systems Research or Legal Reasoning. When then looking at the newer technologies and existing research, an essential concept of old and new research is distilled, the 'Ecotronic Normative Environment'. This is a prime concept to describe at the same time legal and technological or economic systems that can incorporate rules. This concept is then used to put these developments into the context of socio-legal work about networks and describe the technological instantiation as the coming into being of connected digital contracts or contract(ual) networks. Finally, this is connected to thoughts on transnational law and contract law in a liberal society, in which it can be placed.

Through this inter-disciplinary literature review and comparison, new insights are gained about how to describe these developments and what the essence of their being actually is – a very important endeavour, as the actual developments are frequently overshadowed by marketing and other obfuscation. Defining the essence of the normative systems described and placing connected digital contracts in the arena of law – instantiating them – enables us to understand and work with these developments toward a further digitalisation of contract law.

2. BLOCKCHAIN AND 'SMART CONTRACTS' PRIMER

This section describes the development of 'blockchain'[1] technology, a decentralised database. The most prominent implementation of such a system is Bitcoin, best known for its use as an alternative, decentralised and as yet mostly unregulated virtual currency.[2] This is why Bitcoin and related literature will be used to explain certain characteristics of such systems. More advanced blockchain systems such as Ethereum are then referred to with regard to 'smart contracts'. Whereas Bitcoin recreated an Economic System in code, Ethereum tries to recreate norms as code.[3]

Bitcoin[4] and related systems[5] are based on this decentralised database system although they are often described differently in popular media, with a strong focus on the monetary and economic aspects instead. They evolved from a technological and libertarian[6] mind-set and have a strong theoretical and logical

---

1 A. Wright, P. De Filippi, *Decentralized Blockchain Technology and the Rise of Lex Cryptographia*, Social Science Research Network, Rochester, NY, 2015, <http://papers.ssrn.com/abstract=2580664> accessed 12.04.2015.

2 Regional bans (China, Russia) or licensing schemes (NY Bit licence) exist and in many jurisdictions the exchanges with traditional money fall under Financial Services Regulations, but it is uncertain how effective these are.

3 B. Kelly, *The Bitcoin big bang: how alternative currencies are about to change the world*, Wiley, Hoboken, NJ, 2015, p. 156.

4 S. Nakamoto, *Bitcoin: A Peer-to-Peer Electronic Cash System:* www.bitcoin.org 2008.

5 Defined as systems that are, through use of cryptography, similar to Bitcoin and also advertise with 'Coins' or 'Tokens'; Examples: Coinmarketcap, *Crypto-Currency Market Capitalizations*, 2016, <https://coinmarketcap.com/> accessed 15.09.2016.

6 S. Jeong, *The Bitcoin Protocol as Law, and the Politics of a Stateless Currency*, Social Science Research Network, Rochester, NY, 2013, <http://papers.ssrn.com/abstract=2294124> accessed 22.04.2015.

foundation.[7] Based on this development, the basics of a distributed ledger for virtual money and money transactions are increasingly co-opted to use the technology for more general and non-monetary uses.[8] From an economic and legal point of view, Bitcoin represents the first large-scale experiment of certain assumptions that are otherwise only used in a theoretical manner in both disciplines. In economics this is how Bitcoin is attributed with value, how it is used and which market rules it adheres to in comparison with state-issued currencies. In law, this is the definition of money and currency,[9] more specifically private monies and how to deal with those if they are used on a large scale. On a bigger scale, there are issues of disruption regarding the financial services industry and loss or shift of control, which through extension of Bitcoin and new developments such as Ethereum, could potentially spread.

Research into 'Agreement Technologies'[10] more generally which proposes next-generation distributed networking systems based on agreements between computational agents, has been ongoing for a while and takes very diverse forms. These have ranged from markup and annotation techniques over code as law (or instead of law in some readings of Lessig) to legal reasoning and argumentation applied to technology and multi-agent systems where multiple agents negotiate to achieve a certain consensual outcome.[11]

Though there are significant differences between the established models of law and economics and the blockchain technologies presented here, especially with regard to enforcement, it is likely that the technologies described or similar ones can usher in a new era of transparency, recordkeeping and efficiency for the law.[12] However, at this stage it is not possible to say where a profound clash with existing institutions and policy makers would lead.

2.1. THE LEGAL AND TECHNOLOGICAL SYSTEMS UNDER CONSIDERATION

The interactions between legal and technical systems can be looked at from many angles and perspectives, even when just looking at contract law. From a technical perspective, there are many different approaches past and present

7 See P. Franco, *Understanding bitcoin: cryptography, engineering and economics*, Wiley, Hoboken, NJ, 2015, and referenced technical papers for details.

8 Wright and De Filippi, above n. 1. p. 8.

9 W.B. Beck, 'Bitcoins als Geld im Rechtssinne', *Neue Juristische Wochenschrift* 580–586, 2015.

10 S. Ossowski, *Agreement Technologies*, Springer, Dordrecht, 2013. This is only one of many approaches and similar research is done under other names, but for the purpose of this paper the scope is limited to Agreement Technologies.

11 *Agreement Technologies Project*, 2008, <http://www.agreement-technologies.org/project>.

12 Wright and De Filippi, above n. 1. p. 17.

on the borderline between law and technology. Because of this, the present examination is restricted to certain specific cases.

On the side of law, this analysis will deal with contract law specifically, but with notions of law in general when this is referenced as such by outside literature. The notion of contract used is a general one, with references to principles and the general (western) understanding of contract and not specific national implementations or provisions. In the future, country or region-specific regulation can be an issue, but at this point it is too early to discuss the results of this or potential future regulation. On a technical level, the present analysis will examine the Ethereum[13] system for decentralised rule-making and decentralised institutions and similar systems to analyse their uses for forming agreements and contracts.

The technology behind it is based on and inspired by Bitcoin, a decentralised network for value storage and accounting, so many explanations refer to Bitcoin literature or publications, as this is more expansive and better developed and is often analogous.[14] I coin the term *Ecotronic Normative Environments* for the systems under examination in this chapter[15] because of their specific properties, which will be explained further below. This section will now first explain the general properties of Bitcoin, Ethereum and related systems, from now on also called 'blockchain' technologies or simply blockchain(s) as a common term of these systems, used also in popular media due the unique structure of the their database.[16]

2.2. GENERAL (BLOCKCHAINS)

While this description is focused on Bitcoin, in principle it works similarly with other systems based on the same codebase or the same principles.

To begin with, it has to be explained how the system of the blockchain functions, which is the basis for any further consideration of the Bitcoin and Ethereum systems. The main part of the system is a decentralised database which catalogues all balances and transactions. This called a *blockchain* due to its structure, where one *block* of data, containing multiple transactions, succeeds the next.[17] The blockchain database is synchronised between and verified by all *nodes* (computers) on the network. No existing entry in the database may

---

13 See table of definitions; Vitalik Buterin, *Ethereum White Paper*, Ethereum, 2014, <ethereum.org/pdfs/EthereumWhitePaper.pdf> accessed 18.02.2015.

14 Nakamoto, above n. 4. pp. 1–2.

15 This is a neologism of this contribution, developed in detail below at section 4.2.

16 Franco, above n. 7. pp. 95–105.

17 Franco, above n. 7. pp. 99–101.

be modified once it has been added in consensus with other network nodes. A key part of a blockchain's integrity is that one block is always dependent on the previous block, so that a chain of interwoven blocks is created, therefore called blockchain.[18]

The interwoven blocks are secured through a network function called *'Proof of Work'* which, in abstract terms, is a simple but effective way of representing work, represented by computing power in an algorithm.[19] It is described as 'moderately hard' to solve, but easy to verify.[20] This is achieved by requiring a given algorithm (hash function)[21] to achieve a result with a certain number of zeros at the start, while the main content of the hash is represented by the contents of the block, describing the transactions included in it.[22] To do this, an otherwise unimportant number '*nonce*' is included in each block for it to be included in the blockchain. This number plus the other hashed content has to result in the certain number of zeros at the start. As this is unpredictable and statistically not optimisable so far, the nodes involved just increment the nonce until they find a number that results in a hash with the required characteristic. This process is also called 'partial hash inversion'. The difficulty of the process can be adjusted by changing the number of leading zeros required, makin.[23] There are also developments that try to move y from the Proof of Work algorithm (PoW), to one that bases its metric for 'work' on other factors that are more easily available to a greater number of people and is resistant against optimisation to keep its economic properties due to this 'work' intact.[24]

This mechanism, combined with the interlinked blocks of the blockchain and a time-stamping mechanism employed alongside it, form the blockchain and assure its security and consistency.[25] To include transactions in the blockchain, clients broadcast a transaction prepared in the right format to the network. This network can be public (such as Bitcoin), private (such as within one company) or semi-private (such as used by banking consortia). The latter two, however, cannot offer many of the benefits of public blockchains while gaining more centralised control.

---

18 Franco, above n. 7. p. 105; Each block relies on the existence of all its preceding blocks, thereby creating a unique chain of blocks, where no single block or part thereof can be changed without affecting all subsequent blocks in the chain.

19 Franco, above n. 7. pp. 95 and 101.

20 This means that the creation of these hashes is not so hard as to take an inordinate amount of time, but once a hash is known it can be verified with just one computation.

21 Nakamoto, above n. 4. p. 3.

22 Franco, above n. 7. pp. 105–108.

23 Franco, above n. 7. pp. 101–103. (This applies to Bitcoin as described. Ethereum at time of writing uses a more complicated system to make it harder to optimise with specialised hardware but the important essence described is the same.)

24 Franco, above n. 7. pp. 233–237.

25 Franco, above n. 7. p. 105.

2.3. BITCOIN

Bitcoin is a specific implementation of the blockchain technology and the first one that was widely successful.[26] 'Widely successful' in this context does not mean mass-market adoption, but compared to many other cryptocurrencies or e-payment solutions the volume of trade and investment is relatively high and at least certain merchants accept it.[27] Some of Bitcoin's success and popularity can also be attributed to actual and potential illegal uses such as unregulated online markets that offer payment in Bitcoin for a perceived anonymous use.[28] For a more legal introduction, see Boehm and Pesch.[29]

Briefly summarised, it represents a peer-to-peer version of electronic cash, with no central point of direct authority.[30] Apart from its 'fame' Bitcoin and many of its users also have ties to libertarian ideas and some forms of the Austrian Economic School.[31] In particular, the (unknown) founder of Bitcoin stated that he saw it as a response to the failure of banks during the economic crisis and that he wanted to show that a different way, without needing to trust a bank, is possible.[32]

To use Bitcoin, every user has a 'Wallet' associated with one or more virtual addresses, consisting of a public and a private cryptographic key per address.[33] These are used to tie transactions to a particular address. When a new node connects to the network or reconnects after a period of absence, it obtains the latest state of the blockchain from other nodes, trusting the longest chain with the highest total difficulty.[34]

The Proof of Work algorithm described above is referred to as 'mining' as it is likened to mining for gold due to the incentives it entails. In the Bitcoin network, the difficulty of 'mining' is adjusted about every two weeks, measured in blocks, which is possible as the time between new blocks is stable under the assumption that the 'Hashrate' of the network (the rate at which it guesses solutions to the

---

26 Franco, above n. 7. p. 37.

27 Franco, above n. 7; Humboldt Universität Berlin – School of Business and Economics, *CRIX – CRypto IndeX*, 2016, <http://crix.hu-berlin.de/> accessed 17.09.2016.

28 Nakamoto, above n. 4. p. 6. P. De Filippi, 'Bitcoin: a regulatory nightmare to a libertarian dream', 3 *Internet Policy Review* 2014, <http://papers.ssrn.com/sol3/papers.cfm?abstract_id=2468695> accessed 11.05.2015. p. 2.

29 F. Boehm, P. Pesch, 'Bitcoins: Rechtliche Herausforderungen einer virtuellen Währung – Eine erste juristische Einordung', *Multimedia und Recht Zeitschrift für Informations-, Telekommunikations- und Medienrecht* 75–79, 2014.

30 Nakamoto, above n. 4; Franco, above n. 7. p. 169.

31 A school of theoretical economics focusing its method on the subjective choices of individuals instead of empirical findings.

32 Nakamoto, above n. 4. pp. 6–8.

33 Nakamoto, above n. 4. p. 2.

34 Franco, above n. 7. p. 115.

algorithm described above) stays the same. Each time a 'block' of a transaction is mined the checksum (hash) incorporates a time-stamp, the previous hash, the nonce (which computing power is spent on looking for) and the actual transaction values.

The primary use for this and its original intent (as expressed by its anonymous unknown creator) was a virtual currency and virtual macroeconomic system. However, as the system became more popular, a variety of alternative uses for such a distributed database were envisioned.[35] For example, the contents sent with a transaction were replaced with arbitrary data that was then hashed and replicated by all nodes. This could for example be used to hash a document or image and, through the tamper protection and time-stamping mechanism inherent in the system, be used to prove that at a certain time this document already existed.[36] However, quite soon it became apparent that for non-currency uses, the Bitcoin system was not ideal and hard to adapt; especially as it already runs a currency with a certain value, and so adjustment, even if only for scalability, is done extremely slowly and cautiously – as parties with large holdings of Bitcoin have a vested interest against changes to the algorithms or governance.[37]

This led to the development of alternative technologies that incorporate the main features of the Bitcoin blockchain, but try to adjust and improve it for different use cases. One big advancement is the development of technologies that allow not only for the provision of a medium of exchange and accompanying transaction mechanism such as Bitcoin, but provide facilities to codify a variety of financial instruments and a plethora of alternative uses. The most advanced and progressive of these is currently Ethereum.7[38]

2.4. ETHEREUM

Ethereum[39] takes the basics of the technology as described above for Bitcoin and goes one step further, combining its security and assurance qualities with proper computation within the system. Through its deterministic characteristics, it enables coordination and synchronised calculation that were not possible before. It employs existing blockchain technology and some new approaches, taking account of discovered shortcomings, to provide a programmable ledger

35 Wright and De Filippi, above n. 1. pp. 8–17.

36 Bitproof.io, 'Bitproof', 2015, <https://bitproof.io/> accessed 11.05.2015; ascribe.io, '*Take* control of your intellectual property', 2015, <https://www.ascribe.io/> accessed 11.05.2015.

37 Franco, above n. 7. p. 171.

38 ethereum.org, *ethereum*, 2014, <https://www.ethereum.org/>; Vitalik Buterin, above n. 13.

39 Franco, above n. 7. p. 199.

on which many kinds of assets, logic, rules and calculations can be codified.[40] Similarly to how Bitcoin blocks are distributed and checked by the whole network, the Ethereum network executes and verifies these codifications and calculations.

At its core, it consists of a blockchain as described above. The structure of a block is different though, as it includes the possibility for arbitrary data insertion and code execution[41] within the system. This code (in Ethereum jargon called 'smart contracts' but in theory better referred to as reactive agents)[42] can interact with other agents on the blockchain and (within limits) can be relatively complex.[43] Within the system, it has even self-enforcing qualities, similar to Bitcoin. However, these self-enforcing qualities depend on data already available in the blockchain or inserted into it by another agent. Then the agent running on the blockchain could access this data and act on it. Thus, Ethereum adds to Bitcoin a homogenous environment for rule-making that is deterministic and runs within a known environment.[44] Below, this technical environment is related to existing research in the area such as research on Artificial Intelligence (AI) and Law and Agreement Technologies.[45]

When we look towards systems such as those described in *Agreement Technologies* by Ossowski, they try to approach the law as it is from an academic view and try to create systems through the use of ontologies, machine learning and other techniques that teach artificial agents or other machines to understand the law (or other concepts) and apply them and work with them. This is so far mostly used in the research environment, though also some start-ups

---

40 Wright and De Filippi, above n. 1. p. 24.

41 This means that the size and kind of data it is possible to embed are not as limited (if you can pay for it) than with Bitcoin and that it can contain (programming) logic that will be followed.

42 'Reactive' due to only being reactive to invocation. To be consistent with other publications, either 'smart contract' will be used or just 'agent' if in relation to agent literature.

43 J.S. Czepluch, N.Z. Lollike, S.O. Malone, *The Use of Block Chain Technology in Different Application Domains*, The IT University of Copenhagen, Copenhagen, 20 May 2015, <http://lollike.org/bachelor.pdf> accessed 29.01.2016; Wright and De Filippi, above n. 1. p. 17; An example of too complex code: Thoughts on The DAO Hack, Hacking Distributed, <http://hackingdistributed.com/2016/06/17/thoughts-on-the-dao-hack/> accessed 15.09.2016.

44 G. Wood, *Ethereum: A secure decentralised generalised Transaction Ledger, gavwood.com*, <http://gavwood.com/Paper.pdf> p. 7.

45 Ossowski, above n. 10; G. Sartor, A. Rotolo, 'AI and Law', in *Agreement Technologies*, pp. 199–207, Springer, Dordrecht, 2013; P.C. Romeu (ed.), *AI approaches to the complexity of legal systems : AICOL 2013 International Workshops*, AICOL-IV@IVR, Belo Horizonte, Brazil, 21–27 July 2013 and AICOL-V@SINTELNET-JURIX, Bologna, Italy, 11 December 2013 : revised selected papers, Springer, Heidelberg, 2014; JURIX 2007, 'Legal knowledge and information systems: JURIX 2011: The twenty-fourth annual conference' in K.M. Atkinson (ed.), IOS Press; IOS Press distributor in USA and Canada, Amsterdam: Fairfax, VA, 2011.

are experimenting with AI and Law.[46] Contrary to that, Ethereum gives the opportunity to recreate norms in code, similarly to how Bitcoin recreated an economic system in code. The main benefit is that a system such as Ethereum is much easier to interface with for other nodes (independently of whether they are a computer or human) and has requirements that are far less onerous than a system simulating a virtual agent capable of 'negotiating' on its own, as described in some contributions to *Agreement Technologies*.

'Agreement Technologies' can be said to describe what was or is desired by blockchain technologies such as Ethereum, but a solution incorporating something like Ethereum is more realistic and feasible at present. In any case, to make systems such as Ethereum more accessible, visualisation techniques and intermediary layers have been and will be developed, and in that regard existing work on mark-up languages and legal ontologies will be very useful.

The environment created by Ethereum enables the creation of rules and norms that do not help the machine to understand the real world, but it instead creates a virtual world with electronic norms that can easily be understood by machines and humans alike.[47] This 'environment' or legal virtual world will be described with reference to and using terms of existing scholarship below. On a user level, the development this could lead to is often described as 'business-logic' when referring to the algorithm representing a legal or business process (such as the algorithm used by a gambling site or a bank) with the ability to retrace how it works and verify how it worked in a particular instance. Alternatively, in combination with additional decentralised technologies it is often described as a 'piece of the puzzle' for a potential 'next web'.[48] This refers to the next evolution of the internet, in this case characterised through decentralisation and new structures that have the goal of being less dependent on centralised structures such as the DNS[49] system, thus being more resilient, more transparent and interoperable.[50] This is made evident by the fact that IBM 'forked'[51] Ethereum a while ago, to develop it as a further basis for a decentralised 'Internet of Things' and other firms and consortia are also working on use cases for auditing, banking,

---

46 Examples: Kira Systems, Machine Learning Contract Search, Review and Analysis, <https://kirasystems.com/> accessed 15.09.2016; PETER, *Peter | Your AI-Based Business Lawyer*, <https://hirepeter.com/> accessed 15.09.2016.

47 H.L. CARDOSO ET AL., 'ANTE: Agreement Negotiation in Normative and Trust-Enabled Environments' in *Agreement Technologies*, pp. 549–564, Springer, Dordrecht, 2013 at pp. 551–552.

48 K. FINLEY, 'Out in the Open: Teenage Hacker Transforms Web Into One Giant Bitcoin Network', ('Business') WIRED, 27 January 2014, <http://www.wired.com/2014/01/ethereum/> accessed 06.09.2016.

49 Domain Name Service, the system translating domain names into numeric network addresses.

50 FINLEY, above n. 48.

51 Taking the existing program code and using and adapting it for one own purpose.

virtual goods, crowd-funding, insurance and supply-chain transparency.[52] In the following section, these technical descriptions will be put into the context of existing research and analysed in more detail.

3. LOOKING FOR THE CONTRACT IN 'SMART CONTRACTS'

With the recent advent of blockchain technology and its development[53] and application beyond purely financial transactions,[54] it has become important to actually define which part of these technologies, and under which conditions, can be qualified as a contract in the legal (or any) sense. In principle, as on the internet or in real life, everybody otherwise being capable and allowed to conclude a contract can conclude a contract on the blockchain, or 'take part' in one, thus smart contracts can be legal contracts. Their main advantage is bringing security, 'trustlessness', pseudonimity, legal certainty and some degree of automation to legal contracts. Instead of smart contracts these could also be called (reactive) software agents and, independently of blockchain, they have been described before in the literature on AI and Law.[55] It should be noted that the term 'smart contract' was not chosen by legal professionals or politicians, but by developers and other progressive thinkers that found the merging of law and code – the automation of law – appealing. As a result, the legal nature of 'smart contracts' is not congruent with that of legal contracts, though as explained, this does not mean that 'smart contracts' cannot be legal contracts.

To draw an analogy, a legal contract, at its core is an agreement between one or more parties, valid and qualified as a contract within the confines of a particular environment of rules, made up of the geographic location, legal

52 IBM Institute for Business Value, Paul Brody, Veena Pureswaran, *Device Democracy – Saving the future of the Internet of Things*, IBM Global Business Services, 2015, <http://public.dhe.ibm.com/common/ssi/ecm/gb/en/gbe03620usen/GBE03620USEN.PDF> accessed 30.04.2015; ADEPT demo by IBM and Samsung, *TheProtocol.TV*, <https://www.theprotocol.tv/adept-demo-ibm-samsung/> accessed 18.02.2015.; See also: R.H. Weber and R. weber, *Internet of things: Legal perspectives*, Springer / Schulthess, Berlin / Zürich, 2010; Czepluch, Lollike and Malone, above n. 43.

53 Deterministic, predictable computer agents meant to codify business logic and certain legal relations.

54 Czepluch, Lollike and Malone, above n. 43.

55 G. Sartor, 'Cognitive automata and the law: electronic contracting and the intentionality of software agents', 17 *Artificial Intelligence and Law* 253, 2009; G. Sartor, *Intentional Compliance with Normative Systems*, 2012, <http://cadmus.eui.eu/handle/1814/24300> accessed 31.01.2015.

jurisdiction, agency of the parties and based on these (and additional) factors, the specific rules applicable to a particular contract such as particular rules applicable to consumer contracts or sales.[56]

A smart contract, then, is also subject to a limited environment, though its environment is at first primarily defined by the constraints imposed by the technological environment. This is defined by the limits of the blockchain and networking technology involved and the virtual machine running on top of that, executing computer code in conjunction with a smart contract programming language such as 'solidity'[57] for Ethereum, targeting this virtual machine.

This technological environment, then, defines what is possible, to some extent defining which kind of legal relations can be codified meaningfully on the blockchain. In many situations, these technological limits would then be subject to the same restrictions and regulations that 'traditional' contracts are subject to. However, unless these smart contracts are established and used by known entities such as companies or private legal persons, there is no general way of assessing which law would in a given situation be applicable to ephemeral smart contracts. This is to some degree the perfect example of creating a decentralised, somewhat pseudonymous and mostly 'trustless' system to codify relations meant to be of similar value to legal relations, even when potentially violating certain regulatory measures or laws, pursuing a kind of super-powered 'lex digitalis' as described in transnational law literature.[58]

As a result, until there is an established system to integrate with regulators (and in certain jurisdictions there is still the threat of outright bans, although technically very unfeasible) it is even more the responsibility of companies involved and of individual users to assess the legality of legal relations they enter into via smart contracts such as adherence to Terms of Service restrictions ('*AGB Kontrolle*') for companies, as they are responsible for their actions by established means. Taking into account the restrictions outlined above – there is no reason why smart contracts should not be regarded as legal contracts and legal status be attributed to them, assuming they have the intent to codify some sort of legal relationship and do not violate any of the restrictions outlined above. If, however, they do not seem to codify a legal relationship as understood by existing legal systems – such as when they perform merely administrative or auditing functionality or when there is no agreement – they are likely not to be classified as legal contracts.

---

56 J.W. Rutgers, P. Sirena, *Rules and principles in European contract law*, Intersentia Uitgevers NV, Mortsel, 2015.

57 Czepluch, Lollike and Malone, above n. 43. pp. 16, 18.

58 Wright and De Filippi, above n. 1. pp. 45–47; On smart contract governance and drawing from contract law: B. Marino, 'Smart-Contract Escape Hatches: The Dao of The DAO', *Hacking, Distributed*, <http://hackingdistributed.com/2016/06/22/smart-contract-escape-hatches/> accessed 14.09.2016.

To further specify the characteristics outlined above, in both smart and traditional contracts, there will be either one, two or more parties that agree with common intent (a contract with one party being either a promise or a contract with oneself, such as a savings account). Traditionally a bank would then constitute the second party in a savings contract, but in case of a smart contract the rules otherwise enforced by the bank (such as when savings become available) could be enforced by the blockchain network and the rules built on top by the smart contract directly, in which case this construct would not qualify as a legal contract in most jurisdictions. There are certain characteristics that make the technological environment described very enticing to those wishing to codify legal relationships. From a libertarian perspective this is the use of an economic system and incentives free of state intervention and in a more general, but also simplified understanding of contracts,[59] this is the non-malleability of present and past states (under certain assumptions)[60] so that the details of who executed performance, who did not, and who owns what number of assets may not be retroactively changed.

To recap, as explained above, both the traditional legal system and a system for smart contracts such as described above adhere to freedom of contract, through their own separate environments of rule-making (though these environments might intersect), with the technological environment having additional features through encryption, pseudonimity and decentralisation meant to work as censorship resistance and some automation and easier accessibility to machines. This can either be seen as an advantage or as making up for generally easier surveillance in the digital sphere.

Bigger differences emerge with regard to enforcement, as some degree of automatic enforcement is possible with 'smart contracts', within the constraints of the system, though in borderline cases non-digital and digital contracts would both have to resort to the legal system, where the outcome is uncertain. Much has and will be written[61] about it, but as this is outside the scope of this chapter, this will not be discussed further. It suffices to state that laws still apply, such as consumer protection rules and restrictions on terms of service. This analysis will return to the examination of smart contracts as connected contracts, as networks and how this might help us understand them.

---

59 Which became apparent when there was discussion whether by mutual agreement of key players and community, it would be acceptable to reverse a major theft or if immutability, 'code is law' (even if it was written with different intention) and the libertarian attitude behind it should prevail. (Summer of 2016).

60 Assumptions: No centralised control of contributed computing power (a.k.a. '51% attack'), sufficient incentives and working encryption.

61 Marino, above n. 58; S.D. Palley, 'Determining Jurisdiction When a DAO is Sued', *CoinDesk*, 22 May 2016, <http://www.coindesk.com/legal-liability-dao/> accessed 15.09.2016. Marino, how to sue dao, smart contract escape hatches, and primavera or other German source?

4. WHAT CAME BEFORE, AND WHAT CAN BE DEDUCED?

When investigating the interconnection between legal rules and technological 'smart contracts' trying to implement legal rules independently of jurisdiction, the investigation led to a great amount of literature in related fields that could either be seen as predecessors to smart contracts or at least give valuable input on how these rule-making systems can be described. Already in the '90s there was research about how to display or digitalise legal agreements, such as semantic formats and ontologies / knowledge-bases designed to make legal rules accessible to machines and the first notions of digital agents acting in a legal capacity, only without the networked, decentralised system for record-keeping, security and enforcement; these were potentially the predecessors of today's 'smart contracts'.

This led to the analysis of research called 'Agreement Technologies', mainly conducted in a research project in Spain and the associated Universities and projects.[62] This will be presented below, especially how this more technical research describes the use of 'normative environments' and how they can be transposed to the legal realm or techno-legal realm. In the course of this explanation, it also becomes necessary to give a brief account of how normativity is understood in this context. In the following section, these more techno-legal developments are presented. Furthermore, research into the use of legal ontologies, the semantic web (semantic data), legal reasoning and logical representation will be presented, as they are all valuable sources for understanding codification of rules in 'smart contracts' and could make this technology much more usable and governable and thus harness its proper power.

4.1. WHAT ARE AGREEMENT TECHNOLOGIES?

Briefly alluded to above – Agreement Technologies is a term not known to legal professionals but primarily used by technical researchers. It describes technologies used to negotiate or conclude agreements between physical or digital agents, independently of whether somewhere along the line a contract is concluded or not and it can also incorporate the negotiation part.[63] It could also be called 'contract technologies' giving a very specific and broad meaning to contract, although agreement technologies is certainly less loaded and broader, as lots of discussion with legal professionals is avoided.

62 Agreement-Technologies Project, above n. 11.
63 Cardoso et al., above n. 47.

Some of this research is very technical and some can also incorporate process management and similar models between agents, as to how to optimally negotiate or contract in a certain scenario. Research about how nodes 'negotiate' with each other[64] or how human or digital agents might behave in a virtual economy is important for creating useful and stable blockchain systems, but this shall not be discussed here.

Despite the technical nature, a very useful concept discovered while perusing this more technical literature is the idea of a 'Normative Environment' as a requirement for digital agents to operate.[65] This is necessary for the agents, as they can only act on what they know and also any new rules would necessarily depend on the existing environment. This fits perfectly for 'smart contracts' as (reactive) digital agents, as they need a technical normative environment to function, and it fits for the classical conclusion of contracts, as every legal contract cannot be established in a vacuum, but is based on assumptions, norms and principles established by the (layers of) the legal system.[66]

These two normative environments then interact as well, in specific ways dependent on the situation. This model can be made even better by introducing the concept of layers found in the description of network connections as an alternative to the '*Normenpyramide*' – just as the technical environment for the digital agents has different normative layers, so the legal environment has different layers with different governance models and different priorities as well.[67] Thus, these descriptions are perfect to describe a symbiosis between law and digital agents such as smart contracts.

4.2. ECOTRONIC NORMATIVE ENVIRONMENTS

As established above, both in law and technology we can observe the concept of normative environments, though not always called by this name. To better differentiate between different kinds of normative environments such as those used by Bitcoin and many other blockchain systems this contribution extends the basic term 'normative environment' to account for differences between different technological or legal systems.

First, one can differentiate between Electronic Normative Environment and Non-Electronic Normative Environments. As an example, a blockchain

---

64 Ossowski, above n. 10.

65 Cardoso et al., above n. 47. pp. 551–552.

66 A. Fisahn, W.M.R. Ciftci, 'Hierarchie oder Netzwerk – zum Verhältnis nationaler zur europäischen Rechtsordnung', *Juristische Arbeitsblätter* 364–370, 2016 (description of the hierarchy of norms including a network analogy).

67 H. Zimmermann, 'OSI Reference Model – The ISO Model of Architecture for Open Systems Interconnection', 28 *IEEE Transactions on Communications* 425–432, 1980. and Fisahn and Ciftci, above n. 66.

system for 'smart contracts' or an environment for negotiation between software agents, is necessarily electronic. Traditional legal rules and structures, however, can also be set up and applied non-electronically. As this analysis focuses on smart contracts on blockchain systems, Electronic Normative Environments are the primary model concept to be used. This concept of the Normative Environment can also be extended in a different direction by taking into account the economics-based nature of relevant blockchain systems. This includes the incorporation of a built-in currency to reward participation with computing power and prevent abuse through the requirement of transaction fees for storage and computation and the use of this currency for commerce, investment or any type of economic activity.

This is partially a technical feature as described, but it also undoubtedly has an influence on how the legal quality of these environments works. As a counterargument, it could be said that also the established, offline-based legal systems involve certain fees for specific services and might be easier to use for legal persons with a certain wealth. Whether this deep embeddedness of the economic system and specific incentives into a system also used for (private) legal codification in the form of contracts has profound effects on the way contracts are used or the legal quality of the system more generally remains to be seen. It might also be that existing implicit or explicit ties between actors and services will just become more visible, so that ideally it would be easier to calculate how costly the average contract or legal procedure is and who is influenced by whom. This is assuming that public blockchains become a mainstream tool to some degree, as many benefits would not be available to the public if only private or consortia blockchains become widespread.[68]

Then, when these two extensions, the electronic normative environment and the economic normative environment are combined, the result can be described as an Economic Electronic Normative Environment or as a shortened neologism – *Ecotronic Normative Environment*. So far, all current systems offering the possibility of 'smart contracts' as understood in this chapter are based on blockchain technology and all can be qualified as Ecotronic Normative Environments. Thus, this concept accurately describes the characteristics of blockchain systems developed so far and can help to delineate them against traditional legal systems and other normative environments.

In the course of the above explanation of the value and development of normative environments, it becomes necessary to give a brief definition of normativity. For the description of the 'normative environment' given above and its further use below, normativity or a normative rule is seen as any new rule that sets new conditions that did not exist before. In principle, similarly

---

[68] V. Buterin, *On Public and Private Blockchains*, Ethereum Blog 2015, <https://blog.ethereum.org/2015/08/07/on-public-and-private-blockchains/> accessed 17.09.2016.

to how above the constraints by the programming environment and those by the legal system were compared, it is also possible to differentiate between legal normativity and technical or programmatic normativity. However, for the course of this chapter, whenever a new, normative rule or normativity is mentioned, this is meant to refer to a legal rule, or with some sort of 'legal' quality and not merely a programmatic or procedural rule.

4.3. FURTHER EXISTING WORK

Below, certain works from research into legal ontologies, knowledge-bases and legal reasoning and logical representation will be presented as far as is helpful for understanding smart contracts.

4.3.1. Ontologies/Knowledge-Bases

Since the '80s there has been research about making real world information, such as legal information, more accessible to computers (or humans) by structuring it according to pre-defined parameters.

In metaphysical philosophy the term ontologies is used to describe the nature of being, either in general or with regard to specific cases, so this is a fitting term for how to structure information and capture 'the essence' of its being.[69] Depending on the field or context, it can also be found under the name knowledge-base, whereas the accessibility of this content through the internet is in research circles often termed 'semantic web' or semantic data.[70]

These have also been described extensively to structure legal information such as bodies of legal texts or legal reasoning.[71] In part, these techniques have had some practical application in empirical research on legal texts[72] and attempts at having virtual agents conclude answers through ontologies, though this has

---

69 T. Hofweber, 'Logic and Ontology' in E.N. Zalta (ed.), *The Stanford Encyclopedia of Philosophy*, 2014, <http://plato.stanford.edu/archives/fall2014/entries/logic-ontology/> accessed 17.09.2016; M. Fernández-Barrera, G. Sartor, *Classifications and the Law: Doctrinal Classifications vs. Computational Ontologies*, 2010, <http://cadmus.eui.eu/handle/1814/14314> accessed 01.06.2015.

70 Axel Polleres, 'Agreement Technologies and the Semantic Web' in *Agreement Technologies*, pp. 57–67, Springer, Dordrecht, 2013; G. Sartor, *Legislative XML for the semantic web: principles, models, standards for document management*, Springer Science and Business Media B.V, Dordrecht, 2011.

71 P. Mazzega, D. Bourcier, R. Boulet, 'The Network of French Legal Codes', *Proceeding ICAIL '09 Proceedings of the 12th International Conference on Artificial Intelligence and Law* 2009, <https://arxiv.org/ftp/arxiv/papers/1204/1204.6284.pdf> accessed 17.09.2016; P. Wahlgren, *Automation of legal reasoning: a study on artificial intelligence and law*, Kluwer Law and Taxation Publishers, Deventer, Boston MA, 1992.

72 S. Macaulay, 'An Empirical View of Contract', *Wisconsin Law Review* 465, 1985.

not become too widespread yet. Nonetheless, research is ongoing in academia and private businesses, and more interesting and visible applications for digital contracting are very likely.

4.3.2. Legal Reasoning/Logical Representation

In relation to the provision of structured (semantic) content mentioned above, there is also ongoing research into the science of legal argumentation, legal reasoning and how this can be represented. In this field, methods from philosophy and logic are used to describe ways of reasoning, either to explain a certain outcome or to reach said outcome from a predefined set of data.

This could potentially be used with semantic data mentioned above to power a virtual agent with specific legal knowledge or to analyse ways of argumentation by courts, which could then possibly be compared to what students are taught or to decisions by courts. With regard to the representation of contractual clauses, it has also been proposed by some research that it can be easier to analyse a 'smart contract' built for a 'Ecotronic Normative Environment' or for legal professionals to work with it, if it has a representation in a logical format[73] or some other format more easily readable than computer code. In any technical system either dealing with law as such or digital 'smart contracts' in a digital normative environment, formalised legal reasoning and analysis are very enabling.

5. NETWORKS IN SOCIETY

The descriptions and analyses above have provided insight into the technical and legal nature of research and products on the borders between law and technology in general and into the specific legal and technical nature of smart contracts as based on blockchain technology. To get a comprehensive interdisciplinary picture and build a more complete concept that helps us understand normative environments in general and smart contracts in Ecotronic Environments (blockchains) specifically, without a targeted legal or technical perspective, it helps to look towards sociology and see what some of its scholars who are active in the research of the Moderns in general and research about science and technology specifically have to say and how this can be useful.

[73] F. Idelberger et al., 'Evaluation of Logic-Based Smart Contracts for Blockchain Systems' in J.J. Alferes et al. (eds.), *Rule Technologies. Research, Tools, and Applications*, pp. 167–183, Springer International Publishing, 2016, <http://link.springer.com/chapter/10.1007/978-3-319-42019-6_11> accessed 09.06.2016.

As the technical systems under consideration are actual networks – and law, especially contracts, can also be described as a network – the next point of investigation is research with a sociological understanding of the Moderns and law and technology as Networks (sometimes also called 'Actor Network Theory').[74] It will be seen that this enables us to see the normative environments described above not as a homogeneous blob but as a network, with multiple nodes, multiple layers and connections on the inside (such as between agents in a negotiating system) and connections to the outside.

One of the foremost scholars when it comes to a networked understanding of sociology is Bruno Latour with his 'Actor Network Theory' (ANT), which he developed in his works on science studies. This culminated in his 'AIME'[75] project where he brought this together in a much bigger, ambitious project to combine it with his other works of critiquing parts of sociology, connecting them all in one network, examining nodes, connections and actors. A good lawyer, legal professional, business person or IT professional might view such a project quite sceptically, as it is seemingly removed from the everyday practice of their profession and can seem very vague, philosophical and malleable. However, especially in interdisciplinary projects it is helpful not only to focus on the peculiarities involved but to aim to get a hold of the connecting pieces. These can often be found at the edges of the separate disciplines, but it can be very helpful to see where these edges are and what they are connecting to. In the case of law and technology, the overarching disciplines of critical sociology, of social studies and especially of science studies are especially important – as law is a social discipline in its own right and more and more work is done on the interaction between the social (such as law) and technology.

Latour's main points, are always in some way 'everything is connected' and 'it depends on the context' or to use his term, on the preposition [PRE]. This is very appealing for legal theory, as lawyers or legal researchers will know the sentiment 'It depends'. He, man of anthropological and social science background, a man fond of words, describes very methodically the world and everything in it and outside of it, through the eyes of a hypothetical young anthropologist. He works towards a systematisation of diverse phenomena, trying to unite everything and anything that can be studied. This is achieved by definition and deduction of 'modes of existence'. He starts by describing why strict boundaries between areas and disciplines are not useful and are too rigid, whereas multiple modes

74 B. Latour, *An inquiry into modes of existence: an anthropology of the moderns*, Harvard University Press, Cambridge, MA, 2013; An Inquiry into Modes of Existence, <http://www.modesofexistence.org/> accessed 29.04.2015.

75 Latour, above n. 74; AIME, above n. 74.

of existence can intersect ('cross') or be applied to the same set of facts, similarly to different points of views. This categorisation (though Latour would object to that term) is combined with a critique of 'the moderns' as described in sociology. Though in his wording and argumentation Latour sometimes relies maybe too much on language and wording, it can be important to think about terms and phrases used and what they actually mean, especially when talking about new fields of study such as investigating networks in law.[76] When describing networks, he is also careful 'not to confuse what circulates once everything is in place with the setups involving the heterogeneous elements that allow circulation to occur'.[77] This is important and worthwhile when engaged in interdisciplinary research, as something might for example be theoretically outside the domain of law and not traditionally be dealt with by lawyers, but still have legal consequences. This deduction is particularly relevant when investigating the boundaries between law and technology. In the present chapter, the analysis will focus on the modes of [NET], [PRE], [REP], [TEC] and [LAW] as these are most relevant for investigating the reality between law and technology.

The foremost mode that Latour identifies is [NET]. He uses it to define complexity and connections between elements, deconstructing separate domains and areas, whereafter he employs it to reconstruct what was before described as an 'area' or domain.[78] When he takes a description of law as a network as an example (which makes his account particularly suited to this inquiry) he observes that the legal 'network' is partially made up of 'non-law' but when established, encompasses and 'sustains' a 'supply of law'. This is, in his view, applicable to most things that are made up of elements from other domains, to create something new. This is not only true for law, but also for technological networks such as the internet, and as such is very fitting for the present inquiry.

Furthermore, based on the phrase 'legal means' he goes on to define the essence of a networked substance through the notion of PASS, namely of a trajectory that encounters a series of discontinuities and continuities or in his words 'hiatuses'. He sees this series, this trajectory of defining the continuity of the PASS, so that it is either a 'legal means' for law or in other cases 'scientific proof' or other continuity. While his focus on language can be seen as problematic, it can be seen as a process or a 'PASS' that is transformed and directed, so that it achieves a certain quality, such as a 'legal quality'.

Then, coming back to the layers of a network alluded to before – Latour introduces [PRE], the preposition which according to him sets the 'interpretive

76 This will also be seen below when examining Teubner and his writings on connected contracts.

77 Latour, above n. 74. p. 32.

78 Latour, above n. 74. AIME 'all composed in a heterogeneous fashion of unexpected elements revealed by their investigation' p. 35.

key' of a mode which he says explains why the same things can be seen in a different way by science, law, religion and others. With [NET] x [PRE] he introduces 'crossings' for the first time, the intersection between two modes, where he sees fit to compare modes, to 'get their specific, irreducible character'.[79] This might be seen as just a repetition or specification of the first general part of Latour's inquiry and just using this phrase so well known to lawyers – 'It depends', saying that point of view and circumstances matter. His account goes on to explain this as 'describing at once what people are doing and what they care about'; this leads to the conclusion that the common concepts of reason and rationality are too narrow and 'only interrogated truth and error in a single key',[80] whereas his [PRE] mode and crossings introduce a 'multiplicity of reason' in contrast to the old 'singular reason'. If we take this back to earth and compare it to the interdisciplinary work at hand, it is a great description of the differences between law and technology as 'domains' or modes and of different legal regimes, and how they and the actors associated with them work and view things differently.

A third mode of importance to all others is [REP], reproduction.[81] Latour illustrates this with a map of a mountain and the actual mountain (saying that the map is only really useful if you are at the mountain), describing them as 'aligning networks' that are never the same and always change but still 'align'. This works well to represent legislation and policy, as legal rules in any form are modelled on the real world or a specific model of (part of) the real world, without these two being the same or aligning, as can be very well observed when studying norm compliance or contract compliance and interpretation specifically.[82] This particular mode of existence is a reminder that any orderly structure (of [LAW]) needs some form of repetition or reproduction to sustain itself or be sustained. The same goes for any kind of network that we know of. Especially connected contracts and digital networks, such as the internet and other peer-to-peer networks built on top of it, always need some sort of sustenance, as otherwise they cease to function (in the case of electronic networks), or are put into disarray (as in the case of connected contracts, where the respective contracts have to be kept in order and functioning). In the case of connected digital contracts, technology tries to keep the contracts connected and in order, but this requires technology [TEC], for which some sort of sustenance is also required.

---

79 Latour, above n. 74, p. 62.

80 Latour, above n. 74, pp. 65–66.

81 Latour, above n. 74, p. 91 [REP] (reproduction) 'as the name for the mode of existence through which any entity whatsoever crosses through the hiatus of its repetition'.

82 S. Macaulay, 'Non-Contractual Relations in Business: A Preliminary Study', 28 *American Sociological Review* 55–67, 1963; Macaulay, above n. 72; S. Macaulay, 'Private Legislation and the Duty to Read – Business Run by IBM Machine, the Law of Contracts and Credit Cards', 19 *Vanderbilt Law Review* 1051–1121, 1965, <http://heinonline.org/HOL/Page?handle=hein.journals/vanlr19&div=48&g_sent=1&collection=journals> accessed 05.04.2016.

This technology [TEC] enables networks of all kinds, and reproduction is required to maintain and create technology. Similar to the above distinction between the network of law and the legal quality of its content, for technology Latour decries that we should no longer 'confuse technology with the objects it leaves in its wake'. For the present research, this can be understood in such a way that we should not confuse the fascinating transformation that transforms copper cables and fiberglass into the internet or the software that creates peer-to-peer sharing platforms (or peer-to-peer normative environments) with their intent and purpose. Thus it is best to describe them as a network right away,[83] and describe them as a normative environment (i.e. where rules exist and can be implemented) without going to Lessig[84] and saying 'Code is Law'; instead saying 'Code is what we make it' and 'Law is what we make it'.

As [LAW] is its own mode of existence in the sociological exercise of Latour it cannot be omitted, but it required mention of the modes above first. Latour states that law is its own explanation and thus easy to talk about 'legally'.[85] Furthermore, it is described as 'promis[ing] fairly satisfying correspondence between a domain, an institution and a contrast', instituting a 'state of law' and overall it has its own force.[86] This goes along with the concept of a normative environment described above that has its own internal rules.[87] Further, to understand the law, one 'has to take things legally' and law as a 'preposition' changes what follows or how it is viewed. These points ring true for many legal professionals as the law really often does have its own language, mode of analysis and mannerisms to engage situations. Because of this, Latour describes [LAW] as the best mode to analyse due to its self-referential, tautological nature. This self-contained nature is substantiated by referring to H.L.A. Hart, saying:

> Such rules of law do not imply duties or obligations. Instead they provide individuals with the means to fulfil their intentions, by endowing them with legal power to create, through determined procedures and in certain conditions, structures of rights and duties within the limits of the coercive apparatus of the law.[88]

According to Latour this tautology is of no concern, but is exactly what gives the law strength and resistance, such as against flawed rationalities.[89]

83 A similar description is given by Teubner, in the introduction of *Netzwerk als Vertragsverbund*, below n. 102.

84 L. Lessig, *Code and other laws of cyberspace*, Basic Books, New York, 1999; L. Lessig, *Code: version 2.0*, Basic Books, New York, 2006.

85 Latour, above n. 74. p. 357.

86 Latour, above n. 74. p. 358.

87 Also found here Cardoso et al., above n. 47 and in systems theory literature.

88 Latour, above n. 74, p. 359.

89 Latour, above n. 74, p. 359.

The [LAW] account goes on to identify a distinctive legal quality that everyone is able to experience in cases such as contracts or signatures. This, however, still requires an acute awareness (*Achtsamkeit*), and is very subjective. This leads to the identification ascribing legal quality to signatures and other formalities also found in Ecotronic Normative Environments, and Latour then feigning surprise at 'How could this little obstacle have the power to stop us?', in reference to a missing signature.

It is also stressed how the law is hard and flexible at the same time, or has the potential to be, and thus stays on its own and absorbs other areas. Due to the self-contained nature of law described earlier, it is only a structure, an empty shell that has to be given a purpose.[90] To do this, it needs to absorb other areas and this also determines to some degree whether it can make us civilised. Broadly speaking, based on the definition of 'civilised', law can create this civility or also create the opposite, without any rules of grounding or a framework. It should be noted here that this is the language of sociology and Latour – there can be many names for this, but it can be summarised as such – like any tool, law can be used for 'good' and 'evil'. This is also especially true for norm(ative) systems and legal technological systems – often there will be some collision or intersection with traditional legal systems that provide a basic frame of reference such as a constitution, human rights or other frameworks – this then determines the content and direction of this tool.

The 'Inquiry into Modes of Existence' also gives an account of the economy denoted by the acronym [ORG],[91] whereas in many earlier chapters 'the economy' was sometimes referenced like a mysterious being but not discussed. Due to this chapter's previous focus on 'Ecotronic Normative Environments' it would be great to contrast their economic existence with the account given by Latour, but due to space constraints and less focus on Economics as such in this contribution, this will have to take place elsewhere.

The sociological account by Latour thus gives a good grounding framework to anchor any future discussions on contract law and technology, and how they interact, but most importantly how they relate to 'the social' as sociologists would call it; the world around them, to which they have to connect back at some point. This give a much better understanding of Normative Environments of any kind and a description of how they can be described as interacting with practice and reality.

Since legal scholars have broadened their horizons more and more with interdisciplinarity, there have been a few scholars who have expanded the borders of legal scholarship beyond black-letter law and discussion of case law. Apart from the more techno-legal and social scholarship discussed above, in the following

---

90 Latour, above n. 74, p. 362.

91 Latour, above n. 74, p. 381.

sections, scholars from law and policy fields will show their vision of how law is a network, how law and code are alike and working together, and especially how contract law likes to form connections and thereby, networks.

6. BLOCKCHAIN TECHNOLOGY AS A TECHNICAL MATERIALISATION

6.1. THE NETWORK STRUCTURE OF LAW

This section demonstrates the support of established scholars for socio-legal claims that are made in this chapter. However, let there be another claim – blockchain technology and its network topology are a technical materialisation of the network-like structure of the law, of the fact that the law likes to be a network or is drawn to be one. This holds true for many, if not all of different layers, combinations and modes of existence of law and technology for contract(ual) relations. The scope of this chapter does not allow for going through all possibilities meticulously; thus particular key examples are given.

6.2. CONNECTED (DIGITAL) CONTRACTS

The authors most valuable for this excursion are Niklas Luhmann, due to his early discovery of the law as a social system, including systems theories and descriptions of law and norms in a formalised way, similar to computer code; Gunter Teubner, who took Luhmann's concepts and expanded them and applied them more specifically to contract law and the German and European legal system; as well as Stefan Grundmann, who in some works reconsiders these developments and tries to verify them.[92] The findings of these authors will be explained, as far as possible within this scope, below.

Luhmann[93] published extensively about his systems theoretical approach to sociology – though for the present chapter his work on the sociology of law (*Rechtssoziologie*) is the important one. He described understanding of law as a system not influenced or steered by politics or outside forces but only indirectly reacting thorough internal feedback such as if a case did not give a desirable outcome.[94] This description of law and the whole of society as self-referential systems and devoid of moral thinking or any learning process is foreign to many,

92 S. Grundmann, 'Die Dogmatik der Vertragsnetze', 207 *Archiv für die civilistische Praxis* 718–767, 2007.

93 N. Luhmann, K.A. Ziegert, F. Kastner, *Law as a Social System*, Oxford University Press, Oxford, 2004.

94 Luhmann, Ziegert and Kastner, above n. 93, p. 468.

though if compared to the description of law as a 'mode of existence' with its own particularities by Bruno Latour, this echoes the same sentiment, in that law as a structure without content is devoid of meaning – neither good nor bad. Only when filled with content – in the case of Luhmann by the system's own internal feedback mechanisms – does law sway toward what other authors call moral or immoral.[95] He describes law as permeating all the other systems (also similarly to Latour) and, describing it as self-referential, he says it does this by 'following the legal coding rather than any other coding or even no coding at all'.[96] Even the method by which Luhmann conducts his inquiry is similar to Latour when he seems interested less in the essence of law but in how to observe it at is work. This is comparable to the observations Latour made of scientists or legal professionals. The observation of law as permeating and stabilising leads him to the conclusion that law's primary function is this stabilisation and fixation of 'something legal' – similar to the 'legal quality' that Latour quickly identified. Luhmann also constructs his claims with more detail through setting up a suitable '*Rechtsdogmatik*' and 'structural couplings' such as contract and property.[97] According to him, they operate inside each system but perform differently in each place and play an important role in the economic system.

Most importantly, even before his modern successors he already foresaw a sad description of law in the times of globalisation, with decreasing rule of law, de-nationalisation and de-territorialised commerce, war and transnational societal disintegration which, as is par for the course, would call into question the legal system. This idea of his is expanded by his successors with regard to an increase in norm-producing entities; for him already early on, 'society' meant 'world society'.[98] These two developments foreshadow what is discussed in the present chapter, which might describe the beginning of the end of the 'legal system' as has been long heralded. This is because the Ecotronic Normative Systems described are partially designed to transcend nation states and enable one law, one contract, for the world society. This would then also potentially contribute to the denationalisation and disintegration of the nation state foreseen by Luhmann. These points have also in part been echoed by the marketing materials of marketers and activists for technology companies and Ecotronic Normative projects such as Ethereum.[99] Thus, this 'emergence of new actors

95 Luhmann, Ziegert and Kastner, above n. 93, pp. 255, 268; As opposed to Habermas' description in J. Habermas, *Between facts and norms: contributions to a discourse theory of law and democracy*, MIT Press, Cambridge, MA, 1996.

96 Luhmann, Ziegert and Kastner, above n. 93, p. 467.

97 Luhmann, Ziegert and Kastner, above n. 93, pp. 381–382 and 391–398.

98 Luhmann, Ziegert and Kastner, above n. 94, p. 490; N. Luhmann, 'Die Weltgesellschaft', *ARSP: Archiv für Rechts- und Sozialphilosophie / Archives for Philosophy of Law and Social Philosophy* 1–35, 1971.

99 Ethereum, *Ethereum: the World Computer*, <https://www.youtube.com/watch?v=j23HnORQXvs> accessed 19.09.2016.

and new forms of production render the application of our nation-state toolkit redundant and the memory of international law's normative utopia ever more existential',[100] as was stated in a review of a long overdue English translation of Luhmann's book 'Law as a social system', making more of his work accessible in English. His work had already put down a lot of far-reaching roots, as shown above, and will be built upon below.

Where Luhmann was much more a sociologist, Gunther Teubner, as another proponent of systems theory, tries to incorporate system theoretical findings properly into the body of (German) legal doctrine.[101] His main works deal with connected contracts[102] and the state and legal system in the course of legal pluralism.[103] Similarly to Latour (from a sociological point of view) and Luhmann, he describes the phenomena of connections and networks, though with a stricter relation to law and (German) legal doctrine. Similarly to Latour, Teubner (and his mentor Luhmann before him) described the phenomena of connections and networks. In his articles he identifies problems that legal systems are faced with in respect of connected contracts or networks across the relevant legal fields, primarily in the areas of liability and contract law. He finds that these systems are unable to solve all the problems on their own, though some commenters think he goes too far, overstating the necessity for a doctrine of connected contracts.[104]

A further relation to networks from a sociological point of view and favoured by proponents of alternative societal and economic theories is the claim that companies are more and more evolving into conglomerates, connecting to networks, and this in turn leads to a dilution of the distinction between the market and hierarchy or, legally speaking, between contract and society. This establishes a great parallel with the alternative economic and legal system of Ecotronic Normative Environments generally and blockchain systems specifically, as these to some degree also question the traditional concept of the firm[105] and the distinction between the market and hierarchy or, legally

[100] P. Zumbansen, 'Book Review: *Law as a social System*', 453–468 *Osgoode Hall Law School of York University*, York, 2006, <http://digitalcommons.osgoode.yorku.ca/cgi/viewcontent.cgi?article=2216&context=scholarly_works> accessed 06.09.2016.

[101] G. Teubner, *Netzwerk als Vertragsverbund: virtuelle Unternehmen, Franchising, Just-in-time in sozialwissenschaftlicher und juristischer Sicht*, Nomos, Baden-Baden, 2004; G. Teubner, M. Everson, H. Collins, *Networks as connected contracts*, Hart Publishing, Oxford, 2011; S. Jung, P. Krebs, G. Teubner, *Business networks reloaded*, Nomos / Ashgate, Baden-Baden / Farnham / Burlington, VT, 2015.

[102] Teubner, Everson and Collins, above n. 101; Teubner, above n. 101.

[103] 'Global law without a state' in G. Teubner (ed.), Dartmouth, Aldershot / Brookfield, 1997; G. Teubner, *Global Bukowina: Legal Pluralism in the World-Society*, Social Science Research Network, Rochester, NY, 1996, <http://papers.ssrn.com/abstract=896478> accessed 05.04.2016.

[104] Teubner, above n. 101, p. 20 and relevant chapters.

[105] I. Allison, 'Ethereum reinvents companies with launch of The DAO', *International Business Times UK* 2016, <http://www.ibtimes.co.uk/ethereum-reinvents-companies-launch-dao-1557576>

speaking, between contracts and society, which as a consequence questions the role of the state, contracts and the market.

The present chapter, then, takes the position that to a large extent it is useful for researchers and users to classify smart contracts as connected contracts in an inclusive sense. For this qualification, however, they have to meet certain criteria to distinguish them from other types of legal relations ('*Rechtsgeschäfte*') or from smart programs not meant to have legal functions. One criterion that is examined here on an exemplary basis is the number of contracting parties and how they are connected. For this assessment, the legal relation between parties has to be taken into account as well as the computational or physical action in the on- or offline world, i.e. who instantiated a contract or a program.

The relevant legal relations that can be identified are (1) one party with another party, (2) one party contracting with multiple parties, (3) multiple contracting parties contracting with multiple other parties or (4) 'self-contracting'.[106] From a physical and technical point of view, physical actions or programmatic actions can represent any of those cases; they would not by default qualify as 'connected contracts' but could qualify if they were to import or 'call' other existing 'smart contracts' that specify legal relations or are connected with vertical 'sub-contracts' and through one of these they would qualify as a legal contract.[107] As such, self-contracting, as specified above, does not constitute a connected contract and neither does a bilateral contract unless it is dependent on other program parts or contracts.

From a legal point of view, Teubner references particular examples to describe his view of connected contracts such as 'just-in-time supply' for automobile manufacturing, where multiple suppliers work in a network of specific configurations.[108] An analogous virtual example is the distribution of music, where one track is manufactured from multiple components, produced by one or more artists. Based on licensing agreements, royalties can be automatically and transparently distributed if a track is purchased or licensed downstream.

In certain literature (see Grundmann below) connected contracts are classified based on their topology into stars, circles, polygons or chains which might also be combined.[109] This is a great classification as it complements the

accessed 20.09.2016; C. Metz, 'The Biggest Crowdfunding Project Ever Was Supposed to Create Manager-free Companies. But It's a Mess', WIRED 06.06.2016, <https://www.wired.com/2016/06/biggest-crowdfunding-project-ever-dao-mess/> accessed 20.09.2016; P. De Filippi, R. Mauro, 'Ethereum: the decentralised platform that might displace today's institutions', *Internet Policy Review* 2014, <http://policyreview.info/articles/news/ethereum-decentralised-platform-might-displace-todays-institutions/318>.

106 Such as a savings 'contract' where instead of contracting with a bank, savings conditions are specified in a smart contract in the Ecotronic Normative Environment.

107 One example could be the establishment of identity with all potential specifications that this entails.

108 Teubner, above n. 101, p. 15.

109 Grundmann, above n. 92, p. 723.

analysis of connected contracts as networks by analogy to law in sociology and technical networks and their abstraction through Ecotronic Normative Environments very well, as technical networks also have diverse topologies depending on their use.

Teubner's work shows that there is no 'network contract' as such in law, but only specific provisions intended for connected contracts, and yet it still argues for the usefulness and necessity of the concept of connected contracts and networks, although others disagree. In other areas of law, such as in the discussion of supranationality in the European Union, the concept of network in law has also been examined in the past.[110] Going beyond Germany, see Sciuto for an analysis under Italian law.[111]

Following his predecessors,[112] Grundmann does a renewed analysis of connected contracts in legal doctrine, specifically in German law as his native jurisdiction, as does Teubner. Distinguishing between (too) visionary and (too) conservative accounts of connected contracts and networks in law, Grundmann takes a critical look at the developed literature regarding connected contracts.

His principle finding is that one cannot support connected contracts based on Teubner's arguments, though he identifies room for an intermediary doctrine of connected contracts between too visionary and too conservative. He starts by examining the existing German legislation, where contractual networks are doctrinally non-existent.[113] Various authors have supported them over the years[114] in one way or another, but this did not have much influence on the doctrine. It is described that one way in which authors tried to reason for a 'whole' of the network is by founding their claim on a common 'Networkobject(ive)'. This seems plausible, but is rightly refuted when looking just at legislation or probably also just at the contracts in question (though these are seldom known), as we are told. Despite this, Grundmann acknowledges that contractual networks are at the core of today's globalised economy, constituting the core value creation, as can be observed in production relations between producer and just-in-time suppliers.[115]

---

110 K. Ladeur, 'Towards a Legal Theory of Supranationality – The Viability of the Network Concept', 3 *European Law Journal* 33–54, 1997.

111 M. Sciuto, *The Network Contract in Italy: A Third Route between 'Contract' and 'Organisation'*?, Social Science Research Network, Rochester, NY, 2014, <http://papers.ssrn.com/abstract=2486311> accessed 10.09.2016.

112 Grundmann, above n. 92; S. Grundmann, 'The Future of Contract Law', 7 *European Review of Contract Law* 490–527, 2011.

113 Grundmann, above n. 92, p. 719.

114 Grundmann, above n. 92, p. 720, e.g. referring to F. Niklisch (ed.), *Vertragsnetzwerke komplexer Langzeitverträge*, Beck, Munich, 2001.

115 Grundmann, above n. 92, p. 721 ('Marktwirtschaft').

This finding of contractual network structures and their topologies as the backbone of the economy is a great foundation and analogy by which to describe digital contractual networks based on Ecotronic Normative Environments as the backbone of emerging digital markets. As mentioned, for Teubner, there are several topologies described that can also exist in combination.[116]

Furthermore, the examination of the legal basis of connected contracts is important. Following up on the 'network purpose' mentioned above, concrete examples are analysed, most importantly inter-group agreements that all participants agree to, where all other participants are known and where there is a common purpose (contrary to supplier networks). In Grundmann's analysis, he concludes that such an inter-group agreement does not lead to a contractual network, as he says that no network contract comes into being and would lead to wrong results.[117] If it would lead to a contractual network, he looks towards possible consequences of such a 'traditional contractual network' with the question whether legal consequences could be different in comparison with a single contract and distinguishes between somewhat illusive network contracts and contractual networks, with the latter having the potential to arise organically without the knowledge of all participants.[118]

This comparison is hard to apply to connected digital contracts right now, as they are still emerging and it is uncertain which uses and thus what constellations and topologies will prevail. In principle however, both contractual networks and network contracts according to Grundmann's definition are possible. Other evaluations might also apply to Smart Contract Networks running in Ecotronic Normative Environments, such as the question whether company law could be applied to a contractual network – which is said to be not too far off, since they have the same goal.[119] Further similarities might be observed for joint-venture or research and development agreements.

As discussed above, the renewed evaluation argues that the theoretically possible classification of inter-group agreements as network contracts is contrary to company law tenets and potentially also principles of private autonomy and freedom to contract.[120] Finally, it shall not be forgotten that the author references an American trade and company law scholar in stating that 'Network is not a legal concept' in his paper to examine networks in law.[121] With Weitzenboeck[122]

---

116 GRUNDMANN, above n. 92, p. 723.

117 GRUNDMANN, above n. 92, p. 725.

118 GRUNDMANN, above n. 92. p. 726.

119 GRUNDMANN, above n. 92. p. 727. And at 730, arguing that TEUBNER argued for a superior qualification that is not very consistent but sometimes arbitrary.

120 GRUNDMANN, above n. 92, p. 737.

121 R.M. BUXBAUM, 'Is "Network" a Legal Concept?', 149 *Journal of Institutional and Theoretical Economics (JITE) / Zeitschrift für die gesamte Staatswissenschaft* 698–705, 1993.

122 E.M. WEITZENBOECK, *A Legal Framework from Emerging Business Models: Dynamic Networks As Collaborative Contracts*, Edward Elgar Publishing, Cheltenham, 2012, p. 20.

analysing in more detail and Teubner concurring, but still seeing 'networks and hybrids' as separate, relevant concepts, even if they cannot be subsumed under the categories of contract, market or organisation and do not create a 'new legal form'. However, there are also other opinions[123] that at least validate the subject of study and for the present chapter network is considered 'enough' of a concept IN law, especially as network patterns and topologies can certainly be identified from multiple perspectives when going beyond mere doctrinal law.

7. NETWORKS AS TRANSNATIONAL LAW

In this pre-conclusion, a brief outlook toward further research is given and the present chapter is placed within the broader research into transnational law[124] and the future of contract law in a liberal state. More detail will have to be provided elsewhere, but as these broader concerns are important and the previously described research should be understood in their context, it is vital to mention these 'bigger pictures'.[125]

While the research is ongoing, there is good evidence that the Ecotronic Normative Environments described, especially if used to run 'smart contracts' with certain legal functions – can be subsumed under the existing literature of 'Transnational' law, especially when this references 'lex digitalis' or similar concepts.[126] The notion of transnational law as a law beyond (but not instead of) the state, with a multitude of coexisting legal regimes and institutions, was made

123 I. Augsberg, L. Viellechner, P. Zumbansen, 'Introduction to the Special Issue: the Law of the Network Society. A Tribute to Karl-Heinz Ladeur', 10 *German Law Journal* 305, 2009; A. Kemmerer, 'The Normative Knot 2.0: Metaphorological Explorations in the Net of Networks Special Issue: The Law of the Network Society: A Tribute to Karl-Heinz Ladeur: Legal Theory and Legal Sociology', 10 *German Law Journal* 439–462, 2009; P.F. Kjaer, 'Embeddedness through Networks: A Critical Appraisal of the Network Concept in the Ouevre of Karl-Heinz Ladeur', 10 *German Law Journal* 483, 2009 .

124 Calliess und Renner, 2009; Calliess und Renner, 2007; Calliess und Zumbansen, 2010 P.F. Cafaggi, P.G. Vettori, P.S. Grundmann, *The Organizational Contract: From Exchange to Long-Term Network Cooperation in European Contract Law*, Ashgate Publishing, Ltd., 2013; F. Möslein, K. Riesenhuber, *Contract Governance: Dimensions in Law and Interdisciplinary Research*, Oxford University Press, 2015 .

125 G.-P. Calliess, P. Zumbansen, *Rough consensus and running code: a theory of transnational private law*, Hart Publishing, Oxford / Portland, OR, 2010; P.C. Zumbansen, *Transnational Law*, Social Science Research Network, Rochester, NY, 2008, <http://papers.ssrn.com/abstract=1105576> accessed 28.05.2015; P. Zumbansen, 'Neither "Public" nor "Private", "National" nor "International": Transnational Corporate Governance from a Legal Pluralist Perspective', 38 *Journal of Law and Society* 50–75, 2011; R.A. Miller, P. Zumbansen, *Comparative law as transnational law: a decade of the German Law Journal*, Oxford University Press, New York, 2011.

126 A. Fischer-Lescano, G. Teubner, *Regime-Kollisionen: zur Fragmentierung des globalen Rechts*, Suhrkamp, Frankfurt am Main, 2006. pp. 66, 159.

widely available through a famous lecture by Jessup[127] and later on expanded by many others.[128]

This development 'next to the state' has been described for cases such as transnational copyright or cyber-crime, but could also apply to globalised commerce in general. As it is used for the description of network structures such as copyright and international cyber-crime it can also be used to described the emerging field of digitally codified law, or more specifically 'smart contracts' running in Ecotronic Normative Environments, as laid out above.

8. THE WAY FORWARD (CONCLUSION)

In this chapter, the developments of blockchain technology generally and smart contracts specifically were contextualised with previous research and the legal and social aspects were highlighted. For this, it was important to clarify the scope of these technologies and compare them to earlier developments. Based on previous research conducted in AI and Law and interfacing law and technology, similarities between blockchain networks, smart contract networks and legal and social networks were discovered. To ease this comparison, the device of 'Ecotronic Normative Environment' was introduced, which described a rule-making environment based on digital networks and with economic structures as an essential part of its design. Similar to what Latour did in his own way, this investigative device showed us that the technological networks, legal networks (connected contracts) and potential social and economic networks are inherently linked and have similar characteristics. This places connected digital contracts as described here squarely in the area of transnational law and its societal and social context, even though the excursion to the more detailed analysis of 'connected contracts' showed that there are no provisions (at least in Germany) for differentiating between bilateral and connected contracts, it also showed that these constructs can still be traced in practice, even if not so envisioned by the legislator. In the process of locating transnational (digital) law as described here in society, it will also be important to see in how the presented instruments can be described as 'liberal', neutral or illiberal.

127 P.C. Jessup, *Transnational Law*, <http://iglp.law.harvard.edu/wp-content/uploads/2014/10/IELR-3-Jessup-Transnational-Law.pdf> accessed 06.04.2016; C Tietje, A Bruder and K Nowrot (eds.), 'Philip C. Jessup's Transnational Law Revisited – On the Occasion of the 50th Anniversary of its Publication' – *Beiträge in Transnationalen Wirtschaftsrecht*, Heft 50, <http://www.wirtschaftsrecht.uni-halle.de/sites/default/files/altbestand/Heft50.pdf> accessed 06.04.2016.

128 D.V. Snyder, 'Molecular Federalism and the Structures of Private Lawmaking', 14 *Indiana Journal of Global Legal Studies* 419–445, 2007.

THE SILK ROAD REVISITED – MONEY TRANSACTIONS INSIDE THE BITCOIN SYSTEM

Kristoffer SCHOLLIN

ABSTRACT

The chapter sets out to show a chain between the many aspects of Bitcoin as a regime of exchange and contract-based transactions, and to lay a basic groundwork of understanding for Bitcoin as a framework for transactions. Relevant aspects are Bitcoin's status as money, the different and functional qualities that it shares with other types of money, its distributed technical nature and structural integrity, as well as its ideological roots incorporated in technology. An exciting addition onto the open final link of this chain is the advent of new decentralised Bitcoin-based marketplaces where the goal is to include the transactions themselves *inside* Bitcoin's 'blockchain' – the foundation of this digital regime of exchange. Historical lines are drawn between Bitcoin and the ancient cultures of Mesopotamia in 3000 BC. While the attributes of the monetary system used in the Cradle of Civilisation are the antithesis of Bitcoin when it comes to the dichotomy of geographical centralisation/decentralisation, it evinces strong similarities concerning the relative unimportance of material tokens. A further shared trait is traced, one that is likely to prove revolutionary in the future: the intimate connection between the monetary system itself and the transactions performed using it.

The Silk Road was launched in 2011. That is to say, this was when an online marketplace that called itself the 'Silk Road' was launched. The principal items on sale at this digital market were, unsurprisingly, various illicit substances, and the parties frequenting this marketplace settled their transactions by a direct transfer of something called 'Bitcoin'. In this online version of buying drugs for cash in dark back-alleys, there were no banks or bank-backed payment systems involved, only this money-like thing called 'Bitcoin', which purported to sustain its integrity upon a technology without a central point of control. Now, years after the new Silk Road was shut down, Bitcoin is being used by wholly legal online stores as well as some banks and even state authorities.

1. HIGH PRIEST NAKAMOTO

> The key realization was that there's no difference between modern culture and Sumerian. We have a huge workforce that is illiterate or alliterate and relies on TV – which is a form of oral tradition. And we have a small, extremely literate power elite … who control society because they have this semimystical ability to speak magic computer languages.
>
> N. Stephenson, *Snow Crash*[1]

In 'Bitcoin: a Peer-to-peer Electronic Cash System', written under the pseudonym 'Satoshi Nakamoto' in 2008, a system was laid out that would allow for online payments to be sent directly from one party to another without going through a financial institution.[2] In January the following year Nakamoto released a computer implementation under open source licence, with the first transaction

---

1 N Stephenson, *Snow Crash* (New York, Bantam Spectra 1993).

2 S. Nakamoto, 'Bitcoin: a Peer-to-peer Electronic Cash System' (2008) p. 1. The real identity behind the moniker Satoshi Nakamoto has always been an intriguing conundrum. Based on the fact that the original article consistently uses 'we', one would conclude that it was a collective of individuals, though the wording could have been chosen to evoke an air of respectability, or simply to obfuscate the identity further. Recently Australian entrepreneur

of Bitcoin taking place a few days after release.[3] Since then Bitcoin has grown exponentially and is perceived as a boon by some and a threat by others.[4]

The rules in Bitcoin were designed by engineers with the express purpose of getting rid of the need for trusted third parties. Its digital code is a software incarnation of an ethos that holds up an ideal of decentralisation and contains a core of distrust of monolithic authorities. Rather than storing transactions on a single cluster of computers, Bitcoin works because of a network wherein the transactions' ledger is distributed across all participants.

1.1. THE MONEY STATUS OF BITCOIN

There is an ongoing debate about what Bitcoin is, or perhaps rather what it should be regarded as. That Bitcoin has perceived value is obvious since it is used in transactions. That Bitcoin cannot be the subject of traditional possession is also not in doubt. Though there are various forms of technical safeguards to ensure that each user's control of their Bitcoin is exclusive, the idea of possession of an intangible good is a legal fiction, albeit a useful one.[5] The term 'Bitcoin wallet' is used to denote a set of files on a computer or phone needed to manage each user's virtual coins; in particular there is an encrypted digital file called 'wallet.dat' which, if irretrievably lost, means that the user has forever lost his or her Bitcoins. However, the word 'wallet' is intellectually misleading since it

---

Craig Wright tried to mathematically prove that he was Satoshi Nakamoto. Though accepted by some, the mathematical evidence was also heavily criticised by crypto specialists. It seems this conundrum will not be laid to rest yet, as Wright seems to have ended his attempt. On his website, drcraigwright.net, he published this message on 5 May 2016: 'I'm Sorry. I believed that I could do this. I believed that I could put the years of anonymity and hiding behind me … but I know that the world will never believe that now. I can only say I'm sorry. And goodbye.'

3 Currently the code-base for Bitcoin is managed and developed through the GitHub code depository and development-platform. The management is done by computer developers mostly in a volunteer capacity. Decisions are taken through a consensus-driven process under the auspices of what seems like a localised form of meritocracy that involves name-recognition, seniority and brute commitment of time.

4 More than 100,000 stores accept Bitcoin as payment, while regulators in many countries, particularly when it comes to anti-money-laundering schemes but also concerning consumer warnings and advisories, have taken a variety of steps such as imposing licensing requirements on some firms involved in the Bitcoin market, issuing warnings to consumers, banning financial institutions from using it or outright banning the use of Bitcoin completely. International Monetary Fund, *Virtual Currencies and Beyond: Initial Considerations*, January 2016, SDN/16/03, 'Regulatory and Policy Challenges', pp. 24–35, 'Annex', p. 42.

5 Lindskog holds that while being inspired by an image in legal interpretation is a fiction in the sense that it cannot be verified physically, this does not prevent such a legal fiction from being a good tool, not just for lawyers but also for the business community and society in general. S. Lindskog, *Betalning – Om kongruent infriande av penningskulder och andra betalningsrättsliga frågor* (Stockholm, Norstedts Juridik 2014) p. 27.

creates the illusion that the Bitcoin is residing in the digital file, when in reality the Bitcoin wallet works like a key that unlocks access to making alterations in certain sections of a massive decentralised transaction ledger.

Defining 'money' strictly legally is of course a question for each jurisdiction's legislation and legal tradition. In this discourse cash money is typically treated differently from account-based money, with the former being viewed as some form of generic property while the latter is merely a claim on another entity, usually a bank.

Whether Bitcoin can ultimately be understood as some form of physical or intellectual goods, or as a type of commodity that can be adequately treated under any of the existing legal constructions regarding property, has been the subject of some debate. Though doubtless interesting, at least theoretically so, this text will as far as possible steer clear of those particular types of arguments and instead focus on the subject of Bitcoin's functional qualities when used as 'money'.[6]

1.2. MONEY – PART SOCIAL CONSTRUCTION, PART OBJECTIVE FUNCTIONS

Defining what is money and distinguishing it from what is not money is a delicate problem. This delicacy arises from the fact that there are many different functional qualities that we expect from money, but for something to be recognised as money, it does not need all of these functional qualities, nor does each such function need to be fulfilled to 100 per cent. If you list all the functions we associate with money, there are, out of all the things we recognise as money, probably none that can be said to be 'perfect money'. When one matches Bitcoin against the functional qualities below, one finds that Bitcoin is certainly not perfect money either, but in many functional aspects it is better money than other things whose status as money we take for granted. To this picture must be added that money cannot strictly be defined through its functional qualities, but also through its history; something that has been accepted as money is likely

6 See Section 3 below. Bergstra and Weijland distinguish between possessing 'moneyness' and being 'money-like' with the first denoting a system that is suitable to being used as money while the latter's functionality only partially resembles money, J. Bergstra and P. Weijland, *'Bitcoin: a money-like Informational Commodity'* (Informatics Institute, Amsterdam, University of Amsterdam 2014) p. 8. In their report from 2012 on crypto-currencies, the European Central Bank described Bitcoin as being similar to conventional money but not money. The report noted among other things that Bitcoin lacked a clear connection to existing currencies as well as a central authority in charge of the amount of money available, European Central Bank, *Virtual Currency Schemes* (2012), p. 21. The United States' tax authority has classified Bitcoin as property for the purpose of federal taxation.

to continue to be accepted as money because of social inertia.[7] This logic is not without its limits, however. There is a far from trivial number of objective functional qualities associated with money, and while it is not necessary for a candidate to possess all of these qualities perfectly in order to be accepted as money, a candidate possessing none of them is never going to be seriously considered as money. Following this logic, no thing that once was used as money but at a later stage loses all of these functional qualities will be able to retain its status as money merely on the back of social inertia.

In this ongoing debate about whether Bitcoin is money or not, a large proportion of the arguments seem based around this social status – particularly the acceptance by the large traditional actors such as central banks and state treasuries. In a 2016 staff discussion note regarding 'virtual currencies' the International Monetary Fund adopt a tentatively negative approach to all virtual currencies' money-status in stating:

> While money can be created by private parties (for example, banks) as well as central banks, it must generally be denominated in a currency issued by a sovereign authority, and must be intended to serve as a generally accepted medium of exchange within that state.

while still holding the door to this status open by stating:

> monetary systems and the legal concept of money have evolved substantially over time and will continue to change in the future. VCs should thus not be judged solely based on their current characteristics or on how they compare to current monetary regimes.[8]

The European Court of Justice on the other hand seems to have adopted a stance that focuses on Bitcoin's functional nature as a means of payment that when used as an alternative to traditional currencies is seen as viable as the basis for financial transactions.[9]

To draw a functional parallel with the discipline of International Law, the role of acceptance by traditional actors is one that is quite akin to the role being played by other states' recognition concerning the issue of whether an entity can claim statehood or not. While the discussion about what role that recognition itself plays in a constitutive sense is a philosophically fascinating one, this

---

7 According to Luhmann, over time a successful system of money becomes closed to its environment in the sense that it produces its own elements and its own internal structural changes, making it a self-referential and self-perpetuating system: N. Luhmann, *Social Systems* (Stanford University Press 1995) p. 350.

8 IMF, *Virtual Currencies and Beyond: Initial Considerations*, January 2016, SDN/16/03, pp. 11 and 16, citing C. Procter, *Mann's Legal Aspect of Money*, Oxford University Press, 2012.

9 See the Court's Judgment in Case C-264/14 *Skatteverket v. David Hedqvist*, ECLI:EU:C:2015:718, paragraph 49.

chapter will not consider recognition by other entities as a hard criterion, or constitutive, of Bitcoin's status as money. However, acceptance can play an important role in affecting some of the functional qualities of money that will be described below. First however, we must shift our perspective by roughly 5,000 years for a historical parallel that may serve to make Bitcoin seem less hyper-modern and alien to traditional sensibilities.

2. MONEY WITHOUT MONEY IN MESOPOTAMIA

It is interesting to note that the debate about Bitcoin as money is mirrored in the question of whether money was or was not used in the ancient cultures of Mesopotamia – the oldest organised states known in the history of Mankind. These questions seem perfectly natural because they highlight the surprisingly complex problem of defining money and distinguishing it from that which is not money. Like the states in ancient Mesopotamia, the digital network of Bitcoin lacks an easily perceptible, tangible coinage with the face of a famous historical figure and the representations of significant architecture, but it does nonetheless provide a working framework for managing transactions.

What has given rise to the debate about whether money existed in ancient Mesopotamia is the fact that for many centuries the region lacked coinage: archaeology first finds use of coinage at the end of their Achaemenid period (a.k.a. the First Persian Empire), around 300 BC. However, Mesopotamia had been a hub of trade at least since the third millennium BC and was well connected by routes to the Mediterranean, the Indian sub-continent, the Far East and quite likely with East Africa as well.[10] Towards the age of Alexander the Great this network would be known as the western section of the Silk Road, the famous network of trade routes linking the Mediterranean region to China and eastern Asia. Did the Mesopotamians lack money during this lengthy period of time; did they use primitive forms of barter economy? Most certainly the answer is in the negative. The archaeological evidence challenges the importance of coinage and lets us glimpse an economy where fairly advanced aspects of economics were used without a formal system of coinage.[11]

Initially the system of documentation was likely invented at and managed in the *Temple structures* that were so central for Mesopotamian cultures. Here, not only were gods worshipped, but goods were also sold. The Temples, and the Ziggurat-dominated Palaces of rulers that modelled themselves on the

10 M.A. Powell, 'Money in Mesopotamia' (1996) 39 *Journal of the Social and Economic History of the Orient* pp. 224–242, p. 225.

11 Ibid., p. 238.

Temple organisation were gigantic, complex industrial institutions with staffs of thousands where shepherds, weavers and spinners rubbed elbows with dancers and clerical administrators.[12]

Innovative financial instruments such as *interest-bearing loans* existed in these Temples; their invention likely arose from a need to finance the caravan trade, managed through the hubs of the Temples. This centralised system kept balanced accounts divided into three basic sections: assets, expenditures and balance.[13] The administration of debt and assets had to be a highly centralised affair, purely because of the lack of a system of minted coinage, which would have provided a decentralised mechanism for keeping track of wealth outside of the Palace and Temple administrations.[14] In many ways, the concept of money in early Mesopotamia should seem distinctly familiar to the modern eyes of someone long accustomed to managing their assets without actually dealing with, or in any way handling, either notes or coins.[15]

3. THE FUNCTIONS OF MONEY

In alignment with the account sections in the Mesopotamian Temples, money can schematically be categorised as a medium having three functions: *to measure, to trade and to store*. Put differently: money is a medium of exchange which enables the keeping track of debt and the storage of value.[16] These are functions that are not too hard to arrive at, but it is an insight on a highly abstract level. We will have to delve deeper into their more concrete sub-aspects if we wish to say something beyond the facile about Bitcoin as money.

As mentioned above, not every medium provides a good candidate for money's fundamental function: constituting a medium of exchange by keeping track of debt and value. In order to perform this function well, several qualities can be identified which each facilitate the over-arching purpose. On deeper consideration, money can of course be used fulfil other agendas than to optimise this fundamental function, for example ambitions to order society according to

12 D. Graeber, *Debt – The First 5,000 Years* (New York, Melville House 2011) p. 64.

13 M.A. Powell 'Sumerian Merchants and the Problem of Profit' (1977) 39(1) *Iraq* pp. 23–29, p. 25.

14 Money signifies not only value lodged with an individual or other entity, but also the opposite of value: *debt*. Anthropology confirms that debt as a social organization technology precedes the invention of the material tokens to measure it. B.H. Bratton, *The Stack: on Software and Sovereignty* (New York, Massachusetts Institute of Technology 2015) pp. 335–336.

15 Lindskog (above n. 5) notes that during a few years pre-dating 2002, before the Euro existed in the form of bills or coin, the Euro still functioned as a unit of measure for denoting debts.

16 Lindskog (above n. 5) p. 71.

a certain political vision. Thus not all of the qualities below will be viewed as desirable if a wider political perspective is adopted.[17]

A) Commonly, the first practical quality that comes to most people's mind is that the amount of money must be *limited or at least scarce* and it should not be an easy task to add to it by producing more money or falsifying its tokens. This is an ancient problem known from anthropological stories about landlocked cultures using seashells as money: as soon as an easy route to the sea is discovered, the system is understandably weakened. Connected to this basic quality, money also needs to be easily *identifiable* and distinguishable from other things. To aid in transactions, this identification should preferably be possible for a normal consumer to perform without access to specialised tools or facilities. To further grease the wheels of trade, money should obviously be easily *divisible*, preferably without inconvenient limitations. Though digital management of transactions has removed the coarse division inherent in minted currency, it still has to relate to such concepts as 'cents' and thus run into round-off problems. Obviously non-legacy digital money systems (not based on a historical currency) do not suffer from such afflictions.[18] Traditionally, in order to achieve divisibility one had to have access to tokens of many different denominations, something that could conflict with the ideal of money being *easy to carry around*. From a user perspective, perfect money should require no additional space at all and be possible to transport anywhere.

Furthermore, it is desirable that all such transportation can be done *securely*; that even during transportation the risk of losing your money is minimal. A related functional quality of money that is equally desirable is that of not losing money to banks through transaction fees, merely because you have undertaken said transportation. Alongside digital currencies, US Dollars and gold metal possess this quality[19] and are today therefore used as money internationally.

Though it might seem counter-intuitive, money should preferably have no value and functions outside of being a medium of exchange – it should *lack intrinsic value*, i.e. be impossible to consume or use for either sustaining life or enhancing the experience of it. If this is not so, then its value will be partly dependent on how these external functions are valued on the market, not on its qualities to provide a function of exchange on that market.[20]

---

17 Such political purposes are more time-bound and prosaic in nature. Among these, the more noteworthy ones are related to ordering the taxation system, paying military troops, or just trying to dominate the commercial sector.

18 Bitcoin is currently divisible down to a hundred millionth of a Bitcoin, a unit sometimes referred to as a 'satoshi'.

19 At least if we ignore the various national forms of legislation that exist and require declaration and possible taxation on transporting currency and precious metals across borders.

20 The quality of having no intrinsic value is dependent primarily on whether the money in question already possesses stable value that is preserved over time. If these qualities are not

B) *Non-volatility* is a highly desired quality for any medium to be used as money, since risk minimisation is a predominantly desired quality. A close connection to political sensitivities does of course provide an increased risk of tampering with the value of a currency, a story borne out by our knowledge of both ancient Mesopotamia and the modern independent central banks. But volatility is also influenced by various maturity factors, such as the size of its user base and length of time in use.[21] A closely-related quality is *resilience*, the ability to withstand, preserve or even increase value over cycles of economic change – what is often referred to as 'monetary stability'. Related to this we find the issue of having a large base of users, a quality desired in its own right but one that also has a positive effect on resilience. If the money is easily exchanged for rival currencies – what is termed *liquidity* – then the user base is grown by proxy.

That payment should be *prompt* is another desired quality of good money, but one that matters more or less depending on the context at hand. A consumer's need for speed is high when buying a litre of milk, but less so when transferring money into a savings-account or buying a plane-ticket.

The functional qualities listed under A) are those where Bitcoin excels by definition. Its weaker qualities are found under B). Bitcoin has a short history under which the price compared to other established currencies has been highly volatile.[22] Bitcoin is too new for anyone to know whether the system will prove resilient or not. The issue of *speed* in transactions is one where Bitcoin is currently locked to a ten-minute delay due to the need to build on the block-chain in a peer-to-peer network.[23]

Bitcoin possesses one additional quality, one that has not traditionally been viewed as a property of money, but one that was actually present in the

---

present, having some intrinsic value becomes a positive quality since it provides for less volatility. When the Swedish central bank, the *Riksbank*, back in 1740 was freed from the silver- and copper-foot, they lacked the insight or political will to adopt policies to maintain monetary stability, with drastically negative effects for the Swedish economy, resulting in an exodus of 3000 workers per year – a considerable loss for a country whose total population had yet to reach two million. J.W. Arnberg, *Anteckningar om Frihetstidens Politiska Ekonomi* (Uppsala, W. Schultz Förlag 1868) pp. 245–247.

21 Bitcoin has long been seen as an 'anti-currency'; when trust in large governments such as the USA or China has waned, then Bitcoin has surged. At the time of writing, Bitcoin has had a long and fairly stable climb to around $US440 when it suddenly exploded last night (30 May 2016) due to Chinese investors wanting to move capital outside of China. Speculations are high as to what prompted this sudden surge.

22 Coindesk, an information broker specialising in Bitcoin and other digital currencies, runs a Bitcoin price index that aggregates the largest Bitcoin Exchanges' rates. At the start of 2016 it was being traded for US$400. Between mid-May and mid-June it climbed from US$440 to 750. In mid-September 2016 the rate has been holding at around US$600 for the last two months.

23 The 2016 IMF Report *Virtual Currencies and Beyond: Initial Considerations* (above n. 5) makes comparisons between Bitcoin, other internationally used currencies and commodities, as well as historic currencies such as the US Greenback. (IMF 2016) p. 14.

money-system of ancient Mesopotamia: *programmability*; the terms of a contract can be coded into the currency itself, what is nowadays referred to as 'smart contracts'.

A note about 'trust': It is often said that money is a matter of trust, and Bitcoin has across various media been called a 'trust machine'.[24] However, 'trust' is a complicated phenomenon and can be analysed as an emergent function of the many qualities listed above. For example: Mesopotamian money merited a certain amount of trust given its logically and physically centralised nature, where debts, value and transaction were centrally managed and thus could be verified by the feared and respected Mesopotamian priesthood. However, this very centralised nature made it weak when it came to resisting devaluation due to strong political interests. We find an example of this in the *periodical consumer-debt cancellations* described below.

Conversely, a decentralised money-system based around a scarce metal such as *gold* could not be devalued in such a way, but trust still suffered in such decentralised systems because the material coinage itself was always vulnerable to different methods of tampering, most commonly forgery and various techniques for debasing the metallic content. The Bitcoin system, being simultaneously *logically centralised and physically decentralised*,[25] attempts to enjoy the best of both worlds with respect to these qualities.

4. OLD TEMPLES AND NEW

The extraordinary feat managed by Bitcoin is to do without the physical Temple and manage a working, physically-decentralised type of money through a network made up of those who use it. Some would say that the Temple is still there, only digitally distributed now, and that may in some senses be true. The Bitcoin system is unified, logically-centralised and its underlying framework is maintained and developed by a sort of programmers' priesthood.

But the Mesopotamian comparison cannot be extended in all directions. An important weakness inherent in a centralised system has been shed: the political connection. In Mesopotamia, the priesthood or ruler could interfere with the ledgers and thus change the balance of debts and assets, something that they did at intervals in Mesopotamian societies in order to compensate for some of the many shortcomings of their economy and culture. Debt in ancient

---

24 In 2015, the weekly news magazine *The Economist* used this term in its 31 October–6 November issue.

25 By this is meant that the governing logic of the system maintains one clear central point of verification: the accepted blockchain. The physical decentralisation of the blockchain does not pose a threat to its logical unity, but rather guarantees it.

Mesopotamia seems to have been intimately tied to the debtor and his family, and we have no indications that they had any legal institutes to deal with insolvency other than paying it off by any means available. Thus, financial trouble led to the appropriation of possessions, then the same for servants, children, spouses and the debtor himself. In the long run this resulted in a form of eternal debt-slavery that would be almost impossible to break out of, since repaying your debts when you are bound to serve in a temple or in the household of some merchant was an almost insurmountable obstacle.[26] This state of things created strains on their society, as the Mesopotamian indebted would flee their lands and opt for an existence as brigands: the Merry Men of Mesopotamia perhaps? Jokes aside, this obviously ate away at society. The solution was to wipe the slates of the Temple clean from time to time, declaring all outstanding consumer debt to be void.[27] But, the knowledge that such a jubilee would with certainty be declared from time to time affected the volatility and resilience of the monetary system in a negative way and would doubtlessly have weakened its position if there had been alternative money for traders to avail themselves of. Such was not the case in Ancient Mesopotamia, though.

This centralised and monopolised control over the system of money as exemplified here typically provides great economic and political power, and will inherently always expose such a central power to various pressures to use that control to rectify perceived economic or political imbalances – from the ancient Temples of Mesopotamia to its modern counterparts in Frankfurt and Beijing, this remains a constant.[28]

4.1. CENTRALISATION, GOOD MONEY AND BAD MONEY

> When a government overvalues one type of money and undervalues another, the undervalued money will leave the country or disappear from circulation into hoards, while the overvalued money will flood into circulation.
>
> One formulation of 'Gresham's Law'

In 1976 the economist Friedrich Hayek noted that to keep money non-volatile and resilient, it must be protected from politics, or at least it must be protected

---

26 The social innovation of limited liability was still many thousands of years away.

27 Graeber, above n. 12, p. 65.

28 This was very recently illustrated in the political negotiations between the Hellenic Republic and select Member States of the Eurozone last year as the European Central Bank helped to put political pressure on the Greek government by restricting the money supply to Greek Banks. Upon joining the Eurozone, the Greek treasury department had been required to permanently disassemble their Drachma-printing presses, ensuring the integrity of ECB's control of money, should Greece ever entertain the notion to opt out of the Eurozone and return to its old currency.

from the short-sighted and counter-productive instincts of elected officials. He noted the various pressures a central power had always been subject to during the long history of money, and would always be subject to. Certainly, he did not want to question that an independent central bank authority 'run by very intelligent people' could not *potentially* do better than a gold standard or 'some form of automatic system',[29] but in the real world he saw not the slightest hope that any institution subject to political pressure could ever act in such a manner.[30]

Hayek's suggested solution to this problem was to allow for competition between different types of money. The problem lay not in the fact that states were issuing money; it lay in their power to limit the kinds of money for which contracts could legally be concluded and to set the rates at which money could legally be exchanged. With open competition between different kinds of money, money-use would migrate to the money that possessed the best functional qualities; governments would be unable to conceal if their money was becoming bad and would have to adopt healthy long-term policies.[31]

Many readers are presumably familiar with Gresham's famous law that '*bad money drives out good money*'.[32] This is true in the cases where we have two types of money with the same nominal value but where one type of money lacks the level of intrinsic- or commodity-based or functional value possessed by the second type of money. The bad money will be preferred to be used in transactions, if possible, because it will be 'a good deal' to get the same exchange for something that is less good. Hayek pointed out that this maxim only holds true if the two types of money by law have to be accepted at a prescribed rate of exchange. If, on the other hand, people are free to exchange the different kinds of money at whatever rate they agree upon, then exactly the opposite will happen: *good money will drive out the bad.*[33]

One only has to remember the way American Dollars were used when travelling beyond the Iron Curtain to realise the truth of this. Money that is considered to be good as per the qualities listed above will compete effectively if it is allowed to co-exist with other money that is perceived as inferior. The spirit of

---

29 HAYEK was very unlikely to have been thinking of Bitcoin or of a conceptual digital crypto-currency, but the wording is nonetheless quite prescient.

30 F.A. HAYEK, '*Choice in Currency – A Way to Stop Inflation*' (Institute of Economic Affairs, 1976; online edition 2007) p. 14.

31 Ibid. pp. 17–18. By free competition, HAYEK does not mean that a state must allow other money than its own as legal tender when it comes to taxes; they are perfectly free to set these conditions as they see fit. True to form, his prescribed free competition is framed as the freedom from state interference in the businesses of people and enterprises.

32 One of the oldest insights into the mechanisms of money. Named after a 16th century banker, the principle was earlier mentioned back in ancient Greece by Aristophanes and later by Copernicus. It is occasionally also referred to as Copernicus' law.

33 HAYEK (n. 30 above) p. 20.

Hayek's solution, to allow free monetary competition where good money would prevail, is very much alive in the circles around Bitcoin:[34] not only do many Bitcoin evangelists believe that Bitcoin will prove superior to other national forms of money if allowed to compete on its own merits, they also hold that free competition between it and other crypto-currencies will result in a digital evolution that will give birth to better, or at least more well-adapted, money. In their words, the best Bitcoins of the future may therefore not be 'Bitcoin'.[35]

4.2. THE CJEU AND 'NON-TRADITIONAL CURRENCIES'

The European Court of Justice had the opportunity to analyse and clarify their view on the nature of Bitcoin in 2015. Though the case concerned tax-law, it provided for many observations of an ontological and functional nature that establish a basic understanding of how of the Court intends to approach future issues concerning transactions in Bitcoin.

The case concerned a Mr. David Hedqvist, who planned to engage, via the internet, in the purchase and sale of the virtual currency 'Bitcoin' for Swedish Krona. The price of the Bitcoins would be based on the exchange rate on a particular exchange site plus or minus a certain percentage as consideration for the exchange. Before taking up the activity, Mr. Hedqvist requested a preliminary decision from the *Skatterättsnämnd* (Swedish Revenue Law Commission) to establish whether he was required to pay VAT on the purchase and sale of Bitcoins as described. The preliminary decision found the purchase and sale of Bitcoins to be a supply of services for consideration which was, however, exempt from VAT because Bitcoins are a means of payment which is used in a manner corresponding to a legal means of payment. The Swedish tax administration appealed against this preliminary decision.

The transactions envisaged by Mr. Hedqvist would be carried out electronically via the company's website. That company would purchase units of

---

34 Indeed, it can be said that the theoretical roots of Bitcoin can be found in the works of HAYEK, VON MISES, BÖHM-BAWERK, as well as other more modern authors who sympathise with the analyses of the Austrian school of economics. (Anecdotally, my own personal acquaintances who are computer programmers by profession tend to be quite 'Austrian' in their views without ever having read one word of political writing. One can only speculate that this is somehow related to their having acquired their highly-sought-after skills mainly through their own effort and interests, with little formal schooling.)

35 The risk of 'forking', so often dreaded in Open-Source projects, where one group of programmers split from the development team to continue developing the computer code in their own direction while still competing with the original project, is not seen as a weakness in Bitcoin, but rather as a potential advantage. Value would simply migrate to superior frameworks, it is held.

the 'Bitcoin' virtual currency directly from private individuals and companies, or from an international exchange site. The company would then resell the units on such an exchange site, or store them. Mr. Hedqvist's company would also sell such units to private individuals or to companies that place an order on its website. In a situation where the client has accepted the price in Swedish Krona offered by Mr. Hedqvist's company and a payment has been received, the sold units of the Bitcoin virtual currency would be sent automatically to the 'Bitcoin address' indicated. The Bitcoin units sold by the company would either be those that it would purchase directly on the exchange site after the client had placed his order, or those that the company already had in stock. The price proposed by the company to clients would be based on the current price on a particular exchange site, to which a certain percentage would be added. The difference between the purchase price and the sale price would constitute Mr. Hedqvist's company's earnings. The company would not charge any other fees.[36]

After finding that the type of service that Mr. Hedqvist intended to provide was indeed a service for consideration within the VAT Directive, and ruling that Bitcoin could be equated to deposit and current accounts, payments, transfers, debts, cheques and other negotiable instruments[37] the European Court turned to the question of whether Bitcoin was, instead, of the same general status as currency, bank notes and coins used as legal tender. The Court thus steered away from drawing analogies with older instruments and concepts of a financial- or business-related nature, instead focusing their energy on finding comparisons on a practical and functional scale.

As concerns virtual currencies generally, the Court had already held that such digital currencies have no purpose other than to be a means of payment and could thus not be viewed as any form of tangible property.[38] In this they based their finding on the reasoning of Advocate General Kokott, who observed that 'The only purpose of possessing [Bitcoin] is to reuse them as a means of payment at some point.'[39, 40]

The Court characterised Bitcoin as a direct contractual means of payment between the operators that accept it,[41] and made a distinction between traditional- and non-traditional currencies. The latter type of currency was

---

36 ECJ Judgment in Case C-264/14 *Skatteverket v. David Hedqvist*, ECLI:EU:C:2015:718, paragraph 13.

37 Ibid., paragraphs 39–42. The Court also ruled that, as a matter of common ground, Bitcoin could not be viewed as a security conferring a property right, nor as a comparable security. Paragraph 55.

38 Ibid., paragraph 24.

39 Opinion of Advocate General Kokott in Case C-264/14 *Skatteverket v. David Hedqvist*, ECLI:EU:C:2015:718, paragraph 17.

40 Elgebrant examines the difficulty of determining whether a medium really has no other purpose than to be used as a means of payment. E. Elgebrant, *Kryptovalutor* (Stockholm, Wolter Kluwer Sverige 2016) pp. 76–75.

41 ECJ Judgment in Case C-264/14 *Skatteverket v. David Hedqvist*, ECLI:EU:C:2015:718, paragraph 42.

characterised in the negative as 'currencies other than those that are legal tender in one or more countries.' Functionally, however, the Court found no difference between Bitcoin and traditional currencies as long as they were accepted by both parties in the transaction. That Bitcoin has no other purpose than to be a means of payment and that it is accepted for that purpose by certain operators was deemed as common ground in the case at hand. Thus, to exclude Bitcoin from the same treatment as traditional currencies would deprive the exemption at hand of part of its effect.[42]

5. DECENTRALISATION AND CONTRACTUAL EXCHANGE IN BITCOIN

> So you think that money is the root of all evil? Have you ever asked what is the root of money? Money is a tool of exchange, which can't exist unless there are goods produced and men able to produce them.
>
> A. Rand, *The Ayn Rand Letters*[43]

As stated above, Bitcoin achieves something quite extraordinary in eschewing central control over money by lodging it in the physically-distributed structure of those who use the money. As opposed to the ledgers being kept by the Mesopotamian clerics and the central banks of today, the ledger that regulates Bitcoin has, and must have, two systemic properties: that it is practically impossible to tamper with it, and that, in order to achieve this goal, it is open to inspection by everyone and anyone.

Since Bitcoin is a direct contractual means of payment between two parties, this does of course raise the interesting question of whether governments will have the practical ability to interfere in, maybe even prevent, Bitcoin transactions between such contracting parties. Hendrickson et al. find that in order to effectively do this, the government must control a sufficiently large part of the economy, and even in these extreme cases some transactions will effectively be beyond the reach of the state.[44]

5.1. TECH OVER TRUST

> We need a way for the payee to know that the previous owners did not sign any earlier transactions. For our purposes, the earliest transaction is the one that counts,

42 Ibid., paragraphs 51–52.

43 A. Rand, 'Hunger and Freedom' *The Ayn Rand Letters* (1974), vol. 3, no. 22.

44 J.R. Hendrickson, T.L. Hogan, W.J. Luther, 'The Political Economy of Bitcoin', 54 *Economic Inquiry* 929–935, 2015.

> so we don't care about later attempts to double-spend. The only way to confirm the absence of a transaction is to be aware of all transactions.
>
> Satoshi Nakamoto[45]

The Bitcoin designer's conceptual solution to integrity and transactional tampering is in many ways ingenious: *any 'tampering' with the ledger establishes the official ledger*. Thus there can by definition be no tampering, since any work done that is sufficient to establish the accepted ledger is the work that drives the system. This is a bold conceptual move, but will it prove practically satisfactory to the parties engaging in the exchange of Bitcoin?

5.1.1. Transactions in the Blockchain

The ledger in Bitcoin is called the 'blockchain'.[46] Technically it is a distributed database consisting of a constantly growing list of transaction records arranged in 'blocks'. Each such block contains a time-stamp and is a function of the previous block. Actually, every block in the blockchain is a series of numbers that, through a cryptographic function, incorporates all the previous blocks combined with the latest one – all the way back to the first block, the so-called 'Genesis Block'. The original Nakamoto paper expresses it thus:

> For our timestamp network, we implement the proof-of-work by incrementing a nonce in the block until a value is found that gives the block's hash the required zero bits. Once the CPU effort has been expended to make it satisfy the proof-of-work, the block cannot be changed without redoing the work. As later blocks are chained after it, the work to change the block would include redoing all the blocks after it.[47]

Each new block of transactions gets tacked onto the existing chain in a process that provides the driving engine behind attracting computer power to the network, and then uses this power to maintain its own integrity.[48]

---

45 Nakamoto (above n. 2) section 2.

46 In Nakamoto's original paper the term is not used specifically, though the author(s) speak of blocks that are chained or a chain of blocks. The term proper seems to have cropped up on the cryptography mailing list where Bitcoin was discussed, in 2008. The Satoshi Nakamoto Institute (satoshi.nakamotoinstitute.org) has made these emails available online: *'Cryptography mailing list emails'*, http://satoshi.nakamotoinstitute.org/emails/cryptography.

47 Nakamoto (above n. 1) section 4.

48 This text does not address the issue of low integrity at the exchange level, such as when a third-party who undertakes to exchange your assets for Bitcoin acts in a fraudulent way. Many Bitcoin exchanges also suffered from a combination of poor management, neglect and raw inexperience, as the story of Mt. Gox, detailed in *Wired* magazine on 3 March 2014, illustrates.

5.1.2. An Example of Exchanging Bitcoin

Alice and Bob, of course, are our contractual parties. They are going to be exchanging an amount of Bitcoin. When they agree to do so through the Bitcoin peer-to-peer network, their transaction information is broadcast across the entire network. Through Alice's public key encryption, Bob can verify the identity of Alice and that she has the Bitcoin, although he cannot verify that she does not try to spend the coin somewhere else simultaneously. But now everyone in the Network also knows, theoretically at least,[49] that Alice and Bob are going to participate in this exchange. All the information that identifies Bob's and Alice's unique digital wallets, the number of Bitcoin's transacted, any contractual conditions set on the transaction as well as the optional transaction fee – it all becomes publically available information. The network now automatically rejects transactions that include the same Bitcoins and thus prevents them from going toward two separate ends, thus nullifying the risk of Alice double-spending, and thereby double-crossing Bob.

The same goes for the other transactions that happen in the network at this time. The collated product of all these transactions provides the basis for the next proposed block in the Bitcoin blockchain. Alice and Bob's transaction is not finished until the next block has been accepted by the network. That is, until a node in the network has solved the cryptographic puzzle generated from all the proposed transactions. Solving this puzzle takes a lot of computational 'horse-power'. But once a node in the network has found the right solution, it is easily and quickly verifiable (see below for details). The node will broadcast its solution to the rest of the network and the other nodes can verify that the solution is indeed correct; they will then cease trying to find their own solution to the puzzle and will start working on the basis of this new block in the chain – the block that incorporates Alice's and Bob's transactional record:

New proposed block = *f* (AB transaction, XY transaction … etc.)

5.1.3. Practical Transactional Irreversibility

At this point, the transaction between Alice and Bob is complete and irreversible at a systemic level. To edit a Bitcoin ledger post-transaction is unlike the situation where the transaction was handled by a bank, or indeed by Mesopotamian clerics. Here, the system is set up so that to edit a transaction *ex post* requires the power to modify a past block in the blockchain, and to modify a past block you would have to 'attack' the system. In effect, such an attack requires redoing the

49 Users who are not directly involved in the transaction only 'know' of it in the sense that it is encrypted in their instance of the blockchain that resides on their computer.

proof-of-work of the block and all blocks after it and then catching up with and surpassing the work of the honest nodes.[50]

However, outside of the systemic level, at the level of the contracting parties, they retain the freedom to 'reverse', by undertaking whatever second Bitcoin transaction they deem fit to compensate for any errors in the first transaction.

5.2. PROOF-OF-WORK PUZZLES, MINERS AND THE INCENTIVE FOR VERIFICATION

As per above, each new proposed addition to the blockchain of Bitcoin is a result of the cryptographic combination of the new transactions in the network. This string of numbers provides the challenge in a mathematical puzzle – in Bitcoin this is a mathematical hash-function.[51] The most important aspect of such a function is that it is hard to solve, but at the same time it is very easy to verify that the solution is the correct once it is proposed.[52] Anyone with computational power can become part of the Bitcoin network and try to find a 'response string' of numbers that when combined with the challenge will solve the puzzle. These days only serious actors with huge farms of dedicated computers have a realistic chance of solving this puzzle before any of their competitors do.[53]

The incentive for those who dedicate computer power to this effort is twofold: they can set one transaction of a mathematically-determined amount of Bitcoin to themselves, and they are also allowed to claim any of the rewards that the primaries have included in their transaction.[54]

---

50 Nakamoto (above n. 2) section 4.

51 Unlike the other two traditional cryptographic algorithms, Secret Key and Public Key, the Hash function provides one-way encryption. In a good hash function, the only way to arrive at the data string that will recreate a cryptographic hash function's output is to try a large number of possible data strings to see if they produce a match. The level of difficulty can be ratcheted up by increasing the number of bits required in the output. For example, finding the correct string in a 128-bit function can be compared to throwing a coin and having it land heads-up 128 times in a row. In effect, the computer has to 2128 tries before finding the correct string. 2128 is more than the expected number of stars in the known universe, including all known galaxies. S. Northcutt, 'Hash Functions' *Cryptography in Business Series* (Sans Technology Institute 2008).

52 Proof of work puzzles have been around long before Bitcoin. They can, for example, be used to deter email-spamming activity by requiring each sender to solve such a puzzle before being allowed to send an email. Solving a puzzle once is not a noticeable effort if you are only sending to a few recipients, but becomes insurmountable when you are an email spammer. Conversely, since the effort of verifying the puzzles requires a fraction of the effort, the effort required by the service that asks for the puzzle-solution is almost negligible.

53 At the time of writing, 29 May 2016, Swedish Bitcoin miner KNC has filed for bankruptcy, citing the high energy taxes of Sweden as the chief factor behind their inability to compete with their Asian counterparts.

54 The ability to reward oneself with a new Bitcoin is sometimes referred to as mining. Mathematically, the system will 'mine out' in 2050, when there will be around 21 million

Trying to trick or in any way hack a system such as the one at hand cannot be done by attacking any one point in the system, since that kind of weakness is missing in a non-centralised system. Instead an attack has to be made against the entire network and all the instances of the blockchain in it; in essence you would have to 'out-compute' all the other current miners as well as all the work previously made.

5.3. BLOCKCHAIN SUMMARY

Put shortly, the blockchain is shared, trusted and public; qualities that by definition puts it outside of any single user's control. The participants in the system collectively keep this encrypted ledger up to date: it can be amended only according to strict rules and by general agreement. The blockchain of Bitcoin prevents double-spending and continuously keeps track of transactions.

6. OLD AND NEW PRIESTHOODS

Changes to the codebase of Bitcoin are decided by consensus, in an informal circle of merit among involved programmers. Such systems are common in software-developer projects, particularly Open Source, but bring with them their own difficulties and limitations concerning scalability. Certainly this system of consensus-driven governance has been the subject of frustrations that may be long-standing and sometimes made public.[55]

The pride in having established a monetary system that does not have a Temple or a Palace, and thus possesses the inherent integrity to resist political demands, seems to have made it quite sensitive to discussion of any significant changes to the underlying architecture. This is understandable, since any such discussion will at least have the potential for inviting political deliberations and thus risk criticism for allowing the short-sighted and counter-productive instincts of elected officials or other special interests to 'play politics' with the codebase of Bitcoin.[56] Thus, opening up a debate about reforming the underlying

---

Bitcoin in circulation. At that point, incentives will be provided solely by the rewards included. The optional rewards are sometimes called 'miner's fees' and also give the miners the incentive to prioritise your transaction when constructing a new block.

55 Such frustrations sometimes take the form of alternating codebases. For an example, see Bitcoin core developer Mike Hearn's argument on upgrading the Bitcoin code, 7 May 2015, 'Crash Landing – What Not to Do' <medium.com/@octskyward/crash-landing-f5cc19-908e32#.ymitlcxqd>.

56 This resulted in Bitcoin core developer Mike Hearn leaving the project and claiming that Bitcoin was an experiment that failed due to 'people problems', 14 January 2016: 'The Resolution of the Bitcoin Experiment' <medium.com/@octskyward/the-resolution-of-the-bitcoin-experiment-dabb30201f7#.jn65ucc4z>.

code of Bitcoin could further damage its money-qualities such as non-volatility and resilience; but not reforming the code to adapt to changes such as a radically increased user-base for example, could hurt other qualities such as promptness and possibly security.

The respected developers who dominate these circles reject state-created law and regulation, and will likely continue to resolve policy issues within these circles. It would seem likely that their current methods of resolving such conflicts are underdeveloped and rely on fairly primitive ideas of consensus, but it is unavoidable that more elaborate sets of rules be developed as time passes and more conflicts have to be managed while still keeping Bitcoin working and relevant.[57]

7. A RETURN TO THE MERCHANT TEMPLE – A GLIMPSE OF THE FUTURE?

Though Bitcoin itself has many interesting properties, it is when used with an equally decentralised system of contract that its revolutionary potential shines through properly. Like in the Mesopotamian temples, there is a potential for a connection between the monetary system itself and the contractual relationship prompting the transaction within it, a connection inherent in Bitcoin's logical potential, but managed at a physically decentralised level. Though any such decentralised trade system involving programmable crypto-currencies could draw on this potential, this text will use the newly-launched OpenBazaar network to provide concreteness.

Touted as the next 'killer app', OpenBazaar is an open source project to create a decentralised network for peer-to-peer commerce online, using Bitcoin, without fees and restrictions on the types of goods traded.[58]

The people behind OpenBazaar see themselves as bringing a new approach to online commerce. Their stated intention is to put the power back in the users' hands. Instead of buyers and sellers going through a centralised service, this system provides a marketplace where they can connect directly to each other.[59]

---

57 A study of this system of private governance within the circles of the lead software developers would be an intriguing topic for future research, but is not the topic for this text.

58 Currently, online commerce means using centralised services. eBay, Amazon, and other big companies have extensive policies and charge fees for listing and selling goods. They only accept forms of payment that cost both buyers and sellers money, such as credit cards or PayPal. They require personal information, which can lead to it being stolen or even sold to others. Buyers and sellers are not always free to exchange goods and services with each other, as companies restrict entire categories of trade.

59 The OpenBazaar project was initially spun off from the 'DarkMarket' project, a concept developed during an intense computer-coding competition but never taken further than a first draft. As the code was under open source licence, the team behind OpenBazaar picked it up, though the name was dropped.

Let us for example imagine that Alice is looking to sell her old computer. Using the OpenBazaar client application she creates a new product-listing of her computer with a type of detail exactly like what can be found on any e-commerce site, such as eBay. When Alice publishes that listing, it is sent out to the distributed peer-to-peer network of other people using OpenBazaar and becomes searchable by all others thereon. Let us then assume Bob is also on the network and finds Alice's listing. If they both agree on a price, the software client creates a contract between them both, and sends it to a third-party called a moderator. The moderators are other human nodes on the OpenBazaar network whom Alice and Bob trust in case something goes wrong. The third-party witnesses the contract and creates a so-called *multi-signature Bitcoin account* that requires two of three people to agree before the Bitcoin can be released.

Bob then sends the agreed amount to the multi-signature address. Alice subsequently receives a notification informing her that Bob has sent the funds, and she ships the computer to him and notes that it has been shipped on the network. When Bob finally receives it he marks it as received on the network, which releases the funds from the multi-signature account to Alice.

Further interesting qualities envisioned for this network are that with Bitcoin and its programmable property the inclusion of contracts readable by both humans and machine becomes possible. With these so-called 'Ricardian contracts',[60] disputes in more advanced contractual arrangements can be resolved directly between two parties, or in cooperation with a mutually-selected third-party that needs only to verify certain facts rather than render a more traditional judgment. Thus OpenBazaar aims to leap-frog the deeply embedded and highly involved 'paper institutions' rather than wait for them to adapt themselves to a digital globalised world.[61] Needless to say, if this vision attains traction within the business world and establishes some form of critical mass, then national legislation – particularly concerning creditor protection – will come under a high level of pressure to adapt.

60 Not to be confused with the English economist David Ricardo. This variation on smart-contracts was initially a format developed by Ian Grigg and Gary Howland as part of the Ricardo payment system. I. Grigg, 'The Ricardian Contract', <iang.org/papers/ricardian_contract.html>. The over-arching philosophical goal is to provide a unified document that will work for both man and machine.

61 Szabo characterises this development as a move from static to dynamic media, where software 'literacy' will have massive impact on law and legal institutions. N. Szabo, 'Formalizing and Securing Relationships on Public Networks', <http://szabo.best.vwh.net/formalize.html>.

8. THE SILK ROAD REVISITED AND A RETURN TO THE SUMERIAN TEMPLES?

Given the over-arching historical comparison in this text, it is quite fitting that OpenBazaar was supposedly conceived of as a response to the shutting-down of the internet-marketplace called 'Silk Road' mentioned in the first paragraph of this chapter. It was, of course, on the surface an infamous hive of scum and villainy best known for its abundant and varied supply of illegal drugs, but this obfuscated market was also hailed as a libertarian zone of free trade by its evangelists. It was shut down in October 2013 when a United States citizen was arrested by the Federal Bureau of Investigation and subsequently sentenced to life imprisonment. As a response to the fact that the Silk Road had been shut down by the arrest of one single individual, the idea of a decentralised marketplace gained traction.[62]

However, it might be a mistake to think of OpenBazaar as a project that embraces the same criminal ideals as the Silk Road did. The roots that connect the project are only as deep as the computer code they share, and do not seem to be lodged in shared ideology; the current development team inherited the code from the original developers who had left it to chase other projects. OpenBazaar's financial backers and spokespeople see themselves as competing with services like eBay or Amazon and have not implemented the type of anonymity aimed at avoiding law enforcement that was the very core of Silk Road.[63]

The ancient Mesopotamian Temples were places of commerce, where goods were sold and purchased, business ventures were proposed and planned – all under the watchful eyes of the clerics who kept records in their ledger of how value changed hands, and to what purpose. In its physically-decentralised network, decentralised markets such as OpenBazaar aims to repeat the same process – by tacking each transaction and its contractual terms onto the ledger that is the Bitcoin blockchain.

In this replacement temple of OpenBazaar its developers even envision a function called an *Oracle*. An oracle can be another person, a group, or even an autonomous organisation governed only by self-sustaining code. Oracles can act as reporters on the *state* of any object or event in the future. They can thus provide the necessary data input needed to settle disputed contracts between other users. These users would have little or no interaction with the Oracle directly. Oracles can also serve as the escrow agent or moderator, where the

---

62 This is an exact parallel of what happened in the online file-sharing community 20 years ago: centralised services such as Napster were replaced with decentralised protocols such as Bittorrent.

63 Forbes.com, 'OpenBazaar Is Not The Next Silk Road – It's An Anarchist eBay On Acid', 3 March 2016.

future state of the object or event, which they report on, is the basis of releasing funds from multi-signature accounts to the appropriate party. Releasing funds would be done in cooperation with the winning party, since a multi-signature contract requires two out of three parties to agree.

In line with the spirit of free competition even between forms of money itself, OpenBazaar sees an open market for Oracles as a way to introduce competitive forces and diversity, in order to improve the quality and range of data sources. Oracles can advertise what categories of objects or events they will report on, and why they are uniquely qualified over their peers. Each Oracle's reputation within the system will reflect how accurately they report correctly and cite reputable sources.[64] In this, the project holds up the direct contractual transaction between two parties as the central hub second to none, thus tying in with the 'Austrian' economic ideological roots inherent in the Bitcoin currency that, at least for the moment, will provide the means of payment in the lion's share of transactions.

Just as the Temples that provided the hub of Mesopotamian trade were complex industrial institutions with staffs of thousands, where craftsmen, caravan-organisers and clerical administrators mingled, so Bitcoin can be seen as a complex ecosystem with many actors making up that which has the potential to be truly novel and valuable. The various existing forms of alternative crypto-currency that try to keep the cryptographic base around a block-technology but in a centralised form merely provide a new technological vessel for an ancient tradition of centralised money. The unique selling point of Bitcoin lies in its attempt to create a competing form of money that eschews the weaknesses inherent in a physically centralised system, where the trusted party can always be put under pressure to meddle with the properties of its money. As a juxtaposition to established forms of money, Bitcoin is a more natural fit for the decentralised markets of the future without being a requirement for them.

As has been discussed, the Bitcoin of the future may not be termed 'Bitcoin'. While the technological framework seems to be strong in theory, there are at least some weaknesses in the practical governing framework that may prevent the necessary evolution needed for Bitcoin to achieve the critical mass needed to exert real pressure on the legal constructions in the commercial arena. Currently, Bitcoin performs well on some fundamental functional qualities required by good money, but is found to be lacking concerning volatility, speed and its (current) ability to handle large amounts of transactions. In keeping with the Austrian meta-competitive spirit that Bitcoin has built-in, if 'Bitcoin' does not resolve these issues, then another version of it is likely to do so instead. In the future, if open competition between different kinds of money is allowed to take place on the international stage, money-use will migrate to the form of money

64 See the OpenBazaar blog of 3 November 2015, 'Oracles and Risk Contracts' <blog.openbazaar.org/oracles-and-risk-contracts-in-openbazaar>.

possessing the best functional qualities, perhaps away from traditional currencies. Good money will drive out bad money. In the event that Bitcoin becomes a serious contender used in transnational transactions, its technological structure has the functional qualities to maintain integrity and resist pressure from the political sphere in a way that centralised monetary authorities can never hope to do. The integrity that comes from Bitcoin being logically centralised while physically decentralised, allied with the attraction of decentralised markets and smart-contracts, would thus constitute a tripod strongpoint around which political currents and legal debris would likely have to change their course.

PART IV

DEVELOPMENT AND IMPLEMENTATION OF CONTRACT – MORE DIGITAL, MORE LIQUID

CONTRACTS IN THE INFOSPHERE

Giovanni Sartor

ABSTRACT

As information machines become increasingly autonomous, not only partial and predetermined aspects of contracting are delegated to them, but also the very deliberations pertaining to whether to enter a contract, with whom, and with what content. After considering the different aspects of autonomy, I argue that the use of autonomous contracting agents involves the delegation of cognitive tasks. Consequently, such agents should be considered the real authors of the contracts they conclude. Not only do they exercise discretion in contracting, but they also have those cognitive states that are relevant to the contracts they form (beliefs, goals and intentions). Consequently, the rules that apply to human agents should in principle also apply to autonomous digital agents. This does not presuppose that digital agents should be granted legal personality, understood as the ability to bear rights and duties, since the normative effects of their activity will fall upon their users. Finally, I consider some of the legal and social issues that may result from the widespread delegation of contracting to digital agents.

1. INTRODUCTION

Contracting takes place today in a new socio-technological space, the so-called infosphere, based on digital information and information machines.[1] In such a

---

[1] L. Floridi, 'The Onlife Manifesto: The Onlife Initiative' in L. Floridi (ed.), *The Onlife Manifesto: Being Human in a Hyperconnected Era*, Springer, 2013, pp. 7–13.

context, several contract-related tasks are either accomplished with the support of machines, or are completely delegated to them. As information machines become increasingly autonomous, not only are partial and predetermined aspects of contracting delegated to them, but also the very deliberations pertaining to whether to enter a contract, with whom, and with what content.

I shall address some emerging dimensions of contracting in the ICT-based infosphere, focusing on artificially intelligent contracting parties.

First, I shall address the embeddedness of contractual activities in active, responsive, and connected informational environments. I will argue that in such environments a vast expansion of contractual interactions is likely to happen, since contracting enables distributed autonomous collaboration between humans and artificial entities, and between such entities themselves. Contractual relations will be entered into by both virtual artefacts (e.g., online bots) and physical artefacts (e.g., autonomous cars), as interactions with physical artefacts take place through their interconnected digital interfaces.

I will then focus on how contracting may take place with and between Autonomous Contracting Agents – 'ACA's. I will characterise the idea of autonomy as including three aspects: independence of action, high-level cognitive skills, and adaptive/teleologic architecture. I will deploy the concept of cognitive delegation to characterise the relation between ACAs and their users. The latter entrust contract-making to ACAs, relying on the ACAs' ability to collect information, process it, and adopt appropriate determinations.

Finally, I will consider whether and to what extent we need to change our legal conceptions for dealing with ACAs, and whether we need to assume that such contracting agents are 'mere tools', so that all their declarations (and accompanying attitudes) are traced back to their users. I will argue that, on the contrary, we may attribute intentional states – intentions, goals, and beliefs – also to ACAs, and that such systems may indeed be able to make declarations and engage in commitments. Even though ACAs have no legal personality, the commitments they undertake can be legally binding, having effects on their human or corporate users. In fact, while not possessing a human psychology, an ACA may possess those basic cognitive attitudes and capacities that are needed for contracting, namely, those attitudes that are needed to express and finalise a contractual instrument.

Therefore, in principle, we should be able to apply the basics of contractual law to ACAs as well. Adjustments may, however, need to be devised, considering that digital contracting agents may possess certain capacities (e.g., critical reflection, ability to understand contextual information) at a sub-human level, while possessing other capacities (e.g., speed, ability to process vast amounts of digital information) at a super-human level. The law also has to cope with the interconnectedness of computer systems, whose cognitive processes may involve distributed intelligence.

2. THE RISE OF COMPUTATION

In the last few decades, we have witnessed an accelerated growth in the number of linked computer devices, their computational power, and the amount of electronic data they collect, store, and process. Our social world has progressively become a hybrid infosphere, populated not only by humans, but also by a huge and growing number of increasingly pervasive, autonomous, and intelligent computational entities. Such entities have become an essential aspect of today's social ecology. On the one hand, we work, play, learn and communicate by symbiotically interacting with computations, and depend on them for most aspects of our social fabric (production, logistics, administration, transport, communications, services, etc.). On the other hand, an increasing number of tasks – involving data acquisition, communication, and processing, as well as engaging with the physical world – has been transferred to automated procedures, often taking place without human involvement.

It is important to stress that not only information processing, but also communication is increasingly delegated to computer systems. Communications have migrated to computer infrastructures, as computer systems have been linked into networks, and these networks into worldwide networks of networks (such as the internet). Not only is a vast part of human communication today computer-mediated, but computer-initiated communications – directed at humans or at other computer systems – play an important role in social and economic interactions. Computer systems are increasingly proactive in communicative interactions, determining when to engage in communication, with whom, and with what content.

In fact, computer systems perform a multiplicity of speech acts. On the one hand, they provide information about the state of the world, engaging in speech acts that have a world-to-word direction of fit,[2] such as assertions, hypotheses or guesses (e.g., when a system provides data about persons or events, or when it makes forecasts about the weather or about markets). On the other hand, computer systems increasingly engage in speech acts having a word-to-world direction of fit. This may happen through acts that are meant to influence human behaviour, such as suggestions or commands (e.g., by a flight or driving Sat-Nav). It may also happen through acts that are meant to produce institutional-computational effects, such as when a person gains or loses permission to access online resources depending of his or her behaviour, or when a contract is formed in an automated way. These effects are institutional-computational, since in computer-governed environments, institutional changes are accompanied by corresponding changes in the functioning of the computational environments. For instance, when a computer system grants or

---

2 J.R. Searle, *The Construction of Social Reality*, Free Press, 1995, p. 208.

removes permission or prohibition to access a resource, it will also enable or disable access. This is indeed a simple example of how human behaviour may be influenced through technological architectures.[3]

The rise of computation is not merely quantitative, since computational entities have also increased their cognitive capacities, i.e. their abilities to understand, act, and adapt. In the last few years we have indeed witnessed a rapid growth of investments in artificial intelligence (AI), accompanied by significant applications. Various definitions of AI have been proposed, referring to a system's ability to act rationality or humanly or to simulate rationality or humanity.[4] As far as we are concerned, it may be sufficient to say that the purpose of AI is to construct systems having high-level cognitive capacities, namely, systems that are able to perceive, understand, and predict the environment; to modify their environments according to their goals; and to communicate and co-operate with other artificial or natural agents. After the overoptimistic expectations of the 1960s and '70s, and the crisis of the '80s (the so-called 'winter of AI'), the new century has indeed seen an AI boom in research, funding and applications. A wide range of AI systems have left the laboratory for many commercial applications, some of them reaching the general public. Many functions that were considered futuristic only a few years ago have become or are becoming reality: automated translation, face and voice recognition, autonomous air and land vehicles, industrial and health robotics, understanding and generating spoken language, etc.

3. AUTONOMY OF ARTIFICIAL SYSTEMS AND CONTRACTING

For our purposes, it is significant to focus on the aspect of intelligent technologies that is most relevant for contracting, namely, their autonomy.

The characterisation of a concept of autonomy that applies to artificial systems is not straightforward. If the standard is too high (autonomy requires all the human cognitive capacities), no existing artificial entity can be classified as being autonomous. If the standard is too low, all algorithms qualify as autonomous.

In the discussion on autonomous systems and their regulation, distinct concepts of autonomy have been put forward.

---

3 As argued, among others, by L. Lessig, *Code V2*, Basic Books, New York, 2006 and R. Brownsword, 'So what does the world need now? Reflections on regulating technologies' in R. Brownsword and K. Yeung (eds.), *Regulating Technologies Legal Futures, Regulatory Frames and Technological Fixes*, Hart Publishing, Oxford, 2008, pp. 23–48.

4 S.J. Russell and P. Norvig, *Artificial Intelligence. A Modern Approach*, 3rd edn., Prentice Hall, 2010, p. 1ff.

For instance, the US Military Defense Science Board provides the following definition: 'Autonomy is a capability (or a set of capabilities) that enables a particular action of a system to be automatic or, within programmed boundaries, "self-governing."'[5] In a similar spirit, the roboticist George A. Bekey describes autonomy as 'the capacity to operate in the real-world environment without any form of external control, once the machine is activated, and at least in some areas of operation, for extended periods of time.'[6] According to both definitions, autonomy consists in the capacity for 'sustained independent action'. Thus, a system is autonomous to the extent that it can accomplish a task by itself, without external directions. Once the system starts its activity, there is no need for other human or artificial agents to monitor its behaviour and govern its functioning.

Stuart Russell and Peter Norvig adopt a different perspective, characterising autonomy as 'an agent's capacity to learn what it can to compensate for partial or incorrect prior knowledge'.[7] According to this definition, the focus is on cognitive capacity and, in particular, on the capacity to obtain new knowledge, interacting with the environment. Thus, an agent is autonomous to the extent that it is able to appropriately expand or revise its initial stock of knowledge, so as to face the challenges of its environment. There is no need for others to reprogram an autonomous system or to provide it with new directives when novel situations are met.

Cristiano Castelfranchi and Rino Falcone adopt yet another approach by grounding the autonomy of a system on the fact that the system tends toward certain specific results due to its internal constraints or representations; it perceives and interprets its environment, defines and selects what stimuli to take into consideration, has internal states, and its behaviour also depends on such internal states.[8] Here the focus is on the cognitive architecture of the system and on the way in which this architecture mediates external inputs and system behaviour. A system is autonomous to the extent that it does not merely react to external stimuli but, rather, integrates such stimuli into its cognitive structures, by modifying appropriately its internal states, according to its own standards and procedures, so as to determine its behaviour.

These aspects of autonomy are connected but do not necessarily coexist and converge. Thus, I propose that autonomy is understood as a scalable capacity,

---

5 Department of Defense, Defense Science Board, *The Role of Autonomy in DoD Systems* (July 2012, Washington D.C.), 1, available at: http://fas.org/irp/agency/dod/dsb/autonomy.pdf.

6 G.A. Bekey, 'Current trends in robotics: technology and ethics' in P. Lin, K. Abney and G.A. Bekey (eds.), *Robot Ethics: The Ethical and Social Implications of Robotics*, MIT Press, Cambridge MA, 2012.

7 S.J. Russell and P. Norvig, *Artificial Intelligence: A Modern Approach*, n. 4 above, 39.

8 C. Castelfranchi and R. Falcone, 'Founding autonomy: the dialectics between (social) environment and agent's architecture and powers' in M. Nickles, M. Rovatsos and G. Weiss (eds.), *Agents and Computational Autonomy: Potential, Risks, and Solutions*, Springer, Berlin, 2004, p. 40.

merging three dimensions, all of which must be present, at least to some degree, for a device to be autonomous: independence, cognitive skills, and teleonomic architecture.[9]

We will say that a technological device, within a system, is independent, relative to a certain high-level task of that system, to the extent that the device can accomplish that task on its own, without external input. As examples in the contractual domain, consider two software components of a typical e-commerce site: the contract-drafting component and the recommendation component. The contract-drafting system of a website is independent in filling in the variable elements in the contract for a particular purchase, inserting the relevant data (object, price, delivery site, counterparty name and address), and in communicating the final contractual declaration. A recommendation system is independent in finding convenient purchase opportunities, given the user's preferences, and in presenting such opportunities to the user.

Note that independence, as defined, is task-relative, and does not presuppose high-level cognitive skills in the system being considered (while not being incompatible with such skills).

For instance, the software of a simple website may be fully independent in making a single contract (it makes an offer or accepts it, without further human input). However, this does not mean that the software has any independence in determining the content of the contract, or that it deploys advanced legal skills. Human designers and programmers may have built the contractual machine by engineering its outputs for every possible input and anticipating the input–output function in every detail.

---

9 See, also for references to the literature on autonomy, G. Sartor and A. Omicini, 'The autonomy of technological systems and responsibilities for their use' in N. Bhuta, S. Beck, R. Geiss, C. Kress and H.Y. Liu (eds.), *Autonomous Weapons Systems: Law, Ethics, Policy*, Cambridge University Press, Cambridge, 2016, pp. 39–74. The notion of autonomy is understood in a more specific sense by some moral and legal philosophers, who often focus on an agent's capacity to select the criteria for its choices, rather than on its ability to choose according to its preferences. For instance, from a Kantian perspective we could say that a system is autonomous to the extent that it acts out of respect for the moral law rather than to serve its preferences, i.e., to the extent that it acts according to maxims it would like to become universal laws, applying to all rational beings, which involves viewing all such being as ends rather than as mere means. Similarly, Ronal Dworkin conceives autonomy 'as a second-order capacity of persons to reflect critically upon their first-order preferences, desires, wishes, and so forth and the capacity to accept or attempt to change these in light of higher-order preferences and values' (R.M. Dworkin, *The Theory and Practice of Autonomy*, Cambridge University Press, Cambridge, 1988, p. 20). He argues (ibid.) that 'by exercising such a capacity, persons define their nature, give meaning and coherence to their lives, and take responsibility for the kind of person they are'. While these more specific (and demanding) notions of autonomy point to aspects that may be relevant to the design of future intelligent systems – to what extent would we want an artificial system to act according to the rules it considers to be universalisable, or according to self-determined preferences? – the broader notion above seems more appropriate to the analysis of current intelligent technologies.

The second dimension of autonomy consists in the ability to perform high-level cognitive tasks. An autonomous system should be able to engage in high-level cognition (involving the ability to discriminate facts, actions, or outcomes) using its own abilities in one or more of the following domains:

- Acquisition and classification of input data (e.g., gathering market prices and trends, information on potential clients, counterparties and competitors);
- Information analysis to extract further information from the input data (e.g., determining trends or profitability, assessing credit ratings, understanding voice and natural language);
- Action selection, and construction of plans of action (e.g., defining negotiation strategies, designing proposal and counteroffers);
- Action implementation (e.g., making offers and counteroffers, assembling contractual clauses, monitoring the implementation of contracts and compliance by the counterparty).

The larger the cognitive task assigned to the artificial system, the more we can say that this system is autonomous under this second dimension. It is autonomous, indeed, in the sense that it performs a significant cognitive task by using its own abilities, which means that the resulting knowledge is, to a larger extent, the outcome of the activity of the system itself (rather than being provided to it as an external input).

Now we turn to the third dimension of autonomy, namely, a cognitive architecture enabling the adaptiveness of the system.

An adaptive system can change its patterns of behaviour to better achieve its purposes in the environment in which it operates. It interacts with the environment, receiving and selecting inputs and providing outputs. Based on environmental inputs, it changes the internal states on which its behaviour depends. The system has a feedback or homeostatic mechanism that keeps it focused on its objective by changing its internal state as the environment changes, and so enabling it to act as appropriate in view of the changed environment.

As an example of an adaptive system, consider a recommendation system that makes updated suggestions according to information it has on the available offers. Another example is provided by a system that, in making purchases on the stock market, changes its behaviour according to market trends and its previous experiences. Finally, consider a credit assessment system that dynamically changes its assessment criteria based on information about past defaults.

A particular kind of adaptive system is represented by teleologic (goal-directed) systems. A teleologic system has explicit cognitive states:

- goals, i.e., representational structures that specify objectives to be achieved by the system (e.g., making profits, expanding the market share, or making a particular contract given certain minimal conditions);

- beliefs as representational structures meant to track aspects of the environment (e.g., beliefs about the goods being traded, or about the identity and reliability of counterparties);
- plans as representational structures that specify how to reach the system's goals through its actions, given its beliefs (e.g., the plan to implement a certain contractual strategy in dealing with certain clients);
- intentions as selected plans, which the system is committed to implementing (e.g., the intention to execute a certain contract).

These cognitive states are differently implemented than the corresponding human mental states. They are simpler, but they perform the same basic functions: indicating objectives, tracking the environment, storing executable commitments. As an example, consider a digital assistant that supports its user in managing various tasks, and proposes plans of action (intentions), taking into account the objectives and priorities of the users (goals), and information about the current situation and its future developments (beliefs). In fact, not only have a number of systems whose architecture is based on the teleological model – usually called Belief-Desire-Intention (BDI) systems[10] – been realised at the prototypical level, but advanced programming platforms exist and many applications of this model are industrially available (in areas such as unmanned vehicles, trading agents, logistics, e-health and air traffic control).

It is important to stress that teleologic systems do not necessarily perform better than adaptive systems that are not teleologic. It depends on the task in question, and in any case a teleologic architecture can be placed on top of a system that uses different adaptive architectures for performing certain subsidiary tasks (e.g., tasks involving pattern recognition).

As an example of a teleologic system, consider a system that sells and buys on the stock market, according to its estimations of the profitability of different choices, bearing in mind the state of the market and the information that can be extracted from past trends, with the purpose of maximising profits and also of expanding the market share. Similarly, consider a digital bot engaging in online purchases, which selects counterparties according to offers and reliability. As an example of an adaptive, but not teleologic system, consider a neural network that delivers credit assessments by estimating the probability of defaults by individuals, based on a database of cases.

The examples I have provided so far concern isolated devices, but a relevant aspect in the deployment of artificial intelligence is the possibility to integrate or even merge different levels of information processing.

---

10 S. Rao and M. P. Georgeff, 'Modelling rational agents within a BDI architecture' in R. Fikes and E. Sandewall (eds.), *Proceedings of Knowledge Representation and Reasoning (KRR)*, Morgan Kaufmann, 1991, pp. 473–84, M. Wooldridge, *Reasoning about Rational Agents*, MIT Press, Cambridge MA, 2000.

On the one hand the autonomous behaviour of a system may emerge from the interaction of lower-level elements. Consider, for instance, the case of evolutionary algorithms. Such algorithms produce increasingly refined patterns of behaviour (e.g., for online trading) by recombining with a higher frequency the 'genes' (basic units) of the most successful pre-existing patterns (e.g., those leading to the most profitable trading). A marketplace of teleologic traders may overall also function in an adaptive non-teleologic way (the hidden hand), as it supports the elimination of the less successful traders and the persistence and imitation of the most successful ones.

Intelligent systems, thanks to their ability to exchange information at the highest speed, may exhibit what we may call 'fluid agency'. This consists in the fact that individual agents may be flexibly integrated into higher units of agency through information and decision-sharing. For instance, consider a fleet of autonomous cars governed by a unified management system. Each car collects knowledge and processes some of it locally, but the management system can access all the distributed knowledge and direct, substitute, or override the local decision-making processes of each car. Therefore, the client approaching one such car may wonder whether he is really interacting with the particular car he is approaching – which is proposing a price and other conditions for the ride – or with the central management system. Similarly, consider a house where different devices (refrigerator, oven, heating, vacuum cleaner, etc.) are endowed with some intelligent functions, but the behaviour of those devices is orchestrated by the house manager. When the refrigerator, having sensed that the milk has run out, sends an order to the supermarket, we may wonder whether it is the refrigerator itself that is making the order or whether it is the house manager, which controls the device and makes it issue the order.

4. COGNITIVE DELEGATION

When using an autonomous system to make contracts on our behalf, we delegate cognitive tasks to it. The delegation to engage in contracting may involve, for instance, finding the best offer, assessing the reliability of the counterparty, drafting a contract, deciding whether to agree on it, etc.

The delegator chooses to assign such tasks to the cognitive skills of the delegated system. She does not know, and thus does not intentionally pre-select, the epistemic or practical determinations of the delegated system. She is not anticipating the behaviour of the delegated system, but this is not a limitation or failure in the use of that system. In fact, the very reason why a cognitive system is used, is to replace human cognition when the latter is not desired or not available. The requirement that the human delegator always anticipate the cognitive activity of the delegated system would frustrate the very purpose of the delegation. Consider, for instance, a taxi service company that decides to rely on autonomous cars rather than on human drivers. It would not make sense for the company to have, for each car, a human driver remotely following and anticipating each move of the car. This would indeed frustrate the very purpose of relying on autonomous cars, namely, to replace the human cognitive activities involved in driving (planning a route, monitoring distances, avoiding obstacles, complying with traffic rules, etc.) with corresponding cognitive activities performed by the car.

This raises the issue of how the law should understand and consequently regulate cognitive delegation to an intelligent artefact, and in particular to an autonomous contracting agent (ACA). It seems to me that the necessary premise for an adequate regulation of ACAs is that they are not messengers but rather autonomous agents acting in the interests of their principal, by implementing, with a degree of discretion, the principal's instructions.

The legal understanding of the activity of ACAs does not require a legal fiction, namely, the fiction that the human principal rather than its artificial agent is determining whether to contract, and is agreeing to all contractual clauses. More precisely, regarding the aspects of the contract that are determined by the ACA, we do not need to pretend that the ACA expresses the will of the principal, merely transmitting the principal's declaration. We rather should accept the idea that the ACA expresses its own will on the basis of its own knowledge. This, however, does not exclude the full contractual autonomy of the principal. The principal of an ACA – similarly to the principal of a human agent – exercises its contractual autonomy precisely by choosing to delegate certain cognitive tasks (which will contribute to determining the content of the contract) to its ACA. This choice also includes the choice to delegate those very choices that are involved in the execution of those tasks.

Thus, the user of an ACA intends to rely on the autonomous determinations of the ACA, and this intention is made known to the counterparties of the ACA, usually by the ACA itself (except in cases of fraudulent impersonation). Thus, the user of the agent will be responsible for the contract in the sense that he or she will bear the rights and duties resulting from the activity delegated to the ACA. However, as I shall argue in the next section, this presupposes the legal relevance not only of the declarations made by the ACA, but also of its behaviour and cognitive states and processes.

5. CONTRACTS WITHOUT AGREEMENT, OR AGREEMENTS BY ARTEFACTS?

The possibility of having contracts whose formation is delegated to the determinations of ACAs raises the issue of how we should approach such contracts from a legal perspective.

On the one hand, it could be assumed that digital agents cannot have mental states (beliefs, goals, and intentions), so that all contracts formed by digital agents should be viewed as 'exchanges without agreement', to be considered from a purely behaviouristic perspective. According to this perspective, contracts with ACAs should be addressed differently from contracts between humans, since in contracts between humans the cognitive states of the parties involved may have legal significance. For instance, to determine whether there has been a mistake or deceit in a contract between humans, we need to consider what a party to the contract believed or what the counterparty intended to have that party believe; to interpret a contract, we may need to consider what information the parties shared or presupposed, etc. All such considerations would be irrelevant when it comes to ACAs: to determine the formation, content, and effects of a contract only conventional actions would matter, regardless of how such actions and their context are understood by the ACAs.

However, a different perspective is also possible, which would preserve the unity of contract law, namely, the possibility to apply the same rules to both humans and ACAs. We can, indeed, accept that even ACAs, when forming a contract, can have appropriate cognitive states. To reach this conclusion we need to approach the legally relevant cognitive states by focusing on those minimal functional aspects that are shared by humans and ACAs, and assume that these minimal aspects may be sufficient for the application of the law. In fact, as we observed above, even autonomous artificial agents – at least those having a teleologic architecture – may have beliefs (in the sense of internal states tracking reality), goals (in the sense of internal states indicating objectives), and intentions (in the sense of internal states prompting action). Consequently, such beliefs, goals, and intentions can be attributed to ACAs without engaging in fictions. For instance, the counterparty of an ACA, when the agent's linguistic and non-linguistic behaviour provides adequate clues, can interpret its contractual declaration accordingly, i.e., by attributing intentions (e.g., the intention to purchase an object) and the epistemic states that are presupposed by such intentions (e.g., the belief that the object has certain features). Moreover, under appropriate conditions, we may affirm that the ACA has committed a mistake or has been deceived, or has deceived the counterparty. We may also derive the appropriate legal consequences of these cognitive states – for the validity of the contract and for obligations to pay damages – without falsely attributing the same cognitive states to the user of the ACA, rather than to the ACA.[11]

In conclusion, I think that the second approach, namely assuming that ACAs can possess, and be assumed to possess, legally relevant cognitive states,

---

[11] G. Sartor, 'Cognitive Automata and the Law: Electronic Contracting and the Intentionality of Software Agents' (2009) 17 *Artificial Intelligence and Law*, 253–90.

is preferable. On the one hand, it corresponds to the cognitive architecture of ACAs, at least those having a teleologic architecture. On the other hand, it corresponds to the natural, and in a sense inevitable, way in which we will approach interactions with ACAs. In fact, when interacting with an intelligent system (be it natural or artificial), we tend to adopt what has been called the 'intentional stance', i.e. we approach the purposeful behaviour of that system by assuming that it has objectives (goals) and commits to choices (intentions) that are suited to achieving these objectives, given the information (the beliefs) it has.[12]

The assumption that ACAs have cognitive states is not incompatible with protecting the reliance that individuals place on the ACAs with which they interact. On the contrary, this assumption is required for protecting such reliance, since humans interacting with ACAs will inevitably form expectations based on the attribution of mental states to ACAs. Imagine yourself interacting with a humanoid robot acting as a salesperson, and imagine that you negotiate your purchase with the robot, asking for information about the items you are interested in, and requesting a discount, to which the robot agrees. You would assume that the robot believes what it is telling you, and you would claim that it lied if you found out that it had the correct information but provided false information to induce you to buy the item. Similarly, you would assume that the robot intends to sell you the item at the discounted price, if it agrees to do so.

Thus, the counterparty of an ACA is entitled to assume that the ACA's cognitive attitudes correspond to its behaviour. Thus, according to the idea of the protection of reliance, the owner-user of an ACA cannot avoid the legal implications of the intentional states that (a) have been attributed, in good faith, to the ACA by the counterparty and (b) are reasonable interpretations of the behaviour of the ACA, according to the conventions which are applicable to the interaction. For instance, if an ACA performs a speech act that appears to be a statement of fact, the counterparty is entitled to assume that the ACA believes what it is declaring. Consequently, the counterparty of an ACA can declare himself to have been deceived, if it appears that the ACA has chosen to provide him or her with false information. The counterparty may indeed accuse the ACA of lying, with the consequences this implies for the owner of the ACA, e.g., contractual liability, rescission, etc. Similarly, when the counterparty of an ACA receives a declaration of will or intention (typically, a contractual offer or a declaration of acceptance), the counterparty may justifiably assume that the ACA intends what it declares.

It is important to stress once again that the deployment of artificial intelligence devices having high-level cognitive skills involves the delegation of the exercise of such skills to the autonomous activity of the device. Human operators may

[12] D.C. Dennett, *The Intentional Stance*, MIT, Cambridge MA, 1989.

anticipate certain features of the cognitive determinations that will be adopted by the device. However, these anticipations will usually only concern abstract features of the working of the device; it would be impossible, or in any case impractical, for humans to repeat each single information-processing operation performed by the device. Therefore, the cognitive states that are associated with such operations, can only be attributed to the AI-based ACA performing such operations (e.g., issuing a contractual declaration).

This raises the issue of what kind of legal position we should attribute to an ACA in order to enable it to autonomously perform legal transactions. We need to distinguish three kinds of normative capacity:

- the capacity to have legal positions vested in oneself, i.e., to have rights and duties;
- the capacity to acquire rights and obligations through one's intentional actions;
- the capacity to cause others to acquire rights and obligations through one's intentional actions.

In modern legal systems, the first capacity is attributed to humans as well as to public and private legal persons (e.g., corporations and foundations). The second capacity is also attributed to all humans, except for minors and incapacitated individuals. It is also conferred on legal persons that exercise it through their legal representatives. The third capacity, too, is attributed to both humans and legal persons, when empowered by a principal, who may be a human or a legal person.

For the use of ACAs in contracting, only the third capacity is needed, namely their capacity to act as agents or representatives for a principal, the latter being a human or a legal person. By using this delegated capacity, the ACA can propose or accept a contract whose effects, as presented to the counterparty, are going to fall upon the ACA's principal. Therefore, the ACA itself is not required to have the legal capacity to acquire the rights or duties established under the contract.

It has been recently discussed whether it might be useful to assume that intelligent agents have the capacity to bear rights and duties on their own, and to act in such a way as to acquire or transfer new rights and duties. This would require such agents to have assets of their own upon which their counterparty might rely.[13] The idea that robots might be granted legal personality has been recently upheld by the European Parliament, which has affirmed the need to create

13 S. Chopra and L.F. White, *A Legal Theory for Autonomous Artificial Agents*, University of Michigan Press, 2011, p. 153; U. Pagallo, *The Laws of Robots – Crimes, Contracts and Torts*, Springer, Dordrecht, 2013, p. 40.

> a specific legal status for robots, so that at least the most sophisticated autonomous robots could be established as having the status of electronic persons with specific rights and obligations, including that of making good any damage they may cause, and applying electronic personality to cases where robots make smart autonomous decisions or otherwise interact with third parties independently.[14]

I think that a cautious approach is required in this regard, considering that existing legal frameworks – such as the laws of agency and representation, and company law – interpreted with sufficient flexibility, may provide adequate solutions for the present deployments of ACAs. Some adaptations of agency law may be needed considering that ACAs, lacking legal personality, cannot be subject to the obligations and sanctions that apply to a human agent. However, the guiding and deterrent function that obligations and sanctions can exercise upon a human agent can be substituted, with regard to the ACAs, by the technological controls exercised by users and developers, which may include – when necessary, technologically feasible and economically sustainable – endowing the ACAs with an inclination to follow legal norms, or ethical standards,[15] or even with the ability to develop and assess normative arguments,[16] or to participate in shared norm-based institutions.[17]

6. CONCLUSION – HOW TO REGULATE ARTIFICIAL INTELLIGENCE IN CONTRACTS

In concluding this analysis on contracts in the infosphere, I would like to propose some considerations on what legal regime may be most appropriate for ACAs. I would argue for the view that a minimalist approach may be sufficient.

---

14 European Parliament, Resolution of 16 February 2017, with recommendations to the Commission on Civil Law Rules on Robotics (2015/2103(INL)).

15 The idea to endow artificial agents with the ability to follow norms was implemented in the BOID (Beliefs-Obligations-Intentions-Desires) architecture, proposed by M. Broersen, J. Dastani, J. Hulstijn, Z. Huang and L. Van Der Torre, 'The BOID architecture' in *Proceedings of the fifth international conference on Autonomous agents*, ACM, 2001, pp. 9–16. See also G. Governatori and A. Rotolo, 'Bio logical agents: Norms, beliefs, intentions in defeasible logic' (2008) 17 *Autonomous Agents and Multi-Agent Systems*, 36–69.

16 An architecture for agents based on argumentation is presented in J.L. Pollock, *Cognitive Carpentry: A Blueprint for How to Build a Person*, MIT, Cambridge MA, 1995 and J.L. Pollock, *Thinking about Acting: Logical Foundations for Rational Decision Making*, Oxford University Press, Oxford, 2006. On legal argumentation in AI, see H. Prakken and G. Sartor, 'Law and logic: A review from an argumentation perspective' (2015) 227 *Artificial Intelligence*, 214–45.

17 D. De Jonge, B. Rosell, and C. Sierra, Human interactions in electronic institutions, in *Proceedings 2nd International Conference on Agreement Technologies*, Springer, Volume 8068, Beijing, 2013, pp. 75–89.

In fact, we could just assume that rules for human parties can also apply to contracts with ACAs, the latter being viewed as quasi-representatives or agents of their human or legal principals. Not only the behaviour, but also the cognitive states of ACAs (beliefs, intentions, goals) can be likened, in principle, to those of human parties, under the same legal rules.

There are, however, some relevant differences between artificially intelligent agents and humans. ACAs (will) have some super-human capacities (speed in processing and communicating, memory, persistency) as well as some sub-human capacities (creativity, understanding natural language, detecting contextual clues, etc.). Their human counterparties need to be protected against the malicious deployment of super-human ACAs' skills, and ACAs themselves need to be protected against the malicious deployment of superior human skills, so that neither of the two parties profits from its superiority to take advantage of the other (e.g., ACAs may take advantage of humans in high-speed trading by pre-empting human choices, while humans may take advantage of ACAs by proposing contractual terms that an ACA may misunderstand). Standards may need to be defined to support reliable and fair interactions between humans and ACAs.

An interesting issue is whether the regulation of ACAs should limit their autonomy or rely on their autonomy to reconcile flexibility and fairness. For instance, it may be argued that by embedding in the ACAs' architecture the ability and the inclination to comply with ethical requirements, a fair behaviour could be obtained without imposing rigid constraints on the ACAs' decision-making processes, thus enabling fair and efficient adaptations.

Another important difference between humans and AI pertains to what we called fluid agency, namely, the fact that the information processing of AIs can be decentralised or centralised, or both, depending on circumstances. So, we may wonder which intelligent entity – the individual device or a central manager (e.g., the single car or the car-management system) – has the situational awareness that is relevant to the legal assessment of the contracts, e.g., for the purpose of contextual interpretation or to determine whether there is deceit or a mistake.

A further issue pertains to the extent of the user's civil and criminal liability for the contractual behaviour of an autonomous agent, and the extent to which the user may be bound by the declarations of the agent. Consider, for instance, the case in which an autonomous agent is purchasing or selling illegal goods (drugs or weapons) in the pursuit of the economic interest of its user, but without the knowledge of the latter. Or consider the case in which a high-speed trading system is making contracts that negatively affect its user in a way that might be recognised as such by the counterparty.

Finally, more general social issues are also related to the use of ACAs. First, the availability of ACAs, in combination with access to extremely cheap micropayment systems, may lead to a pervasive spread of economic exchanges, including in areas which are currently covered by non-economic interactions based on reciprocity (e.g., with regard to giving access to one's digital content or personal material objects). Will this have a negative impact on human relations, on the development of friendship and solidarity?

Secondly, we may wonder to what extent the widespread deployment of ACAs will affect our concrete ability to shape our legal sphere through contracts. In many instances of automation, it has appeared that once an activity is delegated to technological devices, humans tend to lose the concrete ability to engage in that activity (since this ability requires training and persistent exercise). Will an extensive delegation of contractual activity to ACAs lead us to lose the ability to exercise this activity directly? As in the Hegelian master-slave dialectics, will we substantially lose part of our real contractual freedom, and consequently an important aspect of human autonomy, as a consequence of its delegation to our intelligent servants?

PART V

DIGITAL OBJECTS OF CONTRACT – CESL II AND MORE

CONTRACTS FOR THE SUPPLY OF DIGITAL CONTENT – THE PROPOSAL OF THE COMMISSION FOR A DIRECTIVE ON CONTRACTS FOR THE SUPPLY OF DIGITAL CONTENT

Gerald SPINDLER*

* An earlier version of this contribution was published as 'Contracts for the Supply of Digital Content – Scope of Application and Basic Approach – Proposal of the Commission for a Directive on Contracts for the Supply of Digital Content' (2016) 12 *European Review of Contract Law* 183.

ABSTRACT

In December 2015, the European Commission made a proposal for a Directive on contracts for the supply of digital content as a part of its digital agenda. The proposal breaks new ground in multiple ways, encompassing all kinds of different services, from music downloads to social networks. This chapter analyses the Commission's proposal both with respect to its broad scope of application and departure from regulating particular types of contract, as well its approach towards harmonising the standards for contractual liability, termination and rights to damages.

1. INTRODUCTION

The Digital Agenda, as one cornerstone of the Commission's Europe 2020 strategy, has steadily gained momentum and is starting to take increasingly concrete shape. While the Directorate-General CONNECT's attempts to reform European copyright law sparked intense controversy and have thus been postponed,[1] the Directorate-General Justice submitted two new proposals on 9 December 2015 – one tackling the issue of consumer protection regarding the supply of digital content[2] and the second concerning contracts for the online and other distance sales of goods.[3] Though the second proposal entails

---

[1] Communication from the Commission on 9 December 2015, towards a modern, more European copyright framework, COM(2015) 626 final, available at: https://ec.europa.eu/transparency/regdoc/rep/1/2015/EN/1-2015-626-EN-F1-1.PDF. The Commission has not entirely given up on this project, however. See at p. 12.

[2] Proposal for a Directive on the European Parliament and of the Council on certain aspects concerning contracts for the supply of digital content, COM(2015) 634 final, 2015/0287 (COD), available at: https://ec.europa.eu/transparency/regdoc/rep/1/2015/EN/1-2015-634-EN-F1-1.PDF.

[3] Proposal for a Directive on the European Parliament and of the Council on certain aspects concerning contracts for the online and other distance sales of goods, COM(2015) 635 final, 2015/0288 (COD), available at: https://ec.europa.eu/transparency/regdoc/rep/1/2015/EN/1-2015-635-EN-F1-1.PDF.

changes of practical significance, such as prolonging the presumption for a lack of conformity with the contract from six months to two years (Article 8(3), recitals (22), (23)), the proposed 'Directive on certain aspects concerning contracts for the supply of digital content' (CSDC Directive) is of far greater importance due to its far-reaching application and its innovative regulatory approach. Drawing inspiration from the (ultimately unsuccessful) proposal for a Common European Sales Law (CESL)[4] as well as from preparatory studies,[5] the proposed regulatory framework has the potential to severely shake up the traditional typology of contracts in many Member States.

The following discussion seeks to describe and analyse the Commission's proposal, focusing on the remarkably broad scope of application (section 3) as well as its provisions for contractual liability (section 7), termination of contract (section 8) and rights to damages (section 9).

2. GENERAL APPROACH

Despite the proposed framework's character of an all-encompassing, binding set of fixed rules, the Commission has decided not make use of its authority to issue a regulation, but has instead proposed a fully-harmonising Directive to facilitate the implementation into national civil law (Article 4, recital (5) CSDC).[6] In the light of the proposal's broad scope of application, this approach is indeed the best way to achieve the law's purpose while avoiding friction with many Member States' pre-existing systems of various distinct types of contracts – even though a one-for-one transfer may nonetheless be a feasible option for many states. On the other hand, the fully-harmonising nature of the Directive appeared to be necessary due to the dawning prospect of an increased

---

4 Explanatory Memorandum CSDC, n. 2 above, 2; Proposal for a Regulation of the European Parliament and of the Council on a Common European Sales Law, COM(2011) 635 final, 2011/0284 (COD); available at: http://ec.europa.eu/justice/contract/files/common sales law en.pdf. For a detailed discussion of the CESL's proposed changes see M. Loos, 'The Regulation of Digital Content B2C Contracts in CESL' 18 October 2013, Centre for the Study of European Contract Law Working Paper Series No. 2013-10; Amsterdam Law School Research Paper No 2013-60. Available at SSRN: http://ssrn.com/abstract=2343176, last access 9 April 2016; Proposal for a Regulation of the European Parliament and of the Council on a Common European Sales Law, 2012, 9 *et seq.*; S. Arnerstål, *Gewerblicher Rechtsschutz und Urheberrecht, Internationaler Teil* 2015, 882, 884.

5 M. Loos, N. Helberger, L. Guibault, C. Mak, L. Pessers, K. Cseres, B. van der Sloot and R. Tigner, *Analysis of the applicable legal frameworks and suggestions for the contours of a model system of consumer protection in relation to digital content contracts*, Final Report, 2011, available at: http://ec.europa.eu/justice/consumer-marketing/files/legal_report_final_30_august_2011.pdf; M. Loos, N. Helberger, L. Guibault and C. Mak, 'The Regulation of Digital Content Contracts in the Optional Instrument of Contract Law' *European Review of Private Law* 6 (2011), 729.

6 Explanatory Memorandum CSDC, n. 2 above, p. 7.

fragmentation of digital content laws in Europe, with the Consumer Rights Acts in the UK being just one example of recent national activity in this field.[7] Besides protecting the European Single Market (Article 114 TFEU), the Commission also seeks to complement its efforts to foster European Cloud Computing as part of its Digital Single Market Strategy,[8] which is supported by the Expert Group on Cloud Computing Contracts.[9]

This brings us to one of the most significant aspects of the proposal: the absence of any typological distinction between different kinds of contracts, and its primary focus on regulating at an abstract level general duties and remedies. Unlike prior legislation such as the Consumer Sales Directive,[10] the proposal deliberately avoids differentiating between different kinds of contractual agreement, e.g. sales or service contracts, to prevent the new Directive from being outpaced by the rapid technological development and high level of innovation and evolution of new business models in the digital market.[11] Thus, the proposal is not confined solely to data or copyright-protected content, but encompasses all kinds of aspects of the supply of digital content, including accompanying services and other combinations of different contractual obligations which go along with the supply of digital content. It makes no difference whether the contract is limited in time or not.[12]

Furthermore, the proposal includes not only contracts entered into for a monetary price, but also those in exchange for access to (personal) data.[13] This is certainly a step in the right direction,[14] although it also comes with several difficulties in drawing determinate boundaries for its scope of application, which will be discussed later. On the other side, even though the CSDC concentrates on full harmonisation it does not preclude Member States from implementing

---

7 The Consumer Rights Act came into effect on 1 October 2015; part 1, ch. 3 deals with digital content. Available at: http://www.legislation.gov.uk/ukpga/2015/15/pdfs/ukpga_20150015_en.pdf. Other countries such as the Netherlands have enacted or are apparently about to enact similar laws, see. Explanatory Memorandum CSDC, n. 2 above, p. 3.

8 Explanatory Memorandum CSDC, n. 2 above, pp. 4, 8.

9 Expert Group on Cloud Computing Contracts, set up by the Commission on 18 June 2013. For detailed information about the composition of the group, its objectives, and the minutes of their meetings, see: http://ec.europa.eu/justice/contract/cloud-computing/expert-group/index_en.htm.

10 Directive 1999/44/EG of the European Parliament and the Council of 25 May 1999 on certain aspects of the sale of consumer goods and associated guaranties, *OJEC* L171, 7 July 1999, 12, available at: http://eur-lex.europa.eu/legal-content/EN/TXT/PDF/?uri=CELEX:31999L0044&from=EN.

11 Art. 5(b) CESL (n. 4 above) already followed a similar content-centred approach.

12 Cf. M. Wendland, 'GEK 2.0? Ein europäischer Rechtsrahmen für den Digitalen Binnenmarkt' *Gemeinschaftsprivatrecht* (2016), 8, 13.

13 Art. 3(1), recital (13) CSDC.

14 The concept of personal data as a 'price' for the supply of digital content can also be found in art. 5(b) CESL (n. 4 above), see H. Zech, 'Information as Property', *Journal of Intellectual Property, Information Technology and E-Commerce Law (Jipitec)*, 6 (2015). Available at: https://www.jipitec.eu/issues/issue.2016-01-12.5219458400/4315 last access: 8 April 2016.

the CSDC into different contractual types such as sales, services etc. or to opt for a 'sui generis' approach – hence, still substantial differences may exist owing to divergent ways of implementing the CSDC.[15]

While the proposal is generally broad in scope, it also makes sure to exclude other legislative areas in order to avoid friction with European and national law. It neither deals with copyright and other intellectual property related law (recital (21) CSDC) or with the general rules for entering contracts (Article 3(9), recital (10) CSDC), nor does it seek to alter the standards of data privacy law (Article 3(8), recitals (14), (22) CSDC).[16] In fact, the proposal even has its own particular version of the principle of subsidiarity by stating that a conflict between any of its provisions and another Union act governing a specific sector or subject-matter will render this provision inapplicable (Article 3(7) CSDC). Thus, the Directive has no influence on issues like Digital Rights Management Systems (Article 6 Info-Soc Directive), the doctrine of exhaustion of intellectual property rights, or exemptions from and limitations to reproduction rights (Article 5(2), (3) Info-Soc Directive).[17] Thus, important issues for consumers such as the right to resell or to implement the digital content on another device are left untouched.[18]

However, even this cautious approach may result in certain friction and inconsistencies. Take for example Article 8 of the General Data Protection Regulation (GDPR),[19] which generally allows for the processing of the personal data of children of the age of 16 or older based on their own consent,[20] whereas the proposal's protections only apply once a contract is actually entered into – which usually requires the consent of a holder of parental responsibility until the age of 18. If such consent is not provided, the child may be left with only national remedies with varying degrees of effectiveness – at least with respect to his or her non-personal data.[21]

---

15 Also criticised by C. Mak, 'The new proposal for harmonised rules on certain aspects concerning contracts for the supply of digital content' Workshop of JURI-Committee of the European Parliament, January 2016, PE 536.494, 12–13. http://www.epgencms.europarl.europa.eu/cmsdata/upload/a6bdaf0a-d4cf-4c30-a7e8-31f33c72c0a8/pe__536.494_en.pdf.

16 Explanatory Memorandum CSDC, n. 2 above, pp. 5, 6.

17 Directive 2011/29/EC the European Parliament and the Council of 22 May 2001 on the harmonization of certain aspects of copyright and related rights in the information society, available at: http://eur-lex.europa.eu/LexUriServ/LexUriServ.do?uri=OJ:L:2001:167:0010:0019:EN:PDF.

18 Criticised also by H. Beale, 'Scope of application and general approach of the new rules for contracts in the digital environment' Workshop of JURI-Committee of the European Parliament, January 2016, PE 536.493, 27.

19 Regulation (EU) 2016/679 of the European Parliament and of the Council of 27 April 2016 on the protection of natural persons with regard to the processing of personal data and on the free movement of such data, and repealing Directive 95/46/EC (General Data Protection Regulation), OJ of 4 May 2016, L 119, 1.

20 Art. 8(1) GDPR even allows for a national data processing age of consent beginning at the age of 13.

21 Similar problems may also arise with respect to licensing agreements in social networks.

3. SCOPE OF APPLICATION

As mentioned before, one of the proposal's main features is its exceptionally broad scope of application, which seeks to cover almost all kinds of contracts related to digital content.

3.1. DIGITAL CONTENT

The core criterion of the proposal is the concept of digital content as defined by Article 2(1) CSDC. It includes any kind of digital content, such as 'video, audio, applications, digital games and any other software' (Article 2(1)(a) CSDC).[22] Going beyond the former CESL proposal's concept, it furthermore encompasses all related services that allow for 'the creation, processing or storage of data in digital form, where such data is provided by the consumer' as well as 'sharing of and any other interaction with data in digital form provided by other users of the service'. Hence, the proposal goes well beyond just covering the acquisition or use of digital content, which – depending on the Member State and individual nature of the contract – can be qualified as sales, service or rental contracts. Instead, the term 'digital content' deliberately includes all kinds of services related to digital content, thereby covering such diverse services as Cloud Computing, social networks and media such as Facebook or Twitter, e-commerce and trading platforms such as Amazon or eBay, search engines such as Google, blog portals, data storage systems, web-streaming, or visual modelling files for 3D printers.[23] However, the proposal does exclude services that use the digital format mainly as a carrier while the actual services are provided predominantly by human intervention (Article 3(5)(a), recital (19) CSDC). Thus, while carrier platforms like Airbnb or Uber are themselves subject to the proposal, the people ultimately providing the physical services are of course not.

Besides digital content originally pre-generated by a supplier, the proposed Directive is also meant to cover any content tailor-made for the consumer (recital (16) CSDC) as well as any user-generated content created by the consumer themselves (recital (15) CSDC). While the former category encompasses individualised software, expert databases[24] and custom-made models for 3D printers, the latter seems to extend the scope of application even to personal photos, videos, tweets or customer ratings. However, the supplier's contractual

---

22 See, from a US perspective, N. Kim, 'Expanding the Scope of the Principles of the Law of Software Contracts to Include Digital Content' *Tulane Law Review* 84 (2010) 1595-IV at 1598.

23 See also recital (11) CSDC with several examples.

24 Regarding the regulation of medical expert systems: F. Nguyen, 'Regulation of Medical Expert Systems: A Necessary Evil' *Santa Clara Law Review* 34 (1994) 1187–1234, 1187 *et seq.*

duties and remedies as defined by the proposal are obviously only meant to apply to the services provided for this content and not the original content itself.

The most significant – and potentially most problematic – restriction to the Commission's far-reaching approach to regulate all kinds of digital content can be found somewhat hidden in recital (11) of the CSDC proposal, which excludes all embedded digital content operating as an integral, yet subordinate element merely to support the main functionalities of goods. This somewhat vague concept of 'embedded systems' is, however, destined to produce various classification issues in the future.[25] Is the control software of a system really a subordinate part of the product as a whole if it cannot be used without it? What about smart TVs, which increasingly provide online-based services – some of which are not 'embedded' in the narrow sense, but allow for firmware updates or additional applications? Why does it depend on the incidental integration of a system whether it is covered or not?

The same applies to the 'Internet of Things', which is excluded from the proposal to address issues regarding liability and machine-to-machine contracts by a separate Directive. However, the proposal neither tries to define the term, nor does it provide a justification for why commercially used data or control software related to the internet of things shall not be subject to the proposed Directive. After all, there is no reason why a supplier of a separate app designed to control household appliances or cars should not be liable in accordance with the conditions of the Directive.[26] These issues exemplify a fundamental, yet hardly avoidable problem of the Commission's approach to address a wide variety of contracts related to digital content: while the broad scope of application spares the legislator from constantly adapting the legal framework to new technological developments and avoids putting courts in the uncomfortable position of creatively 'filling in the gaps', it is also prone to creating difficulties with setting appropriate limits at its margins.[27]

On the other hand, the proposal successfully solves another problem that has caused a stir in other contexts.[28] According to Article 3(3) CSDC, the Directive

---

25 See also Mak, n. 15 above, 8; B. Lurger, 'Anwendungbereich und kaufvertragliche Ausrichtung der DIRL- und FWRL-Entwürfe' in C. Wendehorst and B. Zöchling-Jud (eds.), *Ein neues Vertragsrecht für den digitalen Binnenmarkt* (Vienna: Manz, 2016) 19, 28; C. Wendehorst, 'Hybride Produkte und hybrider Vertrieb' in Wendehorst and Zöchling-Jud (eds.), ibid., 45, 54; for a discussion of classification problems before CSDC, see Loos, n. 4 above.

26 For classification difficulties in new technologies and old laws, see A. Simpson, 'Content and Copyright in the Digital Age – Impact on Contract' *Journal of Law and Information Science* 12 (2001) 70–86, 73.

27 Cf. also Mak, n. 15 above, 9.

28 R. Mańko, 'Contract Law and the Digital Single Market: Towards a New EU Online Consumer Sales Law?', 15 September 2015, European Parliamentary Research Service (EPRS) in-depth analysis, Brussels: European Parliament, 2015, PE 568.322, ISBN 978-92-823-7932-5 doi: 10.2861/16497, No. 5. Available at SSRN: http://ssrn.com/abstract=2660770, last

shall also apply to every durable medium serving as a carrier for digital content (i.e. CDs/DVDs, etc.) and not just content directly supplied via the internet. Hence, physical data carriers would no longer be subject to the Consumer Sales Directive and would instead fall under the new Directive's rules regarding the reversal of the burden of proof and other standards – irrespective of the way such carriers are distributed.[29] Since the proposal does not, however, regulate copyright law,[30] related issues like the exhaustion doctrine's complex and incoherent application in online vs. offline contexts still remain unresolved and will continue to occupy judicial resources.[31]

3.2. PERSONAL SCOPE OF APPLICATION

The proposal expressly limits its application to the relationship between consumers and traders (or in this context: 'suppliers'), thereby adopting the traditional personal scope of application of earlier consumer protection laws and excluding other groups such as small and medium-sized companies. Consequentially, it also adopts the traditional problems that come with defining these terms, particularly the well-known 'dual use' problem.[32] On top of that, it is particularly hard for the supplier to determine the intended use of digital content, e.g. word processing software, which is frequently used for private as well as professional purposes. While voluntary self-declarations by the consumer and other concepts may help in some cases, they are not capable of solving the problem at its core and as a whole.

---

access: 9 April 2016; asking the question if CESL would had solved consumer's problems: Loos, n. 25 above, No 3.3.2.; with regard to digital content contracts for consumers in general: M. Loos, C. Mak, L. Guibault, L.W. Pessers and N. Helberger, 'Digital Content Contracts for Consumers', 31 May 2012, Amsterdam Law School Research Paper No. 2012-66; *Journal of Consumer Policy* 36 (2013), 37–57; Centre for the Study of European Contract Law Working Paper Series No. 2012-05; Amsterdam Law School Research Paper No. 2012-66. Available at SSRN: http://ssrn.com/abstract=2081918, last access: 14 April 2016.

29 See recitals (12), (13), (20) and (50) CSDC, with (20) stating that in cases of contracts or bundles of contracts with a set of multiple services or goods which do not entirely function as a carrier of the digital content, the new Directive shall only apply to the digital content component of such a bundle.

30 Recital (12) CSDC.

31 The ECJ is about to issue a decision regarding online-based exhaustion for non-software related copyrights, see Case C-174/15 – *Vereniging Openbare Bibliotheken v. Stichting Leenrecht*, ECLI:EU:C:2016:459. Courts in Germany have so far been reluctant to accept such an exhaustion, see OLG Hamburg *Gewerblicher Rechtsschutz und Urheberrecht – Rechtsprechungsreport* 2015, 361, paras. 30 *et seq.* – *eBook-AGB*; OLG Hamm, *Multimediarecht* 2014, 689 – *Hörbuch-AGB*. For software products, see *Usedsoft GmbH v. Oracle International Corp.* Case C-128/11, ECLI:EU:C:2012:407; and furthermore BGH *Multimediarecht* 2015, 530 with comment Heyden – *UsedSoft III*; BGH *Multimediarecht* 2014, 232 with comment Heyden – *UsedSoft II*; BGH *Multimediarecht* 2011, 305 with comment Heyden – *UsedSoft*.

32 See eg Case C-464/01, *Gruber v. Bay Wa AG*, judgment of 20 January 2005, ECLI:EU:C:2005:32.

Since the CSDC's personal scope is limited to the relationship between consumers and suppliers,[33] it furthermore does not extend to the consumer's relationship to third parties, notably to copyright owners and their relationship with consumers based on the widespread End User License Agreements (EULA).[34] While the supplier, e.g. Cloud Computing services or software dealers, may be held liable when selling or granting access to the digital content, the Directive has no influence on liability exemptions and other limitations in the EULA that shield the copyright owner from being held accountable by the consumer. However, if the EULA supplier asks for personal data of the consumer it is arguable that the digital content (software, eBooks etc.) may be covered by CSDC.[35]

3.3. FREE DIGITAL CONTENT

Another novelty of the proposal (which was, however, already part of the CESL)[36] is its application to contracts regarding the supply of digital content for counter-performance other than money, in the form of personal or other data (Article 3(1), recital (13) CSDC). While the digital content appears to be 'free' at first glance, it is indeed justified to extend the Directive's consumer protections to such contracts, since the consumer may nonetheless have a legitimate interest in such content or services being free from defects, and since suppliers would most likely not have offered the content without the benefits he or she may derive from the consumer's data.[37]

---

33 Criticised by Beale, n. 18 above, 28 *et seq.* who favours an optional instrument for small and medium enterprises.

34 It is, however, not yet settled whether the licensing agreement actually come into effect directly between the consumer and the copyright owner ('click-wrap' etc.); A. Gatt, 'Electronic commerce – clickwrap agreements: the enforcability of click wrap agreements' *Computer Law & Security Review* (2002), 404; Y. Bakos, F. Marotta-Wurgler and D.R. Trossen, 'Does Anyone Read the Fine Print? Consumer Attention to Standard Form Contracts' *Journal of Legal Studies* 43 (2014); CELS 2009 4th Annual Conference on Empirical Legal Studies Paper; NYU Law and Economics Research Paper No. 09-40. Available at SSRN: http://ssrn.com/abstract=1443256, last access: 9 April 2016; S.J. Horowitz, 'Competing Lockean Claims to Virtual Property' *Harvard Journal of Law and Technology* 20 (2007). Available at: SSRN: http://ssrn.com/abstract=981755, last access: 9 April 2016; with regard to the relationship between copyright law and consumer protection, see P.S. Menell and S. Scotchmer, 'Intellectual Property Law' in A.M. Polinsky and S. Shavell, *Handbook of Law and Economics*, vol. 2, 1473–1570 (2007); UC Berkeley Public Law Research Paper No. 741724. Available at SSRN: http://ssrn.com/abstract=741424, last access: 9 April 2016; cf also Wendehorst, n. 25 above, 45, 74 *et seq.* for a check of substantial clauses.

35 See also Beale, n. 18 above, 13.

36 See recital (9) CESL, n. 4 above.

37 See also M. Schmidt-Kessel, K. Erler, A. Grimm and M. Kramme, 'Die Richtlinienvorschläge der Kommission zu Digitalen Inhalten und Online-Handel – Teil 2' *Gemeinschaftsprivatrecht* 2016, 54, 57.

The latter does not, however, apply to situations where the supplier collects data necessary for the digital content to function in conformity with the contract (e.g. for geographical localisation purposes) or the (sole) purpose of meeting legal requirements (e.g. security and identification purposes applicable by law), which is why those cases will not fall under the CSDC (Article 3(4), recital (13), (14) CSDC).[38] While this distinction is somewhat clear cut, it nonetheless results in some grey areas. Take for example services with user-generated content like Wikipedia: while users do provide personal data in exchange for using the site's digital content,[39] one could argue that Wikipedia needs the data only in order to link it with the article's version history and thus only for purposes necessary to make its service function in conformity with the contract. If, however, one applies the proposed Directive to user-generated articles, this qualification would entail several problems for the particular service Wikipedia provides – notably with respect to its obligation to delete personal data, which would make it hard to understand and compare the course of discussions the user took part in. Questions like these have also remained unresolved in other contexts, e.g. with respect to the future effects of Article 17(3)(d) GDPR. Moreover, the CSDC does not contain any evidence rules concerning the use of (personal) data by the entrepreneur. Thus, it is likely that the consumer will have to prove that the entrepreneur had used his data in a context going beyond what was necessary for contractual performance – a matter that is likely to be impossible for a consumer to prove.[40]

Apart from these issues, the Commission's proposals also include other exceptions to the applicability of the CSDC to 'free' content, which may not be overly ambiguous, but could lead to a few interesting results. First, the Directive will not apply to cases in which the consumer does not 'actively' provide data to the supplier, i.e. without an individual registration or explicit granting of access to the consumer's data.[41] Hence, classic forms of free digital content like Open Access Data, Open Source Software or Freeware will not be covered, since they typically do not require an active registration. The picture does, however, change once the consumer is provided with further services like patches or additional information if these services require a personal account.[42]

More importantly, the proposal also excludes two other practically important situations from its scope: the users' exposure to advertisements as a 'price' in exchange for the supply of the content, and data collected by cookies, even if the

[38] This resembles art. 6(1)(2) GDPR, n. 19 above. If the supplier does, however, process the date any further or uses it in other commercial ways, the exception does not apply anymore.

[39] At least those users who create an account have to provide Wikipedia with their personal IP address.

[40] Lurger, n. 25 above, 19, 36.

[41] Recital (14) CSDC.

[42] Criticised also by Mak, n. 15 above, 9.

consumer actively accepts the use of cookies.[43] Though excluding advertisements may seem understandable, since they do not necessarily require the supplier to collect consumer data, disregarding cookies requires a reasonable justification. Cookie-based services like Google Analytics are known to collect personal data on a particularly large scale in order to process them for commercial purposes.[44] The sheer amount of data allows for a targeted collection of data and eventually personal identification, as the discussions that evolved around the GDPR have vividly underlined.[45] Still, even services such as Google's data intense search engine would basically not be covered by the Directive's scope as long as the consumer does not create an (optional) account, whereas other services like Facebook would always be confronted with the consumer's new remedies.

While the proposal's general approach to seemingly 'free' digital content in exchange for economically valuable data is a desirable one,[46] it is also important to keep in mind that its implications will not remain without consequence for several other areas of law in many Member States. For example, classifying such contracts as essentially similar to contracts entered into for a particular price may influence how courts view the fairness of certain clauses in consumer contracts.[47] Another question is whether qualifying the supply of data as equivalent to promising a monetary price results in the supply of (personal) data

---

43 Recital (14) CSDC; see, however, Beale, n. 18 above, 13 who argues that cookie collecting activities are covered by 'actively'; criticised also by Schmidt-Kessel, Erler, Grimm and Kramme, n. 37 above, 54, 58 and Lurger, n. 25 above, 19, 35.

44 R. Liebler and K. Chaney, 'Google Analytics: Analyzing the Latest Wave of Legal Concerns for Google in the US and the EU' *Buffalo Intellectual Property Law Journal* 7 (2010), 135. Available at SSRN: http://ssrn.com/abstract=2095434, last access: 9 April 2016; I. Rubinstein, 'Big Data: The End of Privacy or a New Beginning?' *International Data Privacy Law* 2013, doi: 10.1093/idpl/ips036; NYU School of Law, Public Law Research Paper No. 12-56, 4. Available at SSRN: http://ssrn.com/abstract=2157659, last access: 9 April 2016; A. Roosendaal, 'Facebook Tracks and Traces Everyone: Like This!', 30 November 2010, Tilburg Law School Legal Studies Research Paper Series No. 03/2011. Available at: SSRN: http://ssrn.com/abstract=1717563 or http://dx.doi.org/10.2139/ssrn.1717563, last access: 9 April 2016.

45 P.M. Schwartz and D.J. Solove, 'The PII Problem: Privacy and a New Concept of Personally Identifiable Information' *New York University Law Review* 86 (2011) 1814, 1836 *et seq.*; UC Berkeley Public Law Research Paper No. 1909366; GWU Legal Studies Research Paper No. 584; GWU Law School Public Law Research Paper No. 584. Available at SSRN: http://ssrn.com/abstract=1909366, last access: 9 April 2016; W.K. Hon, C. Millard and I. Walden, 'The Problem of "Personal Data" in Cloud Computing – What Information is Regulated? The Cloud of Unknowing, Part 1' *International Data Privacy Law* 1 (2011) 211–228; Queen Mary School of Law Legal Studies Research Paper No. 75/2011, 13 *et seq*. Available at SSRN: http://ssrn.com/abstract=1783577, last access: 9 April 2016.

46 For a discussion about the new economy of information, see B. Laperche, 'Hidden Face of Electronic Commerce between Enterprises' *Information & Communication Technology Law* 10 (2001) 273–284.

47 See generally art. 3(1) of the Council Directive of 5 April on unfair terms in consumer contracts, 93/13/EEC, *OJEC* L95, 21 April 1993, 29–34, available at: http://eur-lex.europa.eu/legal content/EN/TXT/PDF/?uri=CELEX:31993L0013&from=EN.

being an enforceable contractual duty, e.g. when the consumer submits false personal information that is useless to the provider of digital content.[48] In other terms, by classifying personal data as a counter-performance the CSDC runs into problems with the GDPR: Whereas the GDPR stipulates that consent may freely be withdrawn, with the result that all data processing has to be stopped and data even has to be deleted, dealing with data as a counter-performance would be contradicting that right to free revocation of consent, as the consumer is obliged to reveal and disclose his personal data.[49]

3.4. EXEMPT SERVICES AND AREAS

Several services and areas are explicitly exempt from the proposal's legal regime by Article 3(3) CSDC. These areas are all subject to their own intense regulation, which justifies excluding them from the CSDC's additional requirements. This includes Access Providing and all electronic communication services covered by the Framework Directive of 2002[50] (Article 3(5)(b) CSDC), healthcare services (thus, all fitness apps for instance)[51] gambling and – most significantly – financial services (Article 3(3)(d) CSDC). Consequentially, Paypal and other services are not covered by the proposed Directive, but are instead regulated by the Payment Services Directive II, which covers a large variety of internet-based payment and financial services. While 'Bitcoins' still falls through the cracks of much of the financial sector's regulation,[52] they are nonetheless exempt from regulation under the CSDC, since the proposal refers to financial services in general.[53] However, we have to take into account that some of these regulated areas still do not specifically acknowledge digital content and digital services as something to be regulated.[54]

48 While especially Art. 7 GDPR, n. 19 above, places strong emphasis on the fact that the data subject's consent must be freely given, the GDPR does not exclude this possibility once the consent is valid.

49 Similiarly Mak, n. 15 above, 9; Lurger, n. 25 above, 19, 39.

50 Directive 2002/21/EC of the European Parliament and of the Council of 7 March 2002 on a common regulatory framework for electronic communications networks and services, *OJEC* L108, 24 April 2002, 33–50, available at: http://eur-lex.europa.eu/legal-content/EN/TXT/PDF/?uri=CELEX:32002L0021&from=EN.

51 Criticised by Lurger, n. 25 above, 19, 30.

52 See European Central Bank, Virtual currency schemes – a further analysis, February 2015, p. 23, available at: https://www.ecb.europa.eu/pub/pdf/other/virtualcurrencyschemesen.pdf.

53 *Bitcoin* services are, however, usually covered as trading platforms under the MiFID II. Directive 2014/65/EU of the European Parliament and the Council of 15 May 2014 on markets in financial instruments and amending Directive 2002/92/EC and Directive 2011/61/EU, *OJEC* L173/349, 12 June 2014, available at: http://eur-lex.europa.eu/legal-content/EN/TXT/PDF/?uri=CELEX:32014L0065&from=EN.

54 Criticised thus by Mak, n. 15 above, 10.

4. ARTICLE 5 CSDC – TIME AND PLACE OF SUPPLY

Given the broad scope of the proposal and its unavoidable refusal to define different types of contracts that deal with digital content, the CSDC says very little about the specific duties of the supplier, and mostly leaves questions about when, where and how the digital content must be supplied to be dealt with by the individual agreement between the parties. The proposal does, however, state that – absent contractual specifications – the digital content has to be supplied immediately (Article 5(2) CSDC) and that the supplier is not responsible for whether the consumer can actually access the content, as long as he delivers the content to a third-party chosen by the consumer (Article 5(1)(b), recital (23) CSDC).[55] In cases where the supplier offers a bundle of services which includes providing immediate access (e.g. an Access Provider offering additional content), this may of course lead to somewhat inconsistent results.[56] Moreover, the CSDC does not provide for a 'second try' in the case when a download fails – which is quite often the case.[57]

Given that the proposal applies to all kinds of contracts, be it recurring or non-recurring obligations, the proposal does not say anything about the duration of the data supply or possible interruptions – which contracts that deal with digital content frequently exclude from liability, at least if the duration of the interruption is short or for maintenance purposes. As the CSDC does not define different types of contracts, courts may find it hard to determine if such or similar clauses are merely a specification of the contract or a potential breach of duty, triggering the consumer rights of the CSDC.[58] Time will tell if the proposed Directive's high level of abstraction will enable suppliers to circumvent its intentions by redefining contractual duties as predisposed matters of contractual performance.[59]

---

55 This is, of course, appropriate since the supplier usually has no control over internet providers and other carriers.

56 In a bundle of contracts, the new Directive only applies to the part of the contract which deals with digital content (Recital (20) CSDC, n. 29 above), thus an access provider could not be held liable (under the CSDC) if he fails to actually grant the consumer access to the content.

57 Cf. W. Faber, 'Bereitstellungspflicht, Mangelbegriff und Beweislast im Richtlinienvorschlag zur Bereitstellung digitaler Inhalte' in Wendehorst and Zöchling-Jud (eds.), n. 25 above, 89, 94 *et seq*.

58 Which may entitle the consumer to terminate the contract or assert other remedies, see below at section 7.

59 Again, national implementations of the Directive on unfair terms in consumer contracts (n. 47 above) as well as related national laws and regulations may play an important role in this context.

5. ARTICLE 6 CSDC – CONFORMITY WITH THE CONTRACT

5.1. CONTRACTUAL PERFORMANCE AND DEFECTS – SUBJECTIVE AND OBJECTIVE TESTS

In close connection to the time and place of supply, Article 6 CSDC deals with the digital content's conformity with the contract. Following the now prevalent approach of combining subjective and objective elements,[60] Article 6(1) CSDC first refers to the requirements of the contract as agreed on (including pre-contractual information as well as additional instructions) and – in the absence of valid contractual stipulations – the general purposes for which digital content of the same description would normally be used (including purposes that can be inferred from public statements by third parties), as per Article 6(2) CSDC.[61] While contractual agreements thus prevail over objective expectations, it is, however, important to note that the proposal requires that those agreements should be stipulated in a clear and comprehensive (i.e. transparent) manner – be it in general terms and conditions or individual agreements (!).[62]

Article 6(1)(a) CSDC lists a couple of important conformity elements to be included in the contract, such as functionality, interoperability, accessibility[63] and security. Though stressing the importance of the digital content's security is certainly desirable,[64] the proposal does not define what kind of technical security standards are to be expected in a contractual context. Given that most Member States have not yet set concrete, reliable standards, it is unlikely that this element will become clearly definable (and thus practically more important)

---

60 See eg annex, arts. 99–102 CESL, n. 4 above; H.-W. Micklitz and N. Reich, 'The Commission Proposal for a "Regulation on a Common European Sales Law (CESL)" – Too Broad or Not Broad Enough?', EUI Working Papers LAW No. 2012/04, 72. Available at SSRN: http://ssrn.com/abstract=2013183, last access: 11 April 2016.

61 Similar to the Consumer Sales Directive (n. 10 above), the proposal only includes statements which the supplier should have been aware of and that influenced the consumer's decision, art. 2(2)(c) CSDC.

62 Though the ECJ has decided that – for purposes of the Consumer Sales Directive – even the definition of the main subject-matter in general terms and conditions has to be transparent, extending this requirement to individual agreements is a novelty. See *Jean-Claude Van Hove v. CNP Assurances SA*, Case C-96/14, judgment of 23 April 2015, ECLI:EU:C:2015:262, n. 27; *Arpád Kásler and Hajnalka Káslerné Rábai v. OTP Jelzálogbank Zrt.*, Case C-26/13, judgment of 30 April 2014, ECLI:EU:C:2014:282, n. 68; unlike annex, art. 80(2) CESL, (n. 4 above) the CSDC's transparency control will also extend to definitions of the contractual main subject, see recital (18) CSDC.

63 The accessibility is of course limited to the requirements of art. 5(1)(b), recital (23) CSDC.

64 See recital (27) CSDC.

any time soon.[65] Still, the proposal's burden shift will make it easier for consumers to assert and remedy inherent security defects of the digital content, even if those defects could not be foreseen by the supplier at the time the content was initially supplied. On the other hand, the supplier cannot be held liable for security risks which are not an inherent part of the content but merely evolve over time due to subsequent changes of the digital environment, e.g. by a different software later installed by the consumer.

In recognition of the important role digital environments play for the functionality of almost all digital content, the CSDC seeks to place special emphasis on the interoperability of such content – defined as the content's interaction (not portability) with other hard- and software (especially operating systems). While recital (26) CSDC mentions the absence or presence of any technical restrictions such as protection via Digital Rights Management systems or regional coding, it does not bar those restrictions from being part of the contract, meaning that suppliers can still freely restrict their digital content to be used solely within the environment of their own devices or software. The importance of the digital content's interoperability as part of its functionality, however, leads to the question of whether it will be sufficient for the supplier to advise the consumer that the content is designed only for a particular environment, or if he will be obliged to expressly tell the consumer which kind of environments will render the content inoperable in order to meet the CSDC's transparency requirement. In any case, to avoid liability the supplier has to prove that he adequately informed the consumer, as per Article 9(2) CSDC.

The proposal further acknowledges that digital content and software in particular will often demand frequent updates and patches, as per Article 6(1)(d) CSDC. Yet again, the proposal does, however, leave it up to the parties to define if and when updates or patches are deemed to be necessary,[66] allowing for their complete exclusion by means of agreements about the contractual performance, even if the content is prone to malfunction (e.g. beta versions).[67] If the digital content does, however, have (initial) defects, e.g. exploits or lack of security, the supplier will be subject to the consumer's

---

65 Although some countries have taken first steps in this direction already, see e.g. for Germany: https://www.bsi.bund.de/DE/Themen/ITGrundschutz/ITGrundschutzStandards/ITGrundschutzStandards_node.html;jsessionid=852E3D09BB511545F7FFF164368C68B7.2_cid286; and https://www.bsi.bund.de/DE/Themen/ITGrundschutz/ITGrundschutzKataloge/itgrundschutzkataloge_node.html.

66 Despite this, the supplier of course has to supply the most recent version of the digital content if not otherwise agreed, which may warrant updates during long-term contracts, Article 6(4) CSDC.

67 Similarly, annex, art. 103 CESL (n. 4 above) also clarified that updated digital content does not per se render the product to be defective.

rights and remedies as discussed before. Moreover, Article 6(2) CSDC does not refer to those updates and patches.[68]

While not expressly mentioned in the (non-exhaustive) enumeration in Article 6 CSDC, principles of data privacy law – such as data avoidance and minimisation – should be considered part of the minimum elements of a contract, since they likewise determine the quality of digital content and services.

To the extent that the contract does not stipulate the requirements for digital content (or fails to do so in a transparent manner), Article 6(3) CSDC states that the digital content has to conform with the usual expectations consumers may have for this particular kind of content.[69] While such 'objective' standards necessarily carry an unavoidable level of uncertainty, the Commission's attempt to clarify this standard makes things somewhat worse in several ways. First, Article 6(2)(a) CSDC differentiates between digital content supplied for a price and that supplied for other counter-performances in money, thereby thwarting the proposal's intention to create a level playing-field for business models based on direct payments on the one hand and those based on the commercial use of (personal) data on the other.[70] The second problematic attempt to clarify the standard is the proposal's instruction to take into account 'any existing international technical standards'[71] and industry codes of conduct and good practice, as per Article 6(2)(b) CSDC. While deferring to such standards does seem to make sense, it is troubling that the Commission does not set up any requirements whatsoever with respect to standard-setting institutions or process, entirely leaving out any kind of mandatory consumer representation or consideration of consumer interest.[72] Given that the Commission seeks to encourage trade organisations and 'other representative organisations' to establish codes of conducts to support the uniform implementation of the Directive (recital (28) CSDC), leaving out consumer interests for the benefit of swift implementation appears to be a deliberate choice. The benchmark of reasonable expectations of a consumer is missing completely.[73]

Taking all the above into account, it is not very likely that Article 6 CSDC will actually improve the level of consumer protection for digital content.[74] Article 6(1) CSDC leaves the contract's content almost entirely to the parties' individual stipulations (which in practice usually means to the supplier's pre-designed terms and conditions), while the proposal's high level of abstraction

68 Faber, n. 57 above, 89, 109.

69 Criticised by Faber, n. 57 above, 89, 105.

70 Annex, art. 130(6) CESL (n. 4 above) already made a similar distinction, likewise failing to explain which practical consequences this approach is supposed to entail.

71 It is not clear whether the term 'international' rules out every kind of national or (solely) European standards.

72 In the same sense Faber, n. 57 above, 89, 112.

73 Cf. also Faber, n. 57 above, 89, 111.

74 Same assessment by Mak, n. 15 above, 15.

makes it harder to counterbalance those stipulations with consideration of the common requirements of comparable types of contracts.[75] Only if those stipulations are missing or not sufficiently transparent do the objective criteria of Article 6(2) CSDC comes into play, potentially replacing invalid elements without rendering the contract invalid as a whole. If the suppliers manage to meet the transparency standards, they are free to define the main subject-matter of the contract, which permits the limitation of liability, e.g. for beta software or software 'as such', to only those (security) deficiencies currently known. In addition to that, reasonable consumer expectations are neither an explicit part of the objective requirements, nor will they necessarily be included in technical industry standards.

Something that will, however, become even more important in future are the pre-contractual obligations of the supplier to inform the consumer about the interoperability of the digital content, i.e. what kind of technical environment, operating system or additional software (like Adobe's Flash Player, etc.) is required allow the digital content to function in accordance to its (stipulated) purposes.

5.2. INCOMPATIBILITY WITH SYSTEM ENVIRONMENT AS A LACK OF CONFORMITY WITH THE CONTRACT

Specific problems arise out of the fact that the functions etc. of a digital content may depend largely on other digital contents/software/environment. Digital content can itself be free of any defects but may turn out to malfunction when the environment changes or another service provider stops his services upon which the digital content depends.

Since the use of digital content depends on a system environment, Article 7 CSDC classifies the incorrect implementation of goods in the consumer's digital environment as a lack of conformity with the contract. Even if the digital content itself is faultless, an incorrect installation can lead to non-conformity. This rule corresponds to those already known from the Consumer Sales Directive[76] and likewise confines the supplier's accountability to an installation performed by him or herself or incorrect instructions given by the supplier.

At first sight, this term seems like a useful addition and a continuation of the principles known from the sale of consumer goods, but again this approach may become blurry at the margins. In particular, it is questionable when the

75 Criticised also by Beale, n. 18 above, 20/21.

76 Art. 2(5) Directive 1999/44/EC classifies an incorrect assembly as a lack of conformity with the contract if the assembly is part of the sales contract or if the seller took responsibility for it. An incorrect assembly caused by incorrect assembly instructions is also equivalent to a defect.

provider conducts an implementation: can an installation routinely activated by the consumer properly be considered as an act of the supplier?

Or how about an installation of an App on a consumer's smartphone accomplished by an App routine, such as that used within the iTunes Store or GooglePlay Store? Can this process be called an installation performed by the supplier? Considering that the digital content is now beyond the supplier's sphere of influence and the supplier is not able to control the consumer's digital environment, it seems reasonable that only in case of incorrect installation routines should he be held accountable. Of course, this does not include any incorrect use by the consumer.

In this case especially, problems are caused by the burden of proof for a correct implementation of digital content. According to Article 9(1) of CSDC, the supplier bears the burden of proof for the correctness of the given assembly instructions, and furthermore he must prove the digital content's conformity with the contract. On the other hand, according to Article 9(2) CSDC, the consumer bears the burden of proof for his digital environment. However, those regulations do not solve all problems. Since an assembly instruction for a correctly performed installation depends on the consumer's digital environment, strict responsibility of the supplier to hand out faultless instructions can only result from Article 9(3) CSDC if the consumer fulfilled his obligation to cooperate with the supplier in examining his digital environment. Similarly to regulations known in banking and capital market law, a rudimentary obligation to 'know your customer' would be helpful, since an evaluation regarding online goods and services can be performed automatically. Of course, this practice would not include goods used offline, which do not use an internet connection after installation.

However, Article 7 CSDC does not deal with digital content which once was correctly implemented but now – after a change of digital environment not imputable to the supplier – turns out to lose its functions, e.g. connection to a specific service provider who ceases his services. As liability for specific purposes or functions of digital content depends upon the description of the digital content and the promises by the supplier, a change of digital environment may often not be treated as a defect – as long as the consumer cannot expect the supplier to safeguard the perpetuation of the specific digital environment.

Since it is within the nature of the digital environment to change its appearance, which may be caused by newly installed software or different digital content, in the case of a one-time sales contract, the seller would be well advised if he recorded the consumer's digital environment at the time of the implementation of digital content and held on to it for purposes of proof. The consumer's digital environment should be recorded even if the supplier did not carry out the implementation, because instructions or an installation routine performed by the consumer also depends on his digital environment.

5.3. NO DEFECT OF TITLE

Article 8 CSDC claims that the digital content which is supplied must be free of any right of a third-party, including a right based on intellectual property – a formula which is somehow misleading, as the consumer needs precisely the rights of third parties in order to use the digital content (in case of intellectual property rights). If the digital content is supplied in terms of a continuing contract, this regulation is of course limited to this period. Of course, this does not violate the principle of territoriality, since the scope depends on the stipulated terms of the contracts, which may include territorial restriction rights (irrespective of the proposal for a cross-border-portability regulation).[77] While Article 8 CSDC seeks to protect the consumer from third-party rights, it should not be misunderstood in the sense that it could limit any right of the title owner. The proposal expressly excludes copyright law from its regulatory scope, thus leaving any (national) right of the copyright owner to withdraw the content in order to protect his or her personal right untouched. If this does, however, occur, the supplier can be held liable, since this 'defect' is inherent in the digital content from the beginning of the contract, even though it may manifest itself much later.[78] This result must of course be modified if the reason for the withdrawal lies within the consumer's sphere of influence (e.g. by disfiguring works of art).

5.4. PATCHES

If a supplier uses patches to fix defects and other problems which may not have existed when the digital content was first supplied, the question arises whether those patches are still covered by the CSDC liability framework. As long as the original contract does not include additional technical maintenance services, patches are to be considered new digital content.

Unfortunately, these patches will usually be provided neither in exchange for a monetary price, nor in exchange for personal data. While the consumer may of course refuse to implement additional patches (which he almost certainly will not do), it would be thus be advisable for the final version of the Directive to include a clarification that patches are nonetheless covered by its scope. Moreover, the issue of undesired patches which change the scope of digital content (e.g. interoperability etc.) are not dealt with in the CSDC.[79]

---

77 Proposal for a Regulation of the European Parliament and of the Council on ensuring the cross-border portability of online content services in the internal market COM(2015) 627 final 2015/0284 (COD), available at: https://ec.europa.eu/transparency/regdoc/rep/1/2015/EN/1-2015-627-EN-F1-1.PDF, last access: 15 April 2016. http://ec.europa.eu/newsroom/dae/document.cfm?action=display&doc_id=12524.

78 If, however, the copyright owner asserts his or her rights after the statute of limitation has expired, this leaves the consumer without contractual remedies.

79 Profound analysis by Wendehorst, n. 25 above, 45, 78 *et seq.*

6. ARTICLE 9 CSDC – BURDEN OF PROOF FOR UNLIMITED TIME

Just like every right or remedy, the effectiveness of the CSDC's consumer rights depends on their enforceability in practice. Article 9 CSDC helps the consumer by stating that the onus of proof with respect to the conformity with the contract at the time of supply shall be on the supplier. Interestingly – and unlike the Consumer Sales Directive[80] – this burden shift is not subject to any kind of time restriction, as digital content is not subject to wear and tear.[81] However, this does not lead to an infinite liability of the supplier, as will be explained later when discussing the CSDC's statute of limitation.[82] Hence, it depends largely on the way in which Member States will implement the CSDC with prescription limits – it could also be argued that the timeless burden of proof should be limited per se to a certain time, such as two years.[83]

The shift in the burden of proof does not apply if the supplier can prove that the digital environment of the consumer was not compatible with the digital content (and the supplier has transparently informed the consumer about the limits of interoperability and other technical requirements), as per Article 9(2) CSDC. The proposal tries to ease the supplier's burden of proof by requiring the consumer to cooperate in order to determine his or her digital environment, while also limiting the supplier's efforts to the means that are least intrusive to the consumer's fundamental rights to the protection of private life and his or her personal data, as per Article 9(3), recital (33) CSDC. Though the Commission considers automatically generated incident reports to be a less intrusive form of determination, it may turn out to be hard for the supplier to collect the necessary data without collecting personal data at the same time. On top of that, suppliers will usually have a difficult time determining whether the consumer has altered the parameters of the digital environment or if e.g. malware hidden in the system data caused the content to malfunction.[84] In any case, the Commission sees direct virtual access to the consumer's digital environment only as a last resort.[85]

---

80 Art. 5(3) Directive 1999/44/EC; for a discussion about the burden of proof; see B. Kristensen, H. Lando, P. Møgelvang-Hansen and O. Schützsack, 'New Rules on Consumer Sales – An Empirical Study', April 2006, CBS Law Studies Working Paper No. WP 2006-04, 15 *et seq.* Available at: SSRN: http://ssrn.com/abstract=1022624, last access: 12 April 2016.

81 Explanatory Memorandum CSDC, n. 2 above, 13.

82 See below, section 10. Defects Liability Period and Statute of Limitation.

83 See the arguments brought forward by Mak, n. 15 above, 19–22.

84 Sceptical Faber, n. 57 above, 89, 125 *et seq.*

85 Recital (33) CSDC.

7. LIABILITY OF THE SUPPLIER AND REMEDIES FOR THE CONSUMER

According to Article 10 CSDC, the supplier is liable for any failure to supply the digital content, for any lack which exists at the time the content is supplied, and for any lack which occurs during the duration of a contract for the supply of digital content over a period of time. The supplier's liability results in various remedies for the consumer – all of which are a staple of European consumer protection laws, but also come along with a number of characteristics specific to the supply of digital content.

The CSDC follows the traditional hierarchy of remedies: first, the obligation of the supplier to bring the digital content into conformity to the contract; and second, in the case of failure to do so, then price reduction and/or termination of the contract (Article 12(3) CSDC).[86]

In contrast to other Directives regarding consumer contracts, the CSDC does not provide any norm concerning commercial guarantees.[87] However, there is no reason why commercial guarantees should be excluded from the scope of the CSDC.

7.1. ARTICLE 11(1)–(4) CSDC – SUPPLEMENTARY PERFORMANCE AND REDUCTION OF PRICE

Following the principles of prior legislation like the Consumer Sales Directive,[88] the consumer is entitled to have deficient digital content brought into conformity with the contract (Article 12(1), (2) CSDC) or – if the supplier fails to do so within a reasonable period of time[89] – may pay a reduced price proportionate to the decrease in value (Article 12(3), (4) CSDC).[90] Taking into account the diverse nature and different types of contracts covered by the vast scope of the Directive, the proposal is right in not trying to state any fixed period of time

---

86 Cf. also X. Fauvarque-Cosson, 'The new proposal for harmonised rules for certain aspects concerning contracts for the supply of digital content (termination, modification of the digital content and right to terminate long term contracts)', Workshop of JURI-Committee of the European Parliament, January 2016, PE 536.495, 8; Mak, n. 15 above, 23–24.

87 Cf. Beale, n. 18 above, 22; Fauvarque-Cosson, n. 86 above, 12.

88 Joined Cases C-65/09 and C-87/09, *Gebruder Weber v. Wittmer* (Polished tiles case) and *Putz v. Medianess Electronics GmbH*, ECLI:EU:C:2011:396.

89 This includes cases where remedying the non-conformity is impossible, disproportionate or unlawful, not completed in time, significantly inconvenient for the consumer or simply refused by the supplier, art. 12 (3) CSDC.

90 Not that the proposal explicitly refers to the reduction of a (monetary) price. A 'reduction' of (personal) data or similar remedy for contracts not entered in exchange for a price is not provided. Consumers will of course have the right to terminate the contract under additional circumstances (section 7.2).

to be considered reasonable for every kind of digital content (Article 12(2), recital (36) CSDC).

Building on ECJ decisions specifying the Consumer Sales Directive,[91] the proposal exempts the supplier from the duty to bring the digital content into conformity free of charge for the consumer, if this duty would impose unreasonable costs upon the supplier. Article 12(1)(a) and (b) CSDC flesh out this (un)reasonableness standard by taking into account the eventual value of the content and the significance of the deficiency. Consumers will thus often find it hard to remedy a lack of conformity e.g. of low-value apps, unless they are able to prove an exceptionally high personal interest in the conformity of the digital content. Apart from that, it may prove difficult to define the (market) value of digital content offered against counter-performance other than money.

7.2. ARTICLE 11 CSDC – TERMINATION FOR FAILURE TO SUPPLY

According to Article 11 CSDC, the consumer is entitled to terminate the contract if the supplier has failed to supply the digital content, which usually means that if the supplier does not provide the content immediately (Article 5(2) CSDC), the consumer can unilaterally end the contract right away, without having to set any deadline or giving the supplier a second chance to provide access to the content.[92] If, however, the contract is designed as a continuing obligation over a period of time, short[93] interruptions of the supply are not deemed to be a failure of supply under Article 11 CSDC, but are instead supposed to be treated as non-conformity with the contract under Article 12 CSDC.[94]

This brings us back to the aforementioned interruptions for maintenance purposes and lack of accessibility to the site of (the supplier's) Access Providers or Cloud Computing Services, which – as part of (transparent!) Service Level Agreements, etc. – can be incorporated into the contract and thus shield the supplier from liability, indirectly limiting the consumer's remedies. On the

---

91 For the seller's duties regarding removal of non-conforming and installation of conforming goods, see Joined Cases C-65/09 and C-87/09 *Gebruder Weber v. Wittmer* and *Putz v. Medianess Electronics GmbH*, ECLI:EU:C:2011:396.

92 Recital (35) CSDC justifies this strict approach to the seriousness of such a breach of the main contractual obligation.

93 Yet again, the variety of contracts regarding digital content makes it impossible to define the duration of what is considered to be a 'short' interruption, leaving this determination to the courts in the case at hand.

94 Recital (35) CSDC. While the proposal seems to indicate that long-term interruptions are considered to be failures to supply, they should of course be treated as (serious) non-conformities with the contract, thus allowing the consumer to either terminate the contract or assert any of the other remedies of art. 12 CSDC.

other hand, the proposal does not adopt Annex, Article 107 CESL's exclusion of contracts that are not in exchange for a (monetary) price, granting consumers who 'pay' with their data the exact same rights as everybody else.

Article 11 has been criticised for not taking into account the principal differences between tangible goods and digital content concerning the failure to supply, in particular supplying only some digital content.[95] However, this criticism seems to be overstated, as courts mostly assess a gross failure of supply as a non-supply in the end, thus granting the consumer the right to terminate. There is no evidence why, for instance, an obligation to deliver a certain amount of goods should be treated otherwise when the subject-matter is digital content.

7.3. ARTICLE 12(5) CSDC – TERMINATION FOR LACK OF CONFORMITY

If the supplier fails to remedy a lack of conformity and this deficiency also 'impairs functionality, interoperability and other main performance features of the digital content such as its accessibility, continuity and security', the consumer is entitled to terminate the contract without further notice. However, the consumer has no right to terminate the contract without giving the supplier a second chance to bring the digital content in conformity.[96]

Again, the supplier bears the burden to show this is not the case (Article 12(5) CSDC). Interestingly, the proposal does explicitly mention a failure to meet the digital content's contractual purpose (if specifically agreed upon, see Article 6(1)(b) CSDC), although this should at least fall under the open category of 'other main performance features'.

However, the Commission also failed to mention cases where minor non-conformities add up over time and thus may warrant a termination of the contract even though the single deficiencies themselves would not warrant such a reaction. This includes cases of continuous short-term interruption, e.g. when a social network frequently cannot be accessed by the consumer over a longer period of time. Though one may try to argue that an accumulation of minor performance failures also essentially impairs a 'main performance feature', it would be preferable if the Commission expressly includes this category to avoid future controversy.

On the other side, and more from the perspective of industry, Article 12 CSDC has also been criticised for not dealing explicitly in the first place with 'minor' non-conformity cases.[97] Although it may be true that a more

---

95 Fauvarque-Cosson, n. 86 above, 9.

96 Criticised by Fauvarque-Cosson, n. 86 above, 9 as some jurisdictions do not know such a hierarchy.

97 Cf. Fauvarque-Cosson, n. 86 above, 11 *et seq.*

transparent and clear wording for Article 12 CSDC may be advisable, yet the structure and encompassing of 'minor' non-conformity cases seems to be clear, at least for a legally educated person.

As clarified by the Commission, the consumer's right to terminate a contract also encompasses partial terminations.[98] If a contract is entered over a period of time, the consumer is entitled to terminate only the part of the contract which corresponds to the time when the digital content was not in conformity (Article 13(5), recital (42) CSDC). Though not expressly mentioned, the right to partially terminate the contract should also apply to contracts or bundles of contracts with different digital content or additional services.

7.4. FULL HARMONISATION AND ADDITIONAL NATIONAL REQUIREMENTS

The Commission has been very clear about the need for a fully harmonising Directive that would allow consumers to assert their rights in the same manner irrespective of their Member State's law, thereby precluding any additional national requirements with respect to the consumer's remedies regarding contracts that deal with digital content.[99] Thus, any formal or substantive provisions requiring the consumer to notify the supplier of the lack of conformity or pay for the use of the (non-conforming) digital content before termination could not be introduced or maintained by Member State legislation (recital (9) CSDC).[100]

8. ARTICLE 13 CSDC – LEGAL CONSEQUENCES OF TERMINATION

The proposal contains various well-known, as well as a couple of interesting, new approaches regarding the legal consequences of a termination by the consumer (due to the content's non-conformity with the contract or for other reasons), some of which coincide with rules of the GDPR. First, Article 13(1) CSDC states that the consumer may exercise the right to terminate the content by notice to

98 Contracts in exchange for (personal) data are again excluded from this right, since it is unfeasible to proportionally apportion a counter-performance other than money (recital (42) CSDC). Considering contracts or bundles of contracts with different digital content and services, this may of course not always be the case.

99 See Explanatory Memorandum CSDC, n. 2 above, recitals (5)–(9) CSDC.

100 Again, the proposal explicitly incorporates former ECJ decision on the Consumer Sales Directive to avoid future uncertainties, see *Quelle AG v. Bundesverband der Verbraucherzentralen und Verbraucherverbände*, Case C-404/06, ECLI:EU:C:2008:231 (no charge for the use of goods not in conformity).

the supplier 'given by any means', e.g. via telephone, email, etc.[101] Thus, neither Member States with a particular focus on formalities nor the supplier may force the consumer to use a particular form of their choice – although this probably does not preclude the supplier from demanding some kind of authentication by the consumer. Moreover, there is no need for the consumer to go to court and seek a judicial termination of the contract – as obviously is the case in French law.[102]

Along the lines of other consumer protection laws, Article 13(2)(a) CSDC states that the supplier has to reimburse the consumer no later than 14 days after the receipt of the notice.[103] As a matter of course, the consumer has to refrain from using the digital content (and return any durable medium), while the supplier may prevent any further use (e.g. by deleting the consumer's account) (Article 13(2)(d), (e), Article 12(3) CSDC). On the other hand, the consumer is neither obliged to pay for the prior use of the digital content, nor does he have to bear the costs of returning a durable medium (Article 13(2)(e), (i), Article 13(4) CSDC). Regarding the obligation to delete or render unusable the digital content, it may be difficult for the supplier to ensure that the consumer really has deleted the digital content[104] – the similar discussion concerning the transfer of software is a good example of how difficult it could be for the supplier (as well as for the consumer) to get reliable evidence that the digital content has been removed. DRM-Systems can be of help here. Some commentators plead for an obligation of consumer to pay for the non-deleted digital content after termination of the contract.[105] However, this would enable the consumer to continue de facto the contract and make use of the digital content without the consent of the supplier – which contradicts, for instance, intellectual property rights.

However, the CSDC does not specify like the Consumer Rights Directive (Article 13(1)) how the reimbursement should be carried out (like in the same way as the payment etc.). Moreover, Article 13 CSDC does not provide any specifications concerning interests to be paid in case of late reimbursements.[106]

While the supplier must of course reimburse the consumer any (monetary) price paid, things again become a little more complicated for counter-performance other than money which cannot actually be 'reimbursed'. The Commission seeks to resolve this issue by requiring the supplier to refrain from

---

101 Criticised by Fauvarque-Cosson, n. 86 above, 13: more detailed provisions of means necessary.

102 Cf. Fauvarque-Cosson, n. 86 above, 13.

103 The only thing that might potentially cause problems for consumers here is proving that the supplier actually has (or could have) received the notice.

104 See also Fauvarque-Cosson, n. 86 above, 15/16; Mak, n. 15 above, 25–26.

105 Mak, n. 15 above, 26.

106 Cf. Fauvarque-Cosson, n. 86 above, 14 referring to the art. L 121-21-4 al 3 of the French Code de consommation which has a form of escalation of interests according to the delay of reimbursement.

using any personal or other data provided in exchange for the digital content once the consumer terminates the contract (Article 13(2)(b) CSDC). While at first glance, Article 13(2)(b) CSDC seems to apply only to 'free' contracts, its second part states that any data collected during any contractual relationship for the supply of digital content may also not be used after the termination, thereby mimicking Article 17(2)(b) GDPR. Only user-generated content jointly created by several consumers is exempt from this duty, if the other consumers are still using it. Since the proposal does not, however, cover copyright law, these other creators may still be subject to potential copyright remedies by the consumer if provided by national law.

Besides being obliged to refrain from using the consumer's data, the supplier also has to provide the consumer with technical means to retrieve all content provided by the consumer and any other data produced or generated through the consumer's use of the digital content (Article 13(2)(c) CSDC).[107] This consumer right is designed as one of the most important portability provisions in European law and may thus facilitate and encourage enhanced competition among different suppliers of similar services. Unlike Article 18 GDPR, the proposal does not clearly state if 'any other data' also includes personal data.[108] However, the provision is phrased in such a broad way that it should encompass not just personal data, but any kind of user- and supplier-generated content as well as usage data. This also becomes apparent when looking at recital (37) CSDC, which follows a broad understanding of consumer data similarly to the GDPR, and states that

> the supplier should take all measures in order to comply with data protection rules by deleting it or rendering it anonymous in such a way that the consumer cannot be identified by any means likely reasonably to be used either by the supplier or by any other person.[109]

---

107 Those technical means have to be provided free of charge, excluding internet costs (recital (40) CSDC).

108 Regarding art. 18 GDPR, see W.K. Hon, E. Kosta, C. Millard and D. Stefanatou, 'Cloud Accountability: The Likely Impact of the Proposed EU Data Protection Regulation' Queen Mary School of Law Legal Studies Research Paper No. 172/2014; Tilburg Law School Research Paper No. 07/2014, 44 *et seq*. Available at SSRN: http://ssrn.com/abstract=2405971, last access: 13 April 2016; C. Kuner, 'The European Commission's Proposed Data Protection Regulation: A Copernican Revolution in European Data Protection Law' *Bloomberg BNA Privacy and Security Law Report* 2012, 1, 11. Available at SSRN: http://ssrn.com/abstract=2162781, last access: 13 April 2016; C. Cuijpers, N. Purtova and E. Kosta, 'Data Protection Reform and the Internet: The Draft Data Protection Regulation', forthcoming in A. Savin and J. Trzaskowski (eds.), *Research Handbook on EU Internet Law* (Cheltenham: Edward Elgar, 2014); Tilburg Law School Research Paper No. 03/2014, 11 *et seq*. Available at SSRN: http://ssrn.com/abstract=2373683, last access: 13 April 2016.

109 Compare with art. 17 GDPR.

Again similarly to the GDPR,[110] the proposal does not, however, require the supplier to make sure that all consumer data which the supplier has provided to third parties is deleted.[111] By the same token, the consumer cannot require the supplier to delete or retrieve anonymised or aggregated data, since identifying the consumer as the origin of such data is no longer possible.

Unlike Article 17(3) GDPR, the proposal does allow for balancing the interests of the supplier or third parties to legitimately keep and use the data even after termination with the conflicting interests of the consumer. Hence, there is no chance for either of those parties to successfully claim that deleting the consumer's data would render their own data useless – which might be the case even if the data was not generated in cooperation with the consumer. One example of such a scenario would be deleting communication data or online discussions, where the discussion itself cannot be properly understood without the consumer's questions or answers.[112]

9. ARTICLE 14 CSDC – RIGHT TO DAMAGES

Finally, the proposed Directive also provides for damages as a remedy for the consumer (Article 14 CSDC). Because of the broad scope and fully harmonising character of the Directive, the precise requirements for holding the supplier liable are, however, somewhat nebulous. The supplier is

> liable to the consumer for any economic damage to the digital environment of the consumer caused by a lack of conformity with the contract or a failure to supply the digital content. Damages shall put the consumer as nearly as possible into the position in which the consumer would have been if the digital content had been duly supplied and been in conformity with the contract.[113]

---

110 See art. 17(2)(a) (which does, however, require giving third parties notice of the consumer's effort to delete the data).

111 This corresponds with the protections granted to sub-licences under many national copyright laws. See eg Bundesgerichtshof *Multimediarecht* 2009, 838 – *Reifen Progressiv*; Bundesgerichtshof *Gewerblicher Rechtsschutz und Urheberrecht* 2012, 914 – *Take Five*; Bundesgerichtshof *Multimediarecht* 2012, 684 – *M2Trade*; G. Spindler, 'Lizensierung nach M2Trade, Take Five und Reifen Progressiv', *Computer und Recht*, 15 September 2014, 557; J.F. Hoffmann, 'Der Bestandsschutz von Unterlizenzen – Abstraktionsprinzip und Sukzessionsschutz in neuem (immaterialgüterrechtlichem) Licht' *Zeitschrift für Geistiges Eigentum / Intellectual Property Journal* (2015), 245; regarding Data Privacy Laws in Malaysia, the Philippines and Singapore, see G. Greenleaf, 'ASEAN's "New" Data Privacy Laws: Malaysia, the Philippines and Singapore' *Privacy Laws & Business International Report* 116 (2012) 22–24; UNSW Law Research Paper No. 2012-14. Available at SSRN: http://ssrn.com/abstract=2049234, last access: 13 April 2016.

112 This problem of tripolarity does, however, also occur under art. 17(3)(a) GDPR.

113 Art. 14(1) CSDC.

Apparently, the Commission wants to restrict the supplier's liability for damage to the digital environment, which seems to indicate that the consumer cannot assert consequential damage. This view may find support in the fully harmonising nature of the Directive as well as Article 14(2) CSDC, which leaves the precise rules regarding the exercise of the right to the Member States,[114] but not the subject and scope of the right itself. However, such an interpretation would of course have harsh consequences for consumers that were probably not intended by the Commission's proposal.[115] While suppliers could be held liable if their digital content contained, for example, viruses or malware and thereby caused damage to the consumer's other software, consequential damage like that arising from third parties retrieving the consumer's online banking passwords would not (and could not) be covered, even if those were foreseeable losses for the supplier.[116]

There are, however, other parts of the proposal that – despite its fully harmonising character – can be interpreted in a way that the Member States may nonetheless provide additional remedies for the consumer. First, recital 16 CSDC states that while the Directive does cover visual modelling files for 3D printers, it should not regulate goods produced with the use of 3D printing technology or the damage caused to them – which implies that the Member States may of course still provide corresponding remedies for such (consequential) damage. Apart from that, Article 14(1) CSDC offers a particular strong remedy without requiring the supplier to be at fault, and thus imposes strict liability on the supplier even without the slightest degree of negligence. While this may be appropriate for damage to the consumer's digital environment (which the supplier has the opportunity to analyse in advance), it would be too harsh to hold the supplier liable for any kind of distant event based on the non-conformity of the digital content. Though this principle does not apply to every kind of consequential damage, e.g. for damage resulting from a failure to meet a particular purpose the parties agreed upon,[117] the proposal should thus be

114 See also recital (10) CSDC.

115 Strongly criticised by Beale, n. 18 above, 24; see also B.A. Koch, 'Rechtsbehelfe des Verbrauchers bei Verträgen über digitale Inhalte' in Wendehorst and Zöchling-Jud (eds.), n. 25 above, 131, 152.

116 For a detailed discussion of liability in such cases under German law, see G. Spindler in E. Lorenz (ed.), *Karlsruher Forum 2010: Haftung und Versicherung im IT-Bereich* (Karlsruhe: Verlag Versicherungswirtschaft, 2011) 3, 24; G. Spindler, 'Verantwortlichkeiten von IT-Herstellern, Nutzern und Intermediären – Studie im Auftrag des BSI', 2007, para. 100, available at: https://www.bsi.bund.de/SharedDocs/Downloads/DE/BSI/Publikationen/Studien/ITSicherheitUndRecht/Gutachten_pdf.pdf?__blob=publicationFile&v=2. Micklitz and Reich, n. 60 above, 24; with regard to unfair terms relating to disclaimers for damage on consumer's software, see Loos, Mak, Guibault, Pessers and Helberger, n. 28 above.

117 Unfortunately, the Commission has not included such damages in art. 14 CSDC, even though they are part of the conformity with the contract, art. 6(1)(b) CSDC. Under German law, this idea can be found in §443(1) BGB. See A. Matusche-Beckmann, in *Staudinger*

interpreted (or modified) in the way that it seeks to confine strict liability to direct damage to the digital environment while not precluding further rights to (consequential) damages based on national law.[118]

On the other hand, there is little reason to assume that the Member States would also be allowed to add a negligence requirement to those damages covered by the proposal. Since the proposal expressly states that other Union acts take precedent over the CSDC, the new Directive would also not preclude any rights to damages based on other Directives. For example, the aforementioned liability for visual modelling files for 3D printers does not preclude additional rights to damages under the Product Liability Directive,[119] e.g. for damage caused by the use of a defective instruction manual.

Though the Article 14 CSDC generally provides consumers with a strong remedy for non-conforming digital content, it falls short with respect to the consumer's burden of proof. The Directive neither contains a burden shift with respect to causation, nor does it effectively protect the consumer if the supplier tries to avoid liability by claiming contributory negligence on behalf of the consumer – e.g. due to installing non-compatible software by a third-party developer or other digital content. While both scenarios are of practical importance and may place considerable obstacles in the way of claims for damages, consumers might at least be able to rely on a potential shift of the evidential burden regarding a (mutual) obligation to cooperate, Article 9(3) CSDC.

10. DEFECTS LIABILITY PERIOD AND STATUTE OF LIMITATION

Probably the most surprising aspect of the CSDC proposal (at least at first glance) is the Directive's determination of the period during which the supplier can be held liable for digital content not conforming with the contract – or more precisely: the lack thereof. While the Consumer Sales Directive establishes a liability period of two years,[120] the Commission now simply states that since digital content is not subject to wear and tear, it will not provide any liability period whatsoever and that Member States should refrain from introducing such

(Revised edn., Berlin: Sellier/de Gruyter, 2013) §443 paras. 1, 2 *et seq*; F. Faust, in *Beckscher OnlineKommentar BGB*, §443 para. 1 *et seq*.

118 See also the criticism of Fauvarque-Cosson, n. 86 above, 17; Mak, n. 15 above, 27.

119 Council Directive 85/374/EEC of 25 July 1985 on the approximation of the laws, regulations and administrative provisions of the Member States concerning liability for defective products, *OJEC* L210, 7 August 1985, 29–33, available at: http://eur-lex.europa.eu/LexUriServ/LexUriServ.do?uri=CELEX:31985L0374:en:HTML.

120 Art. 5(1) Consumer Sales Directive.

a period themselves.[121] However, what may at first seem like infinite liability proves to be not much more than a different legislative technique: although the Member States are pre-empted from establishing a period of liability, they can still rely on limitation periods instead.[122]

Thus, the Member States are free to limit consumer rights by virtue of a statute of limitation for digital content.[123] Even though the principle of *effet utile* should hinder states from choosing too short a period of time, this approach is not only quite a liberal one for purposes of a fully harmonising Directive, but may even thwart the Commission's intentions by ultimately creating a diverse landscape of national rules on a central issue of consumer protection. It is finally up to the Member States to define the end of the liability period – which is quite the opposite of a European harmonisation.[124]

11. ARTICLE 15 CSDC – MODIFICATION OF THE DIGITAL CONTENT

Since the proposal covers all kinds of contracts that deal with digital content – including recurring obligations over a period of time – it has also had to deal with potential changes to the contractual content. Article 15(1) CSDC gives the supplier a right to alter the digital content's functions, interoperability and other features, e.g. to adapt to changes in the digital environment such as new operating systems, but sets up a couple of conditions: the right to modify the contract has to be stipulated in the contract; the consumer has to be notified reasonably in advance; and the consumer has to be allowed to terminate the contract within 30 days of the receipt of said notice.[125] While the consumer may exercise his right to terminate the contract by any given means (Article 13(1) CSDC), the supplier has to submit his notification on a durable medium (Article 15(1)(b) CSDC). Just like in other consumer protections laws, this requirement is meant to prevent the supplier from altering the notification *ex post*.[126] However, Article 15 CSDC does not provide a test of whether the changes to the digital content adversely affect the consumer; given the wording

121 Recital (43) CSDC.

122 Recital (43) CSDC ('prescription rules').

123 Cf. also Fauvarque-Cosson, n. 86 above, 12.

124 Criticised also by Lurger, n. 25 above, 19, 38.

125 Art. 15(1)(a)–(c) CSDC. Of course, the right to terminate entails all termination-related rights as provided by art. 13 CSDC (and specified by art. 15(2) CSDC), which also includes the right to retrieve one's digital content (art. 13(1)(d) CSDC).

126 Hence, a notification on websites, social networks or other non-durable media does not suffice. *Content Services Ltd.v. Bundesarbeitskammer*, Case C-49/11, ECLI:EU:C:2012:419; furthermore C. Wendehorst in R. Schulze (ed.), *Common European Sales Law* (Baden-Baden: Nomos, 2012) art. 2 para. 54 with regard to the comparable article in the CESL, see art. 8(2) CESL.

of Article 15 CSDC, the right to terminate the contract would even apply in situations of a reasonable modification of the digital content.[127]

On the other hand, Article 15 CSDC lowers considerably the requirements for modification which already has been developed by national courts as well as the ECJ, for instance modifications of price in energy or power contracts.

Article 15(2) CSDC provides for similar consequences to the consumer's termination of the contract as Article 13 CSDC, by also requiring that the supplier refrain from using any (personal and non-personal) data of the consumer.[128] While the proposal appears to specifically (and exclusively) determine the consequences for an Article 15 termination,[129] it fails to include several necessary provisions, such as the consumer's obligation to refrain from using the digital content after termination or the means by which the consumer may exercise his or her right. One is thus left to assume that all provisions of Article 13 CSDC are nonetheless supposed to apply to Article 15 terminations – as long as the article itself does not explicitly specify them for its purposes.

12. ARTICLE 16 CSDC – RIGHT TO TERMINATE LONG-TERM CONTRACTS

Article 16 CSDC provides for another consumer right to terminate the contract in cases where this is stipulated to last for an indeterminate period or a period of time that exceeds 12 months. Since provisions like this are always prone to be circumvented by contractual agreements designed to have similar effects (e.g. by automatic extensions, subsequent agreements, etc.), the Commission has made clear that Article 16 CSDC should cover all kinds of contracts that effectively bind the consumer for more than 12 months, irrespective of their particular design (recital (46) CSDC).

The consequences of terminating the contract under Article 16 CSDC reflect those set out by Article 13 CSDC. However, there are some differences in detail. As the supplier may immediately restrict the access of the consumer to the digital content, the consumer may be confronted with difficulties in order to retrieve his data; Article 16(4) CSCD just refers to a 'reasonable time' without specifying it further.[130]

The period of (and limitation to) 12 months seems to be arbitrarily chosen – investments may be also worthwhile to protect for a longer term or

[127] Cf. FAUVARQUE-COSSON, n. 86 above, 18/19.

[128] The clause thereby also entails the same problems as discussed above.

[129] One argument for the article's exclusiveness may be seen in art. 13(1)(d) CSDC, which only refers to a specific provision of art. 13 CSDC, seemingly leaving out the rest intentionally.

[130] Cf. FAUVARQUE-COSSON, n. 86 above, 23.

vice versa. Hence, a case-by-case approach and a more flexible regime have been proposed by some commentators.[131] However, even though it may be arbitrary to fix the threshold at 12 months, the right to terminate long-term contracts has also to take into account legal certainty and reliability.

13. MISCELLANEOUS PROVISIONS

13.1. ARTICLE 17 CSDC – RIGHT OF REDRESS

Similarly to the Consumer Sales Directive,[132] the proposed Directive would encompass an independent right to redress for a supplier against other persons in the chain of transactions. The details are to be determined by national law.

13.2. SEMI-COMPULSORY NATURE

As a matter of course for a consumer protection Directive, the Member States may only deviate from the Directive's rules for the benefit of the consumer. This comes along with the well-known problem of determining whether the effect of deviating national rules is actually beneficial for the consumer or not.[133]

13.3. ACTIONS BY CONSUMER INTERESTS ORGANISATIONS

Finally, Article 20(3) CSDC would amend Directive 2009/22/EC[134] to allow public interest organisations and independent public bodies to help protect consumer rights under the CSDC by way of action.

14. CONCLUSION

The Commission's proposal for a Directive on contracts for the supply of digital content (CSDC) is a bold step in the right direction, which unlike the CESL proposal, dares to break away from the traditional model of typological

---

131 Cf. Fauvarque-Cosson, n. 86 above, 22.

132 Art. 4 CSD.

133 Assessments of this kind always have to take into account the individual consequences of the contractual agreement, not the overall effect.

134 Directive 2009/22/EC of the Parliament and of the Council of 23 April 2009 on injunctions for the protection of consumer's interests, *OJEC* L110/30, http://eur-lex.europa.eu/LexUriServ/LexUriServ.do?uri=OJ:L:2009:110:0030:0036:EN:PDF.

distinctions between different kinds of contracts and contractual obligations regarding the supply of digital content. The Commission is right in choosing a new path of regulating such contracts, making regulatory use of a high level of abstraction as the only way to keep pace with the industry's high level of technical innovation and the continuous appearance of new business models.

On the other hand, the proposal comes with multiple different problems and legal uncertainties – some of which are more or less inevitable due to its broad scope and abstract nature, while others call for changes of the Commission's current version of the Directive. Among them are several issues regarding the precise scope of and exceptions to the Directive, the objective and subjective criteria by which the digital content's conformity with the contract is determined, and the level of transparency required stipulating the parties' contractual obligations – by both general terms and conditions and individual agreements.

Furthermore, several aspects of the Commission's proposed framework for the consumer's rights to damages should be reconsidered or clarified, particularity with respect to the scope of the Directive's concept of strict liability. As a major contradiction and threat to the proposal's intention to fully harmonise national laws, the statutes of limitation for contracts that deal with digital content should not be left unregulated since this serves as the only actual period of limitation and thus as a pivotal element to the consumers' rights and remedies. If the Commission is, however, successful in resolving these issues in the final version of the CSDC, the benefits for consumers as well as for the Single Market as a whole should greatly outweigh the challenges it entails.

DIGITAL CONTENT – A DIGITAL CESL II – A PARADIGM FOR CONTRACT LAW VIA THE BACKDOOR?

Christina Ramberg

ABSTRACT

This chapter critically examines some features of the proposed directive on sale of digital content, namely its scope of application, defects with respect to digital contents, the contract term, remedies for breach of contract and the right to redress. These aspects are compared with general contract law. The chapter concludes that the nature of digital content does not necessitate any special legislation and will likely contribute to more confusion than clarification. Thereby the proposed directive will be detrimental to cross-border transactions.

1. INTRODUCTION

The EU Commission has an ambition to create directives and regulations. Sometimes the ambition appears to be more to do *something*, than to do *good*.

Directives and regulations are often too narrow,[1] too detailed, too shallow and too fragmented. The proposed directive on sale of digital content (adopted by the EU Commission in December 2015) is an example of this.[2] I doubt that the proposed directive will facilitate EU cross-border transactions;[3] instead I fear that it will create greater hindrance.

2. EXAMPLES OF SALE OF DIGITAL CONTENTS AND THE SCOPE OF APPLICATION

There are many examples of sale of digital content:

- Streaming services of film, books and music;
- 'Cyberbutler' services;
- Dating services;
- Gambling (expressly not covered by the proposed directive if they involve wagering a stake with monetary value, Article 5(c));
- E-learning products;
- Networking products (Facebook, LinkedIn);
- Accounting/book-keeping products;
- News subscriptions;
- Storage of digital material (cloud services);
- Healthcare services (healthcare services as defined in Article 3 of Directive 2011/24/EU are not covered by the proposed directive);
- Fitness services;
- Financial services (expressly not covered by the proposed directive);
- Subscription for contracts and other template documents adapting in response to users' answers to questions posed.

---

1 See Statement of the European Law Institute: Unlocking the Digital Single Market – An Instrument for 21st Century Europe, 2nd Supplement of the European Law Institute on the Proposal for a Regulation on Common European Sales Law, 2015, p. 9 ff., for a description of the drawbacks of a narrow scope of application.

2 Proposal for a Directive of the European Parliament and of the Council on certain aspects concerning contracts for the supply of digital content, COM(2015) 634 final – 2015/0287 (COD). It is a full harmonisation directive.

3 Quote from the European Commission Press release: 'Commission proposes modern digital contract rules to simplify and promote access to digital content and online sales across the EU', Brussels, 9 December 2015: 'This will open up new markets, especially for small and medium-sized enterprises (SMEs), increase competition and contribute to economic growth: lower consumer prices are expected to boost consumption in the EU by €18 billion and EU GDP is expected to increase by €4 billion from its current level.'

Generally, the proposed directive's scope of application is hard to discern.

The proposed directive covers also non-electronically stored data. This may entail a huge scope of application. The proposed directive does not, however, cover embedded digital content, which implies a huge carve out from the application.[4] It is very hard to understand the concept of embedded digital content and consequently to understand when the proposed directive is applicable.[5]

The proposed directive does not apply to personal (physical) services.[6] The distinction between purely digital services and services that consist partly of physical services is becoming increasingly blurred as new products are invented. There is no reason to have different legal regimes for the two situations. Take for example translation services. The users rarely know whether they are interacting with a purely automatic translation program (covered by the proposed directive) or with a mainly automatic program supported by persons translating 'behind the screens'. Another example is medical services which may consist of a mixture between automatic and personal services, unknown to the users.

In the future we will not be able to distinguish between online and offline transactions. The proposed directive tries to deal with this matter by applying the concept of functional equivalence. But this does not make any sense when the objective is to regulate 'digital' content specifically. It is like saying: 'We want to regulate only digital content, but we do not want to create special rules for digital content.'

In sum, it is hard to determine which transactions the proposed directive covers.[7] This will lead to uncertainty and confusion among lawyers giving advice to the digital content industry. Confusion is a great hindrance to cross-border

---

4 Recital (11): 'In particular it should cover services which allow the creation, processing or storage of data. While there are numerous ways for digital content to be supplied, such as transmission on a durable medium, downloading by consumers on their devices, web-streaming, allowing access to storage capabilities of digital content or access to the use of social media, this Directive should apply to all digital content independently of the medium used for its transmission … this Directive should not apply to digital content which is embedded in goods in such a way that it operates as an integral part of the goods and its functions are subordinate to the main functionalities of the goods.' Also the Commission's proposal for a directive on certain aspects concerning contracts for supply of digital content [2015/0287(COD)], paras. 3.2.2–3.3.1, notes that the scope is 'not entirely clear' in several respects (see also paras. 3.4.3–3.4.5).

5 From the Commission's proposal for a directive on certain aspects concerning contracts for supply of digital content [2015/0287(COD)], para. 3.4.5.

6 Recital (17): 'This Directive should apply only to those services whose main subject matter is providing digital content. Therefore, the Directive should not apply to services, which are performed personally by the supplier and where the digital means are only used for access or delivery purposes, such as a translation offered by a person or other professional advice services where only the output of the service is delivered to the consumer by digital means.'

7 Statement of the European Law Institute: Unlocking the Digital Single Market – An Instrument for 21st Century Europe, 2nd Supplement of the European Law Institute on the Proposal for a Regulation on Common European Sales Law, 2015, p. 8 ff., emphasises the need for a simple and precise approach to scope.

transactions, as has been clearly demonstrated by the uncertainty and confusion caused by the directive on e-signatures (Directive 1999/93/EC of 13 December 1999 on a Community framework for electronic signatures) – which will not be cured by the new EU regulation No. 910/2014 of 23 July 2014 on electronic identification and trust services for electronic transactions in the internal market.

3. SPECIAL FEATURES OF THE SALE OF DIGITAL CONTENTS

The sale of digital content has some special features. Do these special features justify special legislation, separate from general contract law rules?

Some special features of digital content are:

- Low distribution costs for the service supplier;
- Often high production costs for the first product and low production costs for the following products;
- The digital content is often provided as subscriptions – delivery takes place over a period of time;
- Payment is not always by money but often instead through allowing the use of personal data;[8]
- The transactions often refer to detailed standard terms (take-it-or-leave-it), for instance so-called EULAs, End-User License Agreements.

These special features are, however, not very special. We see the same features in many other contract types. Low distribution costs are frequent for all types of intellectual services. High costs for the first product and low costs for producing the subsequent products are common in design contracts and other types of intellectual services. Subscriptions are common in many types of contracts (traditional newspapers, storage, rent, etc.). Barter is a common example of payment by other means than money. We also see an increasing amount of goods and services provided for 'free' as a means of marketing in the broad sense also outside of the digital environment. Standard terms are frequent in almost all types of contracts.[9]

8 The proposed directive Recitals (13) and (14). Empirical research has found that personal data have an economic value and may be 'monetised', A. Acquisti, L.K. John and G. Loewenstein, 'What Is Privacy Worth?' (2013) 42 *Journal of Legal Studies* 24, and N. Purtova, *Property Rights in Personal Data: A European Perspective*, Tilburg University, 2011.

9 Statement of the European Law Institute: Unlocking the Digital Single Market – An Instrument for 21st Century Europe, 2nd Supplement of the European Law Institute on the Proposal for a Regulation on a Common European Sales Law, 2015, p. 11 ff., proposes a directive dealing only with non-individually negotiated, standard form, mass communication digital contracts.

The 'special' features of sale of digital content are not very special, and do not justify specific rules for digital content.[10]

4. SPECIAL LEGAL PROBLEMS RELATING TO THE SALE OF DIGITAL CONTENT

In the following I will provide an overview of some legal problems associated with digital content and how the proposed directive tries to solve them.

4.1. VAGUE CONTRACTS

Contractual texts regarding the supplier's performance are often vague, with references to 'reasonable care' and 'best efforts'. It is impossible to determine what such notions mean in an individual case.

To handle the problem of vague undertakings, the proposed Article 6.1 states that the digital content must primarily conform to what was *promised in the contract.*[11] In the absence of explicit contractual provisions, the digital content must be *fit for the purpose* for which digital content of the same description would normally be used (Article 6.2). The notion of 'fit for purpose' is as vague as 'reasonable efforts'. The guidelines to establish the meaning of 'fit for purpose' are not sufficient to create any increased certainty. We see that the proposed directive does not solve the problem of vagueness, but only substitutes one kind of vagueness for another.

4.2. DEFECTS

Digital content entails new types of defects, for example:

- Some products cannot be integrated with the user's appliances (a problem of interoperability). The proposed Article 7 states that this equates to a lack of

---

10 I will not deal with the problem of implementing in national law the proposed directive's creation of a new contract type, see the Commission's proposal for a directive on certain aspects concerning contracts for supply of digital content [2015/0287(COD)], para. 3.4.2 with references.

11 See criticism against freedom of contract in this respect, mainly pointing to the fact that consumers do not read the contractual text: V. Mak, *The new proposal for harmonised rules on certain aspects concerning contracts for the supply of digital content*, Workshop for the JURI Committee, Policy Dept C in-depth analysis, PE 536.494 (2016), pp. 15–16; and H. Beale, *Scope of application and general approach of the new rules for contracts in the digital environment*, Workshop for the JURI Committee, Policy Dept C in-depth analysis, PE 536.493 (2016), p. 23.

conformity of the digital content itself. However, if the supplier has clearly indicated that the product is only intended for a particular software or hardware, it is unreasonable to hold the supplier liable for the defect, see Recital (30). The provision's reference to 'incorrectly' integrated should probably be understood as referring to how the product was described in the contract or manual.
- Some products are attached to a user's individual device and cannot be used if that device is broken or stolen. This problem is nowadays limited, as the products are often attached to the users' accounts and not their devices. The proposal does not deal with this matter.
- Some products can only be used in certain regions and countries. The proposed directive does not deal with this matter.

The liability for defects specific to digital content is not comprehensibly covered and is left to be resolved by explicit contractual provisions. Consequently, the proposed directive does not resolve any problem in this respect.

4.3. INTELLECTUAL PROPERTY RIGHTS

The use of a product may entail copyright infringement. The proposed Article 8 states that the digital content must be cleared of any third-party rights, including those based on intellectual property.[12] This follows already from general contract law. I would be most surprised if this is not the general default rule in all EU Member States.

According to Article 19 the provision on liability for intellectual property infringements is mandatory. It is controversial not to allow the supplier a possibility to limit its liability for third-party rights, particularly since it is not clear what the remedies for such a breach are (the proposed directive does not clarify whether third-party rights constitute 'lack of conformity' and whether the remedies in Articles 10–14 apply). A provision regarding mandatory unlimited liability for third-party rights will function as a strong deterrent for the development of digital business in EU.

4.4. THE USER'S RIGHTS

It is sometimes unclear to what extent the product can be used on several devices, simultaneously or at all. Furthermore, it is sometimes unclear whether the user can transfer or resell the product. The proposed directive does not deal

12 Recital (31).

with these matters. It is presupposed that these matters will be governed by the contractual terms.

4.5. THE CONTRACT DURATION

The contract duration is usually specified in the contract. When the duration is indeterminate or longer than 12 months, Article 16.1 in the proposal establishes a mandatory right for the consumer to terminate with 14 days' notice. This is probably a fair rule for most transactions and could preferably be included in the Directive 93/13/EEC of 5 April 1993 on unfair terms in consumer contracts.

The supplier is, quite self-evidently, liable for defects throughout the contract duration (the proposed Articles 6.3 and 10).[13]

Frequently the supplier introduces improvements and other changes in the product during the contract term. The proposed Article 15 allows unilateral changes that are beneficial for the user. Detrimental unilateral changes are allowed provided that certain conditions are met, in particular that the user has an opportunity to terminate the contract free of charge. This is in harmony with Directive 93/13/EEC of 5 April 1993 on unfair terms in consumer contracts, Annex (j)–(l). The proposed directive does not provide anything in addition to what is already established by EU-law.

The proposed directive does not give the user any right to receive updates, unless stipulated by the contract. The user is only entitled to receive the latest update at the time of formation of contract, Recital (29) and Article 6(1)(d). This default law rule is in harmony with general contract law and does not add anything useful.

4.6. REMEDIES FOR THE SUPPLIER'S BREACH

Article 12 in the proposed directive lists the remedies available to the consumer. The primary remedy is specific performance, as the consumer is entitled to have the digital content brought into conformity (cure or redelivery) within a reasonable time. This provision regarding specific performance may cause problems in common law jurisdictions, at least in theory.[14] Furthermore, it is

---

13 See also Recital (29).

14 For a brief comparative overview on the hierarchy of remedies, see The European Parliamentary Research Service, R. Manko, *Contracts for supply of digital content, A legal analysis of the Commission's proposal for a new directive*, PE 582.048 (May 2016), p. 27 ff.

questionable whether cure is generally efficient as compared to termination with respect to digital contents.[15]

The secondary remedies are price reduction and termination.

The proposed directive indicates that the price reduction is calculated according to general civil law rules on price reduction, i.e. proportionate to the decrease in value.[16] Defects in digital content often entail that the product lacks all value and therefore the user is often entitled to a 100 per cent price reduction. It is consequently questionable whether price reduction is a useful remedy for defective digital content compared to termination. I believe that this provision regarding price reduction may cause problems in common law jurisdictions, at least in theory.

The proposed directive's requirement for termination in Article 12.5 appears in essence to be in harmony with the general contract law rule, that termination due to breach requires a material (fundamental) breach. Regrettably, the proposed directive uses different language but seems to intend a similar rule (Recital (37)). The proposed directive Article 12.5 stipulates a deviation from the traditional burden of proof to the effect that the supplier has the burden of showing that its breach is not fundamental. This deviation may cause confusion and is not likely to make any real difference in practice.

According to Article 14 the remedies can be combined with damages that put the user as nearly as possible in the position which the user would have been in had the product been in conformity with the contract, i.e. the expectation interest, Recital (44). The user's right to damages appears to be limited by the proposal – as it refers only to damage 'to the digital environment of the consumer' – but at the same time the objective is to compensate for the expectation interest (Recital (44)). This contradiction or ambiguity will likely cause confusion.[17] I do not see any reason to introduce a new regime for damages in relation to

---

15 B. Fauvarque-Cosson, *The new proposal for harmonised rules for certain aspects concerning contracts for the supply of digital content (termination, modification of the digital content and right to terminate long-term contracts)*, Policy Dept C in-depth analysis, PE 536.495 (2016), p. 9. See also V. Mak, *The new proposal for harmonised rules on certain aspects concerning contracts for the supply of digital content*, Workshop for the JURI Committee, Policy Dept C in-depth analysis, PE 536.494 (2016) p. 24; and The European Parliamentary Research Service, R. Manko, *Contracts for supply of digital content, A legal analysis of the Commission's proposal for a new directive*, PE 582.048 (May 2016), p. 27.

16 See for example CISG Article 50.

17 There are additional ambiguities in relation to the provision on damages, see H. Beale, *Scope of application and general approach of the new rules for contracts in the digital environment*, Workshop for the JURI Committee, Policy Dept C in-depth analysis, PE 536.493 (2016) p. 23; V. Mak, *The new proposal for harmonised rules on certain aspects concerning contracts for the supply of digital content*, Workshop for the JURI Committee, Policy Dept C in-depth analysis, PE 536.494 (2016) p. 27; and The European Parliamentary Research Service, R. Manko, *Contracts for supply of digital content, A legal analysis of the Commission's proposal for a new directive*, PE 582.048 (May 2016), p. 25.

digital content. The ordinary rules on damages for breach of contract are suitable also for the sale of digital content.[18]

The proposal is generally in harmony with the general contract law on remedies. The deviations are of theoretical interest but hardly of any importance in practice. The proposal on remedies is not specific to digital contents and there is consequently no benefit in introducing a special directive regarding remedies. The articles on remedies could be deleted for the same reason as the proposal does not contain rules on formation and validity of contracts.

4.7. RESTITUTION

A quite specific problem in relation to digital content is restitution of performance in case the contract is terminated or invalid. The return of the parties' performances is problematic for three reasons:

1. *Parts of the supplier's performance that the user has already consumed cannot be returned.* The proposed Article 13.4 establishes that termination has retroactive effects in the sense that the user does not have to pay for use prior to the termination. This is contrary to general rules on restitution, according to which the terminating party normally has to pay compensation for use that it has enjoyed and cannot return. However, Articles 13.5 and 13.6, which seem to contradict Article 13.4, make clear that termination is *not* made retroactively and that the user shall pay for the use it has enjoyed. The user shall refrain from using the content after termination (Article 13.3). The proposal states in Article 13.6 that termination has effect as from the time of the defect, Recital (42). This is different from ordinary rules on termination of services in many states, which provide that termination normally takes effect at the time of notice of termination or invalidity. Generally, paragraphs 13.2–13.6 of the proposal are incomprehensible, or at least very difficult to understand.[19]

---

18 The proposed directive does not give any right to damages for non-pecuniary harm (e.g. when my family photos have disappeared), as in Article 2.5, damages are defined as compensation for *economic* damage to the consumers' digital environment. It is not easy for the reader of the proposal to find this limitation in the definitions section. It would have been more user-friendly to include it in Article 14 dealing with damages. Anyway, the proposal does not add anything to the existing law, since contractual damages for non-pecuniary loss is normally not allowed in national law. The proposal does not deal with notice of damages, but refers in Article 14.2 to national law. This will likely entail discrepancies in the Member States.

19 The explanation in Recital (42) does not provide any help: 'However when the digital content is provided against a counter-performance other than money partial termination is not feasible because it is impossible to proportionally apportion a counter-performance other than money.' See criticism against inconsistencies on termination and restitution, Statement

2. *If the user has not paid any money, no money can be returned.* According to the proposed Articles 13 and 16, the supplier shall refrain from using data about the user after termination. The supplier may, however, have received personal data about the user which has already been used or resold and therefore cannot be returned or deleted. According to the proposal, the supplier is not obliged to act against persons that have before the termination already acquired personal data from the supplier (Recital (37)). The proposed directive does not contain any rule on standardised rates of reimbursement, providing for a graded system of amounts depending on the kind of personal data used and on whether it is technically possible to prevent future use of the data by third parties to whom the supplier may have passed on the data, as suggested by some experts.[20] It is surprising that the proposal limits the consumer's rights in this respect, but understandable as a means to enhance the willingness of businesses to provide digital content for 'free' without facing liability for damages etc.
3. *The users may have generated content through the product which they want to retain also after termination.* Content generated by consumers comprises a wide range of matters including digital images, video and audio files, blogs, discussion forums, text-based collaboration formats, posts, chats, tweets, logs, podcasting, content created on mobile devices, content created in the context of online virtual environments, ratings and collections of links referring to online content. The proposed directive gives the users a mandatory right to retrieve all their generated content for free, Article 13.2(c) and Recitals (39)–(41). This is a useful rule about something specific to digital content services. The proposed rule makes clear that, for example, the users have a right to retrieve all the documents they have created and saved in the cloud when the users end the cloud storage. For some types of service, it is unclear what 'generated content' consists of. Does, for instance, a user have a right to retrieve a list of relevant cases when the user ends a subscription to a case-law database? Another uncertainty is for how long the supplier must keep the users' content retrievable for the users.

Article 13 on restitution only deals with the effects of termination by the user. It is uncertain whether the provision on restitution can be applied by analogy

---

of the European Law Institute on the Proposal for a Regulation on a Common European Sales law COM(2011) 635 final, 1st Supplement: Response to the EP Legislative Resolution of 26 February 2014 p. 32 ff.

20 M. Loos, *The Regulation of Digital Content B2C Contracts in CESL*, Centre for the Study of European Contract Law Working Paper no. 2013-10, p. 287. See also V. Mak, *The new proposal for harmonised rules on certain aspects concerning contracts for the supply of digital content*, Workshop for the JURI Committee, Policy Dept C in-depth analysis, PE 536.494 (2016), p. 26.

when the supplier terminates due to the user's breach. This lacuna causes uncertainty and will inevitably entail differing rules in the EU Member States.

Apart from the Article 13.2(c) on the consumer's right to retrieve generated content, I do not see any need to regulate restitution specifically for digital content. It would be better to regulate it generally for all contracts and until such regulation is in place, we can live with general national laws on restitution, which do not vary much in practice.

4.8. THE SUPPLIER'S RIGHT TO REDRESS

The proposed directive Article 17 provides the supplier with a mandatory right to redress in case of an act or omission by a person in an earlier link of the chain of transactions which triggered the supplier's liability for lack of conformity or a failure to supply towards the consumer.[21] It is controversial to introduce mandatory rules in B2B transactions. I find it particularly controversial since often the supplier contracting with the end user is a big company, whereas its sub-suppliers are smaller businesses unable to foresee the financial consequences of a defect and in need of limitations of liability.

The protection in the proposed directive is generally directed towards SMEs more than consumers. However, the provision on the supplier's mandatory right to redress will in practice have negative effects for small businesses and benefit big business.

5. CONCLUSION

The modern knowledge society needs norms clarifying the rights and obligations for suppliers of services. The most appropriate way of introducing such norms is not a question of Legislative Regulation vs. Self-Regulation. Instead it is a question of Regulating Specifically vs. Regulating Generally.

It is only appropriate to regulate the sale of digital content specifically if:

1. *Many users encounter problems, which are likely to harm the industry's growth and potential.* The proposed directive, Recital (4) states that consumers experience problems regarding quality and access to contents. I doubt that these problems are great. I also doubt that the provisions in the proposed directive will resolve these problems. 'If it ain't broke, don't fix it.'

21 The modalities for exercising this right are to be regulated by the national laws of Member States.

2. *The legal problems are specific to digital content.* The proposed directive, Recital (3) states that there is a need for 'tailor-made rules' to deal with the specific problems related to digital content. Since the problems are not specific – as explained above – regulation on a more general level is preferable.
3. *A regulation would considerably contribute to creating more certainty about the rules.* The EU Commission states that there are no rules available and applicable to the sale of digital content.[22] This is incorrect, since general contract law rules are available. The proposed directive, Recitals (4) and (7), state that consumers are uncertain about their contractual rights. I doubt that the proposed directive will contribute to greater certainty.
4. *The rules are different in the various EU Member States.* Some Member States have taken initiatives to regulate contractual breach in relation to digital content.[23] The differences in the way those types of conflicts are resolved in the Member States have been reported as one of the barriers for the advance of the Digital Single Market.[24] I do not believe that the law as it stands today creates any significant barrier to trade of digital content. I certainly do not share the EU Commission's view that a new directive would enable 120,000 more businesses to sell online and would entail that intra-EU exports increase by 18 billion Euros and EU GDP increase by 4 billion Euros.[25]

It is not advisable to create regulations and directives with a narrow scope of application. Micro-rules are a hindrance to trade as they entail great uncertainty. The problem to categorise the type of contract – i.e. to determine whether the directive is applicable (its scope) – is often more problematic than managing general contract law rules. Categorisation is a legal-technical problem which greatly harms the industry. Only lawyers are happy about definitions and scope of application problems. The efforts to categorise the legal nature of various contract types are not a viable way for the future.

It is not possible to capture the many different natures and relationships involved in the sale of digital content. The innovative knowledge society will

---

22 Explanatory Memorandum, p. 3 COM(2015) 634 final.

23 Namely the UK, the Netherlands and Ireland. See Explanatory Memorandum, p. 3 COM(2015) 634 final.

24 Digital contracts for Europe – Unleashing the potential of e-commerce, p. 3, COM(2015) 633 final and the proposed directive Recital (6).

25 Quote from the European Commission Press release: 'Commission proposes modern digital contract rules to simplify and promote access to digital content and online sales across the EU', Brussels, 9 December 2015: 'This will open up new markets, especially for small and medium-sized enterprises (SMEs), increase competition and contribute to economic growth: lower consumer prices are expected to boost consumption in the EU by €18 billion and EU GDP is expected to increase by €4 billion from its current level.'

create new services and products at a pace the regulators can never catch up with. The micro-rules will be outdated before they are implemented. Therefore, the rules need to be general. Micro-rules are not suitable for evolving, differentiated contract types.[26] The solution is to move away from micro-rules and instead regulate on a general contract-law level; to go deep and broad instead of shallow and narrow. Directive 93/13/EEC of 5 April 1993 on unfair terms in consumer contracts is a good example of a generally applicable directive.

The proposed directive does not deal with several aspects.[27] It is natural that not all questions are solved in a directive.[28] Since the proposed directive does not deal with all problems, the markets will not be harmonised and businesses will, despite a new directive, need to assess each country's law in addition to the directive. The problems that the proposed directive declines to solve demonstrate that we can manage also without the proposed directive.

As I have demonstrated above, most of the proposed rules for digital content already follow from general contract law. It may be hard for businessmen, consumers and practising lawyers to access the contract law rules (as they are often not laid down in legislation). The problem of easy access to the rules on contract law, should, however, not be remedied by micro-rules for narrow types of contracts. Instead the EU should embark on a bolder project, providing a restatement of general contract law, relevant for all types of contracts, including intellectual services and the sale of digital content. A general approach will be able to cope with innovation. Contrary to the EU Commission, I am of the firm opinion that a non-binding instrument, such as a model law, would be a much more efficient tool to harmonise the law in Europe on a long-term basis and to facilitate cross-border transactions for modern contract types.[29]

The legal problems that occur are not specific to digital content, but of a general nature. The proposed directive will create uncertainty about (1) how to define the scope of application, (2) how to solve the lacunas of legal questions not addressed in the proposed directive and (3) how to interpret the ambiguous

---

26 See the presentations in Part II of this anthology by Vanessa Mak on digital platforms such as Uber and Airbnb and Carmen Estevan on crowdfunding.

27 For instance, the user's rights when digital content is attached to a device that gets stolen or breaks, the user's rights with respect to regional restrictions, the user's right to apply the content on several devices, and the supplier's rights to remedies for the buyer's breach of contract.

28 Inter alia, passing of risk, transfer and/or retention of ownership, licensing; multiple or single-use streaming, right to withdrawal, protection of advance payments, rights to multiple downloads, right to resell digital content.

29 COM(2015) 634 final, at p. 6 ff.: 'A non-binding instrument such as a voluntary model contract would not achieve the objective to improve the establishment and functioning of the internal market. Traders would still be obliged to comply with different mandatory national rules of the consumer's country of residence, when the latter provide for a higher level of consumer protection than the model contract, and would thus still face contract law-related costs.'

articles in the proposal.[30] The proposal does not cover the formation or validity of contracts. The reason is that the problems for concluding contracts on digital content are not different from other contracts, and should not be micro-managed.[31] The same argument is valid for the articles in the proposed directive.

The proposal contains only two mandatory provisions that make a difference: First, the user's right to terminate contracts of a longer duration than 12 months (Article 16.1). Second, the user's right to retrieve the generated content after termination (Article 13.2(c)). These two rules are suitable generally for all consumer contract types and would fit better in Directive 93/13/EEC of 5 April 1993 on unfair terms in consumer contracts.

To conclude: The proposed directive on the sale of digital content does not contain any useful rules and will not contribute to cross-border transactions within the EU; instead it will likely create barriers to cross-border transactions. The proposal demonstrates the need for harmonisation of general contract law as opposed to micro-management of specific contract types.

---

30 The many issues not resolved by the proposed directive create uncertainty. What is the meaning of the silence? That the suppliers are never entitled to terminate (since the proposal does not give any such explicit right)? Or that the supplier should rely on general contract law and may terminate due to the user's material breach of contract? Recital (9) proudly states: 'By fully harmonising all requirements related to the topics regulated by this Directive, it precludes Member States, within its scope of application, from providing any further formal or substantive requirements, such as a period during which the lack of conformity has to become apparent, an obligation for the consumer to notify the supplier of a lack of conformity within a specific period or an obligation for the consumer to pay for the use of the digital content until the moment of termination because of a lack of conformity with the contract.' The statement gives a misleading impression that all topics related to digital content are harmonised, which is not the case. Furthermore, it is not clear from the proposal that there can be no notice periods for lack of conformity, particularly not with respect to the right to claim damages. And, as described above, the proposed provision on when and how termination takes effect is incomprehensible.

31 Statement of the European Law Institute: Unlocking the Digital Single Market – An Instrument for 21st Century Europe, 2nd Supplement of the European Law Institute on the Proposal for a Regulation on a Common European Sales Law, 2015, p. 14 ff., recommends that formation of contract be regulated, including the issue of online fraud.

INDEX

EUROPEAN CONTRACT LAW AND THEORY SERIES

1. *Rules and Principles in European Contract Law*, Jacobien Rutgers and Pietro Sirena (eds.)
2. *European Contract Law and the Charter of Fundamental Rights*, Hugh Collins (ed)